Women

Living

Zen

Women

Living

Zen

JAPANESE

SŌTŌ BUDDHIST

NUNS

Paula Kane Robinson Arai

New York   Oxford

Oxford University Press

1999

Oxford University Press

Oxford   New York

Athens   Auckland   Bangkok   Bogotá   Buenos Aires   Calcutta
Cape Town   Chennai   Dar es Salaam   Delhi   Florence   Hong Kong   Istanbul
Karachi   Kuala Lumpur   Madrid   Melbourne   Mexico City   Mumbai
Nairobi   Paris   São Paulo   Singapore   Taipei   Tokyo   Toronto   Warsaw

and associated companies in
Berlin   Ibadan

Copyright © 1999 by Paula Kane Robinson Arai

Published by Oxford University Press, Inc.
198 Madison Avenue, New York, New York 10016

Oxford is a registered trademark of Oxford University Press

Library of Congress Cataloging-in-Publication Data
Arai, Paula Kane Robinson.
Women living Zen : Japanese Sōtō Buddhist nuns
Paula Kane Robinson Arai.
p.   cm.
ISBN 0-19-512393-X
1. Monastic and religious life for women—Japan.   2. Monastic and
religious life (Zen Buddhism)—Japan.   3. Religious life—Sōtōshū.
4. Buddhist nuns—Japan.   I. Title.
BQ9444.2.A73   1998
294.3'657—dc21   98-17675

1 3 5 7 9 8 6 4 2

Printed in the United States of America
on acid-free paper

For my parents,
Masuko Arai Robinson
Lucian Ford Robinson
and my bodhisattva,
Kitō Shunkō

Reflections on Women Encountering Buddhism across Cultures and Time

Abbess Aoyama Shundō
Aichi Zen Monastery for Women in Nagoya, Japan

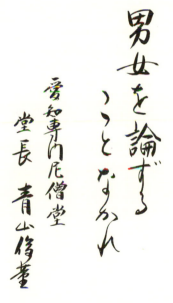

"We must all, male and female alike, profoundly respect Buddhist teachings and practice. We must not argue over male or femaleness."

[excerpt from "Raihaitokuzui," *Shōbōgenzō,* by Zen Master Dōgen]

"I chose the study of comparative religion, because I was born betwixt and between a mother who is a Japanese Buddhist and a father who is an American Christian. In time I was drawn to Buddhism, and in 1987 I sojourned to India where I was able to visit the place where Śākyamuni attained enlightenment. It was there that I met the Zen nun, Kitō Shunkō, who was at the Japanese Temple in Bodh Gaya. I was deeply moved at having encountered a person who genuinely lived according to the Buddhist teachings. At that time, the nun, Kitō Sensei, introduced to me the book written by the Abbess, On Becoming a Beautiful Person. *These experiences and events drove me to come to this Zen monastery for women in Nagoya, Japan."*

This was my first conversation with Paula. When she said, "I encountered a person who genuinely lived according to the Buddhist teachings" a tear glistened in her eye. It was a tear that came out of the joy of having had a profound encounter with a wonderful person and teachings while on a journey in search of the truth.

At that time, I thought that she must have received the seeds of Buddhist teachings from her mother when she was very young, and her Buddhist-seeking antenna were raised from having experienced the complexities of being raised between the two teachings of Buddhism and Christianity. Having met the nun, Kitō Shunkō—who is like a living Buddha—she decided the direction of her search. Since then Paula has come directly and deliberately along this path. These are my thoughts about Paula's actions and commitments.

Buddhist history is about 2500 years long. Nuns' history is the same 2500 years. The first people who began walking this path were the stepmother who raised Śākyamuni, Mahāprajāpatī, and his wife, Yasodarā. Along with the particularities of cultural and historical influence, the Buddhist teachings have been transmitted from India, China, and Japan. Even if there appeared discrimination between monks and nuns, we today continue to receive the unwavering truth as expressed by Zen Master Dōgen's profound heart and mind: "We must all, male and female alike, profoundly respect Buddhist teachings and practice. We must not argue over male or femaleness."

The foundation of nuns' responsibility, conscience, and honor is to have been granted the role to support the spiritual dimension of the efforts of women who bear the responsibility—granted by the gods and Buddhas—to give birth to and raise the people of tomorrow who will saddle the world on their shoulders. We must exert ourselves unremittingly. This is the only path on which we must continuously advance.

In order to write this book, Paula experienced these nuns' path in a personally embodied way; she studied our history, actual circumstances, and various other dimensions. For Paula's posture of commitment and practice, I express respect from my heart.

Gasshō.

Acknowledgments

Giving thanks to people for having helped is one of life's true joys. It is my great pleasure to thank all the people who have contributed to this book with their expertise, time, insights, texts and documents, and hospitality—plus their thoughts and hearts. It is my tremendous sadness, however, that I am unable to thank personally a number of the key people whose efforts were vital to this book, for they have passed on. One of the benefits of writing about nuns, however, is that it has fostered a number of important relationships with truly remarkable people. These relationships have helped sustain me through these losses. Most notably I am grateful for the profound understanding of Kitō Shunkō, who is the inspiration for this work.

I have come to know just how true the heeding of Wilfred Cantwell Smith, my first-year Ph.D.-candidate advisor at Harvard University, was in stressing that the study of religion is the study of religious people. He taught that you must become genuine friends with various religious people. It is only then that you can learn what is in their hearts and understand their religiosity.

Friendships, however, were fostered during my tenure in the monastery, not out of a conscious methodological preference, but because we were engaged in an intense shared experience. Silence being the norm in the monastery, unspoken bonds of mutual respect were cultivated—especially during arduous periods of fourteen-hour-a-day meditation. Having established these bonds of trust and re-spect, at times of crisis we turned to each other for help. Indeed, during a period of personal crisis, unrelated to my research, I found sympathy in a number of my female monastic friends. Not only did they help me through this crisis and heighten my respect for them, but this encounter also became a catalyst for deeper connections that gave me access to intimate information, insight into their private feelings, and clearer understanding of their motivations. Although I do not use this information in any explicit fashion, it enables me to understand the context and import of formal responses given on surveys and in interviews. I am indebted to all the nuns who opened their hearts to me. They are too numerous to mention each by name, but my sincere gratitude extends to all. I would, however, like to highlight a few.

If I had not met the nun Kitō Shunkō Sensei, I would not have written this book. My profound gratitude goes to her, a living bodhisattva. She took care of me while I was in the monastery. She had an uncanny knack of knowing even before I did what I would need, whether it was a *furoshiki* to cover my books, a robe for more formal ceremonies (that was wrinkle-free and dried quickly, even in humid weather), or a reminder that there are many seasons, each with its own valued quality.

Aoyama Shundō Rōshi, the abbess of Aichi Senmon Nisōdō, gave me her trust, an indispensable gift. Without this, I would not have been able to live in the monastery and interview the novices in training, and I would surely not have had much of a response on the surveys. She gave me critical information, clarifying insights, numerous books, free access to the monastery library, and necessary challenges.

I am grateful to the late Kojima Kendō Sensei for sharing that glorious week together at Lumbini-en and giving me a visceral sense of the caliber of women that changed Sōtō history, as well as more documentation of their history.

Special thanks are also due to a number of others. One is Yanaga Jissho, for a depth of friendship that requires few words to communicate volumes. She gently showed me how to survive in the monastery by her kind and insightful advice and stellar example. Tomio Sensei brightened me up each time she appeared in the monastery, and she arranged for me to stay in an apartment in her temple building, located near the monastery. Kuriki Kakujō Sensei, my tea ceremony teacher who let me continue taking lessons at her temple twice a week after I left the monastery. She was always conscious of my research and freely gave information that she knew would be helpful in furthering my understanding. There is also Okamoto Sensei, for her care in teaching me how to sew a *rakusu*, my favorite class at the monastery. Thanks also to the late Miyata Baijun Sensei for her healing laughter, and to Tsuneda Sen'e Sensei for her gifts of time, texts, and the cherished plum blossom incense burner that I have used to bring the smell of temples to my study during the entire process of working on this book—in Nagoya, Tokyo, Cambridge, Hong Kong, and Nashville. Nozawa Wakō provided texts and informative conversations. All the nuns at Aichi Senmon Nisōdō in Nagoya, whom I was cloistered with in the fall of 1989, will remain in my heart for their patient understanding, cooperation, and honesty. My thanks to the numerous nuns who responded to the survey and who offered interviews.

I am deeply indebted to Ōgishi Emiko and her late husband, Sakichi, for their invaluable assistance in sharing their knowledge of Sōtō nuns' history and activities, for helping me gather materials and discussing the findings, and for driving me around to important sites in the nuns' history. I am especially grateful for the eleventh-hour assistance Mrs. Ōgichi so freely gave.

Mrs. Kurokōchi is due my thanks for an unforgettable night of hospitality at a point in the field research phase when I was so extremely exhausted my teeth hurt. She prepared a savory meal, a hot bath, and let me sleep in a warm soft bed with a heater in the room. I felt like I had been blessed with a day in Pure Land.

My gratitude to the Skrzypczak family for their generous help.

I would also like to thank Koyanagi Reiko for her innumerable kindnesses. Gratitude goes to the Nomura family for a place to stay when doing research in Kyoto, and to Suzuki Atsuko for advice on matters of Sociology in a Japanese context. Ihara Kōji helped with scintillating discussion about Sōtō Zen.

I owe the Yanai family deep gratitude for their boundless generosity, engaging and insightful conversations that have deepened my understanding of traditional Japanese culture in Japan today, and for "adopting" me into their family.

Thanks are also due to Dai-en Bennage for invaluable discussions; Coen Murayama for practical advise in the monastery, Jihō Sargent for materials on Sōtō regulations; and Kondō Tesshō, abbess of Yoshimizu Gakuen, for books, information, and extensive discussions.

Throughout my years of study, I have been blessed with numerous teachers who took the time to guide me and help me grow. Without each and every teacher who cultivated and nourished me, I would not be where I am today.

Among the professors to be thanked, foremost is Masatoshi Nagatomi, my beloved mentor at Harvard University, who welcomed me into the world of Buddhist Studies and who had faith in me. His keen insight and commitment to intellectual inquiry have inspired me over the more than ten years under his tutelage. His encyclopedic knowledge of the Buddhist world is daunting, but always a source of illuminating guidance.

Other professors whom I would like to thank are: Miriam Levering for astute questions, numerous discussions, information, and insights. Helen Hardacre for her sound advice. Inés Talamantez for assistance with methodological considerations. Victor Sōgen Hori for helpful discussions and comments. Mineshima Hideo of Waseda University for foundational instruction and helping me make connections with other people. President Koide of Aichi Gakuin University deserves special mention for his assistance. Okajima Hidetaka, also of Aichi Gakuin University, for assistance in understanding arcane aspects of Sōtō sect regulations. The late Ishikawa Rikizan of Komazawa University for information about nuns in early Sōtō Zen history. Paul Swanson and Jim Heisig of Nanzan University Institute for Religion & Culture for their reflections and assistance. My professors at Kalamazoo College who introduced me to the significance of the study of religion.

Conversations with colleagues at Vanderbilt University, especially Daniel Patte, have helped me refine the book. I also thank Beth Conklin for her indispensable insights, editorial comments, and penetrating questions that helped deepen my thoughts. Her assistance significantly improved the book.

The field work required for this project would not have been possible without the financial support given by a Fulbright Dissertation Grant, a Reischauer Institute at Harvard University Summer Research Grant, and the YKK Corporation.

Special appreciation is due to Miranda Shaw for scholarly advice and inspiring discussions, Lisa Hallstrom for careful reading of early drafts and invaluable comments, John Holt for careful reading of parts of the manuscript, helpful encouragement and instrumental advice, and Tara Doyle for helping me get to India in the first place.

I would like to duly acknowledge and express my gratitude to the people of Oxford University Press for their support and careful work, especially Cynthia Read and Lisa Stallings.

My thanks also goes out to Lucy for helpful discussions, and to Wendy for sisterly support.

I am deeply grateful to Chih Wang, my supportive husband, who enthusiastically did whatever he could to enable and empower me to complete this book.

My deepest gratitude goes to my parents, who through their example instilled in me a profound sense of wonder in the rich cultural and religious diversity of our world. My father gets special appreciation for setting me on the path to find the contributions that can be made to humanity through engaged scholarship. His generous assistance in the late stages of preparing the manuscript is also deeply appreciated.

Although my mother will not see this work in its published form, her incomparable generosity and dedicated assistance helped me all along the way. She came to live with me in Nagoya for several months after I left the monastery. Because she was from the same generation as most of the nuns I was interviewing, even when she was not attending the actual interview, it was clear that her presence in my life was a bridge which facilitated deeper conversations that I could never have had on my own. She also addressed the envelopes for the surveys and helped decipher the elegant (but sometimes illegible, to my eyes) writing on the responses. There are more ways in which she freely gave her assistance than I can recount here. But I must mention one of her last gifts to me. It was a gift that also poignantly showed me how to mother a child with unconditional love. She cared for my newborn son, Kenji, while I finished this manuscript. (He was born five weeks early, so I did not meet my personal deadline to finish before his birth.) For several weeks she would send me off to work for long days, expressing concern that I be careful not to push too hard. I now realize that those weeks when I had spent long days away working had not been easy for her, but she never gave any indication. Just a month after the manuscript was submitted, we learned her body was completely wracked with cancer. All I can say is that my profound gratitude for her love moves me to tears.

Gasshō.

Nagoya, Japan
August 1998   P.K.R.A.

Contents

Transliteration Guide

Japanese names appear following Japanese custom, family name first, given name second.

In transliteration of Japanese words and names, the Hepburn System is used, except in familiar names like Tokyo. The Hepburn System follows the common English reading, using diacritics to mark long vowels.

Because this work focuses on the Japanese Buddhist tradition, Japanese is considered the primary language for Buddhist terms. The equivalent Chinese and Sanskrit are sometimes provided for clarification.

For Chinese words, the pinyin system for transcription is employed. Sanskrit words are transliterated according to Whitney, *Sanskrit Grammar*. References in Pāli are limited to citations quoted that use Pāli.

Non-English terms are given in italics, except for words that are frequently used and are basic to the book, for example, words like Nigakurin and Nisōdō, which are explained in the text. In addition, place names do not appear in italics.

Abbreviations: J., Japanese; Ch., Chinese; Skt., Sanskrit.

Prologue

Let me begin with three episodes that were formative and vital in creating this book. They provide keys to my motivation and illustrate the sometimes serendipitous nature of scholarly pursuits. The first episode explains my early impressions of Buddhism in contemporary Japan. The second reveals my initial impulse to move in the direction of exploring the topic of Buddhist nuns. The third episode shows how the research proceeded.

When I was living in Japan in 1980, I was just beginning my formal study of Buddhism at Waseda University. I learned introductory material about major Buddhist leaders in Japanese history and basic Buddhist concepts, including that compassion was a fundamental value in the Buddhist teachings. Therefore, I was rather bewildered when I heard the wife of a priest say, "Our son wants a stereo, I wonder if there are any funerals around?" At the time, I had no idea what the connection might be between stereos and funerals. Finally, a friend explained it to me. Funerals are a temple's major source of income; indeed, funerals make many priests rather wealthy. This incident, as well as casual observances of life in modern Japan, led me to an impression that there was no genuine Buddhism left in Japan. I was disillusioned. I thought that the affluent economic impulse had ruined any vestige of the tremendous history and teachings I had been studying. My cynical, naive, and uninformed conclusion about the state of Buddhism in modern Japan shifted when I met a Japanese Zen Buddhist nun.

I met Kitō Shunkō in the autumn of 1987 when I sojourned to India as a scholar of Buddhism. She is an elderly Sōtō Zen monastic woman who was returning to India for a final pilgrimage to the Mahābodhi Temple in Bodh Gaya. Although I had concentrated my Buddhist studies on Japan, I was not aware of an extant order of Japanese Zen nuns. My first glimpse of her with clean-shaven head and saffron robes—the traditional color of Indian monastics—was compelling. Moving toward her I realized her robes were Japanese in design, but not the black that is common to monastics of Japan. Her aesthetic sensitivity and cultural awareness drew me to her side. In the softened light of evening as we walked around the Bodhi Tree her face glowed with the wisdom of enlightenment. Compassion emanated from her every motion as we moved through wispy clouds of incense carrying the prayers of devotees. Among the spirited pilgrims and the desperate beggars her laughter resounded with the peace of one who has soared the heights and fathomed the depths. She seemed to be a living model of all that I had been studying—embodying harmony in its richest form. What teachings have helped her gain such wisdom? How did she train to be so compassionate? Where is the spring of her ebullient laughter?

I knew after our first conversation under the Bodhi Tree that I wanted to learn as much as possible about her way of life. As we walked along the Niranja river where Śākyamuni once walked, a brilliantly pink sun rose into the sky. She interwove stories of the years she spent in India building the Japanese Temple in Bodh Gaya with poetry by Zen master Dōgen (13th c.) and information about a training temple for monastic women in Nagoya, Japan. We laughed heartily as the image of meeting again in that monastery for women—worlds away—flashed through our minds.

I had found a living treasure of Japanese Buddhism.

(Numerous people, including abbess Aoyama, mentioned that if I had not met this particular nun, Kitō Shunkō, I probably would not have been moved enough to come live with and study Zen nuns. A laywoman very close to many of the higher ranking nuns, Ōgishi Emiko, recounted to me the story of her first meeting with Kitō Sensei. It illustrates how Kitō Sensei is respected among the nuns themselves. Ōgishi-san was visiting Katō Sensei at Seikanji Temple when Kitō Sensei came in and sat at her teacher's (Katō Sensei) feet and began stroking her hand. Katō Sensei looked at Ōgishi-san and said, "There are many kinds of nuns. But this nun, Shunkō-san, is a nun's nun.")

Another event that propelled this book along occurred a few years later, after I had spent one year living with and near the Zen nuns' community. It involved my interaction with one of my important living sources, a nun named Kojima Kendō (1898–1995). In the summer of 1990, I went to visit her in Toyama Prefecture where she was passing her final years at the Lumbini-en orphanage she had helped to establish. I knew I would not be able to conduct a typical interview with this nun, who had taken on the entire Sōtō sect administration to win equal rights for nuns. I just wanted *darśan*: to see and be in the presence of a holy being. In lucid moments, she provided details of various poignant moments in her life: what it was like being among the first nuns to study at Komazawa University, how she laughed when she realized that she was the only nun among a roomful of top-ranking monks as she pounded her fist on the table demanding reforms in sect regulations, and the time she served as the lead celebrant in a religious ceremony at the temple Dōgen founded, Eihei-ji—first nun in recorded history to do so—and how Niwa Zenji, the highest Zen Master in Japan, teased her about how masculine she was and she teased him about how feminine he was. She also gave me numerous original texts that shed light on the inside story of Zen nuns' activities that I would never have known about otherwise.

We were inseparable for the entire week, holding hands walking down the corridor to the dining hall, napping on the floor in the heat of midday, snickering in the bath, and giggling past lights out as we lay in our twin futons. As I was packing my suitcase, she scooted her tiny frame—a shadow of her past form—across the floor, and she offered me a cookie that she had already started nibbling on. She announced, "These are from Shunkō-san." Then she impishly smiled as she finally remembered that the cookies in the pretty lavender tin that we had been snacking on all week were the ones I had delivered to her from Kitō Shunkō. Sadness weighed heavy in the air as we knew the hour of my departure had arrived. Although it had been only a few days, it was as though we had been friends forever, an unlikely pair—me, a graduate student fighting for a little self-confidence, she, a famous Zen nun who fought an entire male-dominated institution and won. I gathered my courage, because I could not return to Cambridge without asking her, "Kojima Sensei, what do you think of me writing my dissertation on the history and activities of twentieth century Sōtō Zen nuns? Is it okay?" Nothing that had transpired in the last days had prepared me for her response. Her tiny curved back shot up—restoring the full extension of her former stature. She squared her shoulders and bowed deeply, placing her brow upon the floor for a two-minute eternity. As she began to raise her body, she spoke in the most eloquent and humble form of Japanese, "Please, I beseech you to complete this project. I have not died so that I could meet you." I sat in stunned silence as she dropped her shoulders, back rounded, head cocked to the side, and flippantly added, "I'm counting on you!"

The ancient Indian text composed by elder almswomen,
the *Therīgāthā*, recounts that the devil Mārā queries,
"Can women attain enlightenment?"
The female Buddhist elder retorts, "Of course!
Only Mārā would imagine otherwise!"

Women

Living

Zen

ONE

Introduction

Buddhist nuns have made generative and perennial contributions to Japanese history. Their contributions, however, have been hidden from the dominant representation of history. They were central agents in cultivating the foundation of Buddhism in Japan in the sixth century. They were active participants during the formative years of the Sōtō Zen sect in the thirteenth century. Monastic women also induced major advancements in the twentieth century. Between these prominent moments of Japanese history, Buddhist women have been a vital and constant presence. They displayed creative vision that navigated them through sometimes foul waters—a testimony to their seriousness of intention, commitment, and ingenuity.

The lives of many Sōtō Zen nuns in the twentieth century embody classical Buddhist ideals. This book focuses on these women. It highlights the women who were not daunted by a male-dominated institutional hierarchy. It gives names to women who did not flinch as they demanded that sect regulations treat male and female monastics equally. It gives voices to the women who have chosen to lead strictly disciplined and refined monastic lives over successful careers and the comparatively unconstrained and unregulated quality of secular lifestyles.

In the face of such resolute determination and historical efficacy, one is justified in wondering why nuns have been largely nonexistent in the scholarship on Japanese Buddhism. Part of the reason is the now unsurprising, but nonetheless significant, androcentric bias that has dominated academic inquiry. Gender has

3

only relatively recently become a salient category in the field of Buddhist studies. Furthermore, Zen Buddhist studies have primarily focused on textual documentation. The field lags behind in ethnographic research, contributing to the lack of examining how the tradition has been lived by the diversity of its adherents. Because nuns' activities and contributions rarely appear in the texts that have attracted the attention of scholars, nuns' assiduous engagement in the tradition has been neglected. Moreover, nuns have been omitted from western studies of Zen philosophy and history in part due to androcentric bias in the translation of Japanese materials. Almost all nongendered words in Japanese are translated in their male declensions in English, rendering female participants invisible.

This volume expands the purview of Zen studies by presenting historical evidence and providing new ethnographic data that advance a critical interpretation of the meaning and significance of female monastic practice. Where the historical record did not reflect why or how nuns achieved what they did, I sought out answers. Where historical documentation and textual sources were insufficient, I gathered ethnographic data. Where prevailing interpretations of Buddhist nuns did not correspond with the historical, textual, and ethnographic evidence gathered, I revised them.

I bring to the surface important moments of Japanese history that help explain why Sōtō Zen nuns are strong today. These materials elucidate the activities of the nuns fighting for and gaining opportunities in this century. They also shed light upon how Sōtō Zen nuns practice Zen in the twentieth century. Changes in Japanese religiosity as Japan rapidly moved from a traditional society with a rich cultural heritage to an affluent, modernized society are also considered. I analyze developments in this century in terms of the features that are unique to monastic women. I attempt to present the nuns' perspective on their history, their practices, and their interpretation of their lives. Without this any study of Japanese Zen nuns would be incomplete.

Scholarly Contexts

This is primarily a study of Japanese women who have chosen a Buddhist monastic lifestyle complete with vows of celibacy and the pursuit of wisdom and compassion. The structure of their lives is regulated by Sōtō Zen monastic practices, which means their daily lives include waking up at predawn, doing zazen, chanting, cleaning, and cooking. Aside from exploring their lives as an example of human religiosity, this book also addresses concerns found in historiography, Japanese studies, women's studies, and ethnographic studies. I am trying to find out what Sōtō Zen nuns consider important as Buddhists. Close examination of a large group of nuns within Sōtō Zen, especially those affiliated with Aichi Senmon Nisōdō, a women's monastery in Nagoya, Japan, is the main focus of this work. It is only an explication of that part of history that helps bring to light the efforts of this group of Sōtō Zen nuns in their struggle to live meaningfully in situations that they wanted to modify.

In order to do this, I had to do a critical examination of the available materials and gather original data. This entailed making value, epistemology, and legitimacy judgments along the way. To clarify what this means, let me explicate a scheme devised by the insightful semiotic scholar, Daniel Patte.[1] He outlines the types of interpretations that are basic to scholarly work by contrasting two main varieties: customary scholarly interpretations and exemplary critical interpretations. "Customary" is used here as shorthand for "Androcentric and Eurocentric."

Patte's scheme, originally designed for literary interpretations, can also apply to field researchers or people interpreting the practice of religion. In general, one's background in language, culture, and education, as well as age, sex, and experiences, influence one's value, epistemology, and legitimacy judgments. Value judgments are judgments made about the significance of the material. For example, I made a value judgment when I decided to explore the religious aims and experiences of nuns. Another type of value judgment would be to choose, instead, to focus on the socioeconomic dimensions of being a monastic in modern Japan. My decision to focus my investigation on the activities of women is also a value judgment, which I make explicit. In "customary" scholarship it was common to limit the focus to men, but frequently to cast it as if men represented all people. Another value judgment found in "customary" historical scholarship was to limit one's purview to western music, for example, and call it the history of music. In these examples the value judgments remain implicit.

Epistemological judgments are judgments made when one chooses the types of sources upon which to base one's conclusions, such as oral interviews, participant-observation, and written documents—published research, institutional records, individual surveys. Although this is true for both "customary" and "critical" scholarship, in "critical" scholarship one is acutely conscious that one's method shapes the knowledge that is gained. Furthermore, one's relationship to the material and the material-gathering process are integral to the epistemology judgment. For example, one's facility in the languages used in the sources affects one's epistemology judgments, compounded if an interpreter or translations were used. Besides methodological and reflexivity concerns, specific epistemology judgments I had to make in studying nuns involved discerning what categories nuns use to interpret and express their lives. I made an epistemological judgment to use Buddhist categories to guide my interpretation. Moreover, I based my judgment upon what nuns think, not upon what monks think. When epistemology judgments remain implicit, there is little to no reflexive analysis. For example, when one does not take into account the differences

	Customary Scholarly Interpretations	Exemplary Critical Interpretations
Value Judgment	Implicit	Explicit
Epistemological Judgment	+/−Explicit	Explicit
Legitimacy Judgment	Explicit	Explicit

that are introduced when a translation is used, the epistemology judgments are not explicit.

Legitimacy judgments are judgments made about the accuracy and reliability of the material. In other words, the researcher must determine what counts as significant evidence. In most scholarship, written documents constitute the preponderance of legitimate sources. Other types of sources, however, can be as valid—or in some cases more valid—than written sources. Validity is related to, and in part assessed by, the value judgments one brings to the research. For example, because I value what the nuns think of their own lives, I made the legitimacy judgment that interviews with nuns yield valid data. Oral, observed, and written sources directly from nuns are essential to my research, because I am trying to ascertain how nuns interpret their own lives.

According to this schema, "customary scholarship" and "critical scholarship" differ mainly in whether the perspective or epistemology and value judgments of the scholar are made explicit or remain implicit. "Critical scholarship" recognizes that each person has a perspective. A scholar, of course, tries to have as informed a perspective as possible. The quality, quantity, and type of information available to the scholar will surely affect the perspective of the scholar, but it will not dissolve the epistemological and value judgments made. Each perspective sheds a distinct light on the issue at hand and therefore makes a contribution. This is all good for advancing scholarly understanding. Thus, for example, androcentric and Eurocentric perspectives are not problematic when these orientations or value and epistemology judgments are an explicit dimension of the scholarship. Problems can arise, however, when the perspective is not explicated in the presentation of one's material.

The raw data I gathered did not always corroborate the types of interpretations I found in the scholarship on women, Buddhism, and Zen monasticism. Therefore, I began to analyze how the perspective of the author shaped the conclusions drawn by the author. In the process, I had to learn to see from the nuns' perspective. From that vantage point, nuns, Buddhist history, Japanese religion, and Zen monasticism looked very different.

The aim of this work is to gain a more comprehensive view of these themes, not to lift women out of context. Women cannot be understood when taken out of the larger historical, cultural, and social context in which they act. Likewise, the larger historical, cultural, and social context cannot be understood without understanding the role of women in these spheres. Particular attention, however, is devoted to positive contributions and activities of women, for these aspects have not been sufficiently explored in a scholarly context. Therefore, highlighting the participation of women in the various fields of scholarly discourse is pursued because of the relative neglect of women in scholarly works in the past, as well as my concern to develop more balanced views of religion, Buddhist history, Zen monasticism, and Japanese religiosity.

Feminist historiography informs my interpretation of the historical section on monastic women. What makes a historiography feminist is the approach to history that assumes women were active participants in the creation of history. Although I take cues from feminist historiographic principles, I would stress that historiography must begin with the notion that all people are agents and actors creating and participating in history. One's gender does not determine whether or not one has a history. The neglect of certain people in historical accounts is a *historiographic* problem. It is not a problem of *history*. All people have been, and continue to be, active agents of history. Therefore the solution lies in expanding the scope of what is deemed important enough to include in historical accounts. It is, furthermore, women's interaction with the "rest" of history that illuminates their contributions.[2]

The historiographical principles applied in this work interpret the lack of historical documentation as an indication of how much has been lost rather than as proof that women were not involved.[3] This interpretation is based upon a notion of historical significance that acknowledges the contributions of those who may not have received official or institutional recognition for their efforts, but who, nevertheless, continued to act and serve. Lack of recognition does not necessarily indicate lack of activity. One must first explain what women were doing in order to determine what they were not doing. In lieu of information, one can only conclude that one does not know. For example, one cannot conclude that nuns did not study philosophy until one can determine exactly what nuns did study. Scholars now realize that the history of women must be reclaimed, not just for the sake of women or for a more balanced account of historical events, but also because current academic exploration into female religiosity reveals important differences between the religious lives of men and women. Such studies help refine our conceptualization of religion, which is incomplete so long as it excludes the activities and thoughts of women. In view of this emerging awareness, study of religious values demands distinguishing male and female experiences and expressions.

Furthermore, studies of people cannot proceed without the benefit of detailed ethnographic studies of people in various cultural settings.[4] These studies primarily focus upon cultural and contextual issues that bear upon the lives of the people. Such studies that explore the women involved depart from feminist studies that are solely concerned with extinguishing androcentrism. It is critical in such studies, however, to be aware of ethnocentric perspectives that can misdirect one's analysis of ethnographic research. Ifi Amadiume, an African scholar, is keenly aware of the ethnocentrism inherent in scholars who think that women are inferior across all cultures and in all social contexts.[5] From her vantage point vis-à-vis western scholarship on women, it is clear that gender is a sociocultural construction that must not be confused with sex, a biological category. She continues with words of caution about racist biases that function like an insidious disease upon the scholarship.[6] Through the insightful instruction of nonwestern scholars, many western scholars are becoming increasingly sensitive to the assumptions they bring to their work. Listening to the voices of women and men in their own context is indispensable to understanding them.

Ever since women during Śākyamuni's lifetime (6th c. B.C.E.) claimed the right to seek ordination and to pursue the contemplative life, Buddhist female monastic orders have been an important mode for women to express and explore their spiritual development.[7] However, the relative lack of scholarly attention to women's distinct religious values and lifestyles obscures the signal importance of the female religious paradigm. Assertions that women have been universally oppressed are unfounded. Too much is unknown to draw any such conclusion. But by not seeking to illuminate the contributions of women—even (or especially) those not recognized by their contemporaries—historians tacitly subjugate women and perpetuate any unfair treatment women might have experienced historically. Looking at what women did do is important. Just looking at what they officially were not supposed to do can be misleading.

The insidious nature of androcentric interpretation is revealed in a 1992 example of an analysis of women that does not fully take into account the perspective of the women concerned. It is found in the volume *Buddhism, Sexuality, and Gender*. One contributor delineates four aspects to early Buddhist attitudes toward women: soteriological inclusiveness, institutional androcentrism, ascetic misogyny, and soteriological androgyny.[8] This is a late twentieth-century male view of Buddhist attitudes toward women. This is not a description of early Buddhist women's attitudes toward themselves. One must question whether women's institutions were indeed androcentric. Furthermore, there is no evidence that Buddhist women practiced misogyny. Considering the available data with the women's perspective in mind would likely lead to different conclusions than those drawn from an androcentric perspective.

I made an effort to discover Sōtō Zen nuns' understanding and interpretations of their own lives and monastic careers. This led me to seek data on the activities of female monastics and their perspectives of their own situations. A picture of strong, devout, and resilient monastic women emerged. In contrast, most scholarship on nuns paints different impressions that would be strikingly modified if the nuns' perspectives were included. Scholarship that does not include the perspectives of the nuns mutes the voices of dedicated monastic women. The literature continues to provide impressions of monastic women as weak social misfits with an occasional powerful, imperially endowed female monastic. Descriptions like the following one from a 1986 work engender such impressions: "The nunnery was a place of refuge for women who did not wish to marry, widows, abandoned concubines, and prostitutes."[9] This statement obfuscates the fact that a nunnery is more fundamentally a place for women to pursue a monastic Buddhist life, regardless of their motivation. Although some women were escaping difficult circumstances, there is no evidence that this was widespread or even the primary reason for women to pursue monastic life. Even when motivation to enter monastic life did derive out of poor life conditions, this does not mean that they were insincere or not dedicated to Buddhist teachings. What most poignantly illustrates the inequity inherent in such statements is that the motivations of their male counterparts are rarely highlighted.

Another statement that indicates the women's perspectives were not the point of reference is illustrated by the following: "Buddhism attracted women who wanted to run away from their gender-determined roles."[10] But interpreting these actions from the perspective of the women concerned would conclude instead that the women attracted to Buddhism were defining their gender and their roles in ways that were not in accord with the roles more common to women. Clearly they were making a deliberate choice against one way and for another, but they were not running away from gender-determined roles to nongendered nonroles. Instead they were redefining their gender and roles in terms of the Buddhist monastic life of women.

Some texts even leave the impression that there are no Buddhist monastic women, especially in Japan. Nearly categorical exclusion from encyclopedia sources, including the *Encyclopedia of Religion* (1987) and the *Perennial Dictionary of World Religion* (1981), helps foster this unwarranted impression. The *Encyclopedia of Religion* entry for "Nuns" does not inform the reader that there are Buddhist nuns in Japan and does not refer the reader to the entry "monasticism," whereas the entry on "monks" does. The information one can cull from the entry on monasticism includes a description of life in a Japanese Zen monastery. Although this information accurately describes the training and lifestyle of female monastics, it fails to mention this. With further investigation of categories like "Women in Buddhism" one can find minimal information on nuns. But it does not inform the reader that Mahāyāna monastic women exist.[11] The *Perennial Dictionary of World Religions* deepens the impression by citing only Christian nuns in their seven-line entry on "Nuns," refers only to monks in its entry on "Zen," and discusses the *Pātmokkha* as the text on monks' *vinaya* regulations with no mention of the *Bhikkhunī Pātmokkha* which contains numerous regulations for nuns.[12]

Other misleading comments can be found, like "The Path of the nun, although theoretically viable as a religious practice in Buddhism from the outset was destined for virtual extinction,"[13] or "While the *bhikkhuni*[14] Order died out in India and Southeast Asia, a women's monastic Order was sustained in China, Taiwan, and Tibet."[15] These statements assume that all Buddhists have the same definition of nun and that all have the same set of monastic discipline (*vinaya*). They do not take into account different cultural and historical developments. Moreover, numerous women in some Buddhist countries, especially Sri Lanka and Thailand, lead lives that are best described as the life of a nun, but current historical and social circumstances deny them official recognition.[16]

Japanese Buddhist nuns practice a kind of Mahāyāna Buddhism in which there is a fundamentally different understanding of monastic discipline. Unlike monastics in other parts of Asia, during most of Buddhism's centuries-long history in Japan most monks and nuns have not taken vows in the full set of monastic discipline laid out in the *Vinaya Pitaka*. In Japan, the definitions of monk and nun do not revolve around the number of precepts one takes nor the lineage into which one is ordained. From the beginning of Sōtō Zen in Japan, Dōgen (1200–1253), the attributed founder of the sect, only prescribed sixteen precepts for both male and female monastics.[17] On numerous occasions Sōtō nun teachers, including abbesses, explained to me that by truly abiding by these sixteen precepts one would not violate any of the other precepts found in the *Vinaya Pitaka*. In short, compared to practices in other Buddhist regions, Buddhist traditions found in Japanese culture allow considerable flexibility in determining who is ordained.

Indeed, deciding who is a nun is multifaceted and controversial. This issue is frequently linked to an issue of dire concern to many women Buddhists in the world: ordination lineage. Some nuns "have" the lineage and other nuns do not care about the lineage. There are also women who want the lineage in traditions that say they cannot have it. This issue sets in high relief the complexity of cultural transformations of an ostensibly shared religious tradition. Nonetheless, one thing is common. There are women in each Buddhist culture who seek to commit their lives fully to Buddhist monastic life. I choose to call all these women nuns and to define what that means in each given context.

When some academics have recognized the existence of female monastics, it is with reservations. For example, the statement that "the order of nuns was never taken very seriously by the Japanese" begs the question, "Which Japanese?" It is safe to assume that at least the women themselves took their own practices seriously. The fact that women were the first monastics in Japan and that women have continued to the present day to ordain other women into the Buddhist path, a time span of more than 1,400 years, denies the validity of such statements.

In the academic literature to date, one of the more detailed evaluations of monastic women in the Sōtō sect does not include the perspective of the women under consideration.

> In Japanese Zen, two facts are striking: there are virtually no prominent women, and the condition of the Zen nun in Japan has been sorry indeed. In Sōtō Zen, the largest Zen sect in Japan, nuns, until the very recent past, were not allowed to function as priests, could not live in temples, and could not hold independent retreats or attend retreats held by monks.[18]

The initial conclusion asserted in this source that "there are virtually no prominent women" lacks the necessary qualification "in published texts." The unambiguously established androcentric bias in historiography has created the illusion that women were not actively involved and prominent in their own spheres of influence. A judgment about the status of women, then, must be withheld until we have a more informed understanding of what women were actually doing. There is little doubt that monastic women did not always receive official recognition for their activities. This indicates the prejudice practiced by the male branch of the monastic institution, but this does not necessarily mean that the women saw themselves as dwelling in sorry conditions. It is inconceivable that women who for centuries have dedicated their lives to Buddhist teachings would continue to choose to remain in a tradition that they did not find valuable in some way. To think that they might have done so is to deny that they had the capacity to make sound and intelligent decisions about the course of their lives.

The fact that women were not "allowed" to function as priests has two sides to it. The inequality of this situation is fundamentally economic. Performing priestly duties is the most common source of income for a temple; not being included in this activity actually has marked—and to some extent continues to mark—deep lines of discrimination. On the other hand, when one begins analyzing from the perspective of Dōgen's teachings on monastic life as the nuns assess it, monastic women appear to be following the tradition of their founder quite closely. Nuns have stressed maintaining a monastic lifestyle.

Prior to recent reforms, female monastics were not allowed to head temples and hold officially recognized retreats, but they did undergo rigorous training and they do lead lives of practice in their sub-temples. Many of these previously unacknowledged centers of female monastic training are still active, and they now receive official recognition. Women worked hard for official status, but the moment they received such status does not mark the beginning of their intense practice or dedication to the Buddhist Path—there is ample evidence that women were active throughout Buddhist history in Japan. One final note of reinterpretation is necessary. In the article on Sōtō nuns previously cited, the final assessment of Sōtō Zen nuns is that, given these poor conditions, "it is scarcely possible that any outstanding nuns could appear" until recent reforms.[19] It is more to the point to say that the recent reforms were won precisely because there *were* outstanding nuns who wrought them.

From these examples, it appears necessary that an interpretation of events takes into account the perspective of the women concerned. Time spent with the nuns convinced me of this necessity, especially since I found that they were not hesitant about acting in the face of oppressive and unfair circumstances. Viewing developments in history from the nuns' perspective also gave me a new vantage point from which to interpret activities of women in the past. Viewing the long history of Japanese religious activities, one sees that women were at the center of things during the formative stages of Japanese civilization.[20] Shamanesses, matrilineal and matrilocal systems, goddesses—including the highest deity in the Shintō pantheon, Amaterasu—and female rulers were features that shaped the Japanese landscape. When one includes these features in a picture of the landscape, Japanese religion looks richer, more diverse, and more egalitarian than it has appeared in the hands of androcentric scholarship.

Some historical elements of Japanese religiosity provide necessary background for placing twentieth-century Zen nuns' views and actions in context. Part of the cultural milieu of sixth-century Japan involved sensitivity to the beauty and ephemerality of natural phenomena—cherry in spring bloom, summer songs of birds, the autumnal moon, and snowy winters. During that time, Buddhism provided a vehicle for new cultural energy in art, architecture, written language, institutional structures, and various technologies, plus new insights into the highly developed civilizations of India, China, and Korea. Buddhism and Japanese culture underwent a mutually transforming process, but one may still trace the impulses that give contour to Buddhism in the Japanese cultural context.

At the time, the concept of a transcendent realm beyond immediate experience of the phenomenal world was not highly developed in the dominant Japanese worldview. As observers of Japanese culture have stated time and again, one of the characteristics of this culture was its primary focus upon the present activity, where the here and now was affirmed. Change was accepted as an inherent feature of the world as experienced.[21] Indeed, taking cues from nature, impermanence was understood as a quality of beauty. The ephemerality of flowers embodied the essence of beauty, with cherry blossoms being the quintessential example. Contrary to being a source of suffering, impermanence was understood to be vital to the experience of beauty. At the core of this interpretation is an affirmation of the beauty of nature because of, not in spite of, its ephemerality.

Moreover, phenomenal reality was not dissected into divergent ontological categories.[22] This holistic view led Japanese Buddhists to understand the term "sentient beings" in a distinctive way. In the Japanese context it was more natural to include plants and rocks as sentient beings rather than to exclude them. Ramifications of this line of interpretation extend to the fundamental concepts of enlightenment, Buddha-nature, and some of the institutional forms Buddhist monasticism has taken in Japan.

Each in its own way, sects of Buddhism in Japan creatively combine the qualities of the indigenous Japanese worldview with Buddhist teachings and culture as they came to Japan from India via China and Korea. My study centers upon nuns in the Sōtō Zen sect said to be founded by Eihei Dōgen. Sōtō Zen is one of the sects of Zen Buddhism that derives from Chinese developments in Mahāyāna Buddhism. There are two other Zen sects that also came to Japan from China, Rinzai and Ōbaku.[23] They each have a distinct way of articulating their concept of enlightenment and the method for realizing it. Dōgen stressed that all "existents" are Buddha-nature.[24] In short, he taught that you realize enlightenment when you act enlightened.

Dōgen institutionalized his distinctive understanding of Buddhism into a strict monastic system that is articulated in his book of detailed monastic regulations, *Eihei Shingi*.[25] Modeled after Pai-chang's version of Chinese monastic regulations, Dōgen translates his understanding of Buddhist truth into Buddhist practice.[26] Dōgen's keen philosophical genius is embodied in this monastic lifestyle. In its structure, form, and spirit one can experience the subtle yet pervasive way in which Dōgen's monastic tradition takes the indigenous Japanese affirmation of the phenomenal world and sensitivity to beauty derived from ephemerality and harmonizes it with fundamental Buddhist teachings on Buddha-nature, enlightenment, and impermanence.

The role Dōgen's teachings play in daily life and decisionmaking continues to vary from era to era and from temple to temple. But his influence on Sōtō Zen tradition has proven indelible through the vicissitudes of time and understanding. Writings attributed to him contain diverse views, perhaps reflecting changing social circumstances and developments in his thought. In turn, these writings have been interpreted in a variety of ways as they traversed over centuries and countries.

What is the role and meaning of being a Sōtō Zen female monastic in twentieth-century Japan? My field research in Japan led me to begin answering this question by exploring the history of women in Japanese religion, the teachings and practices of Sōtō Zen, the motivations of monastics, and the social currents of modern Japanese culture. During the course of my research, it also became apparent that at times the significance of female monastics' activities would be clearer when viewed in contrast to the activities of male monastics.

It is essential to explore the vocabulary male and female monastics use to describe themselves. Difference in vocabulary not only indicates differences in attitudes and self-understanding of monastics in Japan, but it also has ramifications that extend into the translations of terms from Japanese to English. The reasons for such difference include discrepancy between the definition of the term and its corresponding object, plus gender-variant language that has previously gone unacknowledged. The original Sanskrit of the terms in question are *bhikṣu* and *bhikṣunī*. The most common translation of the terms in English are monk and nun, respectively. Careful investigation of female monastics establishes that reexamination of these words and their accompanying definitions and nuances is necessary.[27]

The basic terminology denoting members of the Buddhist Community (Skt. *saṅgha*) is important to mention, to clarify changes in Chinese and Japanese terminology that occurred. The Buddhist Community is generally described as being composed of people in four categories: *bhikṣu* (almsman), *bhikṣunī* (almswoman), *upāsaka* (layman), and *upāsikā* (laywoman).

Sanskrit Terminology

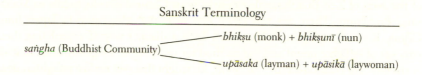

saṅgha (Buddhist Community) — *bhikṣu* (monk) + *bhikṣunī* (nun) / *upāsaka* (layman) + *upāsikā* (laywoman)

The Sanskrit term for Buddhist Community is *saṅgha*. *Saṅgha* means a group, often applied in ancient India to people who belong to a religious order. The Sanskrit term I am rendering as almsman is composed of *bhikṣ*, which means to beg or ask for, and the noun deriving from it, *bhikṣu*, means one who begs, a mendicant, a world renouncer, or a renunciant. *Bhikṣunī* is the feminine form of *bhikṣu* (*nī* is the Sanskrit suffix indicating feminine). The terms for the laity are composed as follows. The prefix *upa* means near or close to. The root *as* means to sit. Thus, the noun deriving from *upa-as* is *upāsaka*, meaning one who sits near, one who waits upon or serves. *Upāsikā* is the feminine form of *upāsaka*. Therefore, *bhikṣu* and *bhikṣunī* are those who beg for food, shelter, and basic necessities for life, and *upāsaka* and *upāsikā* refer to those who supply the renunciants' basic needs.

The Buddhist Community (Skt. *saṅgha*) can be viewed from two perspectives, the ideal Buddhist Community (J. *shihōsanga*; Skt. *cāturdiśa saṅgha*; literally translated "the saṅgha of the four cardinal directions) and the actual Buddhist Community (J. *genzensanga*; Skt. *sammukhī saṅgha*; literally "the present saṅgha").[28] The ideal Buddhist Community transcends time and space. It is the ultimate and universal concept of a Buddhist community eternally living according to the Dharma. At this level *bhikṣu* and *bhikṣunī* are equally world renouncers, as are *upāsaka* and *upāsikā* equally householders. There is no discrimination based upon gender. It is not a historical community. The actual Buddhist Community, on the contrary, is located in a cultural and historical context at a particular place with specific people. This is the Buddhist Community of experience that can be seen with the eyes. It always changes. Each epoch, each culture, and even each community has a unique expression of the actual Buddhist Community. And, unfortunately, among a host of other problems, a number of actual Buddhist Communities have a history of discrimination based upon gender.

The Chinese transliterate the Sanskrit term *sangha* as *seng-chia*. Departing from that point, the Chinese did not use transliterations of the Sanskrit terms *bhikṣu* and *bhikṣunī*. Instead, they dropped the *"chia"* from *seng-chia*, and they used *seng* to refer to monks or *bhikṣu*. For nun or *bhikṣunī*, they added the transliteration for the Sanskrit feminine suffix *ni*, as in *bhikṣunī*, to *seng*, resulting in *sengni*. In other words, the Chinese terms for monk and nun do not etymologically derive from the Sanskrit terms for monk and nun. The Chinese conflation of the Sanskrit lends itself to ambiguity. Therefore, references that are intended for the entire Buddhist Community (Ch. *seng-chia*) are often obscured. They have been mistaken as references only to monks (Ch. *seng*). Nuns were only noted where the suffix *ni* was affixed.

Chinese Monastic Terminology

seng (monk) + *sengni* (nun) = *seng-chia* (Buddhist Community)

The Japanese terminology regarding monastics was modified from its Indian roots and Chinese adaptations. Moreover, a difference has emerged in the terminology regarding male and female monastics in Japan. In androcentric Japanese terminology, male monastics are designated with the character *sō*. "Nun" is *nisō* in Japanese.[29] Etymologically, *sō* is a generic term that makes no reference to gender,[30] but the ambiguity generated by using a portion of the generic, nongendered term for Buddhist Community as the term for monk insinuates that monks are the standard for all monastics (*sō*). In so doing, monks are placed in a hierarchical relationship above nuns. The suggestion is that monks are the "real" Buddhist Community and nuns are a sub-Buddhist Community.

Japanese Androcentric Vocabulary

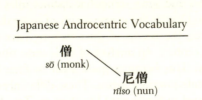

Upon examination of Japanese female monastics' understanding of the terms, however, a different set of terms emerges that is more accurate and specific. Tonsured Japanese women see monastic Buddhists first as *sō*, members of the ordained Buddhist Community (Skt. *sangha*). Within that they make a distinction between male (*nansō*, *nan* meaning male) and female (*nisō*) members. The *sō* taken from the Sanskrit *sangha* is used to refer to all monastics. In this way, monk, or *nansō*, more closely corresponds to the intended meaning of the Sanskrit *bhikṣu*, a male mendicant. The term for female monastic remains the same in the androcentric and the female monastics' vocabulary, *nisō*.

Japanese Female Monastics' Terminology

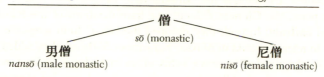

僧
sō (monastic)

男僧
nansō (male monastic)

尼僧
nisō (female monastic)

In strict etymological terms, *nī* designates female gender in Sanskrit. In folk etymology, the *ni* from *bhikṣunī* is the same *ni* used in transliterating Śākyamuni in Chinese and Japanese. Hence, Japanese nuns do not consider *nisō* a word with any condescending nuances. Thus, in accordance with the female monastic's vocabulary, the term *sō* is most accurately translated "monastic," *nisō* as "female monastic" or "monastic women," and *nansō* as "male monastic" or "monastic men." Within this framework, where "monk" is not considered the generic term for "monastics," "nun" for *nisō* and "monk" for *nansō* is also appropriate.

All nuns I interviewed, surveyed, or conversed with knew the terms. Some monks also use them. This terminology is evidence that nuns can create and define who they are. They do not just passively accept the male-dominated patterns. By accurately reflecting the vocabulary of Japanese female monastics, I hope to encourage the adoption of their terminology as the standard. It allows for distinction where necessary, yet does not harbor unwanted discrimination. We in English-language based academe must be careful, for the vast majority of texts in English invariably use the gender-exclusive term "monk" where monastic women would see themselves included. This practice has promoted the impression that Dōgen and other Zen writers only had a few words to say about nuns and nuns' practice.

It is not, however, a simple matter of inserting "and nuns" after each reference to "monks" or changing "monks" to "monastics." "Monk" and "nun" should not be treated simply as parallel terms, because today female and male monastics lead different daily lifestyles and serve somewhat distinct roles in society.[31] My field research bore this out. Despite the commonality of using the same scriptures and doing similar practices, the results of their training have increasingly diverged during the twentieth century. An analysis of their texts, rituals, and training tells only part of the story. This becomes quite clear in their daily patterns of life, motivations, and attitude toward practice. These differences between monks and nuns are not represented in the current literature on Zen, however.

Having gained access to rare original sources on the development of the women's monastery, I have a more complete context in which to understand Sōtō nuns. Although writings of Dōgen assert the equality of female and male practitioners, the available evidence suggests that female monastics have not been treated as equals in the Sōtō Zen institutional system for most of its history in Japan. My study of Zen Buddhist monastic women provides specific data about their recent history of struggle and independence against the backdrop of Japanese Buddhist institutional history. Throughout the twentieth century, Sōtō Zen female monastics have been engaged in an effort to maintain their interpretation of monasticism, but they did not have the advantage of institutional support until they began a concerted fight for such support at the turn of the century. Nuns strove to change the structures that oppressed them by harking back to Dōgen's teachings on equality that had gone unheeded by the institution of the Sōtō Zen sect. They sought to make these teachings an integral part of the Sōtō Zen tradition and demanded that the institutional regulations be rewritten to conform to them. This was at a time when monks were testing the extent of relaxed regulations with regard to monastic lifestyle. Nuns, on the other hand, were fortifying their ranks with strict discipline based on traditional monasticism. Because a traditional mode of monastic practice was at the center of nuns' daily pattern of life, they could face with confidence the powers that were designed to restrict them. The weight of monastic tradition helped establish the legitimacy of institutionalized equality.

The early decades of this century are explored in terms of the activities and goals of the four nuns who founded one of the first officially recognized Sōtō Zen monasteries for women. These early years laid a foundation for monastic women to achieve ranks commensurate with their competence within the Buddhist hierarchy. These four female monastics institutionalized their form of Zen, which strives to both maintain traditional values and practices and create avenues for women committed to Buddhist monastic practice in the modern world. The middle years of the twentieth century are highlighted through the life story of the nun Kojima Kendō. During these years Zen monastic women finally succeeded in establishing sect-supported institutions and equal regulations. Gaining sect recognition for their activities, female monastics prevailed over the social pressure for male dominance and actualized their interpretation of Dōgen's teachings.

The types of teachings and roles of Zen monastics in present-day Japan is illustrated through the biography of Aoyama Shundō, the current abbess of Aichi Senmon Nisōdō. Personal narrative has become recognized, particularly in feminist studies, as a rich source of information to illuminate the specific concerns and insights of the subject. Such information is especially important where little is known or recorded about the subject. But scholars are also becoming increasingly aware of different perspectives yielding different histories.[32] Abbess Aoyama's personal narrative exemplifies the contributions, activities, and accomplishments of a modern monastic woman. Although she is not an example of a "typical" nun, her story contributes to the awareness reflected in recent scholarly texts that women have been active participants and leaders in Zen.[33]

In short, Sōtō nuns had to come up with innovative ways to create the Zen tradition as they understood it. Heralding the teachings of Dōgen, nuns proclaimed their equality with men. Although they were not supported by the institution of their sect at the time, they persevered in their efforts to make their activities officially recognized. They entered the stream that follows the patterns of the past in an attempt to make them viable patterns in the present. Their harking back to "tradition" can be interpreted as a strategy for gaining power and establishing legitimacy.

In order to place the nuns' activities in context, let me remark on what issues monks were addressing. Sōtō monks did not need to establish legitimacy within the sect. They had to prove their relevance in a society that was undergoing rapid modernization. Most male monastics fit into the pattern of those who face the future with a novel vision, who change not to maintain tradition in a new context but in accord with their vision of changing needs. Monks clearly demonstrate that they are modern together with the best in lay society who are concerned about Japan's place in the evolving international environment. The male monastic institution can still be found today at Eihei-ji, the monastery Dōgen founded, and at other Sōtō monasteries, both large and small. The place of the male monastic lifestyle in the prevailing trends of Sōtō Zen, however, has undergone notable— in many instances radical—change. Most train in the traditional monastic life for the minimum requirement of two years, but a sizable number manage to shorten their stay in the monastery due to compensation granted to those with advanced academic training.[34] A majority have changed their roles so much that they are perhaps more accurately called priests, since most center upon liturgical activities and exclude renunciatory practices. Many ordained men marry and lead householder lives similar to laity. They are involved with raising children, concerned with cultivating an heir to the temple, engaged in efforts to support the family economically. A significant number are also notorious for indulging in the consumption of alcohol and other luxury items. These are all activities that fall within the bounds of the government's expanded monastic regulations for monks (1872)[35] and for nuns (1873). It should be pointed out that male monastics who have chosen to become "householder priests" are part of a deliberate tactical decision encouraged by the government. This decision resulted in the formal institution of a hereditary system, the notion of which is not hard to grasp in the Japanese cultural context, where hereditary systems abound.

Some Zen scholars have concluded that "it is impossible to detect the teachings of Dōgen in [monastic practice today]."[36] My research, which focuses on female monastics, differs from this conclusion. The basic explanation is in accord with my assessment of the monks being in the "modernizing" stream of society. The general move away from monasticism is a deliberate strategy to meet the changing needs of the Sōtō sect. The *Shushōgi*—a text widely taught to the laity (and that does not mention zazen)—is cited as the quintessential example of the sect's desire to not scare away the laity by stressing zazen and the strictness of the monastic lifestyle of the founder.[37] The Sōtō sect assessment of itself leaves the impression that men offer pragmatic reasons and popularity as central to their decision to change away from traditional practices.

The fact that a number of academics researching the contemporary situation of Zen in Japan conclude that Dōgen Zen is not alive in Japan today is yet another illustration that confirms Trinh Minh-Ha's conviction that

> [women anthropologists] have for the last decade devoted their energy to denouncing the male scholar's androcentrism, which prevents him from admitting or even recognizing the full impact of women's participation in the creation of society. They have begun challenging his limited descriptions of social reality by reinterpreting data to redefine power, influence, and status and to demonstrate that only within a male-biased perspective does the subjugation of women take on a universal face.[38]

In academic literature, there were almost no texts or documents that mentioned Sōtō Zen nuns. I did not even know about the current existence—much less the contributions—of Sōtō Zen nuns until I met one when I was in my fourth year as a doctoral candidate in Japanese Buddhism at Harvard University. Living and talking with these nuns was the only avenue available for learning their views and practices. After establishing relationships with these nuns, I was introduced to various Japanese original documents that told some of the story, but without the ethnographic data to provide a more complete picture, advancements on the scholarship of Zen nuns would be minimal. After I had researched the topic further, it became apparent that the activities of Japanese Buddhist women challenge the widely accepted concept that women were universally subjugated.

As though Dōgen were anticipating the developments in this century, he issued a warning to monastics who choose to modify the monastic life. As recorded by his disciple in the *Shōbōgenzō Zuimonki*, Dōgen lectured that

> No monk or nun attains it [Buddha Dharma] unless he or she has the mind of one who has left home. There must be a difference in the attitude of laypeople and those who have left home. A layman [or laywoman] who has the mind of a monk or nun who has left home will be released from samsara [suffering]; a monk or a nun who has the mind of a layperson has double faults. Their attitudes should be quite different.[39]

According to Dōgen, you cannot have both the attitudes and lifestyle of a layperson *and* reap the rewards of a renunciant. Since all traditions are like complex chemical compounds—that is, if you change one element the quality of the entire compound is changed—changing one aspect of a tradition inevitably results in a new set of circumstances. When an element, especially a fundamental element like the difference between lay and monastic lifestyles, is changed, the tradition changes. Certainly a tradition is free to transform in response to changing needs.

Looking from a broader sociohistorical perspective, one might analyze the striking differences between Sōtō Zen monks and nuns as a gender-delineated response to Zen in the twentieth century. Most nuns participate in the impulse to establish "traditional" Zen based upon their interpretation of Dōgen's teachings and to create a distinct "traditional" Japanese culture vis-à-vis modernization. Most monks modernize in a different way, trying to modernize in order to prove their significance and insight into the needs of a modern society. The result is that most ordained females lead strict monastic lifestyles and most ordained males act more like householder priests than monastics.

Although Sōtō Zen boasts the highest number of female monastics (just less than 1,000), 52% were born before 1928.[40] Zen monastic women, however, developed and maintain an institutional structure to support, train, and encourage themselves. Therefore, despite the statistical reality and although traditional patterns of life have become obscured in the competing impulses coursing through modern Japanese society, the nuns strive to keep the basic quality of life at the Zen monastery for women today a living kernel of traditional Zen values interwoven with traditional Japanese culture. Inquiry into monastic women as a distinct group within the Buddhist structure is, therefore, indispensable for a better understanding of Buddhism in modern Japan and the role of women in Japanese religion.

In brief, the Sōtō Zen structure includes specialized training monasteries and temples of three different ranks.[41] One must receive a degree from a training monastery in order to become the head of a temple. The higher the rank of the temple, the higher the degree one must have to become its head. The regulations about the amount of time one must spend in monastic training to be granted the basic degree necessary to head a basic Sōtō Zen temple range from a few weekends to two years (in rare cases, four years is required if one does not have a high school diploma upon entering). The amount of time varies according to one's academic background and experience in temple living. If one has been raised in a temple and has a college degree with a major in Buddhist Studies, the regulations allow for minimal time in a monastery. The regulations permit each person to tailor their own program.

Despite the flexibility of the regulations, in practice the shortest period of monastic training in the women's community is two years. However, monastic women consider five years to be the minimal amount of training necessary for the rhythm and quality of the strict monastic life to become a natural part of one's being and body, for one must cultivate habits of mind and body that are increasingly divergent from the habits of the common lay householder in modern Japan. Consistent with the value they place on monastic training, the average time a nun spends in training is actually five years. The physical demands of rising at predawn, sitting in zazen posture, eating with ritual exactness and grace, and cleaning with meticulous determination (using no assistance from convenient gadgets or solutions), requires a keen mind and strong body. Furthermore, without chairs, all activities from chanting scriptures and drinking tea, to sewing and confiding with a fellow adept are done in the formal sitting posture called *seiza* (sitting on the floor on one's legs with back perfectly straight). Since they are monastics, they do not even allow themselves the comfort of sitting on a cushion. The nun's hands, however, habitually hold precious tea bowls with a familiarity and ease uncommon in the highly aristocratic tea ceremony. They frequently take time to enjoy traditional tea and cakes, a time when often the comings and goings of the flowers in the garden are noted with longing and awe. Words that interrupt the silence are ordinarily embellished with graceful and humble turns of phrase. Subtle feelings are expressed through refined sensitivities that are ever aware of the season, while the vocabulary and grammar betray patterns of centuries past. The rigor of the activities and the intensity of human relations within this regulated environment are the grounds from which refinement is cultivated. The polished results are testimony to the serious and continual effort of the teachers and trainees. Upon graduating from the monastery, the majority of women enter a temple in which they continue the practices they learned in training. This training enables Zen monastic women to be self-sufficient in a temple as they become imbued with a traditional way of life. In the world of monastic women, therefore, one may still experience traditional Sōtō Zen monastic values laced with traditional Japanese culture.

Theoretical Considerations

Zen studies has rarely employed ethnographic data to explicate Zen Buddhism. This has resulted in a paucity of information about the lived tradition, especially women's experience. Typical text-based scholarship is insufficient to study the lives of Zen nuns today. The topic requires an ethnographic component. Beginning with the living religion of Zen, rather than with the Zen found in textual sources, expands the purview of Zen scholarship. This work specifically explores Sōtō Zen nuns' views of themselves and the paradigms that frame nuns' experience.

Developing a hermeneutical strategy that is based upon the subjects' own hermeneutical strategy is akin to the performative type of scholarship to which Faure points: "Through the transferential relationship between the scholar and his [or her] object, the shift from the hermeneutic model to the performative model, which characterized the evolution of Chan during Tang, may reappear in Chan/ Zen scholarship."[42] My scholarship is performative in the sense that my hermeneutical strategy is based upon the nuns' own interpretation of their situation. I culled the nuns' interpretation of things from having lived, worked, and practiced with them as well as from having studied Buddhist texts with them. I came to know their approach to dealing with conflict in everyday situations as well as by learning how they interpret various Zen Buddhist teachings. They claim that women have played vital roles in the history of Japanese Buddhism, have been important in Dōgen's circle, and have had a formative role in their own history. The general feature of Sōtō Zen nuns' interpretive bias is to take situations and make them into opportunities for practice. Practice is not limited to overt forms like zazen. The current abbess of Aichi Senmon Nisōdō often reminds her trainees that if you think you are too busy to practice, then you do not know what practice is. Their example teaches that practice is interpreting difficult circumstances as a resource for honing compassion and wisdom. This does not mean mere acceptance of the status quo. On the contrary, their constant practice enables them to change the status quo into a situation more in accord with their interpretation of Buddhist living. (Since they succeeded in making the Sōtō Zen institution more egalitarian, this strongly indicates that the nuns' practice is effective.)

Since they see themselves in a positive light, even under less than egalitarian circumstances, the overall effect of my interpretation of Sōtō nuns is also positive. This does not mean that nuns were not or are not oppressed. Instead, it elucidates the nuns' method of addressing their oppression. Moreover, using the nuns' understanding of themselves to analyze their attitudes, activities, and contributions is one method for overcoming the hazards of androcentric and ethnocentric interpretations of nuns. My analysis of nuns, however, is not limited to their perspective of themselves. That is where I begin and that is my guide, but I also strive to see nuns from other perspectives, including the general Japanese historical and cultural context and Sōtō Zen teachings and trends.

Although the number of monastic women in modern Japan is relatively small, they do make an important contribution to society. One could say that sacred space moves with them. This is facilitated by their sacred appearance (monastic robes and shaven heads—which most monks have abandoned). Nuns are spiritual guides to a society in which competing currents push and pull people between traditions configured in the past and pressures striving to modernize. As living reminders of the values and aesthetic sensitivities at the heart of traditional Japanese culture, traditional monastics become increasingly important in modern society. Intricately tied to traditional Japanese culture, traditional monastics are vital to the creation of traditional Japanese culture in modern Japan.

During the Meiji era (1868–1911), the aim of Zen historiography was to demythologize Buddhism and to make it more rational. "Superstitions" were interpreted as expedient means (*upāya*) for the deluded masses, but the religious leaders made a conscious attempt to make Buddhism conform to a scientific vision of the world[43]:

> The redefinition of Zen as a "pure" tradition was by and large an ideological fallout of the Meiji era, a period when Japanese Buddhists, having lost and/or repudiated their grounding in local culture, were trying to adapt to the spirit of the time by redefining Buddhism as a "philosophical tradition."[44]

The concept of "pure Zen" gained currency. It guided subsequent analysis and explanation of Zen texts and Zen practice.

In analyzing how the actions of nuns and monks are affected by the concept of pure Zen, I saw that nuns' interpretation of Zen monastic life closely adhered to the ideals outlined in the "pure" Zen concept. This was easy to see. It was much more difficult to understand how the typical lifestyle of a monk fit in. At first I could only see those monks who lived householder lives as ignoring this concept of "pure" Zen. Was it because they were aware that it was a fabricated construct? Were they merely acting within the bounds of the expanded monastic regulations that the Meiji government enacted? Then I added another layer of analysis.

The significant activities of Sōtō nuns during the past 100 years are a lucid illustration of an important facet of Japan's cultural development formally launched with the Meiji Restoration of 1868. Since then, the tenor of Japanese society has been characterized by a tension between acting in accord with exalted patterns of the past and racing towards patterns that appeal to a novel vision of the future. Meiji leaders were guided by two principles: restoration of the old order (*fukko*) and renewal through modernization (*ishin*). Although there are impulses in Japanese society fueled by an extreme concern for one or the other of these streams, most people are seeking compatibility between the two. A glance around twentieth-century Japan immediately reveals this effort, from the plots of television dramas to definitions of respectability in the spheres of religion and business, from minutiae in etiquette to competing values within a changing concept of family. The values of a traditional lifestyle and its accompanying virtues, however, are obscured by the accelerated tempo of change and by diverse and competing attractions constantly punctuating the rhythm of life. People still pause to note the flourishing and flitting of cherry blossoms, but the act of securing a location for the festivities has in many cases upstaged the flowers. Fewer and fewer Japanese take the time, or have the leisure, to live according to traditions that have been carefully cultivated over centuries of refinement, including things as mundane as diet and eating practices, clothing, and verb conjugations, as well as "special" things like writing calligraphy with a brush, composing poetry, and arranging flowers.

Those who are propelled by a vision of the past are, however, not merely maintaining the traditions of the past as they were. In a sense, their visions of the past are more refined than the past actually ever was. In a climate of competing visions, convincing explanations for choosing one way over another become necessary. The strongest strategy is to create a vision of the past that highlights certain appealing ideals. This requires, however, a consciousness about one's actions not usually found within the tradition under question. This activity is frequently cast as an effort to preserve tradition, despite the fact that it is almost a deliberate attempt not to follow a pattern of activity found in history. By "traditional," I am not referring to a static entity of the past that is repeated in the present. By "preserving tradition" I refer, rather, to the creative process of basing one's current actions on a perception of a particular heritage.

As to the traditions of Sōtō Zen, both female and male monastics of the Sōtō Zen sect turn to the teachings of Zen Masters Dōgen and Keizan for guidance in their interpretation of the Buddhist view of the world. There is, however, no uniform picture of Dōgen and Keizan, for there are numerous dimensions to their writings and actions. They have been interpreted variously in different periods of history, and they are viewed differently by women and men, academics, laity, and monastics. Taking an anthropological approach to them adds a new dimension to our understanding of Zen studies.

Sōtō nuns have used their interpretation of Dōgen to serve as a symbol of authenticity, a rallying point for legitimacy. Keizan's teachings and practices, on the other hand, are interpreted to represent innovation and adaptation. He is remembered as the historical figure at the root of Sōtō Zen's impulse to accommodate various situations and accept the need to change in accord with the changing needs of the monastic and lay community.

I heard nuns stress that the rationale for monastics leading householder lives can be found in the writings of the historical Keizan. Their textual source for this understanding is found in his *Denkōroku*[45] case on the fourth patriarch, Upagupta, in which a dichotomous scheme between physical and spiritual renunciation is introduced.[46] Dōgen rejected the validity of spiritual renunciation.[47] For Dōgen, it was all or nothing. Keizan, on the contrary, accepts the category of spiritual renunciation, and he articulates his thinking on this issue in his sermon on the fourth case:

> For Buddhists, there are basically two forms of renunciation, which are physical and spiritual. Leaving home physically means that they cast away love and affection, leave their homes and birthplaces, shave their heads, don monks' [sic][48] robes, do not have male or female servants, become monks or nuns, and make an effort in the Way throughout the twenty-four hours of each day. Whatever the time, they do not pass it in vain. They desire nothing else. They neither delight in life nor fear death. Their minds are as pure as the autumn moon; their eyes are as clear as a bright mirror. They do not seek Mind nor do they

hanker [to see] their [original] natures. They do not cultivate the holy truth, much less worldly attachments. In this way, they do not abide in the stage of ordinary folk or cherish the rank of the wise and holy, but more and more become mindless seekers of the Way. These are people who leave home physically.

Those who leave home in spirit do not shave their heads or wear monks' [sic] clothing. Even though they live at home and remain among worldly cares, they are like lotuses which are not soiled by the mud [in which they grow] or jewels which are immune to [contamination by] dust. Even though there are karmic conditions so that they have wives and children, they consider them as being trash and dust. They do not entertain love for even a moment or covet anything. Like the moon suspended in the sky, like a ball rolling around on a tray, live in the noisy city and see one who is tranquil. In the midst of the three realms, they clarify the fact that they dwell beyond time. They realize that exterminating the passions is a sickness, and that aiming for ultimate reality is wrong. They realize that both nirvāna and samsāra are illusions, and they are not attached to either enlightenment or the passions. These are people who leave home in spirit.[49]

Dōgen defines renunciation in a conservative and "traditional" way, and Keizan defines it in a broader and innovative way. These two concepts of renunciation reflect the two streams in modern Japanese society, to follow "tradition" and to change with the perceived needs of the times.

The vast majority of nuns follow the physical renunciation mode of monasticism, the only kind of renunciation Dōgen recognized. In the last few decades their commitment has been challenged time and again when faced with the issue of diminishing numbers in their order. They continue to assess and reconfirm their commitment to a "traditional" mode of monasticism, even if this might discourage would-be nuns. Others who follow a less ascetic mode of Zen monasticism can legitimate their behavior using Keizan's teachings and labeling themselves spiritual renunciants.

Dōgen's and Keizan's practices and views of women, however, are a separate issue from how nuns view Dōgen and Keizan. Dōgen's and Keizan's writings and activities that reflect their attitudes and teachings about women are explored in chapter 2. The actions of nuns discussed in chapter 3 illustrate nuns' interpretation of Buddhist teachings, especially Dōgen's. Although academics have built a case for asserting that Dōgen changed his mind about women (from unconditional acceptance to qualified rejection), the women did not change their minds about Zen monastic practice.

This book is designed to explicate the religious disciplines of Zen nuns in modern Japan. The structure and organization of the monastery illuminates the pragmatic features of their lifestyle and training, while explication of the curriculum and degrees conferred by the monastery gives insight into their education and training. The annual calendar and daily schedule reveals the activities that give contour and depth to their life. This study focuses primarily upon the foremost Sōtō women's monastery in Japan, Aichi Senmon Nisōdō, because its educational system is the lifeblood of the female monastics' tradition and provides the locus of contemplation, study, and practice of their values.

The materials in chapter 4 show how the external structures of the nuns' monastic life are based upon a "traditional" or Dōgen model. In chapter 5, the thoughts and attitudes of the nuns will reveal what the nuns think of their own lives. Based on information gathered while living in the monastery, plus data from interviews and surveys, I reflect upon developments in the attitudes and motivations of female monastics and analyze the significance of their contributions to Japanese Buddhism and Japanese society. I present the first scholarly examination of the internal side of Zen monastic women, a rare glimpse into their personal backgrounds, motivations, and values about religious practice. The views of monastic women seem to be fueled by images of powerful female figures who preceded them, empowering them to overcome the social strictures that have circumscribed their existence. I was led to this line of analysis because my anthropological data show that Zen nuns do not see themselves as fundamentally oppressed. Beginning with a positive valuation of their lives as religious women, they tend to interpret their experiences in terms of what it tells them about their own understanding and practice of Buddhist teachings. It is clear that understanding Japanese Zen monastic women is crucial to the understanding of the transmission and preservation of traditional Japanese and Buddhist values in the face of modernizing impulses in Japan today.

We must, however, be conscious of two levels of interpretation when examining the position of female monastics in modern Japan: the social and the religious. At a social level of analysis, one might cite the fact that male monastics frequently marry and have access to significant financial resources as an illustration of the subordinate position of monastic women. At a religious level of analysis, however, the majority of female monastics recognize themselves as living heirs of "traditional" Buddhist monasticism. As will unfold in chapter 5, most nuns' motivations differ from those of many male monastics who frequently become ordained in the context of a hereditary system. Not being tied to a system of heredity, most female monastics make an independent and personal commitment to a monastic Buddhist lifestyle. They choose to maintain a traditional lifestyle by including traditional arts of Japan as an integral aspect of their religious discipline and by abiding by the traditional monastic regulations laid down by the founder of the sect. They do not want to dilute the tradition. Furthermore, their fight for equality can be viewed from both a social and Buddhist perspective. They are progressive women in the forefront of the twentieth-century struggle for official acknowledgment and equal opportunities. In so doing, they are actualizing Dōgen's thirteenth-century teachings that women be recognized as equals in the monastic profession. Anthropological work sheds new light upon Buddhist Studies, especially Zen. I look forward to the field continuing to explore the vast human resources available; they cannot be overlooked when trying to understand Buddhism.

I strive to show the nuns in their complexity, for they are a diverse group of people. The ideals they hold are not always directly evident in their daily actions. This led me to seek out an understanding of how tensions, frustrations, and anger are expressed in their lives and how these negative emotions function as part of their religious practice. Indeed, there are many things that are rare (and many things that are common) about the way they live. But they are not primarily a forlorn group of people. I tried a number of "negative" interpretations of the nuns' activities and circumstances. Here are some examples of hypotheses I entertained: "Because nuns are oppressed, they are weak," or "Because nuns are weak, they are oppressed;" "The number of nuns is small, so they do not play a significant role in Zen Buddhism or Japanese society;" and "Nuns have not made any real gains in the twentieth century, because they are only able to do what the monks used to do from the thirteenth through nineteenth centuries." None of them seemed to capture the dynamics I saw in the monasteries, temples, and streets, nor the ways in which nuns described themselves. I kept returning to a positive view.

Thus, here are the six hypotheses I decided to explore in this work:

1. Many women in Japanese Buddhist history did not act as though they were defeated by oppressive conditions.
2. In their fight for institutionalizing egalitarian regulations, twentieth-century Sōtō nuns acted as though they were only asking for what history had told them was their due.
3. Sōtō nuns use distinctive strategies to establish legitimacy, relevance, and power in the twentieth century.
4. Most twentieth-century women became Sōtō nuns because they *wanted* to lead traditional monastic lives.
5. The aesthetic dimension to Sōtō nuns' practice helps maintain and transmit traditional Japanese culture in modern Japan.
6. In order to accomplish their goals, Sōtō Zen nuns in twentieth-century Japan became innovators for the sake of tradition.

Methodological Considerations

In this work, the method employed in the research and the content of the research are particularly congruent. Engaging in research on Zen nuns demanded participant-observation field research, for many nuns are suspicious of scholars. They trust lived experience more than just words. After I lived with the nuns for a number of months at the main Sōtō Zen nunnery, Aichi Senmon Nisōdō (in Nagoya), the abbess, Aoyama Shundō, confirmed my sense that just an interview and request for documentation about their lives would have yielded little. The abbess frankly stated that others have come requesting information about them, but they were not interested in seeing how nuns lived firsthand, so she did not even grant them interviews. Indeed, when I requested permission from the abbess to study Sōtō nuns, indicating that I wanted to spend time living at the monastery, she is the one who determined the length of time I had to stay there. Hence, my primary method involved experiencing the life of the nuns by living with and near them for a little more than a year.

I first visited Aichi Senmon Nisōdō in January of 1988. I participated in a *sesshin* retreat and received permission from Abbess Aoyama to return to the nunnery to live for a while as part of my field research. Finally, toward the end of summer 1989, I went to stay at that monastery for women for a period of four months. Afterward, I lived in an apartment within a nearby nun's temple for another nine months. Since this concentrated period in the field ended in the fall of 1990, I have continued to visit and interact with numerous nuns. My investigation of these nuns enabled me to study their relationships with people, the significance of events, the dynamics of their organization, and the meanings of their patterns of behavior. I was able to segue into the rhythm of life there with a minimum of discord primarily because of my sex,[50] but also due to my facility in Japanese, Japanese culture, and Buddhism. I did not take monastic vows nor did I pretend to have any intention of becoming a monastic. This was acceptable, because they have a program entitled *josei kyōshitsu*, which is designed for laywomen who want to experience the lifestyle of monastic women. I made every effort to abide by their rules and learn their pattern of life. At first I was overwhelmed by the minute details that regulate their behavior, and I was constantly making mistakes. My sense of being out of place was eased by the other laywomen and the recent novices who comforted me by confessing that they had also taken time to learn all the details of where a person of low rank is allowed to place her towel in the bath, where and how slippers are to be removed when going from one room to the other, where each person of each rank is and is not allowed to walk and sit, in addition to memorizing various prayers, sundry scriptures, and numerous ritual motions. The monastic women did not question my motivation and my position so long as I behaved as they did. That meant that at times I had to hold my tongue and apologize, even if I was blamed for committing a breach of conduct that I had not committed. At other times I had to hand-scrub floors rapidly, sit in motionless meditation for hours in 45 °F temperatures, rake leaves in gusty winds, wipe cooking pots clean with my finger then lick my finger so as not to waste a morsel of food, polish rows and rows of windows without using a cleanser, cart heavy tables up and down stairs, and go for weeks on end without a moment of privacy. In short, I had to work hard to build trust by not standing out or standing around.

Beginning with this extended period of participant-observation, living in a women's monastery as a lay participant, I gained an understanding of how the ideal of monastic life compares to the daily life. It especially helped me appreciate how the ideal can serve as an aim that enables the nuns to use the inevitable tensions and conflicts that accompany their intense community relationships in a constructive way. Even though the positive results are not always immediate, the ideal serves as a guide and model. All the nuns would agree that to be patient, not driven by personal desires, is preferred behavior. Not surprisingly, however, the strains of being required to eat, sleep, bathe, work, study, and meditate with the same group of people every day give rise to irritations, unhappiness, and con-flicts. What makes examining this aspect of the nuns' lives interesting is the way they deal with their problems. Their discipline of human relationships is the foun-dation of their Zen monastic life. It is both the most difficult aspect of the practice and the dimension that yields the greatest transformation. The Zen monastic ideal pressures the nuns to constantly try to be better in an environment so exacting that you are constantly reminded of how far you are from that ideal. But progress was visible. A quick glance at a corner of a room could usually tell you if a first-year nun or a fifth-year nun had cleaned the floors. Likewise, if something had been done improperly, the response of a more seasoned nun would often differ from a novice. It was evident that more time spent in the monastery's intense "greenhouse" environment made for a greater capacity to absorb blame, others' idiosyncratic habits, and differences of opinion.

Aside from the insight gained from the participant-observation, this method helped me establish bonds of trust that facilitated the gathering of information through personal interviews. It was also instrumental in fostering relationships that led to visits to numerous nuns' temples around the country. These visits, in turn, resulted in not only obtaining a firsthand look at the nuns' lives and circumstances, but also led me to a veritable gold mine of books, journals, and other publications by and for nuns that are not catalogued in any libraries nor in the sect headquarters. But I first had to establish relationships with many nuns in order to find out what might exist and then where it might be located. I heard various things like, "We used to have all the issues of *Otayori* until the fire. I think Dōjun's temple might have a few of the early ones. Why don't you try there." Among other things, I was eventually able to procure a whole set of their regular publication, the *Otayori*. This required winning permission from the heads of Aichi Senmon Ni-sōdō (Nagoya), Seikan-ji (Nagoya), Kannon-ji (Tokyo), and Lumbini-en (Toyama) to copy what they had available. Although this required travel, time, and expense, if the issues had all been neatly catalogued in a library, I would not have learned as much about nuns' lives.

I also conducted a nationwide survey that enabled me to gain a broader insight into the self-perceptions, motivations, and attitudes of Zen nuns from different regions, ages, and backgrounds. This method differs from the data gathered through participant-observation, because it involves the nuns reflecting on and constructing their own personal histories. The results reflect this difference. The direct observations revealed how the ideals are negotiated in real situations, whereas the surveys reflect how the nuns have interpreted their own lives in terms of the ideals.

After my cloistered period in the monastery, I did research with the assistance of a number of Japanese scholars at various institutions, including Komazawa University, Nanzan Institute for Japanese Religion and Culture, and Aichi Gakuin University. As a member of the research group "Japanese Women and Buddhism," composed of a nationwide team of Japanese scholars, I benefited from their perspectives, insights, and feedback.

I approach the study of culture and religion—in this case, Japanese culture and Sōtō Zen Buddhism—as an organic process of creativity. The fundamental basis for my methodological approach is grounded in my disbelief in facts that exist "out there," independent of an experience, interpretation, or perception of them.[51] Therefore, I do not aspire to reveal a definitive truth. Following theorists like Alfred North Whitehead[52] and E. Valentine Daniel[53] who criticize essentialism, eternalism, and objectivism, I consider my work one possible interpretation of the dynamics of Sōtō Zen monastic women in modern Japan. I base my work on people with faces and names familiar to me, writings of monastic women and men, and the frustration, insight, and acceptance that I have experienced.

Research, particularly field research, is direct involvement in the here and now. Moreover, even when doing historical or textual studies, these studies, and the people who engage in them, occur in a particular place and time. The insight found in Dōgen's writings that being and time are indistinguishable in the present moment lends historic weight to the claims of contemporary scholars that research is a matter of an internally organic creation. Research, like all activity, is a phenomenon in the present moment. It is an activity of discovery. It is not the discovery of an entity existing independently of time, but the moment of discovery is itself an event where being and time are created. Whitehead, a modern process philosopher, uses the vocabulary "concrescence of an occasion of experience" to describe this phenomenon. Dōgen uses the phrase "being-time" to explain the same. He asserts that "all being is time" and "time itself is being." "Thus," he continues in poetic fashion, "a pine tree is time, bamboo is time. . . . Mountains are time. Oceans are time. . . . If time is annihilated, mountains and oceans are annihilated."[54]

The exploration of the history, lifestyle, teachings, religious practices, and self-perception of the monastic women outlined in this work clearly depends upon the lens through which I, the researcher and writer, perceive them. I am aware that the researcher and the researched have a mutually transforming effect upon each other. The particular factors that affect my interpretation of Zen monastic women are my female gender, my bicultural and biracial heritage as a daughter of a Japanese mother and Caucasian American father, and my bilingual capability in Japanese and English. My academic background includes ten years of graduate school at Harvard University where I focused on Japanese Buddhism from a cultural–historical approach. The combination of my religious orientation— which includes experience in Protestant Methodist (social activist) Christianity in America and Japanese cultural concerns for social harmony—and the practices of the monastic women—where action is paramount, rather than a confession of beliefs—enabled me to adapt to their pattern of life with little resistance. The composite of these background elements helped bridge the distance between inquiring scholar and Zen monastics,[55] resulting in a rich personal and academic experience. It is a challenge, however, to make contributions to theoretical and intellectual discussions when one begins with a keen awareness of the personal and imaginative nature of scholarly research and writing.[56] Rather than denying that there is a mutually transforming internal relationship between me, the scholar, and my scholarship, I choose to make it an explicit feature of my scholarship by reporting my personal background and experience. Readers can then more critically evaluate the value of my research based upon their own collage of concerns.

I would like to explore the issue of my ethnicity as it bears upon the rubric of insider versus outsider[57]—a convention central to my primary method of research: participant-observation. Although all people create their own identity, my experience of coming from two distinct cultural heritages has sensitized me to the process of *creating* ethnic identity. Since I grew up knowing few people with an ethnic identity similar to my own, I developed a heightened awareness of the construction, flexibility, and fluidity of ethnicity. Although this ability to be "many different things" is actually a capability shared by all people, I think the particular features of a person who is culturally, racially, and linguistically engaged in two cultures (by virtue of parentage, family life, and chosen experience) lead to a complex ethnicity that enables one to respond quite naturally to situations that draw upon one's varied internal resources. This chameleonlike quality challenges the standard definitions of "insider" and "outsider."

To illustrate the complexity, I reveal an early episode in my life when I was being raised in Detroit in the early 1960s. At the age of three, I was overwhelmed with the need to explain my identity, because I was frustrated that it was not immediately apparent to people around me, primarily white Americans. As my mother, a black-haired woman with a dark gold complexion and a heavy Japanese accent, held my fair-skinned hand that was attached to a body topped by a head of blond hair,[58] people would sometimes mistake her for my babysitter. My heart was crestfallen at this innocent moment of mistaken identity, for it rendered my mother invisible. I came up with a solution. Complete with explicit facial gestures, I began announcing to passersby in grocery stores and shopping centers in the greater Detroit area that:

My Mommy's Japanese,	(pulling corners of eyes up)
My Daddy's American,	(pulling corners down)
And I'm just a mixed up kid.	(erratic up and down)

Being neither this nor that makes it difficult to determine my status as an insider or an outsider. I am always both and neither, at least in Japanese and American contexts. This illustrates the creative process of pivotal self-identification.

Embarking upon my field research in Japan, I found my mixed background was helpful in facilitating the gathering of information and gaining insight.[59] I could intuitively highlight my "insider" persona when appropriate and draw out my "outsider" persona when prudent. While living in the monastery, I did my best to remain in the Japanese/insider mode, and while I was conducting research in the universities and participating in the Japanese scholarly community, the outsider/academic American[60] aspects were manifested. These facets, of course, were not always so clearly delineated. For example, during exam period in the monastery I drew upon my academic background in Buddhist Studies to help my friends. I had to be careful about whom and how I helped, however, because it was awkward for someone of my low rank in the monastery to have such knowledge. My assistance could easily turn into an embarrassing experience for my seniors. At other times, while working with Japanese scholars, most of whom have little knowledge of the actual lives of Zen monastic women, I served as their informant on female monasticism in Japan.[61] My experience in the monastery confirmed the theoretical stance that there are no distinct categories of insider and outsider.[62] There is, rather, a continuum that ranges from complete difference in gender, culture, race, education, age, class, religious orientation, etc., between the researcher and the researched and relative similarity between them. The rubric insider-outsider, therefore, must be used with extreme caution and an awareness that the two words are merely relative designations which must be carefully contextualized.[63]

Although the novices in training and the various teachers did not question my purpose, Abbess Aoyama did. Her concern, however, never became an obstacle to my research. On the contrary, her interest in me as a person who is or is not living according to Buddhist teachings gave me the comfort as a scholar that I was on the "inside," and it also drove me to work harder and plunge deeper so as not to be guilty of her suspicion that I was engaged in a vain academic enterprise. The only way I could prove to her that I was not going to waste my life and abuse their generosity was to persevere through all the hardships, conduct my research with high respect and genuine concern for the people I was seeking to understand, smile, and bow in gratitude. Not until our last lengthy conversation in the monastery did she grace me with a twinkle in her eye. She was sending me back to academia with her approval.

TWO

Historical Background

My anthropological research revealed that Sōtō nuns entered the twentieth century with a strong sense of confidence — and less of a sense of frustration than I had expected to find. I began an enquiry of women's contributions and accomplishments in the religious history of Japan to understand why twentieth-century Zen nuns were not debilitated by unfair practices. I discovered a history of women in Japanese religion which reveals that many women maintained a positive understanding of themselves and their capabilities. The following is a possible interpretation of the events that are recorded in the *Nihongi* and the *Gangōji Garan Engi*. Contemporary Sōtō Zen nuns highlight this moment in history as support for their claim that women have been central to the development of Buddhism in Japan.

Pioneering Monastics

In 584 C.E., Buddhism is a fledgling new religion in the land of *kami*,[1] having been officially introduced only about three decades ago. Interaction with Korea is active, bringing fresh cultural energy. In that year, a young woman is moved by the new teachings. She lives in a cultural climate where she has numerous models of women engaged in religious affairs, and so it is natural that she and her family consider her ordination in the new religion precisely *because* she is female. But there is no native role model of a nun, for no one in this island country has been ordained into the Buddhist tradition. Being courageous and compelled by the wisdom of these new teachings, she nonetheless commits herself to them. She makes her historic vows and becomes the first ordained Buddhist in Japan.[2] Well over a millennium later, some people still remember her by her Buddhist name, Zenshin-ni.[3] Shortly thereafter, two women join her. They also devote their lives to Buddhism, and are ordained as Zenzō-ni and Ezen-ni.[4] All three women have a zeal to gain a deeper understanding of the monastic discipline and to become fully ordained; as a result, they become the first Japanese to go abroad to study in Paekche on the Korean peninsula.[5] On the ninth day of the sixth month of the year 587, "The nun Zen-shin and the others addressed the Oho-omi, saying: 'Discipline is the basis of the method of those who renounce the world; we pray thee to let us go to Paekche to receive instruction in the Law of Discipline.' "[6] After receiving full ordination, they returned to Japan in 590 with heightened resolve and determination to establish this new religion on Japanese soil. They resided in a Buddhist temple, an amadera[7] called Sakurai-ji, located in the central region, Yamato.[8] At this time, Shōtoku Taishi (574–622), a prince widely recognized for his contributions to establishing Buddhism in Japan, has not yet made his grand entrance onto the stage of Japanese government and culture.

Such is the bare outline of the story. At the very least, the story of the first ordained Japanese Buddhists is a lucid example of a time when women were favored. Although many specifics surrounding this event lie buried in history, some details are available as follows. The official introduction of Buddhism to Japan occurred in the first half of the sixth century, although evidence of active interaction between Japan and Korea suggests that leading Japanese were aware of the Buddhist tradition in Korea before the Paekche King Song (-myong) sent the gifts of Buddhist scriptures and a Buddhist sculpture to Emperor Kinmei.[9] The Emperor had to face the various powerful leaders of competing clans, most notably the Soga and Mononobe. Although Soga no Iname (d. 570) had a positive response to the Buddhist tradition, the other clan leaders did not. Almost as though anticipating a mixed reception of the Buddhist gifts, King Song chose them carefully. He did not want to stir up tensions in Japan. He was hoping to continue in the Yamato court's favor, because of Paekche's tenuous relations with other states in the Korean peninsula.[10] King Song did not send monks and nuns to serve as teachers, and the statue he presented was probably less than a foot high, hence too small to serve as a central image in a temple.[11] The Buddhist scriptures were apparently books on the life of Śākyamuni, and the sculpture described in the *Gangōji Engi* as the "image of a prince" suggests that the statue was of Prince Siddhārtha, a nonimposing figure of the young Buddha-to-be.[12] The form of Buddhism that came to Japan through Paekche was likely to have been a variety of Southern Sung Chinese Buddhism.[13] The Japanese, however, interpreted the Buddhas in the context of their own relationship with *kami*.[14] This suggests that the reception of Buddhism by the Soga clan and its rejection by the rival Mononobe clan was in large part a strategy to win power, the Soga investing in the possibility that alliance with the foreign tradition would secure their superiority.

That the Japanese understood Buddha to be another form of *kami* is evident in the actions of Soga no Umako (d. 626), the son of Iname. During a personal bout with illness, Umako initiated the Buddhist ordination of young women in the hopes that their supplications to the Buddha would assist in his recovery. It was common for women to be recognized for their spiritual powers. It is difficult, however, to distinguish the function of the Buddhist nuns from that of the role of *miko*[15] in the indigenous religious practices. Nevertheless, Shima, the daughter of Shiba Datto, who was apparently close to Soga no Umako, was ordained Zenshin-ni. Two other young women who were considered pupils of Zenshin-ni were also ordained. One was Toyome, the daughter of Ayabito no Yaho, who took the Buddhist name Zenzō-ni, and the other was Ishime, daughter of Nishikori Tsubu, who took the Buddhist name Ezen-ni.[16] It was not possible for their ordination to be performed according to the practices developed by the tradition in other regions.[17] Ten fully ordained nuns and ten fully ordained monks were needed to preside over the ceremony to fully ordain a nun. Thus, as recorded in the *Gangōji* chronicles,[18] the three women left for Paekche to receive full ordination, where, upon arrival, they first received novice precepts (Skt. *śrāmaṇerikā*).[19] Later they received the six precepts (Skt. *chasu-dhamesu-sikkhā*) of a probationary nun (Skt. *śikṣamāṇā*). There was just enough time for them to serve the two-year period required of female ordinands before receiving full status as nuns.[20] They returned to Japan after receiving full (Skt. *bhikṣuṇī*) ordination in March of 590.[21] The three fully ordained nuns then took up residence in the temple Sakurai-ji, located in the present-day region of Nara Prefecture.[22] Although the nuns did receive full ordination, they were not able to gather a quorum of ten fully ordained nuns (Skt. *bhikṣuṇī*) to establish a nuns' order in Japan that was continuous with earlier Buddhist traditions.

Nevertheless, the following figures show that, within one century, the small trickle that began with Zenshin-ni had become a vibrant stream that continues uninterrupted to the present day. In 623, only four decades after Zenshin-ni inaugurated monastic Buddhism in Japan, there were 569 nuns and 816 monks.[23] Fifty years later (674), records indicate that Emperor Temmu (r. 673–686) had about 2,400 nuns gather for a ceremony.[24] It is not possible to reconstruct with certainty the motivations and concerns of the women and men who took the monastic Buddhist path, but apparently during this time, many became tonsured for the sake of the country. In these cases, the motivation seems to have been to make life better in concrete ways, rather than to attain enlightenment in the sense of becoming a supreme spiritual being. Apparently the country's health and protection from natural calamities such as fire, earthquakes, and drought were their primary concerns.[25] The *Nihongi* records that 1,000 persons, men and women, were ordained when the Oho-omi fell ill in August 614.[26] The *Nihongi* cites many such examples, including two more concerning the Emperor Temmu and Empress. He had 100 people ordained on November 12, 680, when the empress was ill, and she subsequently recovered.[27] She had 100 people ordained on behalf of the emperor's illness on the twenty-sixth day of the same month and year.[28] Again she had seventy-eight people ordained on the emperor's behalf on the seventh month, twenty-eighth day of year 686; eighty people on the first day of the eighth month; and one hundred more on the second day.[29] Another example is that, according to the *Shoku Nihongi*, Emperor Shōmu (r. 724–749) had 3,000 people ordained Buddhists in 725 in order to protect the country from calamity.[30] Aside from illustrating the tremendous growth of ordained Buddhists, this suggests that the indigenous model of "religious professionals" — primarily shamanesses who served as agents of hope and change — had a profound influence on the ancient Japanese interpretation and development of Buddhist ordination practices.

In accord with the notion that women were endowed with various powers to effect change or appease angry spirits, a number of women also held considerable power in ruling the country. Their sacred power infused their political power. Eight empresses reigned during the Asuka (550–710) and Nara (710–784) Periods when Buddhism first began developing in Japan: Empress Suiko (r. 592–628), Empress Kōyoku (r. 642–645), Empress Saimei (r. 655–661), Empress Jitō (r. 690–697), Empress Gemmei (r. 707–715), Empress Genshō (r. 715–724), Empress Kōken (r. 749–758), and Empress Shōtoku (r. 764–770).[31] (In Japanese, the term *tennō* is used for both men and women, but in English it is commonly translated as "emperor" for men and "empress" for women. An entirely different term designates the main wife of the emperor, *kōgō*, but this is also commonly rendered into English as empress.[32]) Therefore, in English it is not obvious which women officially reigned over the country. The on-the-throne empresses and beside-the-throne empresses did many things to further the development of Buddhism in Japan. One example recorded in the *Nihongi* is that on the seventh month, fifteenth day of the year 681, "In the fulfillment of a vow of the empress-consort a great feast of vegetable fare was given, and the sutras were expounded in all the Temples of the capital."[33]

Another figure, Empress Kōmyō (701–760), did not reign on the throne, yet profoundly shaped the contours of Buddhism in ancient Japan.[34] Her biography, contained in the *Shoku Nihongi*,[35] records that it was her urging that prompted Emperor Shōmu, her husband, to issue an edict in 740 to establish national temples for monks (*Kokubun-ji*) and national temples for nuns (*Kokubun-niji*) in each province with Tōdai-ji as the head temple.[36] A gold-lettered copy of the *sūtra Konkōmyō-kyō* (Skt. *Suvarṇaprabhāsottama-rāja-sūtra*) was placed in several seven-story pagodas that were built in conjunction with the national temples. This sūtra teaches that four guardian deities protect a king who properly rules a country. Both the monks' and nuns' temples were to assist in the protection of the nation, but they each had a distinct focus. The national temples for monks were to pray for the protection of the nation, as indicated by their name "Golden Light Temple for the Protection of the Country by the Four Heavenly Deities" (*Konkōmyō Shitennō Gokokushi-ji*). The national temples for nuns were named "Lotus Temple for the Absolution of Sins" (*Hokke Metsuzaishi-ji*). The *Lotus Sūtra* was regarded as a sūtra that helped protect the nation. The nuns were particularly responsible for praying for the absolution of sins for the country.[37] A number of calamities had plagued the nation, particularly fatal disease, which might account for the focus upon the purification of the nation. The types of prayers that were offered at these temples were recorded in the *Shoku Nihongi*. It is easy to see Empress

Kōmyō's influence on this project, because the prayers for individual people revolve around those who are her blood relatives, including her father, mother, and children. Altogether the temples were built on thirty sites around the country. Initially each nuns' temple had ten Buddhist nuns, and after 766 each temple had twenty nuns. Since they received economic support from the government, it was not necessary for them to gather alms or seek donations.[38] These temples were a major factor in the propagation of Buddhism outside the vicinity of the capital.

Empress Kōmyō's pervasive influence upon Nara Buddhism made a lasting impact upon Buddhist development in Japan. She supervised the copying of many sūtras, some of which remain in Tōdai-ji to this day. Among them is the *Lotus Sūtra*, a text highly prized by women during this period because they interpreted the story of the Nāga princess turning into a Buddha as proof that women could be enlightened.[39] The empress is also known for her deep concern for people in need. She was socially engaged in actively helping orphans and people who were underprivileged and those who were hurt from military battles.[40] To this end, in 730 she established the charitable institutions Hiden-in and Seyaku-in. They were designed to dispense medicine and relieve poverty and famine among the common people.[41] In 749 she was tonsured at the ordination platform (*kaidan*) of Tōdai-ji.[42] Empress Kōmyō's monumental contributions reveal the impact one woman had on shaping the course of Buddhist history in Japan.

Women not only forged the way, but they also received support for their Buddhist activities from prominent male members of ancient Japanese society. The most obvious example of such a supporter is Shōtoku Taishi (574–622), who is renowned as a formative figure in firmly establishing Buddhism in Japan. The fact that he had deep feelings and gave tremendous support to women in Buddhism, however, is frequently left out of the accounts. His most striking contribution to women and Buddhism is that, of the seven temples he is attributed with having built, five are amadera.[43] The most renowned of these temples, Chūgū-ji, still stands in Nara beside Hōryū-ji.[44] Others include Tachibana-dera, Ikeshiri-ji, and Katsuragi Nunnery.

From all this, it is evident that Buddhist women were not only *not* discriminated against during this period, but that they were strong leaders and respected members of society.[45] Unfortunately, subsequent historical developments have shrouded the powerful roles women played in ancient history. It is true that the Taika Reform Edict of 646 inaugurated the official influx of Confucian values that promoted patriarchy. Although it was a gradual process, hierarchical structures, including religious organizations, became increasingly male dominated. The matrilocal and matrilineal system gave way to a patrilineal system of heredity that offered women little institutional power. This has left us with the prevailing impression that has guided most historiographical schemes regarding women in Japanese history—that women were largely seen as inferior to men in Japanese social structures and institutions. The history itself seems to be more complex. Although in some contexts women were *treated* in an inferior manner during certain phases of Japanese history, and in certain social classes and certain relationships, in none, however, does it mean that they *were* inferior. Rather, evidence suggests that women did not passively accept and simply succumb to the external pressures designed to unduly circumscribe their actions. Documents dating back to the ninth century record women protesting against unfair treatment.[46] Their genuine strength, however, lies in their creative response to discrimination.

Such events make it compellingly clear that historiography, not history, is at fault in the omission of the contributions of women. Recently scholars have begun to correct the histories that have omitted numerous participants, but some only highlight the story of what women could *not* do. While it is important to include the ways in which women have been oppressed, it is perhaps more important to extend one's purview to include what women *have* accomplished, especially when achieved despite nonegalitarian circumstances.

Dōgen and Women

Sōtō nuns today maintain that the recognized founder of Sōtō Zen in Japan, Dōgen (1200–1253), was part of the social climate of inclusivism characteristic of the Kamakura Period (1186–1333) Buddhist reformers. They point to texts that they claim support their view that Dōgen took an affirmative stance toward women. This grounded their sense of legitimacy and fueled their fight to reform Sōtō Sect regulations to reflect what they thought was the intent of Dōgen's thoughts and writings.

In an interview with Abbess Aoyama Shundō, I learned that she begins her analysis of Dōgen's attitude toward women with her understanding of his experience with his mother. Aoyama surmises that Dōgen deeply felt his mother's pain at having been married off in a political struggle to raise the waning strength and status of her family, the Fujiwaras.[47] Dōgen resolved to understand the true meaning of impermanence upon watching the smoke rise from the incense at his mother's funeral.[48] Although this might be hagiographic account, one can imagine the emotions of a young boy (he was seven years old) who has just lost his mother only a few years after losing his father. Her untimely death only made more acute Dōgen's sensitivity to the ways in which women were sometimes mistreated in Japanese society. Aoyama suggests that his respect for his mother contributed to his positive stance toward women. Whether or not her analysis can be verified historically, it is worth serious consideration as a way a leading woman today within Dōgen's own tradition articulates his attitudes towards women.

Sōtō nuns have noted the texts in which Dōgen mentions women. In his text *Bendōwa* (1231), Dōgen unambiguously articulates that male and female practitioners are equal.[49] He wrote this text after he returned from China, but he was not yet solidly established. He was beginning to articulate his understanding of Buddhist teachings, and he was determined to teach "true" Buddhism. He wrote this text while he had at least one female disciple under his tutelage. Laypeople were also around.

During the following decade, he wrote a number of texts that are considered the core of his philosophical writings. The philosophical orientation that unfolds in these texts supports the statement that males and females are equal in practice. In 1233, after moving to Kōshō-ji, Dōgen wrote a text that has been proclaimed as his most fundamental philosophical treatise, the *Genjō Kōan*. In the spring of 1240, just three years before he left for Echizen (where he established the monastery Eihei-ji), Dōgen wrote the impassioned text *Raihaitokuzui* in order to extinguish the errors of those he thought harbored incorrect thoughts about women and Buddhist truth. In the same year he wrote *Uji*, the text in which he explains his nondualistic view of the relationship between being and time. *Sansui-kyō*, a text that further develops his nondualistic view of reality, was likewise written in 1240. In 1241, Dōgen displayed his independent thinking through his radically nondualistic interpretation of the *Nirvana Sūtra* passage, "All sentient beings without exception *have* Buddha-nature." He deliberately violated rules of Chinese grammar to change the meaning of the sentence to be in accord with his understanding of the Buddhist concept of reality: "All existents are Buddha-nature."[50] This philosophical orientation precludes questioning whether or not Dōgen held that women did or did not have Buddha-nature.[51]

Dōgen was also prolific in 1242, when he wrote a number of other texts that further developed his interpretation of Buddhist concepts. In *Daigo* he says that enlightenment (*satori*) is not something that "comes" or that one "has," but by nature is fleeting. In *Zazenshin*, the concept that enlightenment and practice are one (*shushō ittō*) is hinted at when he asserts that the first *zazen* is the first *zabutsu* (sitting Buddha). In a text also written that year, *Gyōji*, Dōgen first mentions a sentiment that suggests a focus on monastic life over lay life. The social climate in which Dōgen wrote this text is relevant. Dōgen was the first to establish a hall called a *shugyō dōjō*, just for practice. The monastic compound on Mt Hiei was an exemplary establishment Buddhism place for practice, but it did not have a shugyō dōjō hall. Dōgen's innovation was a clear departure from the establishment powers.

Seeing the *Raihaitokuzui* text—the text in which he unambiguously and forcefully expresses positive views of women—in the context of his most important philosophical texts, implies that Dōgen wrote the *Raihaitokuzui* with clear awareness that his emerging philosophy fully supported understanding males and females on equal terms. In the following *Raihaitokuzui* passage, he clarifies the confusion surrounding female Buddhist teachers. "It is irrelevant whether a guide has male or female characteristics, and the like; what counts is that the guide be a being of virtue, of thusness."[52] He continues with advice on the appropriate way to express respect and gratitude to a teacher of the Dharma regardless of their form: "Valuing the Dharma means that, whether [your guide] is a pillar, a lantern, buddhas, a fox, a demon, a man, a woman, if it upholds the great Dharma and attains the marrow, then you should offer your body-mind as its seat and serve for immeasurable kalpas."[53] His point is that women are competent teachers, even qualified to teach men. Dōgen substantiates his counsel with an explanation of the precedents established by those with whom Buddhism flourished in Sung China[54]:

> Today in certain temples of great Sung China there are nuns who train. When [a nun's] attainment of the Dharma becomes known, an imperial edict is issued appointing her abbess of a nunnery, and thenceforth she expounds the Dharma at her appointed temple. All the subordinates gather together in the hall and

stand to listen [to the abbess's words on] the Dharma, and [to exchange] questions and answers of monastics. This has been the rule since olden times.[55]

As with much of Japanese Buddhism and culture, the Japanese turned to the Chinese for inspiration and guidance. Dōgen urges the Japanese to continue the equality accorded women and men in China, especially in regard to recognizing the true Dharma in female form:

> In the case of a nun who has received the treasury of the true Dharma eye through transmission, if [the monks of] the four fruitions, pratyeka-buddhas, and even those of the three wise stages and of the ten holy states pay homage to her and seek the Dharma from her, she should receive their obeisance. By what right are only males noble? The empty sky is the empty sky; the four elements are the four elements; the five skandas are the five skandas. To be female is exactly the same: as for the attainment of the Way, both [male and female] can attain the Way. Hence both should have high regard for the attainment of the Dharma, and not argue about differences between male and female. Such is the most marvelous law of the Buddha-way.[56]

Dōgen includes an even more direct criticism of the practices he finds in Japan in a version of the *Raihaitokuzui* found in the twenty-eighth fascicle of the *Himitsu Shōbōgenzō* [The Secret Shōbōgenzō].[57] It is a poignant example of his frustration with Japanese Buddhist practices that helped increase his sense that he was the first to introduce "true" Buddhism to Japan.

> There is a ridiculous custom in Japan: it is the practice that nuns and women are not allowed to enter the places called "restricted territories" or "training halls of the Mahāyāna." Such a perverted custom has been practiced for ages, without anyone realizing its wrongness in the least. Those practicing the ancient way do not reform it; and those who are learned and astute do not care about it. While some say that it is the work of the incarnated [buddhas and bodhisattvas], others claim that it is a legacy from ancient worthies. Yet all fail to reason about it. Their egregious absurdity is truly hard to believe. . . . If such obsolete practices do not have to be redressed, does it mean that the cycles of birth and death need not be forsaken, either?[58]

This passage is a direct criticism of the prohibition of women (*nyonin kinzei*) practiced by the establishment Buddhist sects of Tendai and Shingon. Based upon this statement, Dōgen might have moved to Echizen in 1243 to actualize his understanding of Buddhism which *includes* inclusive views—not as an indication that he changed his mind about women. The timing of his departure from Kyoto—occurring only three years after his unambiguous articulation (in *Raihaitokuzui*) of the errors of the ways of the established Buddhist institutions in regards to women—suggests that the prevailing currents in society may have made it difficult for him to freely practice his understanding of the Dharma. This would concur with the experiences of Hōnen, Shinran, and Nichiren, who all practiced inclusivism and who, for various reasons, all had serious complications with the authorities. Dōgen's move to Echizen, then, can be interpreted as (in part) an attempt to actualize his understanding of the Buddhist teachings in an unencumbered environment.

Dōgen never wrote that women had to become men to be enlightened, although this was a common notion during his time. Dōgen also did not criticize the *Lotus Sūtra*. On the contrary, in the *Raihaitokuzui* he takes the story of the Nāga princess becoming a Buddha and equates it with a seven-year-old girl being teacher to a 100-year-old monk.[59] This suggests that he interpreted the Nāga princess story in the *Lotus Sūtra* in a light that was favorable to females. Nonetheless, the prevailing interpretation among academics is that Dōgen held egalitarian ideals in his early years, but he did not take them with him when he established his "serious" monastery in Echizen.[60] Kasahara Kazuo,[61] Hokoya Noriaki,[62] and Tagami Taishū[63] are some of the Japanese scholars who have published their views that Dōgen changed his mind from seeing women as equal to thinking that females did not have true enlightenment. They conclude that Dōgen returned to a purely monastic-oriented vision of Buddhist practice that did not include females. This view of Dōgen suggests that he was an inconsistent philosopher with little integrity. Some western scholars seem to have uncritically accepted the view of Dōgen as promoted by Kasahara, Hokoya, and Tagami. A passage from *Women, Religion, and Sexuality* succinctly articulates this interpretation:

> When Dōgen was young he believed in the equality of men and women and criticized the foolishness of the Mount Hiei and Mount Koya temples, which barred women from entering. However, in later years, by the time Dōgen built Eihei-ji Temple he no longer believed in the equality of men and women and prohibited their entry.[64]

Another scholar reinforces the interpretation that Dōgen had a change of heart toward women; she claims that Dōgen's move to Eihei-ji is a "good example of a case in which Buddhist celibate monasticism functioned in practice to prevent women's access to one of the greatest Zen teachers in history."[65]

These claims are based upon one sentence found in one of the fascicles included in the twelve-fascicle version of the *Shōbōgenzō*, the *Shukke Kudoku*. At the *end* of the text it is written that "It is also said that one can attain Buddhahood in a female body, but this is not the Buddhist path of the true tradition of the Buddhist masters."[66] This text was recorded in 1255, two years after Dōgen passed away. It is commonly agreed, however, that the date for this text is not clearly established.[67] Dōgen scholars agree that this text was revised, but no one knows in what way or to what extent. In numerous other passages in Dōgen's writings (those that are clearly dated before he passed away), there are mentions of women in a positive light that stand in direct contradiction to the one sentence that has triggered so much controversy over whether Dōgen changed his mind about women. The possibility that a sentence was edited in later should be thoroughly explored.[68] What makes the significance of this one sentence more problematic is that, even within the same text, there are passages that contradict it. The aim of the *Shukke Kudoku* fascicle is to convey the merits of being a renunciant. Citations from the *Daibibasha-ron* (Skt. *Abhidharma-mahāvibhāṣā-śāstra*)[69] are used to invoke the concern for renunciation held by Śākyamuni. One of the passages in the *Shukke Kudoku* quotes from the *Daibibasha-ron* where Śākyamuni is cited as making Vow 138: "After I attain perfect enlightenment in the future, if there is a woman who decides to become a renunciant but is prevented from receiving the great precepts and attaining her purpose, then I will not attain true enlightenment."[70] Given the contradiction within this one text, it is clear that we must look beyond the *Shukke Kudoku* to understand Dōgen's views of women more thoroughly.

In the face of the sheer number of passages in Dōgen's texts that develop his positive view of women, versus the one sentence to the contrary—especially given that the sentence appears in a text revised after Dōgen's death—the case for Dōgen reversing his views of women is weak. To offer the compromise that Dōgen did not change his stance philosophically, but he just decided it was impractical to have women practicing at Eihei-ji, does not resolve the issue. The historical record does not support such an interpretation.

Funaoka Makoto interprets the two facets of Dōgen's texts as nothing more than emphasizing different things at different times in different conditions.[71] He notes that things written at Eihei-ji were written to an exclusive audience of renunciants. Some had a difficult time enduring this life, so emphasis on the high value of renunciation would have encouraged the practitioners. This is in stark contrast to the earlier texts from the Kōshō-ji period when Dōgen was working among laity.[72] Funaoka argues that Dōgen's writings have contradictions that he plays out differently at different times. They cannot be construed to mean that he went from thinking laity can be enlightened to thinking that only renunciants can,[73] nor that he thought women could be enlightened and then later decided that women's enlightenment was not true.

Kawamura Kōdō follows a similar line of analysis. He also argues from the perspective of viewing Dōgen's writings as a whole. He says we must consider the vision of the "World of Shōbōgenzō" as a conceptual world of an intelligent human being who dared to break out of a narrow-minded framework. He concludes that the interpretation that Dōgen went from understanding women as equal to excluding them once he went to Eihei-ji would be rejected by Dōgen as "not the activities of the Buddhist teachers, but a one-faceted narrow view (*Sansuikyō*)."[74]

Even if one could finally prove that Dōgen changed his mind, the historical record proves that he did not change his actions. A number of monastic women were his disciples through to the end of his life.[75] Moreover, Dōgen's male disciples continued to take female disciples for generations past the founder's death, a practice that continues to the present day.

Although no women took ordination under Dōgen, a number of monastic women had chosen to transfer into his order from the Daruma-shū or another tradition.[76] His first female monastic disciple was given the Buddhist name Ryōnen-ni. She is attributed with being the primary influence in Dōgen's most explicit teaching on the equality of male and female practitioners in the *Bendōwa*. Ryōnen-ni became Dōgen's first female monastic disciple one month before he wrote the *Bendōwa* on August 15, 1231, at Annyō-in in Yamashiro.[77] Dōgen bestows rare praise upon her at the time he was writing the *Bendōwa*. In a Dharma talk he says that Ryōnen-ni had peerless aspiration to enlightenment, *bodaishin* (Skt.

bodhicitta).[78] Also, in the *Eihei Kōroku* (vol. 8), Dōgen wrote that Ryōnen-ni was deeply devoted to the Great Way of the Buddhas.[79] In the tenth chapter of the *Eihei Kōroku* Dōgen wrote a poem upon Ryōnen's death. She probably died in the winter, for the poem makes a reference to snow.[80] Menzan Zenji, in his *Teihokenzeiki Kōroku*, confirms that "Ryōnen Bikuni" was Dōgen's disciple. Although she was an elderly woman when she came under Dōgen's tutelage, she is remembered for having practiced intensely and making great strides in her understanding of the life of the Dharma. She is remembered as one who knew Zen from the marrow of her bones, and is sometimes compared to the prominent nun Dōgen heard about in China, Massan Ryōnen-ni. Both were incontrovertibly highly respected, and they serve as historical proof that women were able to realize ultimate enlightenment. To offer an interpretation that suggests otherwise would, aside from defying historical proof to the contrary, go against the fabric of Dōgen's thoroughgoing nondualistic philosophy.

As recorded in the *Eihei Sansogyōgōki*, Dōgen also received significant patronage from women. The most renowned was Shōgaku Zenni, who donated the funds to construct the Dharma Hall at Dōgen's first monastery, Kōshō-ji.[81] Apparently she was a distant relative of Dōgen's through his mother, a Fujiwara. She was ordained on September 3, 1225,[82] after her husband, Minamoto Sanetomo, died. She chose to devote her life and her riches to Buddhist practice under Dōgen.

Another monastic woman affiliated with Dōgen, Eshin-bikuni, is recorded in the *Eihei Kōroku* (vol. 2).[83] In the section that mentions Eshin-bikuni, Dōgen wrote about life and death in general. In this context it specifically mentions that around 1244–1246 Dōgen gave a service at Daibutsu-ji[84] in memory of her father's death.[85] Although such evidence is disappointingly sparse, it contributes to the picture that Dōgen respected monastic women.

Egi-ni, originally a Daruma-shū nun, was another one of Dōgen's female disciples who is recorded in history. She was originally the disciple of Kakuan, who had been a disciple of the leader of the Daruma-shū, Dainichi Nōnin. She first met Dōgen in the winter of 1234 at Kōshō-ji, and she remained under his tutelage even after he went deep into the mountains of Echizen. The *Eihei Kōroku* (vol. 5) refers to an event where Egi-ni was with Dōgen at Eihei-ji, perhaps on the occasion of a memorial service for Dōgen's mother.[86] Menzan also mentions "Egi-bikuni" in his *Teihokenzeiki*. On July 28, 1253 (exactly one month before Dōgen passed away), Dōgen wrote that Egi-ni was the Dharma sister of Ekan, Ejō, and Eshō. This makes her the Dharma aunt[87] of Gikai (the head of Eihei-ji after Ejō and just prior to Keizan). Altogether she spent a span of twenty years with Dōgen. Near the end, Egi-ni served at his side and assisted him at his sickbed until he left for Kyoto on August 5, 1253.[88] The fact that Egi-ni served the master when he was vulnerable is a clear indication that Dōgen trusted her. In a monastery community, serving in a capacity close to the master is keenly sought. He showed her high respect and honor through the end of his life. Egi-ni remained an important figure during the leadership of the next generation headed by Dōgen's devoted disciple, Ejō.[89] Her story confirms the fact that Dōgen was committed to, and even relied upon, monastic women throughout his life.

Dōgen had one of the lucid voices that sounded the philosophical and practical truth of the equality of female and male practitioners amid the cacophony of doubters. How much of his thought was realized in the 700-year history since then? A successor of Dōgen, Keizan Jōkin Zenji (1268–1325), continued Dōgen's teachings on equality, and he ordained and taught many women.[90] Keizan learned his religious devotion from his mother, Ekan Daishi (d. ca. 1314).[91] According to the records, she was a nun who had been the abbess of Jōjū-ji at the time of Gikai's funeral in 1309.[92] In honor of his mother, Keizan built an amadera, Hōō-ji, the first Sōtō sect amadera. On October 9, 1323, he appointed his mother's niece, his cousin Myōshō-ni, as abbess of this temple.[93] This action is a concrete illustration of Keizan's egalitarian practices in support of women. Again on May 23, 1325, Keizan (age 58) vowed to help women in the three worlds and ten directions in memory of his mother, Ekan Daishi. In the *Jōkin hotsuganmon*,[94] it is said that;

> [Keizan] praised Ekan [his mother] for having dedicated her life to teaching Buddhism to women. Keizan inherited her dedication. His disciple Ekyū was the first nun known to have received a Sōtō dharma transmission.[95] To help her overcome the difficulties of Chinese, Keizan rewrote Dōgen's explanation of the precepts in the Japanese phonetic syllabary.[96]

Records indicate that Keizan had around thirty nuns under his leadership.[97] Many of their names are remembered: Sonin-ni, Ekyū-ni,[98] En'i-ni, Shozen-ni,[99] Myōshō-ni, Ninkai-ni, Shinmyō-ni, Shinshō-ni, Jōnin-ni, Myōshin-ni. Sonin-ni was from a high ranking family. She and her husband had a deep faith in Buddhism, and in 1312 they were ordained together by Keizan.[100] On January 14, 1322, another husband and wife took ordination under Keizan at Yōkō-ji. Shinmyō-ni must have been at an advanced age, for it records that her husband was 83.[101] Keizan is the main figure responsible for increasing respect for nuns by actively implementing Dōgen's teachings on male–female equality.

William Bodiford, a specialist on medieval Sōtō history, concludes that "there must have been many more nuns at medieval Sōtō monasteries than current records indicate."[102] Bodiford's observation about Sōtō Zen's openness toward women suggests that women were welcomed into Sōtō Zen, confirming that inclusive teachings were practiced. Indeed, the precedent of including women in Sōtō Zen practice established by Dōgen and Keizan was maintained by their successors.

At least into the Muromachi Period (1338–1573) it is clear that the direct successors to Dōgen maintained the practice of treating women with equality (table 2-1). Kangan Giin (1217–1300) had four known nuns as his disciples. Gasan Jōseki (1275–1365),[103] Gessen Ryōin (1319–1400), Tsūgen Jakurei (1322–91), and Daitetsu Sōrei (1333–1408) all had nun disciples.[104] Gasan's disciple, Soitsu-bikuni, also had disciples. Among all Gasan's female disciples, she was granted the status of being Gasan's Dharma heir.[105] Records further indicate the active participation of nuns, including the presence of nuns at the funeral services for both Gikai (1219–1309) and Gasan. The *Sōjijinidai oshō shōtō* records that one of the eulogies for Gasan was written by a nun named Zenshin.[106] Gessen and Daitetsu also had nuns help

Table 2-1 Lineage Under Dōgen[108]

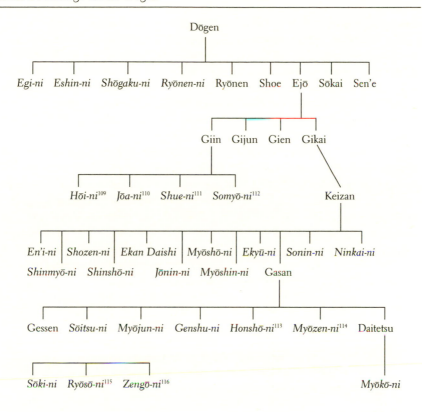

perform their funeral ceremonies. These were probably not unusual instances of nuns being involved in such ceremonies.[107]

The medieval Sōtō school, however, never developed official monastic centers for training large groups of nuns. Sōtō sect temples and activities were primarily concentrated in the provinces, which were controlled by feudal lords (*daimyō*). Nevertheless, in 1334, about 100 years after Dōgen accepted his first nun disciple a number of powerful nuns established the Sōtō-shū Nisōdan.[117] Therefore, it is most likely that the nuns did practice in small groups, but they did not receive recognition or support for their efforts from the male institution.[118] Therefore, only exceptionally superior nuns were referred to in historical texts.

Nonetheless, contemporary Sōtō nuns have a solid sense that women have been a continuous presence in Sōtō Zen. When they look at the history of their sect, they see women seriously engaged with Buddhist practice. When they read Dōgen's writings, they see women being affirmed. That is all they need to know to conclude that regulations that treat women unfairly are wrong. But the twentieth-century nuns had to act within the broader historical situation in which women had been highly circumscribed.

Tokugawa Encroachments

The Tokugawa Period (1600–1867) saw important changes that helped set the stage
for the twentieth-century nuns' concerns and activities. With the establishment of
the Tokugawa feudalistic military regime, the pendulum swung in the direction
of increased demarcation between social classes and distinction between women
and men. The regime maintained peace through tight control in this exclusivistic
period. Buddhist temples and monasteries were vital to the organizational structure
of the unified nation, but the Buddhists' actions were circumscribed by the new
system.

The plight of women interested in participating in official capacities was particularly bleak during the Tokugawa Period. Confucian principles were formally
instituted in governmental policies as the Japanese entered the early modern period. A renowned Confucian scholar of the time, Kaibara Ekken (1630–1714), is
attributed with writing the text which has been most influential in shaping the
education and social position of women: *Onna Daigaku* [The Great Learning for
Women]. In the same vein, Kaibara wrote a 1710 text for the education of Japanese
children. This text includes explicit instructions for women, setting out the Confucian view that women should limit their religious behavior.

> Women should always be careful to guard themselves. . . . They should not fre-
> quent shrines and temples which draw crowds of visitors while they are still
> under the age of forty.

> Women should not be deluded by the arts of male and female mediums, and
> should not pollute, approach, pray or flatter deities and buddhas at will. They
> should concentrate on performing human duties. They must not divert their
> attention to invisible spiritual beings.[119]

This is clear evidence that women in the Tokugawa Period had to overcome social
resistance to their ambitions to follow the religious life before the age of forty.
Forty years was used as a dividing line between women who were of childbearing
age and those who were not. The unambiguous signal was that women's role in
society was to bear and rear children. Their ancient roles in the religious sphere
were being eroded. We find in the twentieth century, however, that the effects of
this erosion are not permanent. Indeed, women have been fighting against these
negative impulses throughout history.[120]

Girls in the Tokugawa Period were taught to adapt to new conditions, because
they would eventually leave their blood-relation's home and move into their husband's home.[121] The aims of their cultivation made them strong by training them
to be flexible and creative. This upbringing enabled women to develop the means
to lead full lives, and it did not always result in the type of behavior that was
deemed socially desirable. An obvious example of this is the response nuns had
to the strict control placed upon women.

Some amadera opened their doors to serve as a refuge for women in need.
They offered these women sanctuary. The two best known of these temples are
Tōkei-ji of the Rinzai sect and Mantoku-ji of the Ji sect.[122] Women could not
receive a divorce in this feudalistic society, but it was not very difficult for a man

to demand a divorce. At a temple, however, women, over a period of time, could be granted a divorce. The temple was also a place where women could receive an education.[123] Thus, for various reasons, women found a safe and interesting path in becoming a nun.

During this period, Sōtō Zen women are found engaged in monastic life in the proximity of Eihei-ji. Hakuju-an, an amadera, was built before 1734 in Dai-kakumura, a few kilometers from the Eihei-ji monastic complex. The temple was founded by a disciple of Shōten Sokuchi Zenji. Shōten served as the first head of the temple, and then a nun named Teijitsu-ni became the second head. It is not clearly established, but there is a high possibility that Teijitsu-ni was the disciple of Menzan Zuihō (1683–1769). Menzan had two female disciples, Teijitsu-ni and Teishin-ni, and he mentions Hakuju-an in his *Sansho Nikki* on September 22, 1734. Today Hakuju-an stands at the edge of Eihei-ji; it was moved in February 1827 to its current location a few steps from the main gate of Eihei-ji.[124] Some nuns stay at this temple when they come to Eihei-ji. The existence of this amadera adjacent to the monastery for men disproves the assumption that nuns were not allowed at Eihei-ji during this period.

The social structure and institutions of the Tokugawa Period were based on feudalistic values that did not offer women much support. Despite this intense discrimination, women often found a way to take control of their own lives, even when limited by intense external control. The types of women who became nuns during the Tokugawa Period included women from the imperial family and samurai families, literary scholars, artists, prostitutes, and many who had a family relative who was already a nun.[125] Nuns continued to create avenues to live in accord with their interpretation of the Buddhist teachings, even in a relatively heightened era of male domination and exclusivism.

Meiji Reclamations

Competing values were woven into the fabric of Japanese society with the inauguration of the Meiji Restoration of 1868. The new Meiji government (1868–1911) had conflicting aims. One was to return to the roots of ancient Japan. More precisely it was an attempt to restore monarchical rule, harking back to Emperor Jimmu (6th c. B.C.E) The other aim was renovation.[126] Japan strove to become a modern nation-state replete with western influences. During this era, there was a strong sentiment that any attempt to maintain traditional culture was superfluous and suggested a lack of concern for the critical situation in which the nation perceived itself. The diametrical impulses and the accelerated pace of change left people disoriented. The times demanded that society rapidly integrate the past and future into the present.

Various changes were instituted at both the public and private levels, from the educational system to the type of clothing people wore. Many conservative people wore kimono as a conscious statement that Japan's traditions were the source of their distinctive talents. They wore their tradition with pride and respect. The progressive factions were frequently seen in western fashions, an unambiguous declaration of their enthusiasm for modernization via westernization.[127] A new intelligentsia emerged out of the keen interest in westernization. Among the most renowned was Fukuzawa Yukichi (1835–1901), who promoted western ideas, especially the equality of all men and women, liberty, and human dignity.[128] In the 1870s, the early years of the Meiji Restoration, he had a bestseller *Gakumon no Susume* [*An Invitation to Learning*]. It appealed to the people because he affirmed that "Heaven does not create one person above another person, nor does it create one person below another."[129] The equality of women was seriously considered in this context, because in the flux of ideas during this time, liberalism focused the thrust of the Meiji drive to expand education across class and gender lines.[130] In 1886, the government decreed that elementary education would be available for all citizens. In 1900, four-year compulsory education was enforced. In 1901, Professor J. Naruse opened the first institution for women that corresponded to university status. He had spent three years studying women's colleges in North America and two years of research in Japan. He wrote the book *Women's Education*.[131] In 1907 the four years of compulsory education were extended to six.[132] Presently, education is compulsory through high school—twelve years of some of the most rigorous primary and secondary education in the world.

Leading the efforts of westernization were the emperor and empress, who encouraged women to get an education and improve their intellectual ability, even to go abroad to study.[133] Western feminism entered Japan and resonated with the roots of women's spirituality in Japan. It was not the original source of Japanese women's concern for fair treatment and opportunity,[134] but it served as a catalyst during this time of change. Western feminism empowered and inspired the women of Japan to reclaim their authority.[135]

Nakamura observes that despite these new regulations and movements, many women spent more time in private lessons such as sewing, cooking, flower arrangement, and tea ceremony than in their formal school education.[136] These are skills that were the focus of a girl's training during the Tokugawa Period. Among these traditional arts, girls were taught to adapt to new conditions. They had to learn to be flexible yet strong, and have refined speech and behavior, which were seen as feminine virtues.[137]

Later, we will see how these qualities persisted as feminine virtues, despite the new manuals that were composed after 1868 to introduce western rationalism and liberalism into female education. The education of nuns in the twentieth century is a living tribute to some traditional feminine virtues. Judgment about whether or not this is a positive or negative remnant of Tokugawa culture is not discussed. Rather, I analyze the role and contribution Zen monasticism has had in Japanese culture. I focus particularly on the changing role it has in modern culture and how the roles of monks and nuns differ.

With the Meiji Restoration of 1868, the relationship of the government and the monasteries went through another permutation more suitable to modern times. Article 28 of the 1889 Constitution says that "Japanese subjects shall, within limits not prejudicial to peace and order and not antagonistic to their duties as subjects, enjoy freedom of religious belief." However, the imperial family promoted its abiding engagement with Buddhism, often mentioning that between Empress

Suiko (r. 592–628) and Emperor Meiji (r. 1868–1912) there were thirty-six emperors, seventy-four empresses, two-hundred thirty-three imperial princes, and sixty-seven princesses who were ordained as Buddhist monks or nuns (while numerous others took various forms of lay vows).[138] Although the government did not try to control Buddhism, it still asked the monasteries and Buddhist sects to follow its regulations, even in matters concerning the interpretation of monastic vows. This was demonstrated nearly two decades earlier; on April 25, 1872, the Meiji government changed the regulations and began officially permitting monks to eat meat, have hair, wear lay clothing, and marry.[139] On January 23, 1873, the government also changed the regulations for nuns, except they did not stipulate that nuns could wear lay clothing.[140] This reinterpretation of monasticism is a radical departure from the ancient tradition of celibacy.[141] Indeed, the laity displayed widespread discontent toward the laxity of priestly morals.[142] Most monks have acted on these new regulations, whereas the nuns have maintained the traditional monastic regulations, especially in regard to celibacy and remaining single. It is suggested that nuns would not be acknowledged as nuns if they had followed the new regulations.[143] In the data I collected, however, the reason the nuns themselves give is that they choose to remain true to the Buddhist tradition. They base their practice upon the regulations of their founder, Dōgen.

In historical and social context, it is hard to establish that nuns had a "real" choice. To fight for the freedom to live according to their interpretation of Buddhist teachings within the sect institution, they had to use something for support. They found it in Dōgen and tradition. For the nuns, the fight for fairness was inextricably bound to maintaining traditional Zen. Perhaps the changes the monks willingly participated in gave the nuns a renewed sense of their own self-worth and a heightened awareness of their genuine commitment to a Buddhist lifestyle. This awareness fueled the nuns in their movement for official recognition of their activities and equal opportunity in practice, education, training, and teaching. This new awareness might also be seen as part of a general wave of transformation that swept through the mountain villages during this time. Farmers "discovered" their own authority and overcame their deeply rooted passive attitude towards the government.[144] A Japanese historian, Irokawa, asserts that "the unprecedented activities in agricultural and mountain villages during the 1880s were supported by the intellectual as well as political aspiration of the common people, and those activities were the fountainhead of 'Meiji vitality.' "[145] Perhaps it is no coincidence that a number of Sōtō nuns came from farming families.

The Meiji Restoration began a stream of countless changes in Japanese society, eventually transforming it from an isolated, nontechnological, feudal society to an international, high-tech, democratic society. The monastic women of the twentieth century are living embodiments of the Meiji government's aims. Although a return to tradition and a heightened zeal for modern innovations may appear contradictory—and in most cases they were in direct conflict—in the case of Zen nuns they find a compelling harmony. In order to reclaim the rights of women worn thin through the years of male dominance, the nuns had to fight for equity. In concurrence with Fukuzawa, who taught "that one should adopt a spirit of skepticism toward all authority,"[146] the nuns challenged the unequal regulations imposed by the sect authorities. In so doing, they became models of modern women organizing and establishing their own institutions. They helped propel the current that was gaining power for women in Meiji Japan.

A sweep of history from the first ordained Japanese Buddhists to the perspicacious monastic women of Meiji reveals an uninterrupted stream of courageous, creative, and faithful monastic women.[147] These women did not act as though they were defeated by oppressive conditions. The first Japanese Buddhist temple in Japan was established and led by a nun. Tenaciously obedient to their concept of the truth, monastic women of feudalistic Tokugawa overcame intensified male domination. When we view the activities of the twentieth-century Sōtō Zen nuns from this historical perspective, it is clear that they are not inaugurating women into positions of religious leadership. On the contrary, they are acting in accord with what history had shown them was their due.

THREE

Twentieth-Century Leadership

In the beginning, woman was the sun, the genuine human
being. Now she is but a moon—dependent on others for
existence and unable to do anything more than reflect the
glory of others—an infirm pallid moon. . . . She must
return to her original state of glory.[1]

—Hiratsuka Raichō (1886–1971),
Leader of Japanese Feminist Movement,[2]
September 1911

As the twentieth century began, Japanese women were engaged in a deliberate
and active attempt to reassert their concerns. The stark proclamation by Hiratsuka reflected the sentiment of forthright women of her age. The shackles of
the male-dominated and markedly regimented Tokugawa Period were shed in
their renewed sense of worth. Monastic women had a similar vision and acted
with swift strength. Fortified with the triumphs of female religious leaders of the
past, they approached their goals with confidence.

Sōtō Zen nuns began the twentieth century with a deep commitment to living
a monastic Buddhist life, plus the conviction that their founder, Dōgen, had teachings that affirmed women's practice. Although academics have become divided
over the significance of Dōgen's egalitarian teachings, practicing Zen nuns were
not and are not divided. Nuns embrace Dōgen's views of women as positive;
empowered by Dōgen's writings, the nuns have affected the course of Sōtō history
in the twentieth century. But they began the century encumbered by misogynous
regulations in a sect administration that did not acknowledge nuns' abilities, contributions, or commitments.

The sect has a hierarchical system, with each rank being symbolized by an
appropriate robe color. A visible indication of the sect administration's policies on
monastic women was that all nuns were required to wear black robes, black being
the color of novices. They were not permitted to receive the requisite monastic
or secular education for the higher ranking positions that would have entitled

49

them to wear the colors commensurate with the rank. The issue for nuns in the twentieth century was not the desire to wear colored robes, but the concern to be as effective as possible as monastics. That means being officially allowed to participate in the decisionmaking process of sect affairs, the level of which is determined by rank. Legend has it that Dōgen refused a purple robe, the color that symbolizes highest respect, for it did not coincide with his commitment to simplicity. In keeping with their founder, many monastics prefer to wear black, regardless of their rank. For male monastics, preferring black was a matter of choice—but it wasn't a choice for women until the middle of the twentieth century.

At the beginning of the twentieth century, nuns did not have training facilities supported or authorized by the sect administration, nor were they permitted to enter the Sōtō sect university, Komazawa. Compounding the limited resources available to them, the requirements for a nun were considerably lengthier than those for her male counterparts, sometimes necessitating one, two, or even three years more training. This extra effort was only rewarded with degrees lower than the lowest male degrees. From this unfair foundation, it was easy to keep nuns out of heading temples of any size or influence. (This, in turn, meant that nuns were not involved with the financial system that would become notably lucrative by the final decades of the century.) The regulations stated that only a monastic with a certain rank could be considered for middle to high positions, but nuns were not eligible to attain those ranks, no matter how long and hard they practiced.

A significant core of Sōtō nuns was determined to rectify these inequities. Their goal of being treated fairly would require a creative mix of established practices and novel methods. Starting in the 1880s, they began to reach their goal by combining monastic discipline and training with secular education. After establishing a firm foundation and cultivating a sizable number of competent nuns, they organized themselves in a concerted effort to force male sect leaders to institute what they held were Dōgen's teachings on egalitarianism. Throughout this period the majority of nuns maintained a lifestyle in accord with their idea of traditional Zen monasticism. On the contrary, numerous male monastics increasingly chose to live according to relaxed monastic regulations permitted by the Meiji government. Many monks also began modifying their practices in an attempt to adjust Sōtō Zen to modern times. Although a number of nuns were engaged in traditionally nonmonastic activities, they appeared more monastic in contrast to the trend in the monks' community. This eventually helped foster an increased perception of monastic women's authority and legitimacy, making it difficult for the male sect leaders to ignore the claims nuns made based upon the founder's own writings.

The nuns' actions tell us much about what they thought of themselves. They did not act like women who were just discovering liberation. They acted like women who knew that historical precedents made them entitled to fair treatment. From the beginning of the century, they acted with deliberate and well-reasoned conduct. They knew that nuns were supposed to be full members of the sect, and they were tired of men leaving them out. They understood Buddhism to be a tradition that was fair to women, and they acted with confidence. The leading nuns managed the competing currents of tradition and modernization to shift toward a structurally egalitarian Sōtō Zen institution.

My exploration into the world of Japanese Buddhist nuns concentrates upon the Sōtō sect of Zen, for it is currently the largest and most organized sect of nuns in Japan. The Sōtō sect has the most nunneries (three: Aichi Senmon Nisōdō, Niigata Senmon Nisōdō, and Toyama Senmon Nisōdō), compared to the Jōdo sect, which has one (Yoshimizu Gakuen of Chion-in). The other sects do not have a special school for the sole purpose of training nuns. Although Sōtō nuns are more diverse than what is examined here, I have focused my attention on nuns primarily affiliated with the Aichi Senmon Nisōdō in Nagoya. The leaders of each generation I explicate were involved with the Nagoya nunnery. These particular nuns represent the largest group within Sōtō nuns. Furthermore, their records are the most organized, extensive, and accessible. I have gained access to this period of their history through sources found primarily in the Nagoya nunnery archives. The major documents include *Sōtōshū Nisōshi* [The History of Sōtō Sect Nuns], the authoritative book on the history of the Sōtō sect of monastic women, edited by Tanaka Dōrin, Katō Shinjō, Yamaguchi Kokan, and Tajima Hakudō; *Rokujūnen no Ayumi* [A Path of Sixty Years], a book that explicates the history of the Aichi Senmon Nisōdō; and *Jōrin* and *Otayori*, journals written for and by monastic women.

I am not seeking to discover what "really" happened to these nuns during the twentieth century. Rather, I am interested in finding out how nuns say they experienced this part of their history that resulted in so many positive structural changes. Therefore, it is more important to find out how nuns represent and understand their actions than it is to ascertain the "facts."

In her analysis of shamans in Japan, Carmen Blacker found a close relationship between suffering, endurance, and gratitude and the spiritual awareness that ascetics sought and achieved.[3] I found a similar correspondence in the nuns I studied. The key to understanding their interpretation of their lives—especially how they do not express oppressive feelings in the face of blatantly unfair treatment—is that they see enduring suffering as part of what will help refine them along the Buddhist path. Therefore, gratitude even for "oppression" is integral to their discipline. They strive to view all experience as a resource, an opportunity to polish oneself. This attitude toward their experiences will become evident through the way they have articulated their activities. In short, they used suffering to further their aims. They were not unaware of the unfairness of their situation. But because they did not see the "official authorities" as having much say in their religious practice, they found effective ways to change the external structures to accommodate their understanding of Sōtō Zen monastic life. They did not wait for the sect institution to support or recognize their efforts. They took action in accordance with their interpretation of Buddhist teachings.

This chapter traces the three generations of Sōtō monastic women who have been responsible for releasing nuns from systematically undue restrictions. The foci of the three generations are (1) the four pioneering nuns who founded Nagoya's official training monastery for nuns in 1904; (2) Kojima Kendō (1898–1995) and the founding of the Nisōdan, the organizing body that helped establish egalitarian regulations; and (3) Aoyama Shundō (b. 1933) and the life and teachings of a traditional female monastic Zen master in modern Japan. The first generation broke through the embankment of inequity by focusing on the fundamental link of the vicious cycle: education. The second generation continued to blaze the trail by forcing the sect administration to revise sect regulations, eradicating rules that had given male monastics preferential treatment. By the third generation, the fruits of the previous generations' toil were beginning to ripen. Structurally and institutionally, a nun could live according to her interpretation of Buddhist teachings and practices. In this sense, third-generation nuns could choose to be more "traditional" than those who came before them. The first two generations had to be more innovative in order to establish a tradition they held was in accord with the founder's interpretation of Buddhist monastic life. Reflecting the different needs of each generation, these women manifest strength of character, creative ingenuity, and a profound commitment to Buddhist monastic life.

First Generation: Rapid Ascent through Education

Monastic women were leaders in the drive for women to seek education outside the home, but it was a path filled with institutionalized obstacles. During the late Tokugawa Period, nuns lived in sub-temples studying and practicing together. The sect did not officially acknowledge their efforts. They did not authorize the sub-temples to grant degrees that would qualify nuns to rise in the ranks of the sect.[4] The sect-administered degrees were part of the hierarchical system that determined who could teach what level of course recognized by the sect and who could run what level of temple. Since nuns were not allowed to study and/or practice at anything but the sub-temples, they had to determine their own fate with discipline and commitment. In a move to increase the quality of their education, the first monastery school for resident Sōtō nuns was established by a nun in Gifu prefecture on April 1, 1881.[5] Nuns had not yet received recognition from the sect administration for their efforts, but shortly thereafter each region established its own school for nuns. In 1887 the second school was established in Aichi prefecture, followed by one in Kyōto in 1888, then Tokyo in 1889, and Toyama in 1892.[6] These monastery schools gave the novice women training in Buddhist practice and a general education. The general education they received at the monastery schools qualified them for middle-school (jogakkō) degrees conferred by the Japanese Ministry of Education, but the schools were not authorized to grant degrees that were conferred by the sect administration. The new monastery schools the nuns established were, nonetheless, more advanced than the sub-temples in which monastic women trained each other and practiced together, for they offered a more organized and higher level of education.

Many temples also ran terakoya, schools for neighborhood children.[7] Although the terakoya was invariably at a monk's temple, the majority of those doing the actual teaching and care of the children were nuns.[8] Nuns also were involved in nursery schools and day care for children during the farmers' busy seasons. Targeting these areas of activity reveals that although they personally renounced the householder life, nuns had insight into the needs of householders. Temples were the predominant facility for education. During the Meiji years of rapid modernization and reexamination of traditional customs and values, temple education was reformed. Sōtō nuns forced the currents of change in their favor, and after a little more than a decade they won the official right to establish schools fully authorized to train women in the monastic life as well as offer a government-authorized general education.

With the administrative barrier removed, Sōtō nuns wasted no time in fulfilling their dreams of higher education. On August 10, 1902, regulations were established for official degree-granting Sōtō-shū Nisō Gakurin (Sōtō Sect nuns' monastery schools). It was originally determined that there would be three locations in the country that would give instruction on various Buddhist teachings and offer courses as found in a regular secular school. But by 1907 monastery schools for nuns had been established in Toyama, Aichi, Nagano, and Niigata prefectures. The schools' curriculum was designed to prepare novice nuns broadly in both Buddhist studies and general academic studies. The requirements during their tenure at the monastery school included Sōtō sect teachings, teachings of other sects, ethics, practice, Japanese, Classical Chinese (*kanbun*), history, geography, math, calligraphy, chanting scriptures (*shōmyō*), and sewing. To receive the Sōtō Sect preparatory degree (*yoka*), one had to attend the monastery school for a year. The Standard Degree (*honka*), involved three years of study and practice.[9] These monastery schools were distinct from a pure monastery, for their aim was to train monastic women to be effective in both the Buddhist community and the community at large. In order to function and be respected by society, the secular component of the education was indispensable. Since most schools were traditionally affiliated with a temple and there were few public schools at this time, it was not unusual to have them combined in this manner. Sōtō nuns persisted until they won both the authority to grant official monastic degrees recognized by the sect administration and grant official academic degrees recognized by the Ministry of Education.

This historical achievement was fostered in large part by the efforts of the women who established the first autonomous school officially authorized to train monastic women. Four monastic women, Mizuno Jōrin, Hori Mitsujō, Yamaguchi Kokan, and Andō Dōkai, established the Aichi-ken Sōtō-shū Nisō Gakurin on May 8, 1903, only nine months after the regulations enabled them to do so. The nunnery designates May 1903 through March 1908 as their founding period. As we look at this period, the background of each founding nun will be illuminated. A brief sketch of their individual backgrounds will elucidate a pattern, especially that education was a commonality that linked them together. It also seems to be of no coincidence that each of the women received significant support from their families, all of which were of good standing. Both the type of women who chose the monastic path during the late nineteenth century and the vision and determination of these particular women will become clear in the ensuing paragraphs.

Mizuno Jōrin (1848–1927) was the key figure among the four nuns who founded the monastery school for nuns in Aichi prefecture. She epitomized the type of woman who was cultivated for a leadership role in the nuns' community. She was a native of Aichi prefecture, and her family was well-to-do and of high standing in the community. So despite the lack of institutional facilities, it was not difficult for her to realize her goal of receiving a high monastic education. Her family supported their daughter when, at age nine, she initiated the request to be a renunciant. She practiced near her home at Bishō-dō under the tutelage of Kankō-ni, a nun renowned among nuns for her strength. Mizuno made quick progress under her and showed great diligence and intelligence. In 1858, she went with her teacher to Kyoto, where Kankō-ni was to become the eleventh head of Yōrin-an. Yōrin-an, originally a Rinzai temple for nuns, has a history that reaches back to Toyotomi Hideyoshi (1536–1598).[10] After Kankō-ni died in 1884, Mizuno became the twelfth head of Yōrin-an. During these years, Mizuno had done an extensive study of classical texts under a recognized teacher, Kanbyō-ni. Mizuno distinguished herself in 1890 when she became the Dharma heir of U Riki. It was quite unusual for a nun to become someone's Dharma heir, for the regulations did not allow for it. She then went to Niigata and Toyama in 1893 to practice Zen further. In the autumn of 1901 she was received by the head Zen Master of Eihei-ji, and she was given the title *Ni-oshō* (Female Buddhist Preceptor).[11] Despite the fact that sect regulations did not permit nuns to be granted this title, the highest Zen Master of the sect saw that she was clearly deserving of such recognition. Establishing such precedent made blazing a path for nuns more acceptable. Mizuno's vision for nuns was taking form. She moved closer to her goal in April 1902, when she was appointed national head of Zen nuns at the behest of the Zen Master of Eihei-ji.

On August 15, 1868, Hori Mitsujō (1868–1927) was born into one of the most prominent families in the Nagoya castle region in Aichi prefecture. It was not unusual that the Hori family consented to tonsuring their child at age nine, for the family was actively engaged in the founding and continuation of a lineage of nuns laterally related.[12] The Hori family is a notable example of the dominant pattern of aunt–niece blood relations in the nuns' community. It is no surprise that the Hori nuns rose to leadership positions, for they had strong financial and social support. Hori Mitsujō became a disciple of her blood-related aunt, the nun Hori Tokujō-ni of Ryūsen-kutsu (later renamed Saikō-ji)[13] in Higashi-ku, Nagoya. At that time, nuns did not have much opportunity for academic study. It was not common for them to have time nor the necessary resources for such pursuits. However, while in training, Mitsujō would create time to study diligently. Like Mizuno, she seems to have understood that education was the vehicle for advancing nuns. Mitsujō began to reveal her promise when on September 27, 1885, she was granted the title Head Nun (*Ni-shuso*) at Eihei-ji. It was almost inevitable that the young Mitsujō would eventually meet Mizuno Jōrin, for they were among an elite category of highly educated and officially recognized nuns. The following year (1886), she began to practice and study under Mizuno Jōrin at Yōrin-an in Kyoto. Her pursuit of Buddhist Studies led her to a series of teachers. She received the teachings of Hakuchōzan at Hōji-ji in Nagoya, where she studied alongside monks. Then from February 1899 through September 1901 she went to Zenbō-ji and studied under Hayakawa Kenryū; in 1910 she received the title *Ni-oshō* from the Sōtō sect head temple. It was rare to have the resources to study extensively and reach a high level of education; Mitsujō's accomplishments are a reflection of her intellect and also the high status and support of her family. In 1911 she moved to Chōsei-an (later renamed Seikan-ji) in Chikusa-ku, Nagoya.

Andō Dōkai (1874–1915) was born in Aichi prefecture, the third daughter of her family. From a young age she showed intelligence and had an affinity for studying. She became a Buddhist renunciant at the age of thirteen at Entsū-an, a temple outside the city of Okazaki. She took initiation (*tokudo*) under the thirtieth generation head of Ryukai-in, Kondō Shuken. She then studied under the nun Andō Daiken-ni at Minami Kifun Yakushi-dō,[14] later renamed Kōrin-ji.[15] Daiken-ni was the second head of Kōrin-ji. Andō Dōkai eventually became the third head of Kōrin-ji. Andō met Mizuno in April 1891. She studied and practiced under Mizuno for nearly thirteen years at Yōrin-an. Andō remained a devoted attendant over the following twenty years, when they worked together establishing and running the nunnery. Once again, an exception to the regulations prohibiting women from high monastic titles was necessary. In 1911 Andō also received the title *Ni-oshō* with a mark of outstanding achievement and a special robe from the Zen Masters of both Eihei-ji and Sōji-ji. Not long after achieving her goals, Andō died at age 42 on August 4, 1915.

Yamaguchi Kokan (1875–1933) was born in Aichi prefecture on November 25. At the age of four she was adopted by the nun Yamaguchi Dōkin-ni. Beginning at age eight, she started studying Chinese classics under the tutelage of Yamaguchi Daikyū. In 1888 she received initiation from Sada Kendō. She subsequently studied the doctrines and teachings of Sōtō and other sects with him. In April 1902 she received the title *Ni-shuso* from Eihei-ji, indicating she was a leader among monastic women. She practiced and studied under Mizuno Jōrin for ten years. Yamaguchi was dedicated to the advancement of monastic women. She was only twenty-nine when the official nunnery was established. Yamaguchi served the nunnery for thirty years, first in the capacity of teacher and later the school superintendent. In 1907 she became the sixth head of the temple in which she received ordination, Ōtaka-machi Yakushi-dō. Completing the quartet of prodigious nuns, Soji-ji bestowed the title *Ni-oshō* upon her in September 1910. The next year, Eihei-ji followed suit and also recognized her as a *Ni-oshō*. Yamaguchi is remembered by nuns as a model of erudition who had an intense interest in philosophy.

Having quickly ascertained their mutual concern for education, in 1902 these four monastic women decided it was time to advance the education of all nuns. They were exasperated at the lack of facilities for running an educational program for monastic women. After a long and careful deliberation over the structure for training and educating monastic women, Mizuno Jōrin created a proposal, and was joined by Hori Mitsujō, Yamaguchi Kokan, and Andō Dōkai. As comrades, the four nuns worked together to establish a nuns' training school, a Nisōdō. Under the guidance of their teacher, Mizuno Jōrin, they divided the various tasks necessary for establishing the nuns' school. Mizuno wrote of her sentiments at that time:

For many years I have been responsible for cultivating nuns. I have encouraged them to practice The Way while walking, stopping, residing, sitting, and lying down. The current group of nuns has come to be dissatisfied with the education at Yōrin-an. We are, therefore, resolved to establish a monastic school for nuns (*nigakurin*) with official recognition from the sect. It will support the future education of monastic women. We cannot quit. Together we vow to establish [the nuns' school] through a spirit of cooperation.[16]

These remarks show that the establishment of an educational facility for monastic women was not initiated by the sect headquarters or the male leaders of the religious community. At the beginning of the Meiji Period, the social and religious status of monastic women was low. Few recognized the necessity for monastic women to have an education. Nevertheless, the nuns' school was finally established, founded upon the vision and dedication of a small group of monastic women under the leadership of Mizuno Jōrin. At first they did not receive any assistance from the sect. These nuns overcame great hurdles to establish the school through their diligent efforts and organizing skills.

Their beginning was modest. They used Andō's small resident temple — Yakushi-dō (Kōrin-ji) — as their shelter and school room.[17] It was surrounded by a verdant and thick bamboo grove at the edge of the countryside.[18] This was the stage for the historical drama where the nuns set precedents in the education of monastic women by establishing a place where nuns could practice and study and receive recognition for their efforts by the sect headquarters. They opened the training monastry on May 8, 1903. They combined the opening ceremony with the entrance ceremony for the first class of novices.

This monastery underwent numerous changes as the nuns responded to the needs of the times and the opportunities they created. The name of the monastery changed in accordance with each major development. In general, I use the term Nisōdō (Nuns' Training Monastery) to refer to their facility. This is the term that is used by most people today, because it is part of the current official name, Aichi Senmon Nisōdō. A number of nuns who started their training before 1949 still call it the Nigakurin (Nuns' Monastery School), for that was the name it used during the years the monastery also offered education in a broad curriculum that even included math and science. Today the appellation "Nigakurin" has an affectionate and nostalgic ring to it. (On a practical note, I have also found more taxicab drivers know how to get to the "Nigakurin" but not the "Nisōdō," even though it is the same place. Perhaps this is due to the fact that more elderly nuns use taxis today than the younger ones who have the strength to get up the steep incline.)

In the first year of the Nisōdō, twenty-two women entered. There were originally eight teachers. All thirty lived together in the two six-mat *tatami* rooms (approximately 210 square feet.).[19] The space served as their sleeping quarters at night. Upon waking, the women immediately transformed it into a meditation hall for zazen. At other times it was used as a worship hall for services. Throughout the day it alternated as a dining area and classroom. They were devoted to their practice day and night. The food was primarily barley. The *miso* soup[20] was mostly salt, with little of the primary ingredient, soybean paste. It was inconvenient to obtain simple supplies like books, pens, and ink, so they had to make a trip into Nagoya once a month. It was also difficult to see a doctor due to the remoteness of the location. Despite the extremely tight conditions, they studied diligently, overcoming numerous obstacles. It is also possible that their practice had to be extremely strict *because* of their tight conditions.

Tanaka Dōrin (1884–1973), a nun who graduated in the fourth class and eventually became abbess, recalls when she first went to the Nisōdō. There were no vehicles to transport her over the three *ri*[21] of mountain roads. She wore straw sandals and carried her baggage over the mountain. She reminisces about an unforgettable moment of sipping water that flowed over a rock along the way. To the east of the Nisōdō were mountains, to the west a woods, to the south a bamboo grove, and to the north a train track—the Chūo-sen. There was no electricity at this time. She also remembers how salty the soup was.

Although at first they had no abbess, they were organized and approached their tasks with seriousness. The curriculum of 1903 was comprehensive and ambitious for these monastic women, who did not have support from the sect headquarters for their actions. Hori assumed the position of school superintendent. Mizuno Jōrin and Hori Mitsujō taught both Sōtō Sect teachings and Zen practice. Andō Dōkai was responsible for explaining the teachings of other sects and Buddhist ceremonies, while Yamaguchi Kokan also covered the teachings of other sects and Classical Chinese (*kanbun*). Eight other instructors came in and taught history, science, math, calligraphy, sewing, tea ceremony, flower arranging, and language.[22] They studied various fascicles of Dōgen's *Shōbōgenzō*, including *Kiesanmon*, *Bendōwa*, and *Fukanzazengi*. The novices also studied the *Eiheishingi*.[23] Many of the Sōtō Zen texts they studied focused on practical instructions on how to live the monastic life. It is significant to point out that the *Bendōwa* text includes explicit statements about males and females being equal in practice. The education novice nuns received was comprehensive, reflecting the expertise and seriousness of the founding nuns.

In 1906 Mizuno Jōrin helped with the construction of a new lecture hall at the Nisōdō. In May of that year they became a *Shūritsu Nisō Gakurin*, a denominational nuns' school. Until that point they were run privately, but their diligence brought them official support from sect headquarters. The first class of nuns graduated in 1907. About ten nuns entered each year. Beginning in 1912, the size of the entering class increased to an average of twenty nuns. By 1945, 150 nuns were studying and practicing there.[24] These nuns' efforts were a driving force for the advancement of monastic women in this century, creating a generation of solidly educated and trained nuns.

The nuns designate April 1908 through May 1945 as the second period of the Nisōdō, known as the "Yanagihara Jidai." The number of student nuns soon exceeded the capacity of the original site of the school. This increase was apparently augmented by economic conditions. Although the Russo-Japanese war (1904–1905) was considered a major triumph because it was the first time in Japan's recent history that Asians defeated a Caucasian race, late Meiji Japan's taxes were high. Famine and epidemics drove the poor into desperation. Many girls left home to seek work in factories and brothels, and some sought refuge in the life of a mo-

nastic. Indeed, in the 1910s the number of novices increased with women from
various backgrounds. This helped prompt the effort to find adequate facilities to
accommodate the increased need.

Hori frequented Chōei-ji, a modestly sized temple renowned for miracles.[25]
She prayed daily to Kannon, the Bodhisattva of Compassion, who was enshrined
there. A wealthy man who lived in the neighborhood named Umemoto Kinzaburō
also came to that temple to pray daily. One day, he asked Hori about what kind
of miracle was sought such that a nun would visit this temple on a daily basis.
She told him of the need for a new location for the nuns' school. Umemoto
answered her prayers with the donation of construction supplies and 1,000 *tsubo*
(3,300 square meters) of land in a nearby region called Yanagihara, which lies just
north of Nagoya Castle.[26] The nuns helped in the construction, and they literally
moved a lot of earth to fulfil their goals. In November 1909 they moved the site
of the Nisōdō to Yanagihara. There were many hardships involved in moving the
Nisōdō to Nagoya, but due to the exceptional effort of Hori at the construction
site, they achieved their goal. Through the help of others and their own hard
work, they made a monastery school that could train and teach the increasing
numbers of women entering the monastic path.[27]

In September 1912, however, tragedy struck the new Nisōdō when a typhoon
destroyed one of their new classrooms and killed three nuns.[28] With resilience and
the generosity of their benefactor, Umemoto, they began building a new worship
hall in 1913. In 1914 they also undertook the construction of a great lecture hall.
The following year, they held a ceremony on behalf of the donors and in cele-
bration of the effort of the numerous people who made the new construction a
success.

On the twentieth anniversary of the Nisōdō (1923), Mizuno Jōrin wrote the
following:

> Although many people thought it was quite a risky enterprise for those with no
> economic support or knowledge about the ways of the world to organize such
> an institution, with unwavering peace of mind we endured hardships of body
> and mind and have surmounted the difficulties. We could not imagine welcom-
> ing in the twentieth anniversary of the Gakurin at that time, but now upon
> seeing the grand anniversary ceremony, I have learned the profound gratitude
> of Buddha's infinite liberation. It is only possible due to the assistance of the
> followers and Buddha's infinite protection. From start to finish with consistent
> sincerity from the bottom of our hearts, this is the requirement of being single-
> minded, not divided in two. Although I have recently been ill, the fact that I
> can attend the twentieth anniversary ceremony in health is a joy beyond all
> bounds.[29]

The twentieth anniversary celebrations were augmented with the publication
of the Nisōdō's first journal, *Jōrin*. Arisaga Tainin, the director of the Jōrin Association (*Jōrinkai*) that published the journal, began the inaugural issue with some
remarks about the founding of the Nisōdō:

> The original Nigakurin was established after the second war in which the coun-
> try was resolved to recover its honor in the Japan–Manchu war. It was a period

in which people were incited to take opportunities, to be diligent in development, to display perseverance and determination in government, economics, education, and religion. The Nigakurin was established for the purpose of waking up those nuns who desire the indolence of many years of having passively accepted the status quo. The spirit of the education was to accommodate the devoted nuns in the sect. By working together, we achieved educational discipline through overseeing the educational level of middle and higher girl's school education while also providing a religious education. This was an alarm bell awakening those who lost sight of the religious mission of teaching the Dharma through education. This is the origin of the Nigakurin and its spirit of education.[30]

The curriculum in 1926 included twenty-nine instructors (many of them nuns) and a greater diversity of courses, adding writing, sociology, geography, biology, music, and English.[31] The school was thriving. By 1927, however, Yamaguchi remained the sole survivor of the original four founders, after Mizuno and Hori died within months of each other. Before passing away, Mizuno said: "I am fast growing old. I ask from the bottom of my heart that you stay devoted to the cause of the education of future nuns. You must not waver and pass any opportunity. I'm counting on you." Yamaguchi responded, "We are in an urgent time, and we will not be lax and hesitate for even one day."[32] Hori Tokuō and Tanaka Dōrin, among others, worked with Yamaguchi from then on, and they devoted themselves to the great task of educating monastic women and gaining various substantial facilities. On September 13, 1933, Yamaguchi also died.

The four founders left a legacy of competent nuns in their wake, so their passing did not interrupt the steady flow of progress. By the Nisōdō's thirtieth anniversary in 1933, the school had added Buddhist history, religious philosophy, pedagogy, logic, and psychology to their curriculum.[33] In 1937, to mark the twenty-third memorial of Andō Dōkai's death, the nuns placed a memorial stone in the grounds of Kōrin-ji to remember the birth of the Nisōdō at Andō's temple, the stone simply inscribed as: "Sōtō-shū Nigakurin Foundation Site."[34]

In 1941, when the Pacific War began, the Nisōdō had 140 student nuns. During the years of war, like all able-bodied people, the nuns in training were mobilized for labor by the government. They left the Nisōdō in traditional monastic work clothes, stopping for a prayer to the Buddha to have that day pass without harm as they went to the factories to work. They had to carry gas masks on their shoulders in case of an air raid with poison gas. Kitō Shunkō, then a young nun, recalls how their elderly teacher, Hori Sensei, brought them hot food and water in the factory.[35] Fortifying their organizational structure even as the country was struggling to fortify its own forces, in 1943 they changed the name of the Nisōdō to "Sōtō-shū Dai-ichi Nigakurin" (Sōtō Sect Primary Monastic Women's Training School).

Nuns designate May 1945 through December 1947 as the third period of their history. It was a time when they were recovering from the ravages of the war that had forced them to move a number of times before they could settle in a suitable permanent location. On May 14, 1945, a time when hunger was incessant, there was an air raid that left the Nisōdō in ashes. All the novice nuns were at the

Nisōdō that day. When the sirens went off, they all went into the air raid shelter with only a few things. A deafening sound burst their ears as the planes flew low, dropping bombs that burned with sharp metallic sounds. The sound of burning grew louder as they realized their school was in flames. Fear was palpable as they huddled together. A faint echo of somber tears resonated in the shelter when the teacher, Hori, became aware of their impending danger. She shouted, "We must escape and separate. Return when the flames have died down!" Everyone obeyed. When the flames grew quiet, they all returned to the Nisōdō garden only to find the air-raid shelter had also burned down. The small items they had brought with them to the shelter had become ash. Fortunately, no one had been hurt. All 131 novices held each other's hands as they stood around their school of ashes.[36]

Takama Shūdō, the regional representative of the Sōtō sect administration, said he will never forget that May 14:

> Hori Mitsujō Rōshi came to report the damages. She bowed deeply with her hands together. She had just come the 6 kilometer distance in bare feet. I invited her in, but she said she must take care of the children [novices]. She ran back without having come in. I had tried to offer her shoes to get her 60-year-old self back through the broken glass and shrapnel, but she would not accept.[37]

After the Yanagihara site was destroyed by the bombings,[38] the nuns stayed in a local temple, Fukugon-ji, until they arranged for more permanent accommodations. From August 1945 through December 1947, the nuns resided at another local temple, Kentoku-ji.[39] They built a new school (and a place for sleeping), adjacent to the temple Shōbō-ji in Nagoya, and on December 3, 1947, they finally moved in. They had passed the previous two and a half years quite literally as *unsui* — clouds and water — the name given to novices to stress their lack of abode and the malleability needed to accommodate to monastic life. They were grateful, however, to have a regular monastery, and they went to the Buddha's relics enshrined at nearby Kakuōzan to offer their prayers. They had survived the war without a single person sacrificed, and they finally found refuge in a pleasant location in a quiet and convenient area of Nagoya called Shiroyama.[40]

The fourth era of the Nisōdō, lasting from January 1948 through March 1963, was a period marked by the restoration of the fundamentals of monastery life. These decades represent the time when the vision of the four founding nuns became firmly established. Knowing that education was the key to becoming effective participants in the sect administration and gaining more power to define the parameters of their monastic life as women, the nuns maintained the centrality of education to their training. In April 1948, under the United States occupation led by General Douglas MacArthur, new regulations for high school education were instituted; the "Sōtō-shū Dai-ichi Nigakurin" (Sōtō Sect Primary Monastic Women's Training School) became the "Sōtō-shū Kōtō Nigakurin" (Sōtō Sect Higher Monastic Women's Training School). The change in name signified that the Nisōdō was no longer responsible for, nor authorized to, grant high school diplomas. This, however, did not prevent nuns from receiving a higher education. Upon the encouragement of the president of Aichi Gakuin,[41] Koide Yūzō, many nuns entered the university to further their academic studies. Novices were allowed to continue monastic training and reside at the Nisōdō while attending the secular school.[42]

In 1949, the Nisōdō assumed its current name, Aichi Senmon Nisōdō (The Aichi Advanced Training Monastery for Monastic Women), which reflects the shift in their focus. From this point on, the nunnery would specialize solely in monastic training. In conjunction with this shift in emphasis, in March 1950 they began an all-out campaign to build a meditation hall. They did alms gathering (*takuhatsu*) for one and a half years.[43] Teachers and students went nationwide seeking support. Their success was celebrated on September 12, 1951, when they had the opening ceremony and an inaugural meditation retreat (*sesshin*). Nuns' reflections of that ceremony and retreat reveal deep emotion, for they had attained their goal despite institutional obstacles compounded by setbacks experienced because of the war.[44]

A clear indication of the nuns' pride in their accomplishments is expressed in their concern to contextualize their activities in terms of Sōtō Zen history. They wanted to highlight the efforts of Dōgen and Keizan, whom they viewed as Sōtō leaders who established the legitimacy of women devoted to Sōtō Zen monastic life. Thus, in 1953, on the occasion of the fiftieth anniversary of their founding and at the behest of the Nisōdō, Tajima Hakudō wrote *Dōgen, Keizan Ryōzenji no Nisōkan to sono Eka no Nisō* ("Dōgen's and Keizan Zenji's Attitude toward Monastic Women and the Monastic Women under Them"). Tajima was chosen to lead the project because he had an important combination of expertise and experience. A professor at Aichi Gakuin, he specialized in the history of Sōtō Zen in Nagoya, he had keen interest in nuns' contribution to that history, and he had firsthand insight into the internal workings of the Sōtō sect—for he himself was a Sōtō monastic. In a capacity as editorial board, a number of nuns were instrumental in bringing the project to fruition. Most notably, Kojima Kendō, the prominent nun, led this effort to establish a strong awareness of the tradition of Zen monastic women. After seven years of research, they also completed *Sōtō-shū Nisō-shi* (The History of Sōtō Sect Nuns), which was published in 1955. By 1963, the curriculum was modified, reflecting the nuns' heightened concern for educating novices about the historical background of their tradition; they added history of monastic women; Zen history; history of Buddhism in India, China, and Japan; poetry (*waka*); and children's sermons. The texts that were studied at that time include the *Shōbōgenzō*, *Shushōgi*, *Gakudō Yōjinshū*, and the *Denkōroku*, among others.[45]

The year 1963 also marked the sixtieth anniversary of the founding of the Nisōdō. To commemorate the event, the nuns had a few more rooms added to the monastic complex, including a formal traditional Japanese drawing room (*shoin*) and library. A nun who was in the first graduating class, Ōtsubo Kōsen (1880–1979), gave these remarks at the anniversary ceremony:

> The four teachers Jōrin, Mitsujō, Dōkai, and Kokan, all endured hardships for which there are no words to adequately express. At the time it was a Gakurin [monastery school] in name only since facilities and supplies were sparse and all the young nuns were not strong. We were dependent on the endurance of our teachers. They were genuinely kind in teaching us. That was 60 years ago,

yet even now the spirit of those four teachers lives on in the heart of a small nun.[46]

The first monastic woman to be officially recognized as the abbess of the Nisōdō was Tanaka Dōrin (1887–1974) in 1963.[47] She was a disciple of Mizuno Jōrin. Tanaka entered in the second class of the Nisōdō in 1904. She devoted her entire life to the school of nuns. Tanaka saw them through a triumph; in April 1970, more than a century of discrimination between monks and nuns was abolished with the establishment of a place to train nuns as high-ranking teachers — Tokubetsu Nisōdō (Special Advanced Monastery for Monastic Women). From this time forward, nuns could train nuns to serve in the highest teaching ranks of the sect. This completed their goal of advancing monastic women's education to equal that of male monastics.

Shortly thereafter, Tanaka died on September 25, 1974, just after the nuns had performed the Autumnal Equinox ceremony. Ever mindful of perfecting detail, she had stopped to teach a novice the correct way to play the complicated rhythms of the wooden fish-shaped drum (*mokugyo*) and gong (*keisu*), and then she quietly retired to her quarters. The following morning they found that she had already passed away.[48] Katō Shinjō became the abbess after Tanaka's sudden death. The death of leaders in the nuns' community does not result in a disruption of their activities — still more testimony to the efficacy of the training the nuns received.

Nuns were now able to direct the course of their actions more freely, and they were officially recognized for their achievements. They had autonomy of decision in administering their own monastery for officially training future monastic women and advanced teachers. The struggle and glory of the establishment and development of Aichi Senmon Nisōdō illustrates the courage and resiliency that characterizes Zen monastic women in general. The background of two other Nisōdō in Toyama and Niigata prefectures reflect the broad extent of the Zen monastic women's activities.[49]

In anticipation of the head temples, Eihei-ji and Sōji-ji, granting official approval for establishing Nisōdō, the Toyama Nisō Gakurin opened in March 1902. They wasted no time in obtaining official recognition after the August 10, 1902, regulations established the right for monastic women to run monastery schools. The Nisōdō there was founded upon the efforts of the monastic women Okumura Taidō, Kametani Esan, Tamagawa Jitsubyō, and Myōgen Soshin. In 1937, sixty-three nuns were in attendance at Toyama, as opposed to approximately 100 in Nagoya. At the end of the war in 1946, there were thirty nuns.

At the Toyama Nisōdō, they now maintain a traditional Buddhist practice of alms gathering (*takuhatsu*) that is designed to build physical and spiritual strength.[50] Deliberately scheduling two cold months and one hot month (March, July, and November), the nuns go out each time for a stretch of five days to gather alms. The practice is designed to train one how to overcome the challenges of cold and hot weather, as well as to learn humility and gratitude. The milder seasons of spring and fall are avoided, for they do not train a person as well. The abbess of Toyama Nisōdō, Hasekawa, is adamant that nuns should be taught by nuns.[51] She claims that monks teach differently, although she would allow a monk to teach the nuns two out of twelve hours of instruction time. Due to the small number of novices and the location in the countryside, the monastery is run more like the training temples of old, where a teacher would train disciples in their own temple. The large institutional training monasteries have become more common in recent history.

Nakamura Sengan, another pioneer in the history of the Sōtō nuns' movement for educational reforms, founded the Niigata Nisō Gakurin on April 1, 1907. Although she worked alone, she made a contribution to the education of monastic women outside the major central regions of Japan. Her work also extended beyond the period of her direct influence during the Meiji and Taishō periods. Like the other nuns' schools, at first all secular school subjects were taught along with the rigors of monastic training. With the change in the Ministry of Education regulations, the schools were no longer authorized to confer junior high and senior high school diplomas. So in 1952 they became the Niigata Senmon Nisōdō (The Niigata Advanced Training Monastery for Monastic Women). Like the other Nisōdō, this new title reflected that their main purpose had shifted to focus only on monastic training. Their meditation hall is located on the second floor, a reminder throughout the year that deep snows blanket the region during the long winter. Although the area is relatively remote, the number of nuns in training at one time reached eighty. In 1972 the nuns built a kindergarten on the land that they had previously used to cultivate their food. Now with the number of nuns greatly reduced, they do not need such a large plot of land, but they continue to grow their own vegetables and run the Niigata Nisōdō like a family unit.[52] They maintain the structure of a monastic training school—holding classes, practicing rituals, and doing zazen—despite the small numbers, for their aim is not quantity. The goal always has been and continues to be focused upon training nuns to excel in a quality of life worthy of a monastic.

The strategy of the leaders of Sōtō nuns to concentrate on education bore the desired results. They set out to train young nuns to think carefully about what needed to be done, and they produced hundreds of nuns who knew how to dismantle the male power structures that sought to institutionalize the nuns' subordinate status. These nuns of the early and mid-twentieth century had become strong under the hardships of war and the frustrations of unequal sect regulations. They were poised for action.

Second Generation: Strategists of Egalitarianism

The educational foundation was firmly established in the first half of the twentieth century, enabling many nuns to direct their efforts to rectifying the other inequities of the sect administration's regulations. During the middle decades of the century, nuns went from ranks below that of all monks to being permitted to attain high levels equal to their male counterparts. The fight for equality in monastic ranks, teaching ranks, and temple ranks was carried out through the *Sōtō-shū Nisōdan* (Sōtō Sect Nuns' Organization), an official organization established by the nuns in 1944 for addressing the needs of Sōtō nuns. Their battle with the *Sōtō-shū*

Shūmuchō (Sōtō Sect Administration), the official organizing body of the Sōtō sect, was led by the invincible efforts of Kojima Kendō (1898–1995). Her biography will be highlighted in this section, for her life story is a series of first-time opportunities claimed by and granted to a Sōtō Zen nun. It is no coincidence that Kojima's most zealous and productive years coincide with the period of most rapid progress toward equality for the nuns. It is notable to mention that this was also the most turbulent period of recent Japanese history, spanning the years before and after World War II when the rhetoric of male military dominance was at a high point. My examination of Kojima will be based on her published autobiography, my extensive interviews with her, and a rare collection of her articles that she entrusted to me.[53]

Kojima was born in Nagoya. When she told her mother of her decision to become a monastic, Kojima still remembers how her mother cried daily. Kojima, however, had been interested in becoming a monastic since she was quite young. Kojima spoke with conviction about those days when she resolved not to be dissuaded. She explained that her family belonged to the Sōtō sect, and as a child she frequently saw monks and nuns. She reminisced about how her young heart was moved by their robes and their chanting, although she later reflected that being a monastic required a commitment of steel. Garments are only external adornments, words easier than action. In 1910, at the age of twelve, Kojima accomplished her first goal: she became ordained. As she grew a little older, she began to recognize clear discrimination between male and female monastics. She said that she could not endure it.

Kojima entered the Nisōdō in Nagoya after she finished the mandatory two years of high school. She mentioned how she entered with excitement and joy, but that she soon realized how difficult it was. The teachers were extremely strict. Kojima, a nun who proved to be one of the most important and powerful nuns in this era, even admitted that at moments she thought she would die. Since she decided to enter the monastery upon her own initiative, however, she could not return home. She persevered.[54] Upon graduation in 1918, Kojima became Hori's assistant, but Kojima was compelled to obtain a higher education. Even after Kojima graduated from Aichi Gakuin, it was not enough to quench her thirst for study. Although no female monastic had been permitted to attend Komazawa University, she was determined to go. She explicitly noted in my interview with her that she was determined to succeed, because she knew such regulations went against the current of egalitarian teachings she had learned from Dōgen and the Dharma. Empowered with this knowledge, Kojima did not hesitate to act.

In 1923, 10% of all monastics were women. The nuns fought for raising the level of education of nuns, which was equivalent to junior high school level at that time. They wanted college-level education and money to support an education equivalent to the monks' educational opportunities. They demanded better texts, teachers, and a library.[55] In 1925 Kojima prevailed, and along with four other nuns—Katō Shinjō, Taniguchi Setsudō, Adachi Teikō, and Kurata Baigaku—became the first monastic women to enter Komazawa University. Kojima studied there for three years. She commented that they were treated well by the dean, and, since they were older than most of the students, they were also treated well by the male student body. Kojima then returned to the Nisōdō. Hori and Yama-guchi requested that both Kojima and Katō take responsibility for the future of the Nisōdō.

After more than ten years of caring for the Nisōdō and participating in the movement to secure egalitarian regulations for nuns, Kojima decided that it was important to expand her scope of activity. This required her to take a recess from her duties at the Nisōdō. She was among a small number of nuns who ministered in Hawaii on behalf of the International Division of the Sōtō Sect Administration. Kojima ministered from 1938 through 1941. Her first year was spent at Mampuku-ji on Maui, and the remaining three years were at the Eihei-ji Betsuin in Hono-lulu. The followers at these temples were primarily *nisei*, second generation Jap-anese. The work the nuns did abroad included running various classes that focused upon the needs and concerns of women and children. Along with teaching Zen practice and teachings, they ran Sunday school, a women's club, a girls' club, a female youth club, and a children's club. They were also engaged in teaching various cultural classes such as tea ceremony, calligraphy, sewing of western and Japanese garments, music, children's stories, and dance. Her return to the Nisōdō was sudden, because of the onset of war. Kojima then resumed her teaching position at the Nisōdō.

The war left many orphaned children. The nuns responded with compassion and dedication. One nun in particular, Taniguchi Setsudō-ni (1901–1986), devoted the rest of her life to helping these children. She established Lumbini-en, an orphanage.[56] Taniguchi followed Dōgen's four virtues of a bodhisattva in running the orphanage[57]:

1. *Fuse*: to give.
2. *Aigo*: to use gentle, loving words.
3. *Rigyō*: to completely forget the self in one's effort to help other people.
4. *Dōji*: to live helping each other out.

Kojima assisted her, and commented on the irony that their commitment to being nuns had led them to be mothers.

The period 1930–1945 marks the Fifteen Years War, a time of general ferment in Japan. All people, including monastic women, made a concerted effort to show their devotion to the nation. Women were joining forces with the realization that they could change their status in society. In 1931, the First All-Japan Women's Suffrage Rally was held.[58] Yet Sōtō nuns led the way one year earlier. At Eihei-ji, on the occasion of a special Buddhist practice session (*sesshin*) for the 650th Memorial of the Second Patriarch Koun Ejō (1198–1280)[59] on May 14, 1930, the Sōtō Sect National Meeting of Nuns (*Sōtō-shū Zenkoku Nishū Daikai*)[60] wrote a statement reflecting their concerns and aims.

The most powerful nuns from all parts of the country gathered at Eihei-ji for a number of national meetings. Nakamura Sen'e, the successor to Nakamura Sengan (the founder of Niigata Nisōdō), served as the leader at this meeting.[61] Nagazawa Sozen,[62] the head nun of one of Tokyo's most important nunneries, Kannon-ji, served as leader at their second meeting.[63] A large number of promi-nent representatives from Nagoya were actively engaged in this historic effort to rectify the position of nuns in the Sōtō sect. Tanaka Dōrin, disciple of Mizuno Jōrin and future abbess of Aichi Nisōdō, served as the leader of their third meeting. Yamaguchi Kokan, one of the four founders of the nunnery in Nagoya, and Hori Tokuō, sibling in Dharma and blood relations to Hori Mitsujō, another of the four founding nuns, made their contributions to this historic event. Katō Shinjō, their blood-related cousin who would one day become an abbess of Aichi Nisōdō, was also present. Kojima Kendō, whose voice would soon reverberate throughout the sect administration, was also in attendance. This group of visionary and de- termined nuns solidified their concerns and wrote a stalwart resolution with de- mands for equal treatment by the sect administration.

The Sōtō Sect Administration records on regulations regarding Sōtō Zen mo- nastic women document the evolution of the official egalitarian advances accom- plished during this century. The Sōtō Sect publishes their regulations annually in the *Sōtō-shū Shūsei*, but there are usually few substantial changes. The regulations from 1941 represent the basic regulations before the Nisōdan instituted reforms. At this time, the highest rank a nun could attain was below the lowest monk rank. Also, even if a nun functioned as the head of a temple, she was not permitted to perform the *zuise*, a ceremony of telling both Main temples (Eihei-ji and Sōji-ji) that a person is officially becoming the head of a temple (*jūshoku*). Therefore, a nun could not technically become the head of a temple. A nuns' census registra- tion (*koseki*) was, therefore, kept at her teacher's temple. This prevented nuns from formally having independence. The record-keeping policies hid nuns' activities. These regulations that circumscribed nuns at the officially documented level, how- ever, did not prevent nuns from actually making the contributions and performing the role of a temple head.

These nuns were empowered by their understanding of the teachings of Dōgen and Ejō.[64] They acted upon their faith in their "original destiny" and what they called their "natural rights" — concepts that had come into currency along with a host of western ideas in the Meiji period. They do not merely claim rights, they *re*claim rights that were theirs before the sect administration institutionalized in- equality:

> We monastic women have largely been neglected by members of the sect, to say nothing of general society. The result has been that the institution of the sect has not granted us our natural rights. Due to this negligence, a great num- ber of monastic women have endured under miserable conditions, and the situation has not changed much over time. However, we will not permit the flow of history to stop and leave us in our current situation. Indeed, we have arrived at a time when the actual day is not far from women in society clamoring with loud voices and claiming the right to participate in government. At the next special meeting of the legislature, the government and the people from both political parties will introduce a bill for the civil rights of women. Is there not a more lucid tale to have seen than this? Even if it is only one day sooner, we monastic women, too, must awaken from our deep slumber; we must free ourselves from the bonds of iron chains. On this occasion, having been granted the opportunity to participate in a National Monastic Women's Meeting at the Head Temple, Eihei-ji, the historic seat of the great Dharma, we monastic women must become self-aware of the important destiny to which we have been

assigned. Along with this, we must claim our natural rights. This will happen soon, for we have the capacity to truly uphold and not doubt the spirit of the Second Patriarch Koun Ejō and the original founder, Dōgen Zenji. The majority are of congenial spirit, namely, we the monastic women of Japan are ever more solidifying our joint forces. We must succeed in attaining our original destiny, and in so doing let us claim the natural rights that we deserve but have not yet gained![65]

Resolutions

I. We monastic women are resolved to work to achieve the important mission of educating the people along with exerting ourselves to increasingly improve, advance, and cultivate belief in ourselves by looking in the mirror to see our duty and the current of the times.

II. Beyond accomplishing our duty as monastic women, we are resolved, in the name of this large association, to petition to the sect authorities and the institution of the sect to claim the rights as follows in each item.

A. We want authorization to designate Dharma heirs.

B. We reclaim the right to participate in the governing of each aspect of the sect and to opportunities for education and the like.

C. We reclaim the capacity to have appointments in each category of religious teacher.

D. We resolve to hold annual seminars that focus upon the various concerns of monastic women.

E. We reclaim the right to be granted positions as heads of temples at least as high as those with the status of full-ranking temple (*hōchi*).[66]

In 1937, at the third Sōtō Sect National Assembly of Monastic Women held at Sōji-ji in honor of the 600th anniversary of Emperor Godaigo (1318–1339), the delegates wrote another resolution, including petitions for authorization to designate a Dharma heir, to wear different colored robes (nuns still were only allowed to wear black), the right to participate in all aspects of the sect governing organization, and to have increased educational opportunities. Thereafter, they decided to present their resolutions annually.[67]

The nuns formally established the *Sōtō-shū Nisō Gokokudan* (Sōtō Sect Nuns Organization for the Protection of the Country) in 1944.[68] Kojima was elected president. Their motto is: "Do not discriminate against [a person's] sex, this is the True Law of the exquisite and supreme Buddhist Way." They stated the three aims they established for this organization as follows.

1. To be authorized to grant Dharma transmission.

2. To build a school for teaching nuns, and to publish a history of nuns before Koun Ejō's 700th Memorial [1980].[69]

3. To be engaged in social work. For example, we started the orphanage Lumbini-en, when we found children who had lost their parents in the war struggling for survival in Ueno Park and the subway station in Asakusa [Tokyo]. Taniguchi Setsudō took sole responsibility for the long-term daily care of the children.[70]

Sōtō nuns saw their aims clearly and proceeded with confidence. They developed their role as protector of the unfortunate, institutionally cultivating and advocating a socially engaged monastic life.

After the war they gave the organization its current name, Sōtō-shū Nisōdan (Sōtō Sect Nuns' Organization), and the nuns received an office in the sect head-quarters building in Tokyo. They organized their various concerns and needs into divisions. The Religious Discipline Division (*Shūdō-bu*) oversees Zen training and practice, ceremonies, and chanting of scriptures. The Encouragement of Learning Division (*Shōgaku-bu*) is concerned with the development of educational funds and dormitory fees. The Education Division (*Kyōka-bu*) is responsible for the women's section, youth section, and the educational writing division. The Division for the Arts (*Geinō-bu*) oversees the music section, drama section, tea and flower section, and the writing section (calligraphy and poetry writing). The Social Work Division (*Shakaijigyō-bu*) promotes activities such as orphanages, nursery schools, kindergartens, child care, youth protection groups, adult protection groups, mother–child groups, and a welfare commission. The final division deals with resources (*Shigen-bu*). At the helm of the Sōtō-shū Nisōdan, Kojima left her mark upon the history of Sōtō nuns through this position of power and responsibility from 1944 until 1963. In that capacity, she fought for and succeeded in winning equal regulations for the nuns.

The timing of the nuns' demands was in the context of a large-scale surge in the cause of women, in part promoted by the Allied Occupation Forces. On October 9, 1945, the Occupation Forces demanded that Japan take five steps. The first step was the liberation of women.[71] The new constitution made with the Allied Occupation Forces in 1946 gave women full legal and political equality.[72] Article 14 reads: "All people are equal under the law and there shall be no discrimination in political, economic or social relations because of race, creed, sex, social status, or family origin."

From December 15 to 17, 1945, the nuns held a retreat (*sesshin*) at Eihei-ji. The text studied during this retreat was the *Raihaitokuzui* fascicle of Dōgen's *Shōbōgenzō*, a text renowned for being Dōgen's most explicit articulation on the equality of women and men. The fact that nuns used this text as the base of their fight for equal regulations proves that these nuns interpreted Dōgen as a founder who held egalitarian views. Unlike a number of academics who a few decades later would develop an interpretation of Dōgen as a man who changed his mind, these nuns in 1945 did not question whether Dōgen modified his views late in life. In fact, the sect showed their approval of the nuns' interpretation of Dōgen, for they eventually granted the women their requests. In 1946 the nuns again made an appeal to establish egalitarian practices within the Sōtō sect, and they submitted their five concerns.

1. Concern: new roles, because nuns must fulfill their capacities.
2. Concern: a method for advancing the education and skills of the nuns.
3. Concern: a petition to decrease the limitations set upon nuns' teaching ranks and appointment to monastic ranks.
4. Concern: the prosperity of nuns' temples and hermitages.

5. Concern: the problem of establishing opportunities for the nuns' disciples.[73]

They gave their concerns to sect leaders along with the following concrete demands as an acceptable way to resolve the issues.

1. Those who graduate from a nunnery should be allowed to enter Komazawa University.
2. The head of a nunnery should be a nun [abbess].
3. Do not discriminate between male and female monastics in monastic rank if they have the same level of practice.
4. To have the same entitlement to teaching ranks as male monastics.
5. To have the same rights to being the head of a temple as male monastics.
6. To have the right to vote on sect matters and to have the right to be elected to office.
7. To receive authorization for a Nisō Senmon Sōdō [a nunnery that confers advanced teaching degrees].[74]

The sect leadership responded with changes that are in accord with the spirit of Dōgen's egalitarian teachings:

1. Equality in Teaching Degrees, hereafter:

    a. Third Subordinate Rank Nun Instructors (*Sankyū Nikyōshi*) to be raised to Third Rank Teacher (*Santō Kyōshi*)
    b. First Subordinate Rank Nun Instructor (*Ikkyū Nikyōshi*) and Second Subordinate Rank Nun Instructor (*Nikyū Nikyōshi*) to be raised to First Rank Teacher (*Ittō Kyōshi*) and Second Rank Teacher (*Nitō Kyōshi*), respectively.
    c. After three years a nun is to be granted the degree First Subordinate Rank Nun Instructor (*Ikkyū Nikyōshi*), and after five years to be granted the degree Second Subordinate Rank Instructor (*Nikyū Nikyōshi*).
    d. A nun who is classed as Second Rank (*Nitō*) or above is to be granted the title *Ni-oshō*. Those who have graduated from the Nigakurin or Nisōdō are to be granted the degree Third Rank Teacher (*Santō Kyōshi*). Those who graduate from Komazawa University Senmonbu are to be granted the degree Second Rank Teacher (*Nitō Kyōshi*).

2. To recognize *Nishisō* [monastic women as teachers].
3. To authorize the titles *Nishisō* and *Ni-oshō* upon their completion of established periods of training.
4. To be eligible to be the head of a temple if one is at least a *Ni-oshō*. One becomes a *Ni-oshō* after five years of practice (*ango*).
5. The right to vote is limited to those with at least the rank of Teacher (*Kyōshi*).

After World War II, just as all women were given the right to participate in national government, the new sect regulations included the authorization for nuns to designate their disciples as their Dharma heir, men and women to be treated equally in attaining teaching degrees, official recognition was granted to female monastic teachers, permission was granted for nuns to have their own training sessions (*ango*), and nuns won the right to vote in sect matters.[75] The sect administration had effectively and fundamentally been reformed according to the demands nuns had resolved to win less than twenty years before.

With Kojima Kendō at the helm of the Nisōdan, the reforms continued to dissolve the bastion of male authority and power over nuns. She traveled extensively in the name of equality (sometimes Kojima had no choice but to stand seven to ten hours on the train to get to a meeting at the sect headquarters[76]). In 1947 she guided other significant changes that marked a move in the direction of autonomy; new regulations allowed nuns to move their census records to their own temples. This modification of the regulations provided high nuns with visible proof of their status. Also, regulation number 536 permitted *Oshō* and *Ni-oshō* to wear colored robes commensurate with their rank.

The inertia of reform continued. Due in large part to Kojima's perseverance, in 1948 nuns also became eligible to hold elected office. In 1949, nuns who studied at Komazawa University were able to matriculate as regular students, the same as male students.[77] Four nuns entered that year. Another major triumph was winning authorization for Dharma transmission in March of 1951. In November of that year, both Katō and Kojima went to Sōji-ji and entered the highest teacher (*shike*) training program that was opened there.

Together Katō and Kojima were successful in establishing a new tradition to reflect the raised status of nuns. Beginning in 1949, each year on October 14 a nun was allowed to serve as *shōkōshi*[78] at Sōji-ji, one of the sect's Main temples.[79] Sōji-ji was chosen, for the nuns maintain the general impression that Keizan Zenji (the founder of Sōji-ji) was actively concerned with the affairs of monastic women. Katō was the first nun to be given the honor.[80] Another example of the strong support Sōji-ji shows for women is Tsurumi Jōshi Gakkō, the all-girls school they run, kindergarten through university. The high school girls attend the annual ceremony. Kojima was the *shōkōshi* the second year. In the beginning, the *shōkōshi* had to be at least seventy years of age, but now the Nisōdan chooses a nun regardless of her age. To serve as *shōkōshi* is a position of honor and a symbol of the nuns' triumph over a period of institutional discrimination.

The most dramatic reforms, however, occurred in the 1953 regulations. The tides of reform had swelled nationwide, and all Buddhist sects in Japan went through a major revision at this point. *Ni-oshō* or above could now be formally designated head (*jūshoku*) of full-rank (*hōchi*) temples. It is important to note that *hōchi* have lay supporters who provide financial resources. The rank of temple above *hōchi* is called *kakuchi*. These are temples with great historical and cultural importance and temples with significant power. Previously, monastic women were only allowed to head *heisōchi* level sub-temples or hermitages. They had no lay supporters, and thus they had little financial resources, because one of the major activities (and a mainstay of income) of a temple is to perform memorial services for the ancestors of their lay supporters.

Another sweeping change was that the nuns' teaching degrees and monastic rank titles were raised all across the board. Prior to the reforms, the requirements for the various degrees were much more stringent for nuns than for monks. For example, after being in training for five years, a nun received the same degree that a monk could receive after just two years of training. Furthermore, there were high positions that a nun was never eligible for, no matter how hard she studied or practiced. The irony of this is that the monastic women became more thoroughly trained than the average monk, because they had to work harder to get minimal degrees.

In 1965, the major revisions to the regulations were stated as follows:

1. The monastic ranks are to be High Seat Nun (*Nijōza*), Foundation Seat Nun (*Nizagen*), Preceptor Nun (*Ni-oshō*), and High Preceptor Nun (*Ni-daioshō*, authorizing these nuns to teach others and train monastics at their temple).
2. Since training sessions for nuns (*Ni-ango*) can only happen in full rank (*hōchi*) temples, all temples ranked sub-temple are to become full rank.
3. Nuns can wear robes commensurate with their rank.
4. Establish a *Tokubetsu Nisōdō* to open the path for cultivating advanced teachers (*shike*).

Kojima documents their fight, recalling her relentless approach to winning fair and just regulations. In her advanced age, she remarked that she was slightly embarrassed for her forthright action, but the twinkle in her eyes reflected no genuine regret.[81] She was notorious for speaking out at official sect meetings, frequently the only nun among many powerful male leaders of the sect. She recounted to me with delight how she had pounded her fist and spoke with conviction. However she was renowned for being even tougher with herself and her fellow nuns than she was on the sect leaders. Kojima reflected that the good fortune of the Nisōdan came through self-discipline and uniting their strength. Reflecting her indomitable spirit she frequently recited the Zen dictum, "Seven times down, eight times up." On September 29, 1952, Kojima's efforts were acknowledged when she was commended with an award of excellence at the occasion of the 700th Memorial for the Founder of the Sōtō Sect. In her mid-90s, Kojima continued to live by her own proclamations of June 1949: "Devote yourself to opening the true path for monastic women. One ought not be negligent in one's duties, for death is in the distant future."

Kojima extended her concern for Buddhist monastic women beyond sectarian boundaries. From October 1951 through October 1961, Kojima served as an administrator of the *Zen Nihon Nisō Hōdan* (Pan-Japanese Buddhist Nun Association), and from 1961 to 1965 she served as its director. They established three aims at the founding of their organization that united monastic women from all sects. Their first aim was to get official recognition for monastic women as Dharma transmitters and heirs, because they assumed these were standard for disciples of the Buddha. In conjunction with that, the monastic women wanted to be authorized to train their successors to be teachers. The third aim was a natural development from the other two, namely, that the monastic women wanted to participate in the Sect Assemblies and have the rights and responsibility to initiate and to be involved in sect activities. Their motto is:

> Brilliant like the sun,
> Pure like a lotus blossom,
> True well-being comes
> From compassion,
> From wisdom,
> From liberation.

The Pan-Japanese Buddhist Nun Association published their first journal, *Hanahachisu* (Lotus Blossom), in the spring of 1961.[82] As with their motto, they took their title from the image of a lotus blossom that is pure, yet rooted in the mud. It is a journal written for and by monastic women across all sectarian lines. They are concerned particularly with realizing the compassion of Śākyamuni. The pages of the journal are filled with pictures, poems, articles on practical aspects of Buddhism, scholarly articles, a series on one's obligation to one's parents, and articles by nuns and laywomen. References to western literature—Goethe and Toynbee—are sprinkled throughout. There are articles of international concern, including a number on the then Union of Soviet Socialist Republics. It also contained messages like "World Peace Begins at Home." There was an article entitled "The Universal Age of Religion." Numerous articles are devoted to South Vietnam and the conditions and plight of the Buddhist nuns there. Children and television shows also come into the scope of their concern. "Food Makes Character" is an example of the types of articles they have included on health and medicine. Many articles highlighted historical nuns' accomplishments and contributions.

Kojima also helped connect the concerns of Buddhist women in various parts of the world. She served thirteen years (1952–1965) as the executive director of the Japanese Federation of Buddhist Women. She was also the sole Japanese representative to participate in the Third International Buddhist conference, held in Burma in November 1954. She also participated in the Fourth International Buddhist conference, held in Nepal in November 1956. At that time, the Japanese delegation went on a pilgrimage to the famous sites marking Śākyamuni's life. In Bodh Gaya, the site of his enlightenment, Kojima noted that although there were temples from various countries of the Buddhist world, there was no temple from Japan.

Although it took a few decades to organize, an organization of representatives from all the major Buddhist sects in Japan decided to establish a Japanese temple in Bodh Gaya. A young nun, Kitō Shunkō (b. 1925), wanted to help in the land of Śākyamuni Buddha. She had been deeply affected by the strength of Kojima, having been disciplined under her tutelage at the nunnery in Nagoya. A lone nun, Kitō went and oversaw the temple while it was still under construction from 1970 to 1974. She went knowing only Japanese to a place where there were no Japanese people or Japanese speakers. Yet, she bore the heavy responsibility for commencing the work of the Japanese temple there. Although there were powerful institutions supporting the establishment of the Japanese temple, she had to carry out the actual task, knowing that the leaders of all Buddhist sects in Japan were depending on her. She quickly endeared herself to the local Indians, and a few dedicated young men learned Japanese from her.[83] The needs of the people in Bodh Gaya far exceeded her ability to serve, but she healed many people with a little aspirin, *seirōgan* (stomach and diarrhea medicine), soap and water, bandages, and a never-ending stream of smiles, hugs, and loving kindness. Kitō left an indelible mark of compassion upon the villagers of Bodh Gaya. She opened the door for the Japanese Buddhist community by firmly gaining the trust of Bodh Gaya's people. It was fitting, even though unintentional, that Kitō's teacher, Kojima, led the ceremony that officially opened Nihon-ji, the Japanese temple in Bodh Gaya, on December 3, 1973. Although a nun named Ichijō Chikō Jōnin, the head of the Pure Land Sect, was scheduled to perform the honors, she did not arrive in time.[84] Kojima had the perspicacity and wherewithal to lead the lavish ceremony without any preparation.[85]

At Koun Ejō's 650th memorial service in 1930, Sōtō nuns were determined to establish parity in sect regulations by his 700th memorial service. In 1980 when Eihei-ji celebrated the 700th memorial service for Koun Ejō, Kojima Kendō led the ceremony as *shōkōshi*.[86] It was a symbol that nuns had attained their goal. Since eighty-three-year-old Kojima had won many of the battles with her own fists—literally pounding on tables—she was the perfect person to be the first nun permitted to lead a ceremony at the temple Dōgen founded. Kojima wore yellow robes, a sign of her high stature in the sect. More than 200 nuns attended the ceremony. It was a grand display of the support of the nuns. In formal statements made on that day, Kojima emphasized the fact that she was not doing this alone; the efforts of numerous nuns hidden in the shadows had made the event possible. The serious nature and gravity of the ceremony was underscored by the twenty to twenty-five nuns who had gathered before the ceremony at Hakuju-an, the nuns' temple adjacent to Eihei-ji, and held a retreat (*sesshin*) from April 23 to May 13.

Kojima remarked from her vantage point as a dedicated leader in the struggle to rectify inequities in the sect:

> I never thought nuns would hold a ceremony at Eihei-ji. We nuns accomplished our goals rather quickly. A true testament to the heart and spirit we put into our actions. It is like being in a dream. The most important thing for young nuns is to educate them and mature them in character and not to dilute the nuns' lifestyle.[87]

Thirty-six years after its establishment, the Sōtō-shū Nisōdan could boast of nearly complete success in abolishing discrimination between monastic women and men; in a few short decades the nuns had claimed their "natural rights" for equal regulations between monastic men and women and egalitarian status within the institution of the sect. Kojima reflected upon her experience, "Anything can be done when you all join strength and work together."[88]

The Sōtō Sect Administration designates 1989 as the year in which total equality was achieved between monks and nuns. In that year, they changed a few more regulations in an attempt to entirely abolish any remnants of unfair and discriminatory practices. Unfortunately, they did not consult with monastic women when they determined which aspects of the sect's regulations were still discriminatory. They decided not to distinguish between male and female when calculating the number of teachers in the sect, and they have removed the designation *ni* ("female" or "nun") from the titles of monastic women. This effectively renders invisible some important distinctions between male and female monastics, because it is generally impossible to determine the gender of a person with a Buddhist name. Without the addition of the character *ni* to distinguish between males and females, it has become increasingly difficult to gather data on the activities and contributions of monastic women. The common opinion of the monastic women is that removing the character *ni* also removes any recognition of them. Rather than removing the *ni*, monastic women think it would be clearer and less discriminatory to add the character *nan* (male) to male monastic titles.[89] As a scholar of Japanese monastic women, I concur with the opinion that making a distinction between female and male monastics is necessary and actually *less* discriminatory, for it does not allow inequities to remain hidden in vague statistics.[90] The fact that sect administrators changed the rules without consulting nuns suggests that the administration is premature in claiming its equal practices.

Kojima's life history is a concrete illustration of the tension between the self-perception monastic women have of themselves as equal in the Dharma and their struggle with the institutional authorities of the sect to claim their equality. Her story, however, is not a story merely about her battle with oppressive male institutions. It is a story of her creative triumph over them. Despite the image that the male institutions tried to propagate, monastic women prevailed with their teachings and practices of an egalitarian Dharma. Kojima felt that nuns had succeeded, because nuns even gained the right to be elected a Zen Master of the head temples. She summed up, in her own words, the secret to her invincible spirit:

> Whether the Nisōdan, the Nigakurin, an amadera, or just one individual monastic woman, no advance will occur without the spirit of an independent way of life. To accomplish the spirit of an independent way of life, though, like I have said, it is important to realize this strength from the outside, but even more important is the inner strength.[91]

Third Generation: Zen Master of a New Tradition

More recently, monastic women have entered into a period where novice nuns reap the fruits of their teachers' struggle for parity. The nuns now control their own religious training, enjoy educational and ceremonial rights, and have the appropriate titles and religious robes. The present lifestyle in the training monasteries shares some of the benefits of an affluent and more democratic society, yet the nuns' practice and education maintain a severity and intensity that the Zen tradition has cultivated (at least rhetorically) for hundreds of years. A major figure in this chapter of their history is the abbess of Aichi Senmon Nisōdō, Aoyama Shundō (b. 1933), widely respected within the tradition for her spiritual excellence and for being among the first women to be granted graduate-level education at the Sōtō sect's Komazawa University. Her influence extends into the broader Japanese society through numerous books and articles written for the laity and into the international scholarly community through her participation in religious dialogue. She exemplifies the current opportunities of Zen nuns and is renowned as a living exemplar of their attainments.

At the age of five, Aoyama entered her aunt's temple, Muryō-ji, located in the shadows of the Japanese Alps in Nagano. Her aunt, Aoyama Ryōkan (1888–1992), became her teacher and raised her in the ways of a nun at the request of her parents. She was strict with the young Aoyama, but being a child, Aoyama was very flexible. Aoyama recalled how her teacher ensured that she would be able to sit in full-lotus posture with a minimum of pain. Since her teacher had experienced a lot of hardship mastering this most fundamental posture of Zen meditation, her teacher did not want the young girl to experience the same. Her teacher made her sit in full-lotus posture while taking a bath, because the warm water would soothe the muscles and the effects of gravity were not as strong. It was a good idea that was conceived in her teacher's heart of gold, but there was one small flaw. When Aoyama would sit in full-lotus in the big Japanese bath, she would flip over and her head would go under.[92] In the end, Aoyama did master sitting in full-lotus posture with no pain. Her teacher made her rise early to chant sūtras—learning scriptures by heart before she could even read them—no matter how low the temperature was in the unheated worship hall in the snowy mountains of Nagano prefecture. Discipline was the key to life there, and although it was hard for a child to endure, Aoyama remembers how her teacher made it seem more like a game with little challenges. She remarked how her teacher effectively taught her the value of work, effort, sweat, and appreciation.

Although Aoyama was raised in the temple, and it was most likely that she would become an ordained nun in the future, the final decision was her own. She explains that the fundamental reason in her decision to become a renunciant was her love for her mother. Her mother would say that she was going to go to hell because she loved her children more than anyone else's. Aoyama wanted to find a way to save her mother.[93] When at age fifteen Aoyama expressed her desire to renounce the householder life, however, her mother was sad. She had hoped her daughter would wait until she was twenty-four or twenty-five to make such a serious decision. Aoyama writes and speaks with deep affection for her mother. Though sadness filled her mother's heart, she sewed her daughter clothing to last her for her entire life as a monastic woman. Aoyama still wears those clothes. She makes a special note to always have some of her mother's handmade clothing with her especially when she travels, even though the clothing is almost threadbare from constant use. Aoyama's mother, however, also included a bridal kimono that she had also made for her daughter, in the hopes that someday. . . . Aoyama is still deeply moved by her mother's display of concern for her daughter. She quotes an old saying, "For every billion people there are one billion mothers, but my mother is a peerless mother." With deep love for her mother, Aoyama did not sway from her original decision to become a nun, and she carried her mother's love—and the bridal kimono—with her into the temple. She had the elaborate silk brocade bridal kimono resewn into hangings for the altar pillars. They are used on special ceremonies. She also made a promise to her father, who became ill and died while she was still young. Aoyama still remembers him saying, "Since I was weak, I was not able to do anything with my life. Please grant me the favor of you becoming a renunciant and do enough disciplined monastic training and meditation for me too."[94] With confidence, certainty, and determination, young Aoyama became tonsured.

The poem she wrote at age fifteen, just after graduating from middle school in the small town of Shiojiri, expresses the enthusiasm she had for her new life:

> Inflame life a crimson red and
> Affect karmic relations.
> Cut black hair and enter The Path!

At that time, Aoyama thought she was choosing the path to the highest happiness in the world. She was aware that there were many paths to take, but she thought you could only live one of them. With no second chances, Aoyama wanted to take the best. Her desire for happiness was so strong that she was not willing to settle for partial happiness. She wanted total happiness. She marvelled at how greedy the path of a renunciant was.[95]

When she went to the monastery, she thought that it would all be people who were on the same path and the teachers would be perfect. She looked forward to being embraced in an entirely perfect Buddhist world where she would quickly realize enlightenment and become a Buddha. It did not take long for Aoyama to learn that the path does not include wandering eyes that judge the ways of others. She said she learned that the Buddhist path is to focus on oneself. Aoyama added, "When you stop to examine others, you cannot see yourself."[96]

Aoyama wanted to study hard and pass the college entrance examinations for Tokyo University. The schedule at the Nisōdō, however, was unremitting. She had little time and light by which to study, but she was determined. She finally arranged to have a light allowed in one room for studying after the "lights-out" bell. Through her high school years, raw desire kept her studying until midnight or 1 A.M. every night, even though wake-up was at 4 A.M. She remembers washing her face with cold water to stay awake. It became clear, however, that despite her best efforts of studying at the Nisōdō, it would not be enough to be successful in this most challenging of university entrance exams. One year before the exams, her high school teacher suggested that she leave the Nisōdō for just one year, then surely she would pass the exam. Aoyama became aware of her quandary. Her dream was to attend Tokyo University, but her Zen training was more important. She wrote a senior student she knew in Tokyo about her dilemma. The response was quite simple: "If you want to be a scholar, go to Tokyo University. If you want to be a religious, go to Komazawa University." Aoyama saw clearly after that. She continued her training at the Nisōdō, and she attended Komazawa University. She eventually went on to graduate work, earning the equivalent of a doctorate degree.[97]

While attending Komazawa University, there was a phrase that circulated. "When a nun comes to Komazawa University, she will renounce the monastic path, so nuns should not go." Aoyama had a professor approach her on this matter, insinuating that she might be one of the first to go since she was intelligent and pretty. She was indignant at the intimation. Aoyama retorted that if she had wanted to marry, she would never have been ordained. As she looked back on this, she realized that her professor's words had actually strengthened her to persevere on the monastic path.

During the fifteen years she was away studying, her teacher tended the fields and the temple, supporting her studies and activities year in and year out. While Aoyama studied in Tokyo, she had lived at a temple, Shōbō-an. When Aoyama returned to her home temple, she put her head to the floor, tears of gratitude welling up in her eyes, and humbly gave thanks. She knew that all those years she had enjoyed herself while studying in Tokyo were possible because of her teacher's efforts and understanding. Her teacher replied, "Welcome home. You did well." That was it. Then they went into the fields to work together.[98] Perhaps this was one of the incidents that eventually inspired her to write the poem:

> Helping donkeys to cross
> And horses to cross:
> Such a bridge I wish to be
> Yet I am merely helped to cross.[99]

In 1970, at age 37, Aoyama became the abbess of the Tokubetsu Nisōdō of Aichi Senmon Nisōdō in Nagoya. This was a genuine sign that discrimination between male and female monastics was diminishing. There was now a nun heading a fully authorized facility that trained nuns to be advanced teachers. It was not long before that a female monastic teacher who had raised a disciple was not even authorized to give them initiation, much less give Dharma transmission, or designate a Dharma heir. The nuns inaugurated Aoyama's tenure as abbess by holding a one-week retreat (*sesshin*). In this capacity, Aoyama has a deep influence upon the novices.

Aoyama has also become the head of Muryō-ji, the temple in Nagano prefecture in which she was raised. Aoyama runs a number of activities at this temple. She reaches laypeople at a personal level with her various temple activities. She teaches tea and flower lessons regularly, and she leads an annual "Zen no Tsudoi" or Zen retreat for laity. The success of the three-day retreat, held at the end of August, can easily be measured by the increasing number of people who attend. Some have been faithfully attending every year for more than thirty years. Some parents now come accompanied by their elementary school children, helping to make up the more than 200 people who gather to do Zen practice together in one small nuns' temple. The worship hall transforms from a Zendō to a dining hall, to a lecture hall, to sleeping quarters, with extreme efficiency born out of a spirit of cooperation.[100]

An even broader group of people have an opportunity to hear Aoyama at lectures around the country and occasionally on national television. These engagements help her reach out to a broad cross-section of people with her teachings on Zen life. She also serves as a role model for women. Her glowing face is so renowned that one of the major Japanese cosmetic companies asked her to give a talk, and they wanted to know specifically how she keeps her facial complexion so well. Her eyes twinkled as she simply stated, "I wash my face with soap and water, and I do not use any cosmetics." She went on to discuss a life of Zen that focuses one's concentration on the present moment and accepting it as it is. There is a lesson to be learned in every event, and something for which to be grateful in everything. Live what is under your feet today. She explained that approaching life in this way is her key to her "glowing complexion."

Aoyama reaches even more people through her numerous books. They range in topic from tea and Zen to the Lotus Sūtra, to biographical accounts, to inspirational reading and spiritual guidance. The titles of her publications include Chazen Kanwa [Quiet Talk on Zen Tea] (1978), Utsukushikihitoni Zen ni Ikiru Nisō no Kotoba [Becoming Beautiful: The Words of a Nun Who Lives by Zen] (1983)[101], Nori no Kemanshō: Hokekyō o Ajiwau [Flower Garlands of the Dharma: A Taste of the Lotus Sūtra] (1984), Imani Inochi Moyashite: Watakushi o Sutete Dou Michi o Hirakuka [Inflame Life Now: How to Unlock the True Path by Abandoning the Self] (1987), Tenzo Kyōkun: Suzuyakani Ikiru ["Admonitions To a Cook": Living Freshly] (1987), and Kokuhatsu-tachite Irishi Michi [Black-Haired Ones Entering the Path] (1989).[102]

A few fellow nuns have expressed concern about the possibility of a conflict between Aoyama's increasingly public and popular profile and her ability to transmit the true Buddhist teachings. They are more conservative than the nuns who earlier this century had worked so hard to enable nuns to live the tradition unencumbered by inequities. The fact that there is tension between nuns who are more traditional and those who are less traditional is testimony to the freedom nuns now enjoy. The concern about Aoyama's effectiveness, however, seems to be unfounded, because Aoyama's prolific writings and public appearances have borne fruit in the hearts of many. There is at least one woman who entered the monastic path upon reading Aoyama's books and another who was moved to pursue the monastic life after seeing her on a television appearance. She receives numerous letters and telephone calls in response to her books, and she is happy to speak with anyone who will do a retreat (sesshin) at the Nisōdō first. Men are also welcome, although they must find sleeping accommodations elsewhere.

Aoyama exemplifies the concerns of many nuns in today's complex world where various religious traditions are engaged in international dialogue, seeking deeper mutual understanding. She was part of a group of Japanese Buddhists who participated in an East–West Spiritual Exchange Program in the summer of 1979.[103] The Japanese Buddhists went to Bonn and Rome, and then for three weeks actively shared in the life of various European contemplative monasteries, including Trappist and Benedictine. In the fall of 1990, the Catholics came to Japan and participated in the lifestyle of the Buddhist monasteries. Benedictine nuns stayed with Aoyama at Aichi Senmon Nisōdō. Having experienced the international Buddhist–Christian exchange, Aoyama thinks that "Truth is one. Words create competition."[104]

Aoyama has said that she does not look for only the sweet things in life. She explains that it is precisely because she does not find disappointment in the complexity and richness in life that she can act as she does. "Birth, old age, illness, and death, as well as happiness and misfortune, gain and loss, love and hate, all these are important tools for weaving the brocade of human life. A brocade cannot be woven with the single color of happiness."[105] She reflects that happiness and sadness often arise merely from changing one's point of view, a point illustrated by a poem she composed as a child in fourth grade:

> The Playground
> "It's small, it's small"
> We complain as we play.
> During morning assembly when we must clean up stones we grumble,
> "It's huge, it's huge!"[106]

She teaches that the mind is fickle. With deep understanding and insight into daily life and human nature, Aoyama advocates, "Go straight by winding along." In her teaching, Aoyama frequently draws upon the lessons in life that happen all around us. She illustrates her point that there are many ways to measure life by recounting an incident a young mother had told her: Some people put one ounce of effort and reap ten; others put ten ounces in and reap one. The most important thing is to do your best. On more than one occasion, I heard her recount the story of a young boy to drive this point home. There was a young school boy who was not likely to win the race over his faster friend, but his friend fell down during the race. The little boy waited until his friend got up before continuing the race. Who wins? Who loses?[107] Aoyama knows how to make her lessons clear. It is always apparent how one might apply them in one's own life. This is one of Aoyama's gifts that people repeatedly mention.

Aoyama frequently draws upon poetry and incidents in her own life to illustrate her teachings. One of her favorite poems is by Aida Mitsuo, known for his simple, yet insightful, Buddhist poetry:

> When one piece of china hits another piece of china, they easily break.
> If one of the pieces were soft, both would be all right.
> Let's keep hearts soft.[108]

This is Aoyama's preface to explaining what she tells herself when she is not flexible and has a heart of "china." She describes monastic life as an environment in which everyone bumps into each other, breaking off the sharp edges. Through this mutual "rounding off" process, all become softer and more human together.

She stresses that the body and mind are not separate. If the body becomes weak, the mind will also become weak.[109] I had the opportunity to witness an example of her refined mind and body working in harmony when I was helping with breakfast preparations in the kitchen of her temple, Muryō-ji. It should be mentioned that nearly all activities in the temple are so well designed that the number of minutes it takes to accomplish the various tasks can be timed accurately. The pace is always fast, so there is little room for changing the schedule once it has been set in motion. This particular morning, Aoyama was unexpectedly called and needed to leave forty-five minutes earlier than planned. She was to have an unrelenting day, as usual, and we could not let her leave without breakfast. Meals are a community activity, so breakfast had to be prepared for everyone with forty-five minutes less than usual. Since Aoyama is usually busy with numerous activities, much to her regret, she rarely has time to work in the kitchen. That

morning, however, she felt so bad about throwing the temple schedule into dis-
array that as she rushed to prepare herself to leave, she came through the kitchen,
picked up two apples and a knife, set out a plate, and peeled the apples. Her
hands were a flurry of motion. Within seconds she handed me the plate—once
again apologizing for the change in schedule—and asked me to take it into the
dining room. Impressed with how quickly she was able to cut and peel the apples,
I took the plate of neatly arranged apple slices. As I was walking down the hall, I
was struck by the most beautiful and thoughtful gesture. There was a perfectly
straight and continuous hairline sliver of red peel left up the middle of each and
every one of the sixteen slices of apple! It became clear to me that she is never
too busy to strive for perfection nor too rushed to do all activities with a keen
aesthetic sense.

If ever a flower represented the life of a Zen nun, it is the plum blossom.
Aoyama expressed the reason why she respected this flower: "Instead of succumbing to severe winter weather, they exude their fragrance, look noble in their garland
of snow, and flourish."[110] But perhaps the most frequently repeated lesson I heard
her say while at the Nisōdō was: "It is not a matter of *cannot*; it is a matter of
whether you *do* or you *do not*."[111] In other words, one has the potential to act, so
to hide behind "inability" is not a valid excuse for not acting. Her words encap-
sulate the spirit of the nuns throughout history. They did not succumb to the word
games like "nuns are prohibited from," "nuns are unauthorized to," or "nuns are
not allowed to." The nuns give these words no power. The nuns just "do." Finally,
in this century, the institution did too.

These three generations of monastic women are connected by their commitment
to actualizing their interpretation of Dōgen's Buddhist teachings in twentieth-
century Japan. The generation that opened the twentieth century was not intim-
idated by a sect administration that wielded regulations that circumscribed the
nuns' lives. They had a lucid vision of what was necessary for nuns to lead lives
in accordance with their understanding of Dōgen's teachings and Buddhist truth.
These perspicacious nuns did not accept the authority of an institution that was
not practicing egalitarianism. They joined forces to dismantle the cornerstone of
the barrier that was designed to keep nuns in a subordinate status to monks. With
their keen intellect, poignant insight, and resolute strength, they quickly won the
authority to establish official training monasteries for women. This first generation
realized that education was the key to their freedom, and they succeeded in seizing
that key for themselves and all subsequent nuns.

During the middle years of the twentieth century, the second generation aimed
to rectify the remaining inequities in the sect regulations. They empowered themselves with their knowledge of Dōgen's egalitarian teachings. The most powerful
leaders in the nuns' community worked in concert and wrote resolutions and
demands to the Sōtō sect administration. They claimed their rights to temple
leadership, Dharma transmission, and advanced education. They did not acqui-
esce until all regulations were the same for male and female monastics.

As a result of the efficacious efforts of the first two generations of nuns in the
twentieth century, the third generation now fully participates in all aspects of

religious and institutional life of the Sōtō sect. They can choose whether or not they want to pursue advanced degrees. Many train their own disciples in their own full-ranking temples. They are respected in Japanese society for their sincerity and commitment to the traditional monastic life. A number of nuns even have the opportunity to interact with religious people around the world. Sōtō nuns began the century with asserting that Buddhist truth and Dōgen's teachings included equality, and they reformed the Sōtō sect regulations to conform to those views. Sōtō nuns in modern Japan can now choose to live a monastic life in accord with their vision of traditional monasticism.

The Monastic Practices
of Zen Nuns

On Becoming a Beautiful Nun

Nuns are forever praying for beautiful things.
The Buddha probably does not like a nun who does not
    have spirit.
A nun whose heart and body are beautiful is an
    incarnation of the Buddha.

Kon Tōkō-ni, inaugural issue of
Hanahachisu [Lotus Blossom], 1961

Nuns' Vision of Monastic Life

An inviting and popular perception of Zen monastic life in the West is that it is
a world where men wise in their foolishness engage in enigmatic conversation
about nondualism. In reality, the more typical Zen monastic life as it has developed in Japan is a highly regulated lifestyle that aims to awaken one's Buddha-
nature by placing a high priority on order and propriety inculcated through a
pervasive hierarchical system and strict discipline.[1]

After a few months in the monastery, I became so exasperated at the intricacies
of human relations that I had to talk about it. I found a safe place in the kitchen,
one of the few places in the monastery where you can talk a little more freely. I
was washing *yama-imo*, a small round Japanese yam that is hairy like a coconut.
Because they are so full of dirt when they come out of the ground, the traditional
way of washing them is to put several in a bucket and bump them against each
other. In this way, the bumping helps them get mutually clean. This conjured up
the image of rocks in a rock tumbler. Before life in this confined environment, I
had never thought so much about the fact that it is the rocks hitting against each
other that does the polishing. I was beginning to appreciate that gems become
beautiful by first applying abrasive measures, banging and cutting off imperfec-

tions. I mentioned this similarity of the vegetable cleaning and rock polishing, and I timidly added that's how I felt life in the monastery was like. I was surprised, and relieved, when the other nuns working in the kitchen burst out laughing. They use the vegetable cleaning image to describe life in the monastery all the time. It was comforting just to know that I was not alone in thinking that I had landed myself between a rock and a hard place.

A monastery is not the place to go if you are looking for a tranquil respite from the pressures of a demanding world. In a way, interpersonal relationships in a monastery are an intensified version of those in the greater society. You live so intimately that you can tell who is walking behind you by their footsteps, and often you can even discern what mood they are in—rushed, angry, sad—by their gait. Even the mere sound of the footsteps of someone you currently are upset with can raise your ire. In the monastery, though, tensions are actively and consciously employed as resources for meeting their ideal: to be like a plum blossom, strong enough to be gentle in even the harshest conditions. This does not mean that everyone manifests this ideal all the time, but that the nuns pressure each other to strive toward it. The learning process is filled with subtle, creative, and sometimes even childish expressions of malcontent. Once the initial negativity has been released, it is not uncommon that all parties concerned will privately reflect on how their own actions contributed to the conflict. This is where their religious practice of mindfulness is most helpful. It helps the nuns gain clarity on themselves and their situation. This is their discipline of human relationships.

Basing his appraisal upon the more popular view of Zen, Victor Turner refers to similarities between Zen life and his concept of communitas. The social dimensions of communitas—unity, fraternity with other people—are readily found in Zen monastic communities, but Turner makes special note that unstructured character, spontaneity, and immediacy are the particularly appealing aspects of Zen.[2] These, however, are the fruits of Zen that ripen only with heavy doses of discipline,[3] and the Zen monastery is the place where that discipline is cultivated.[4] This chapter investigates the meaning, daily pattern, structure, activities, curriculum, and discipline of the monastic lives of modern Sōtō Zen nuns.

Turner is aware that society's attempt to routinize communitas through monastic institutions is a paradoxical endeavor, for qualities inherent in an institutional structure are at odds with many of the qualities that characterize communitas: simplicity, silence, transitional states, homogeneity, equality, and absence of status. Simplicity and silence are unequivocally central values of Zen monastic life, but Turner well realizes that one of the most obvious differences between communitas and monastic communities is that a monastery is an institutional structure that is intended to be maintained. The people within the Zen monastery walls, however, are not expected to continue living in the monastery like Catholic monasteries where a group of people live in continuing community. The Zen monastery has become primarily a place for training leading to certificates of qualification that authorize one to head a temple.[5] Once a monastic has received the level of training desired, he or she generally serves either as an assistant or head of a temple. In this sense, the monastery is a transitional community. However, by entering a temple, one stays tied to the sect institution, of which the monastery is a part. Socially, then, the monastery is only partially transitional. On the other hand, in a more philosophical sense, Sōtō Zen monastic life is designed to train a person to act in awareness of impermanence.

Homogeneity—the dissolution of distinctions among individuals—is perhaps in relative terms higher within the monastery than in the larger Japanese society, for monastics participate in a rigidly prescribed life in which everyone has a similar appearance, wearing the same robes with clean-shaven heads. They share the same space, wash their faces in the same manner, bathe, eat, clean, chant, and do zazen together. The external appearance of similitude, however, often conceals the social diversity within. Backgrounds, motivations, aims, and personalities vary greatly and become magnified in the intensity of monastic life.

Theoretically everyone in Sōtō Zen is equal in terms of Buddha-nature, but Zen monasteries have made a high art out of the hierarchical structure that dictates the details of daily life.[6] From where you take your slippers off, to where you place your towel in the bath, to which conjugation of verb you use when speaking with whom, all is determined by how long you have trained at the monastery and in which division you work. Unlike in the greater society, chronological age is not a strict factor in seniority. A first-year novice at age seventy-eight must respect a twenty-two-year-old second-year novice as her senior. In other words, seniority is determined according to the length of time one has been a monastic.[7] The divisions in which you work, although they are hierarchically organized, are based upon a system of rotation. So at some point each monastic in training will be in the highest ranking division and in the lowest. Although indications of status are prevalent, all divisions are seen as equally necessary. The strict hierarchy is designed to retrain one's focus upon oneself. It demands one's constant awareness of how one's actions affect the people around one, and to act in response to what the environment requires, rather than what the self desires. In the words of a twentieth-century Sōtō Zen Master, Sawaki Kōdō, "Religion is not something for remaking the outside world. It is for remaking our eyes, ears, and point of view."[8]

Nuns teach that Dōgen's understanding of Zen monastic life is an institution that teaches the ephemeral nature of reality. It aims to draw out the fundamental Buddha-nature in all by raising a monastic's awareness to the infinite forms of Buddha-nature. The hierarchical structure pervading monastic life functions as a tool designed to hone a monastic's sensitivity to the interdependence of all. Ideally, a monastic awakens to her actions being a part of a vast web. This becomes clearer to the novice who is trained to notice her position vis-à-vis those around her. Reinforcement of her particular relationship to those around her are made explicit, for example, by which words are appropriate for which person at what time; by making her pause to think who comes before and after her in order to determine the most respectful and least obstructive location for taking off her slippers; and by regulating exactly how much water to use and precisely how to use that water to wash her face so as to not make disruptive sounds and use more water than necessary.[9] These are considered to be concrete acts of compassion born out of wisdom.

A practice of establishing seniority is not seen by the monastics as inequity, for when one is within the monastic community, it becomes natural to treat with respect a person who has been a monastic longer than yourself and who has worked hard helping you develop. Relentlessly paying attention to minute details teaches one *how to actualize* that respect. For juniors (who must arrive at a room before their seniors), respect means to leave just enough space—too much space would indicate a rebellious brand of arrogant humility—for their seniors to take their slippers off close to the doorway, so their seniors do not have to walk on the cold floor very long. The seniority system does not merely train juniors in relation to seniors, but, the senior-most member of a division is responsible for her whole division's performance.[10] Even if she does not know how something is done, she must figure out how to accomplish the task.

Zen monastic life, in Turner's vocabulary, is a quintessential example of a life "betwixt and between." It is an institutional structure (an entity that aims to perpetuate itself) that strives to teach an appreciation of the life of impermanence and the ephemeral nature of reality. For the Zen nuns I studied, their aim in living in such an environment is to cultivate the trainees' understanding of Dōgen's teachings that diverse forms are all Buddha-nature. Seniors teach their juniors these teachings in sometimes simple, even silly, ways. For example, senior nuns will shriek, "Ouch, ouch" if a junior nun treats a sitting cushion (*zafu*) harshly, explaining that it is bad to treat "Buddha" poorly. The strict hierarchy, replete with status and ranks, compels one to see that there are no independent entities, but rather that all are interrelated. The rules of a monastery are designed to show nuns how to act like a Buddha in everyday life.

Certain aspects of Dōgen's approach to discipline are notably similar to the Buddhist monastic discipline in its earliest phases in India. Dōgen was among a number of Japanese Buddhists of his time who were concerned with the laxity in regards to monastic discipline. In Japan, monastic discipline and the meaning of renunciation were quite different from what had been understood in India. Dōgen sought to create a Buddhism in Japan that was in accord with his understanding of true Buddhism. A number of fascicles in his *Shōbōgenzō* and *Eihei Shingi* outline his vision of monastic discipline. Dōgen based many of his specific points of monastic discipline on a text that was widely used in Southern Sung China, the *Ch'an-yüan ch'ing-kuei* (J. *Zen-en Shingi*), compiled in 1103. Dōgen did not directly follow the discipline as laid out in any versions of the *Vinayapiṭaka* (Book of Monastic Discipline). Nonetheless, reflecting on the original intent of the monastic discipline, Dōgen's basic approach to discipline seems to echo the primary concern of the early Buddhist community. John Holt explains that ". . . *śramaṇa* teachers [from which Buddhist teachings emerged] advised that one must *act* in prescribed manners by means of disciplined self-effort in order to gain salvation."[11] Actions that brought one closer to enlightenment were cultivated. In determining the types of acts that should be encouraged, the early Buddhist Community accumulated a list of acts that were not proven to be conducive to attaining the goal of enlightenment. This effort resulted in the *Vinayapiṭaka*, which Holt describes as a "text [that] consists of a systematic endeavor to specify the means by which *nibbāna* might be won. . . ."[12] The points of the discipline are based upon how to act so that one can become enlightened.

Minute acts, *sekhiya*, also became a part of the monastic discipline in India. Holt explains how their apparent triviality betrays a vital aspect of the goal of discipline: "The motive which generated their [*sekhiya*'s] inclusion into disciplinary code was quite simply this: perfect control of inward demeanor leads to perfect control and awareness of outward expression, even the most minute public expressions."[13] Every action, even small ones, affect one's course on the path to enlightenment. Both the *Vinayapiṭaka* and Dōgen's writings on monastic discipline teach that enlightenment is realized with disciplined action. The major point of departure is that Dōgen does not see it as a means (discipline) to an end (enlightenment) nor that the external action is a reflection of inward demeanor. The nuns who train novices invoke Dōgen's teaching on the "oneness of practice and realization" (*shushō ittō*). They stress that disciplined action is enlightened action.

The following section shows how the nuns interpret this concept, and how it is actually taught and experienced in Sōtō monasteries by women in contemporary Japan.

Daily Life in a Monastery of Zen Nuns

Let me draw from my field notes made regarding the day I entered the monastery in order to give you a more direct impression of what I was thinking at the time. The incident shows a cab driver's views on nuns, providing a quick, unsolicited glimpse of how nuns are perceived by an average person unaffiliated with the monastery. The cab driver's advice to me also expresses the common view of the role of women in society. Primarily, this passage reveals some of my thoughts about nuns before actually experiencing life in the monastery.

In terms of methodology, I cannot help but reflect that I could only have done this type of research precisely because I was eager to devote the next several months of my life completely to this life, and I had no previous experience living in a monastery. Had I entered the monastery with any dread of suspending all personal life, right down to when I could bathe and how to position my legs when I sat, I surely would not have been in a state of mind that would have helped me establish a trusting relationship with many nuns. Such negativity would have been seen as a burden to the novices who had enough to deal with already. The abbess would certainly have been suspicious of my sincerity and commitment to do research. Actually, Aoyama, the abbess, is the one who decided how long I had to stay in the monastery for this research. When I asked for permission to do the research, she set the terms. One semester, the longest of the three. I was to be given no preferential or deferential treatment.

Unbeknown to me at the time, my idealistic thoughts about nuns were a critical component of the research method: my naive trust made it possible to gather an unprecedented quantity and quality of information. A positive attitude toward the nuns' lifestyle and respect for them as Buddhists helped bonds of trust develop naturally. Because very little information on nuns was available through public sources, these trusting relationships with nuns were my most important resources. Therefore, it is important to show what it was like when I first entered the monastery:

Thinking that the cool temperature of the air-conditioned cab feels good, I tell the elderly white-gloved taxi cab driver that I would like to be dropped off at the Nisōdō, the Zen Monastery for women. He pauses, then says, "You mean the Nigakurin." He smiles warmly and reminisces about a strong old *ama-san*[14] he used to drive, but he thinks the elderly nun has passed away since he has not seen her in a few years. He remarks how young I am to be going to a monastery, and he urgently inserts his opinion that I am too young to shave my head. I should marry and have children. He stresses that the life of an *ama-san* is hard. I concur that it must be a hard life and assure him my intention does not include shaving my head, as he wishes me well on my visit with the monastic women. They are of the finest people I will find in Japan, he boasts. With a romantic spirit of excitement (based upon sheer ignorance about what cloistered life in a Zen monastery will be like), I alight from the cab, thank him for his kindness and step through the thick wooden gate into the walled-in monastic complex.

Cicadas singing in the late summer air welcome me as I self-consciously bow to the new Scripture pavilion immediately inside the gate. I note that this is my first walk down this path, but I would like to think that one day my body will bow instinctively as I pass the holy sites within the monastery walls. The garden is stark with white stones, moss offers softness as it snuggles against the trunk of an old plum tree. How symbolic that a plum tree grows in the garden of a Zen monastery, since Dōgen Zenji held special reverence for plum blossoms, that delicate flower famous for its late winter blooming. Zen nuns, I imagine, must be like pink plum petals graced with snow flakes — strong enough to be gentle in the harshest conditions. I bow to the left, facing the *sōdō*, monastic hall, and pray that I will grow strong enough to keep pace with the Zen nuns in this hall that trains all kinds of women to be like hardy, delicate plum blossoms. As I walk through the doorway a woman in black robes with a clean shaven head greets me with peaceful eyes and a warm bow.

My romantic rhapsody is broken by a shrill jangle, jangle. Pitter patter go the feet of the wake-up nun running through the dark halls. Rustle, rustle as we don black robes illuminated only by moonlight. Thump. The futon goes in the closet. Splash water on face. Down the steps quickly. Slowly, left foot first, we enter the monastic hall one by one, bow to Monju-bosatsu,[15] the bodhisattva of wisdom, and find our assigned *zafu* meditation cushion. Rustle, rustle. Silence.

Boom   Boom   Boom boom boomboomboomboom BOOM!

Morning zazen ends with a drum roll. On to the worship hall (*hattō*) with images of Dōgen Zenji and Keizan Zenji flanking Śākyamuni. Hot tea and rice cakes have been offered to them. The hour of chanting passes slowly, but with each passing day, as the temperature drops, the tempo increases. One more round of the *Heart Sūtra* to Kannon-sama,[16] the bodhisattva of compassion who

stands at the front entrance, and finally the ritual time and motions of the early
morning are broken as we greet each other in refined Japanese:

> "*Ohayō gozaimasu. Yoroshiku onegaitashimasu.*" [Good morning. May you
> be my kind guide.]

We scurry off to clean floors, breakfast, more cleaning, classes, lunch, a brief
break, classes, tea, evening sūtra chanting, cleaning worship hall, dinner, short
rest, nightly zazen. Thump, the futon is pulled out of the closet.

I spent four months in training at Aichi Senmon Nisōdō in Nagoya, from September 1 to December 23, 1989.[17] This was my first experience living in a monastery
of any variety and inevitably there were rough edges. My transition was helped,
however, by my academic background in Japanese Buddhism, personal religious
orientation, and Japanese cultural heritage (my mother is a native Japanese), all
of which made it a bit easier for me to segue into the rhythm of life within the
cloistered walls of the monastery with a minimum of discordance. Another advantage was that before entering the monastery, I had not studied monastic life in
any depth, so I did not come encumbered with preconceptions of what it should
be like. Mostly, I was nervous, concerned with not becoming a burden to the
nuns, but wanting to learn as much as possible. Above all, I knew that this experience of participating in monastic life would be a rare opportunity to understand at first hand the nuns' daily pattern of study and meditative discipline.

This was my aim: to understand the nuns' lives through an in-depth description
of the structure of the monastery and the nuns' lifestyle, rituals, meditative disciplines, and educational requirements. It almost goes without saying that the ideals
set forth in various teachings are not realized in practice each moment. But what
is interesting about the nuns' practice is that they have managed to use the discrepancy between actual activity and disciplined activity as a resource for understanding the significance of disciplined activity.

The discussion here is based on my experiences and observations of Sōtō Zen
nuns' training and conditions at all three Sōtō Zen monasteries for women, but
primarily Aichi Senmon Nisōdō. Without this time in the monastery, I would not
have insight into how the ideals of monastery life differ from the actual conditions.
Nor would I have understood how the ideals are sometimes achieved through
what on the surface appears to be negative experiences. Every nun I spoke with
mentioned that the hardest but most effective aspect of training was the difficulty
in human relations. Without spending a prolonged period of time trying to adjust
to the structure of monastic life, I certainly would not have gained insight into
how the pervasive hierarchical system functions to make each nun mindful of the
people around her.

Since I did not shave my head, I was always last in the bath (a Japanese bath
is communal), so it was one opportunity I had to be alone and relax a little. I
relished my first bath in the monastery. A nun had walked in to the changing
room while I was bathing, however, and noticed my towel arrogantly lying on a
middle shelf. I was reprimanded for such rude behavior. At first I thought it was
ridiculous that I had to place my towel on the floor below the shelves in the bath,
when I was the last person to take a bath. No one would be needing any of the

shelves, so what did it matter? The act of putting my towel on the floor, rather than a shelf, reminded me of my position, thereafter making it uncomfortable to linger in the warm water. No one else could tarry in the bath, because they had to think about the others waiting to come after them. Being last made me no exception.

Moreover, had I not done this phase of the field research with a modicum of decency, I doubt I would have had in-depth interviews or surveys, been introduced to many nuns, and hence discovered many texts that enabled me to learn more about the nuns' activities and history. Neither would I have understood how beauty is not merely a matter of refined aesthetic sensibilities, but it is the crowning mark of their disciplined practice.

Aichi Senmon Nisōdō is located in a wealthy residential neighborhood in Nagoya. From the moment one steps from the street lined with large modern-style homes through the large temple gate, it is hard not to feel the respect for tradition and discipline that is manifest in the meticulously cared for Zen gardens and the traditional architecture of the buildings. The monastic compound includes all the basic facilities and buildings: a six-sided scripture pavilion, a majestic bell tower, a worship hall (*hondō*) with a patina that only comes with age, a traditional monastic hall (sōdō), a *shoin* for guests, a tea hut, and a newer facility that includes the kitchen, bath, classrooms, library, teachers' rooms, abbess's quarters, guest rooms, office, dining room, and rooms for novices. The temple has a large bell that is struck at sunrise and sunset, sending a deep sound that reverberates throughout the compound and into the neighborhood. The worship hall, like most Sōtō temples, has Śākyamuni in the center of the altar. Fresh flowers, lotus ornaments, and candles flank the Buddha. Daily offerings of tea, fruit, and cakes can always be found reverently placed in front. To reinforce the understanding that the monastic hall is a place of silence, the sign above the sōdō entrance is missing the character for "mouth," which is a component in the characters for "sōdō." Inside, Monju-bosatsu is seated in zazen, rather than wielding his sword of wisdom. His presence in the center of the sōdō reminds those who are also seated in zazen of the centrality of wisdom in their practice.

The traditional architecture creates an environment conducive to quiet sitting, but the traditional windows that slide open and shut on wooden runners are also designed in such a manner as to train one in the art of accepting that cold is cold, for winter winds can always find a crack through which to enter. The *shoin* is surrounded by a garden, complete with a stone well for washing impurities off before entering this special place set aside for highly respected guests. In traditional fashion, the floor is *tatami* straw mats, and there are only cushions upon which to sit. With no furniture to distract one's attention, an intimacy develops between the guests despite the formalities that always accompany a visit to the *shoin*. Tea ceremony classes are also held in the formal rooms of the *shoin*, for it has all the necessary features for serving and preparing tea properly and sets the proper tone for keen attention to intricate details. A stroll through the mossy garden leads to a tea hut only opened for extremely rare and special tea ceremonies. A newer building in the compound is used for most classes, cooking, eating, sleeping, bathing, and studying. Throughout the monastery, the passing of the seasons is enjoyed with winter plum blossoms, spring cherry blossoms, summer camellia, and the flaming yellow leaves of the gingko tree in autumn.

The daily schedule of the monastery is similar to that of any standard Sōtō Zen monastery. Here is a typical day at the nun's monastery[18]:

4:00 A.M.	Wake-up (*shinrei*)
4:15	Zazen
5:00	Morning sūtra chanting (*chōka-fūgin*)
6:15	Daily morning cleaning of monastery (*seisō*)
7:30	Breakfast
8:00–12:00	Classes, *samu* (working together—gardening, cleaning, preparation for events), or private study
noon	Lunch
12:30–3:00 P.M.	Classes, *samu*, or private study
3:00	Tea
4:00	Evening sūtra chanting (*banka*)
4:30	Cleaning of worship hall and monastic hall
5:30	*Yakuseki*, primarily consisting of the days' leftovers[19]
6:00–8:00	Private study in own room
8:15	Night zazen (*yaza*)
9:00	Lights out (*kaichin*)

Nuns rotate the job of waking everyone up. The nun assigned this task must rise earlier than everyone else, dress in the dark, and run through the monastery halls barefoot while ringing a high-pitched bell. At the instant the bell is heard, all must move with planned efficiency, especially the lower ranked people for they must arrive in the sōdō by 4:12 A.M. Seniors may have another minute. In other words, in twelve minutes one must neatly fold all bedding into the closet, dress, brush one's teeth, wash one's face, use the toilet, and get seated in zazen posture facing the center of the mediation hall. After the abbess arrives and makes offerings to Monju-bosatsu, everyone (except the abbess) rotates on her meditation cushion to face the wall for forty-five minutes of sitting in silence. As described in Dōgen's *Zazen-gi*, one rests both feet on the top of one's thighs for the full-lotus posture, or just one leg for the half-lotus posture of sitting. The back is straight, shoulders squared, eyes looking down one meter ahead; the breath is deep and slow. When the drum sounds, the period of zazen is over, and everyone bows and files out to the worship hall. The morning service includes bowing, offerings, and chanting, punctuated by bells and drums indicating what is to be done next. Directly after the service, everyone goes to her respective division to do the assigned cleaning chores. By 7:30 all the floors in the monastery have been hand cleaned, all surfaces dusted, the flowers watered, and the garden spruced up. The cast-iron gong clangs in a pattern that everyone knows means the food is ready. After a perfunctory breakfast consisting of fifteen minutes of chanting, glutinous rice porridge, and pickles, at 8:00 classes commence, more cleaning is done, or private study ensues.

The schedule for each day depends on numerous factors; there is no established routine. Somehow, all that needs to be studied or cleaned is accomplished. Lunch at noon is the biggest meal of the day, frequently the highlight. From 12:30 to

3:00 P.M. there is time for either classes, cleaning, or study. Tea is at 3:00, and the evening service is held at 4:00. By 4:30 everyone has changed back into work clothes and cleans the worship and meditation halls (for the second time in the day). A meal of leftovers occurs with little formal ritual at 5:30. Many days the meal might be warmed-over rice porridge, white rice, and a few vegetables. From 6:00 through 8:00 in the evening, there is more time for study. This is also the time that the head nun thanks each woman for her work that day and assigns the chores for the following day. A final round of zazen is held from 8:15 to 9:00. When the bell is struck to end the session, everyone returns to her division's room, lays out the bedding, and the ceiling light is turned off. Technically this is "lights out," but the various demands of study, memorizing sūtras, and a host of other details frequently keep most nuns up with a desk lamp on until 11 or 12. Silence during this time, however, is imperative.

The nuns base their schedule on Dōgen's teachings on monastic life. He wrote regulations and procedures in a thorough and meticulous fashion. The teachers in the monastery stress that the rules are designed to teach the disciples to act in accordance with the Dharma in each and every activity—to treat all life with respect, to purify the mind of illusions of self and other, good and bad, desire and dislike. The ideal behind this method is to make the regulations and ideals of the *sangha* an internalized mode of living, rather than an external set of regulations to be obeyed.

Zazen is a vital element in the practice of nuns in the monastery, but in keeping with Dōgen's emphasis on practice in each aspect of life, the teachers at the monastery train the novices to do sewing, dusting, scrubbing, eating, washing, walking, and sitting (not just zazen, but all sitting—while listening to lectures, eating, talking, etc.)[20] as practice. The abbess, Aoyama Shundō, often reminds people that if you think you are too busy for "practice," then you do not understand what practice is. Practice is in the way you do everything, not just zazen, for one is enlightened when one acts like a Buddha. A Buddha does not waste water while face-washing. A Buddha licks food bowls clean.

I learned that the key to finding peace at the monastery is to accept the fact that the present moment is all there is. "Now" is the only time when something can be done. The logic is that if you just do what is necessary at the time, then all necessary things will be done. To rebel against this reality only causes you to suffer. To contemplate "maybe" or "later" only means that you must fight against these wishes and keep pace with the others. Yet, to accept the task before you and to do it with your whole heart leads to freedom and peace. When it is cold, it is cold. When your right knee hurts, it hurts. When the morning wake-up bell rings, you wake up. When the bell in the sōdō is struck, you stand up. When the gong is struck, you go to eat. When the *samu* drum is beaten you go to work.

Purity and cleanliness are core concerns in many dimensions of Japanese life. Historically, this concern stems from the purification practices and rituals that were central to pre-Buddhist Japanese religion. Zen Buddhism, in particular, has institutionalized this as a fundamental aspect of monastic life. Maintaining a pure environment requires a pure mind. Since Zen teaches that there is no dichotomy between the body and mind, Zen adepts maintain that while polishing the floor, the heart is also being polished. Therefore, cleaning serves total hygiene, spiritual as well as physical.

How does a Buddha clean? Senior nuns never tire of reminding the novice that a Buddha cleans carefully, not missing a speck of dust or spilling an extra drop of water. Each motion while dusting must be done with efficiency, grace, and respect for the object being dusted. Cleaning is perhaps the aspect of Zen monastic life that comes closest to achieving the ideals of the teachings on a regular basis. During a good part of the time in the monastery, enlightenment *is* cleaning.

Preserving the traditional schedule, the monastery I studied allows the nuns to bathe and shave their heads on dates that contain either the number four or nine.[21] At times when the heat and humidity of Nagoya were intense, I dreamt of pouring the water we used for flowers over my own wilting head. At these moments I felt the oppressive tenacity of tradition. Yet I came to understand that it is precisely because the nuns do not waver on such details that they are living bearers of the traditional monastic Zen life.[22]

No actual system, of course, is as perfect as its ideal appears on paper. Likewise, the pristine image of nuns in public, does not tell the whole picture. It was the actual conditions of everyday life at the monastery that showed me just how human these nuns are. I was initially disappointed that even these nuns displayed petty concerns, but then I saw how they are able to use the tensions and emotional conflicts that accompany intimate community life as resources for "polishing their hearts." I came to understand that this discipline of human relationships is actually the heart of their Zen practice.

The stereotype of Zen monasteries being a haven for like-minded individuals to pursue inner tranquility free from social concerns and constraints—a place to sit in deep meditation—does not capture the dynamics that come into play in actual monastic practice. Many nuns told me zazen was the easiest part of the practice. When you sit you do not have to deal with anyone else directly; you just sit there. Human relations are what make monastic life a training ground. In this sense, zazen is not the central practice. The primary practice is learning how to get along with the people around you. Every nun I spoke with on the matter explained that learning to cope with the challenges of human relationships— idiosyncracies, anger, jealousy, pride—is where the real Zen practice occurs. At times it seemed like what the whole day was about was how not to raise anyone's resentment—or scheming how to gain revenge on someone. The monastery is a virtual greenhouse that magnifies all tensions. Only now from the safe distance of being on the other side of the globe and several years removed can I find the humor in it.

The following vignettes lifted from actual events at the monastery may illustrate. The structure of monastic life is extremely rigid, and the rules and expectations governing behavior are quite exacting. Indeed, interpreting the regulations was a common conversation that was primarily about power. When you are accused of a breach of conduct by a nun who is your senior, the monastic culture dictates that you bow with your head to the floor and apologize profusely. Feelings of anger, frustration, and dislike, therefore, are forced into rather subtle levels of expression. Due to the intensity of the lifestyle, however, even very subdued forms can communicate poignantly. For example, if you are angry, you can roll around in bed and make a fair amount of disruptive sound, so those around you—the target of your anger—may have difficulty falling asleep. Since sleep is at a premium, this technique can be a powerful mode of expression. At the other end of the night, which always comes too soon, another opportunity for expressing dissatisfaction occurs. You can wake up before the wake-up bell and noisily put your bedding away. Loud arising will make your negative emotions clear to everyone.

Mealtimes are another time when negative feelings can be indicated in quiet, yet effective, ways. Food becomes a focus of emotion because it is one of the few things to look forward to in a demanding day of precision cleaning. If you are upset with someone who has a small appetite, you can serve them large portions of food. Since you must eat your bowls clean, this is a particularly direct way to cause discomfort to the person who happens to irritate you. You can always tell who was angry at whom by whose bowls get overly loaded with heavy glutinous rice porridge. Indeed, the cook could have tremendous power to express negative feelings by cooking too little or cooking things that are not very tasty, but I never saw this power abused. On the contrary, it seemed that the person who was the cook for that session was particularly popular among the other nuns.

Work period (*samu*) offers numerous possibilities for expressing resentment and feelings of alienation. You can work extremely quickly and make the others around you look lazy. Or, you can work on easier tasks just slowly enough to not draw attention to yourself, but force your cohorts to do more of the harder work. Another popular strategy is to excuse yourself to go to the bathroom and take a long time. This is an especially preferred technique when the work involves weeding a shady part of the garden where mosquitoes abound. These signals of dissatisfaction may give daily life some spice, and in retrospect they seem quite humorous. When you are in the middle of them, they can be very painful.

At one point I even tried to leave the monastery. I made surreptitious overseas phone calls scheming with a fellow graduate student back in Cambridge about how to get our advisor, Nagatomi Sensei, to call the abbess and explain that I had to leave. Although I never had my advisor call, I did talk with the abbess about leaving. She flatly said that I could not. I was defeated. There was no escape. It was from this point on that for mere sanity I had to start finding out what was redeeming about life in this greenhouse of tensions and seeming pettiness.

I became increasingly aware that I was not alone in feeling defeated and frustrated at not being up to doing all the necessary actions. I ventured out into the hallway after lights out and discovered that this is the time senior teachers informally apply the healing balm of understanding that they themselves nurtured in their own experiences. One teacher in particular, Kitō Shunkō Sensei, was commonly sought out for the compassion of her wisdom. She would instruct novices to let their feelings flow like water, because if they let problems or tensions build up, they would clog and begin to sour. Frequently she drew images from nature to encourage the discouraged. I was not the only one who benefited from her stopping to point to the gnarled old gingko tree out back that had weathered countless seasons. She exclaimed at the sight of the tree aflame with brilliant yellow leaves and explained the natural development of strength over time, the need for each season. Novices find it hard to feel pain very long in the presence of such compassion, wisdom, and beauty, especially since it seems to be in such stark contrast to the rest of the day. Kitō Sensei, along with the other teachers, did her best to keep the novices focused on disciplined action, rather than becoming consumed with self-indulgent thoughts and mindless actions.

On one occasion Aoyama Sensei even revealed that when she first came to train at the monastery she was quite disappointed. There were many aspects of the life and people around her that she thought were not in accord with the Dharma. Her teacher scolded her saying, "Who do you think you are? Nobody is perfect. You have to learn from everything, not just the pure." This teaching, she said, inspired her to see the Dharma in all forms and activities, and to not limit her own practice by judging the behavior of others.

It is here, in the intensity of life within cloistered walls, that tensions over minor matters—issues that would be of little consequence in the broader society—are built up and then resolved. At one time, Miyata Sensei, a well-respected, no-nonsense teacher, came by just as a typhoon was passing over Nagoya. It was a fitting time for her to address the novices about a minor controversy brewing in the monastery over the care of a few stray and unhealthy kittens. Regulations do not permit the monastery officially to keep pets, so some nuns thought they should send the animals away. Others maintained that their intention was not to keep the kittens for pets but to help sentient beings whose lives might otherwise be threatened. Miyata Sensei quietly taught that if we are entrusted with the care of living creatures, we must take good care of them no matter what kind of life form. She reminded the novices that living according to the Buddhist teachings was more than just following rules.

At a time when numerous demands on the abbess called her away from the monastery for an extended period, tension and conflict in the monastery mounted with every whispered conversation and with each set of averted eyes. The air grew thick with insecurity and disharmony. Then at lunch, unannounced, the abbess returned. Upon seeing her, quite by surprise, tears of joy and relief came to the eyes of a number of the novices. Everyone began acting differently. It seemed as if the abbess's mere presence instantly healed the self-inflicted wounds resulting from petty complaints. In public, these nuns appear exemplary, an extremely well-disciplined group of people. Yet, the fact that the abbess's presence (or lack thereof) could affect their actions to this extent is testimony to both the abbess's profound power and the length of time required for training to live a strictly disciplined and refined monastic life.

The pressure of interpersonal tensions in the monastery can be very intense. A senior novice, Baijun-san,[23] explained the situation while helping her junior with some problems with another nun. Though she was still considered a novice herself, Baijun-san wanted to help diffuse the tensions between her juniors. Her tenure in the monastery, she said, had taught her that problems can arise in all phases of monastic life, although the types of problems change. She explained that when you first enter the monastery, you can barely do anything and everybody seems to pick on you. When you get a little more advanced, you begin to worry that you cannot keep up with your peers. Then, as you become even more advanced, if you cannot do something—or even if you can—your juniors complain about you. When you do not do something properly that you are supposed to be able to do, it is more painful than when a new nun does not, because she is not actually expected to do everything properly. She went on to talk about how difficult it is to live with a group of people who are unrelated; but, she added, it is a wonderful place to learn. "In this place," Baijun-san reflected, "you even learn to be kind to people who dislike you. Also, people will tell you when you are wrong. This is a gift, because not many people will tell you." In this sense, she continued, "people here show genuine kindness. They give you the opportunity to improve." Of course, she noted, it is not pleasant when they dole it out, but she added that she still chose to be at the monastery rather than anywhere else. From Baijun-san's comments on the ups and downs of monastic training, it is apparent how life in the monastery continuously challenges nuns to refine their actions. It is precisely these moments—when people are not acting exactly according to the discipline— that train people to pare down their ego.

Completing *Rōhatsu Sesshin*, the most arduous practice of the year, often brings out a lighter and more forgiving spirit in everyone, despite the fact that final exams follow on the heels of the *sesshin*. Since each and every nun has persevered for the duration, minor complaints about this or that style of action seem out of place. At tea time one day during this period, all the novices were giggly while doing a parody of the "Ten Disciples of Śākyamuni." Their upcoming exams would cover this and other aspects of Buddhist doctrine and history. The women started compiling a list of the "Eleven Disciples of Aoyama." By using the Chinese pronunciation of common Japanese words, they came up with formal and eminent sounding names that represented all their bad qualities: Most Eminent Imbecile, Most Revered Chatterbox, Most Honored Indolent One, Most Highly Disarrayed, Most Respected Glutton, Indexterity Incarnate, Most Imminently Provoked, Most Frequently Forgetful, Most Venerable Shrewd One, Most Jealously Guarded One, and Most Beloved of Gossip. The laughter seemed to heal the pain of recent months. They decided to give this to Aoyama as *her* final exam. Baijun-san suddenly stopped with her eyes wide open and queried, "But what if Aoyama Sensei gets them all correct?!" After an instant of utter silence, peals of laughter rang through the monastery.[24]

One last example from monastery life at Aichi Senmon Nisōdō will illustrate how nuns at different stages of training respond to a difficult situation. Although I am choosing one of the clearest demonstrations of the positive effects Zen monastic training can have on a person, it was not an isolated incident. With few exceptions, nuns who trained longer responded to events with more grace and generally a more pragmatic outlook. It seemed they really had had most of their sharp edges worn off after years of bumping angrily around with frustration and hurt. They just did not seem to get as upset by things, because they had learned that it does not make things any easier.

One day the monastery was hosting a large Dharma Lineage ceremony (*Hōmyaku-e*) for laity. It was a full-day affair that included lunch. Since the day before, everyone was involved in the preparations, the most labor intensive of which was a traditional Japanese vegetarian meal complete with individual serving trays and six separate dishes, each carefully arranged. In Zen cooking, the quantity of each ingredient is carefully calculated so as not to make too much or too little. By 10:00 that morning the number of guests who were staying for lunch was tallied up, and the final preparations were well underway. Lunch for the 145 guests was to be served at exactly noon. At 11:30 someone came in and announced that there were fifteen more guests who needed lunch. The next thirty minutes in the kitchen were a brilliant display of the various levels of discipline in human relationships. The newest nuns started muttering under their breath, "Why didn't anyone tell us earlier?" "This is impossible." "We can't make that many more meals in this amount of time." "Who said it was only 145 guests anyway?" The nuns who had been in training for two to three years started moving briskly, barking orders of what should be done, interspersed with inarticulate sounds of frustration, as if to say, "This is not my fault!" The head cook, the most senior of the nuns in training, was completing her fifth year in the monastery. Upon hearing the news, she stopped for about a minute and quietly started running various calculations in her head. Then she swiftly reached into a bin and brought out five more carrots and politely asked a novice to cut them in thin diagonal pieces. She asked another novice if she would please put a medium-sized sauce pan of water on to boil. As she was telling a few other novices to get out fifteen more of each of the dishes, she surveyed the already completed trays. Although effort is made to make each serving equal, variance is common. She found the dishes that had food to spare, and indicated to a few other novices to scavenge from them. In this way, she calmly worked until the meal was served to all 160 guests at noon. She never blamed anyone, nor did she show any sign of tension or displeasure. She thought through the necessary details as she moved quickly around the kitchen, speaking politely.

Although it is not apparent from the daily schedule, language has tremendous impact on shaping the tenor and quality of life in a Zen nunnery. Indeed, a key to the nuns' tendency to interpret or transform negative experiences into a positive aspect of their religious discipline lies in a particular verb conjugation commonly heard in their speech. This form is rarely used in general conversation in modern Japanese society. Grammatically it is a combination of the passive and humble form, but I think its function as a tool of religious discipline is perhaps best described as the "gratitude conjugation." This conjugation enables you to permeate your verbal expressions with sentiments of gratitude. For example, you can respond to the question, "What are you doing?" with: "I am profoundly grateful to the universe for having legs and arms strong enough to carry heavy tables up the stairs." In English this sounds contrived, but in Japanese it sounds eloquent. This verb conjugation belongs to the level of Japanese language known as *keigo*.[25]

Upon hearing a nun utter just a few words, one instantly is drawn into the world of *keigo* where respect and humility are paramount. Donald Shively explains that *keigo* "is one of the features of language most deeply rooted in traditional society."[26] Since language influences the way one understands the world,[27] the traditional Japanese views of the world require traditional Japanese language. This is not just a matter of tradition for tradition's sake; rather, language colors one's perspective and interpretation of experiences. The formal traditional language, or *keigo*, is structured such that the speaker readily humbles himself or herself as a gesture of propriety. The effect is profound.

Keigo draws one into an awareness of the interrelatedness of people in a way that cultivates appreciation. Although a wide range of human emotions can be conveyed in *keigo*, it is difficult to speak in *keigo* and still be grumpy and complaining. One can be sarcastic and express displeasure while using *keigo*, but the grammar forces one to temper and control one's expression. Formalism and coldness are possible too. All these negative things, however, must be filtered through a form that dictates suppressing the ego. Indeed, *keigo* patterns facilitate living according to Buddhist teachings. When speaking in the respectful language of *keigo*, the task of raking leaves on a windy day is suddenly transformed into an opportunity to thank the universe for enabling you to have the capacity to rake leaves on a windy day. Likewise, one does not just "live" (*ikiru*), but one "is grateful for receiving the precious gift of life" (*ikasarete itadakimasu*—passive followed by humble verb form). When the world is experienced as a series of opportunities gratefully reaped, then humility, appreciation, and respect filter out selfishness, ingratitude, and impudence. For the nuns, their use of *keigo* is a fundamental and critical element that helps them maintain their equanimity through strife, and empowers them to turn oppression into triumph.

The following is a simple example of how *keigo* can shape experience. At the age of eighty, a laywoman recalled the details of a day in 1909, when she was only twelve years old, when she met a nun named Tetsugan-ni. Tetsugan-ni had taken the girl to see the play *Oiran* in Nagoya. Upon their return to the temple, the nun placed herself in front of her teacher and sat in strict *seiza* posture with her back perfectly straight. Placing both hands upon the floor, she bowed deeply saying in *keigo*, "We have returned. I express my humble apology for having left you alone. Due to your deep generosity, we have been able to be blessed with an enjoyable experience. We offer up our profound gratitude."[28] Nearly seventy years later, I too was struck by the grace and strictness of the nuns' lives as this elderly woman recalled the words spoken by Tetsugan-ni, articulating an appreciation of how one's actions affect others. Using *keigo* in daily conversation is a critical part of the nuns' practice. I observed how it can pare down the ego and make explicit the Buddhist teaching on the interrelatedness of all things. Understanding interrelatedness is central to the Buddhist concept of wisdom. Living in accord with this wisdom is Buddhist compassion.

The training at the women's monastery seeks to free a person from the three poisons of delusion, passion, and ignorance that plague most sentient beings. The "polishing" occurs as the nuns rub and bump against each other like stones being polished in a tumbler. Dōgen's writings suggest that he too had experienced the "tumbler mode" of Zen monastic life; it seems only someone who has experienced the myriad kinds of things that can become the source of discord would have such an acute awareness of the minute actions that make all the difference between disrespect and respect. For example, in the *Eihei Shingi* he cautions monastics not to make loud gargling noises or rattle their wash basins. This may sound far removed from the Dōgen who discourses on being-time and impermanence, but they reveal that Dōgen was not just an armchair philosopher. Each disagreement on procedure, every difference in attitude toward an activity, each personality conflict—these all are precious opportunities to become smoother and shinier.[29] Zen monastic life is a mutual polishing process. On most days the nuns consider themselves fortunate to live close enough to bump!

Divisions within the Monastery

The structure of the monastery is organized around the various tasks that must be performed to make the monastery function. These are divided according to the system that originated in Chinese Buddhist monasteries.[30] A discussion of these divisions illuminates how traditional values and procedures are preserved and transmitted. Each division has a distinct set of responsibilities, but all are governed by the principles of efficiency and respect.

Since the women's monasteries are small, they function at present with a minimum number of divisions: *ino, chiden, tenzo,* and *anja.* Leadership and organization of the daily schedule are the responsibilities of the *ino.* Worship-related activities are carried out by the *chiden.* The *tenzo* cooks, while the *anja* serves guests. These responsibilities are the heart of the monastery. Together they make the monastery operate smoothly and efficiently. Moreover, this system is tailored to teach various lessons in cultivating harmonious human relations and run a temple aesthetically. A senior nun is placed in each division as the head in order to teach the newer nuns. This is perhaps where the most careful and rigorous training occurs by virtue of the intensity of the relationship in the dynamics of a hierarchical organization. While the senior novice is responsible for the division, she also must teach her juniors how to perform each task carefully. Anyone who has served in a management position can understand that sometimes it is easier to do something yourself to ensure that the task is done correctly and efficiently. Monastic training is designed to cultivate keen attention and patience, especially in seniors who have the sometimes competing responsibilities of seeing that things are accomplished properly on time and teaching their juniors.

The *ino* is in the highest ranked division; those in this role are responsible for making decisions, informing everyone of events, and making sure everyone abides by the rules. It is an honor to hold this position, but it also requires the most work. The nuns in the *ino* division work closely with the abbess and other teachers. This is a treasured opportunity, but their responsibilities often keep them awake hours beyond lights-out. They learn the enviable skill of functioning effectively on minimal sleep for months at a stretch. The abbess, however, must work even harder. In the monastery where I lived, the abbess had slept an average of three hours per night for decades.

Each day the *ino* decides which woman will perform each task, and in the evening she goes to each room and formally tells the nuns their responsibilities for the next day. Deep bows of gratitude are exchanged between the nuns; one expresses gratitude for working hard as was requested the night before, the other expresses gratitude for the opportunity granted. This custom makes everything clear. The hierarchical system dictating one's actions is necessary for organization, but it also means that the individual does not know what the next day will offer until the evening before. It teaches that one is not in control of one's own activities. A nun must accept what is put before her. She does not decide what she will do, not even when she will bathe. This helps break down the ego and retrain one's habits to accept what is given.

The next in rank of importance is the *chiden* division. The primary function of those in this division is to take care of the worship hall and the various ceremonies. They also go out to homes of laypeople and chant sūtras upon request. While in this division they learn to play instruments used in ceremonies, including the large wooden drum for keeping the beat steady while chanting (*mokugyō*), the large round bell (*keisu*), the drum, gongs, and cymbals. This requires coordination and a solid control of rhythm. The skill each nun brings to this varies, but it is essential for all to master the instruments. A ceremony hinges upon the appropriate sounding of the instruments. In the *chiden* division a nun learns the proper motions of the various ceremonies, which must be executed with precision and care. One must be careful to step with the proper foot forward, hold ritual implements with the hands and fingers exactly placed. Each motion has been honed down to its most essential and refined form. It is training of both body and mind.

Performing ritual ceremonies and chanting sūtras are among the most common activities of nuns once they graduate from the monastery, so time in the *chiden* division is an invaluable opportunity for new nuns to learn the various rituals a nun is expected to perform. Even though the official sect regulations have been reformed to enable nuns to have temples with a congregation (*danka*), many of the nuns still do not run temples with congregations. Although their sub-temples were converted into full-ranking temples, this did not guarantee that a congregation would gather. People in a congregation rarely move to a new temple, because they must remain affiliated with the temple in which their ancestors are worshipped. Therefore, nuns primarily go to assist temples with ceremonies. They must be ready to perform any ceremony at any time, so while in training they take the time and care to learn the ceremonies more comprehensively than the average monk. The training received in the *chiden* division will be critical to their lives after graduating from the monastery.

The *tenzo* division, embracing the monastery's cook, is considered by most nuns to be a vital organ of the monastery, for everyone is directly affected by the activities of the *tenzo* three times a day. Fidelity, creativity, and purity are qualities especially cultivated while serving in this division. Its critical importance is eloquently and powerfully explicated in Dōgen's *Tenzo Kyōkun* [Instructions to the Cook]. He counsels that cooking is to "nurture the seeds of Buddha." Therefore, the cook must prepare all food in a nutritious and respectful fashion. The cook also learns how to prepare vegetarian dishes with creativity, for she must wisely use all food without waste. The nuns are taught that each vegetable is a Buddha. To eat vegetables is also an act of nourishing the Buddha with Buddhahood.

With that as the context, the following example will vividly elucidate the types of concerns, challenges, and creative energy of a Zen cook. One morning just after we had finished eating breakfast, already four hours since rising, a man's voice bellowed forth drawing us all out into the crisp autumn air. Sitting in the middle of the compound was a large truck brimming with large white daikon radishes; the truck was manned by a farmer from the far side of the country who had driven all night long to deliver the radishes to the nuns. Excitement filled the air as we fourteen women were warmed with images of the kind farming village while we hauled all 180 of these jumbo radishes, five heavy tubers at a time, down into the cellar. Amid the profuse gratitude that flowed with our laughter while drinking tea with the farmer, no one seemed to notice the serious expression on the face of the cook, Keishin-san, who was quietly at work calculating the most respectful way to treat each and every one of these plump tubers. She was realizing that the generous gift of the farmer was going to challenge her ability to treat all those radish-shaped Buddha bodies with the respect that they deserved. For the rest of the nuns, the farmer's matter-of-fact attitude and modesty in the face of such a tremendous donation made the radishes taste sweeter. Until, that is, after weeks of eating white radishes in every conceivable (and inconceivable form) of boiled, chopped, sautéed, sliced, and fried in the most plain and exotic of sauces and combinations. The *tenzo* began soliciting ideas after her creative juices ran dry. We all knew we had to accept each meal with thanksgiving and appreciate the efforts of the cook. The general consensus, however, was that we had established a case for the Buddha being too full of radishes.

The fourth division, *anja*, is no less important. The members of this division focus their concern on matters regarding people visiting the monastery. *Anja* division members learn how to be gracious to lay visitors, high Zen masters, and guests off the street. Interacting with sundry sorts of people is a time for refining the art of understanding people's varying needs and feelings. The nuns must learn to carefully observe people to discern whether they are hungry or thirsty and offer them refreshment without delay. Serving as an *anja* hones a nun's sensitivity to whether someone would be more comfortable being treated more casually, or that the nature of the visit is serious and therefore all formalities should be adhered to with meticulous detail. It trains her eye to be quick at determining whether a guest will feel cold easily and quietly placing an extra blanket with the guest's bedding. By developing this instinct for anticipating a person's needs before the guest has even become aware of them, the *anja* can then prepare in advance to ensure that things go smoothly. This requires cultivating a heart that cares deeply for the well-being of others—an essential aspect of their training. A modest example brings out the fact that a sensitive *anja* even knows when it is best to bend the rules.

A teacher was entertaining a guest in her room one afternoon, and the *anja*, Dōkō-san, began to serve them formal tea (*matcha*) and cakes when a novice entered the room to discuss an important matter with the teacher. With the novice present, it would have been rude for the teacher and guest to partake of the tea and cakes. A novice, however, is not permitted to be treated with special service, because she is in the middle of ascetic training. Nevertheless, out of respect for the teacher and guest, Dōkō-san brought tea and cakes for the novice, so the teacher and guest could have theirs. The teacher praised Dōkō-san for her awareness of the situation and her quick response. The teacher then lifted her tea bowl indicating everyone could begin. The responsibilities of the *anja* division train nuns in the skill of being concerned about others' needs.

Each trimester, the nuns rotate their divisions, so all the nuns may learn the various essential aspects of running a temple. Since the number of nuns at the Nagoya monastery today is small, nuns tend to get a more thorough training than their male counterparts in larger monasteries. Each nun has the opportunity to be in each division at least once (and half of them twice) during the minimum two-year program. The small number of nuns also necessitates that each nun be responsible for more within each division. This makes them strong and competent members of the Buddhist clergy when they graduate.

The divisions in the monastery train each nun to be skilled in all aspects of monastic life and prepare her to be a responsible member of the community. She can serve as a dependable manager, having gained leadership and organizational skills as *ino*. While in the *chiden* division she masters the intricate gestures and procedures for numerous rituals, enabling her to perform and assist in any ceremony after graduation. A cook who has learned to appreciate food as Buddha will be readily received wherever people are hungry. The keen powers of observation and heightened sense of others' needs are skills that a monastic can use in all types of circumstances and at all levels of interaction. These qualities so carefully taught in the monastery produce women who can affect their spheres of influence in profound and concrete ways.

Another dimension of the division system of organization is that the nuns' rooms, the seating order in the sōdō, the seating order at meals, and bathing order are determined by their division. The result is that the nuns in any given division must do everything together during their tenure in that division. It is an efficient and effective method for a nun to learn to cooperate with any kind of person who crosses her path. The situation is perhaps exacerbated now that the composition of nuns has become more diverse. During the first six decades of this century, novice nuns were all about the same age and had similar backgrounds. The range of ages in recent years (21 to 71 years) is the most striking source of tension and misunderstanding. Furthermore, the nuns come from previous experiences as diverse as having been the general manager of a company to being the daughter of a Japanese Mafia member (*yakuza*). All the nuns agree that human relations are the most difficult aspect of training.

The spatial arrangements and the daily schedule are designed for necessity and efficiency. The result is that there is little private time or space. This aspect of life in the monastery is yet another way in which a nun must discard her personal desires and live in accord with the community. This period of training in the monastery is intensive, not merely because a nun will probably do more zazen and sūtra chanting at this time compared to life in her own temple after graduation, but also because the novice nuns live in a rather insular world where they must work, eat, sleep, study, and practice together throughout their tenure in the monastery. Aoyama adds her insights on life in training at the monastery:

By living in a group without privacy, you learn to control the mind and body out of necessity. Only when you can naturally control yourself, even when no

one is around, are you allowed to have a room of your own. This is the way
Zen living is designed. It is quite effective.[31]

Ceremonial Rituals and Activities

Ceremonial rituals mark various stages in the lives of nuns, plus they give contour
to the nuns' daily lives and accentuate the passing of the seasons. They delineate
who one is through novice initiation ceremonies and teacher certification ceremonies. The time of day can be determined by the ritual activity, whether it be
morning services or night zazen. The annual ritual calendar serves to inform us
when it is spring by performing an equinox ritual. Buddha's Enlightenment Day
celebrations tell you when it is December 8. Rituals help the nuns prepare for
and accept each new phase of life, bring meaning to the passing moments of the
day, and mark the changes of the seasons.

In general outline, the ritual life of the nuns corresponds in many ways to the
threefold scheme of Arnold van Gennep's *The Rites of Passage*.[32] Rites of "separation" in the nuns' lives include ordination ceremonies and precept ceremonies.
The period of monastic training serves as a "liminal period" where the nuns lead
lives isolated from the rest of society and engage in rituals that solidify their commitment to the monastic path. After graduation from the monastery, nuns enter
the "postliminal phase." They then become fully engaged with society as a model
of the Buddhist path, usually running their own temples. In this phase, nuns begin
lives that are filled with close contact with laypeople by serving, teaching, and
leading them through ritual phases of their own lives.

Following van Gennep's insight into the common pattern of ritual phases helps
us observe the changes in the aims and purposes of a nun in different times of
her life. In the separation phase a woman goes through a process of purification
and transformation, as she sheds her individualized clothing and hair and dons
the simple black robes of one who has made a decisive commitment to an ascetic
life. The liminal phase of training in the monastery is essential, for in order to
adjust to entirely new modes and habits of life, the novice must receive constant
reinforcement and strict training. Distractions from the outside world would create
unnecessary conflict when the inevitable doubts and pain arise in adjusting to
monastic life. A postliminal phase accentuates the shift in the life of a nun in
training who lives in a monastery to the life of a nun who heads or assists a temple
whose purpose is to care for the community.

Perhaps the most powerful ceremony in a nun's life is the one when she first
becomes initiated into the ranks of monastic Buddhists, the *tokudoshiki*.[33] The
period prior to this moment is an intense phase of purifying one's body and mind
by casting off one's old patterns of life, familiar possessions, comfortable habits,
and changing one's relationship with friends and family. Many women will practice at a monastery while still a laywoman to ease the transition into a full monastic
life. The day of her ordination becomes her new birthday. Traditionally, a woman
seeking ordination entered the worship hall wearing a formal ornate bridal kimono,[34] for until recent years women sought ordination at the common age for

marriage. It was a stark representation of her choice not to marry but rather to enter the celibate monastic life. More recently, however, women enter at varying ages, and they usually wear a simple and tasteful kimono, with a preference for plain fabrics and muted colors like gray, plum, and blue. A vestige of the bridal kimono remains intact, however, in that a white kimono is worn underneath. This practice graphically symbolizes her death to an old way of life. Having entered the worship hall in her secular kimono, the woman formally thanks her parents and ritually bids them farewell.[35] Her teacher then leads her into another room and establishes an intimate bond of trust by carefully shaving all but a patch at the top of her new disciple's head. The sudden appearance of a white-clad figure with shorn hair prepares everyone for the final metamorphosis of a common woman into a monastic Buddhist. Only moments pass before she dons the pure black robes that will define her role in life from that moment forward. Her teacher presents her with the essential objects of that life, a set of black bowls for eating, a black monastic robe, a surplice (*kesa*) for formal occasions, a black mini-surplice (*rakusu*) for informal occasions, and a cloth for kneeling and prostrations (*zagu*). She is then given a final chance to solidify her commitment to monastic life or return to lay life. The gravity of the ceremony weighs heavily until the final commitment is uttered, and the last remnant of her previous life is removed from the crown of her head. Hereafter, she will be known by her newly received Buddhist name.

Although it is not necessary to perform both rituals on the same day, frequently the ordination ceremony segues into the precept ceremony, in which the precepts of the monastic life are received. There are numerous interpretations and forms to the Buddhist precepts.[36] The founder of Tendai Buddhism, Saichō (767–822), developed an abbreviated set of precepts.[37] Dōgen followed Saichō's lead and established a set of sixteen precepts based upon the central core of Saichō's already abbreviated precepts.[38] Since then, women and men have taken the following precepts upon entering the Sōtō Zen monastic tradition. Three Refuges are taken in the Buddha, Dharma, and Sangha. The Three Pure Precepts—do good, do good for others, do not commit evil—comprise precepts four through six. The remaining ten are known as the Ten Great Precepts: do not kill, do not steal, do not lie, do not become intoxicated, do not commit sexual misconduct, do not talk about the faults of others, do not elevate self and do not demean others, do not be angry, do not be stingy, and do not speak evil of the three treasures (Dharma, Buddha, Sangha).[39] Having vowed to live in accord with these precepts, the woman completes her transformation into a Buddhist nun. The following years of training will develop the necessary skills of a nun who can perform various rituals herself. Her actions and thoughts will be refined through numerous chanting and offering services, *sesshin*, and sundry rituals both simple and complicated, daily and annually.

The most common pattern is for a novice to enter a monastery shortly after becoming ordained. Marking the transition into the liminal phase is the ceremony for entering the monastery (*nyūgakushiki*). It brims with commitment, excitement, and hope for the future. Yet it is also a time of uncertainty and readjustment. Everyone is learning how to put on their monastic robes, how to chant sūtras, how to eat properly, and where to place their slippers. They must even learn to respond to their new Buddhist names. The time I attended this ceremony, April 8, 1990, was an especially joyous time, because for the first time in ten years the monastery received ten new women at one time. The numbers of entering nuns had been steadily diminishing for the last few decades, but that year there was a turn in events. This brought joy, relief, and hope to all.

Daily rituals include chanting sūtras in the morning after a round of zazen. The *Kannon Sūtra* and the *Heart Sūtra* are chanted between prostrations, incense, the recitation of the names of all the ancestors and leaders of the nuns, and offerings to Śākyamuni, Dōgen, and Keizan on the altar. Aside from numerous minor rituals accompanying nearly all daily activities, bells and drums punctuate the day, starting with wake-up, then announcing the beginning and end of classes and work period, opening and closing of sūtras chanted at meals, bath time, evening services, night zazen, and finally lights out. In this way, daily life in the monastery is highly regimented and organized, leaving little to no room for privacy or individual decisionmaking. The rituals train each novice to move as a punctual, polite, and hard-working group.

Although zazen is done in the predawn and night of most every day, once a month a *sesshin* is held for more concentrated zazen. Aside from the two longer *sesshin*, *Rōhatsu* in December and *Nehan* in February, *sesshin* at Aichi Senmon Nisōdō are three days in duration. Daily lectures on Zen philosophy add to the intensity of eight-hour days of zazen. These *sesshin* are open to the public, but they are mainly for the deepening of the nuns' training:

4:00 A.M.	Wake-up
4:15	Zazen
5:00	*Kinhin* (walking practice)
5:15	Sūtra chanting in zazen form
6:00	*Kinhin*
6:15	Breakfast in *zazen* form
7:00	Daily cleaning of monastery (*seisō*)
8:30	Zazen
9:15	*Kinhin*
9:30	Dharma lecture (*go-teishō*)[40]
11:00	Break
11:15	Lunch in zazen form
noon	Rest
1:00 P.M.	Zazen
1:45	*Kinhin*
2:00	Dharma lecture (*go-teishō*)
3:30	Tea
4:00	Zazen
4:45	*Kinhin*
5:00	Zazen
5:30	*Yakuseki*, evening meal of days' leftovers
6:00	Break
7:00	Zazen

7:45   *Kinhin*
8:00   Chant *Fukanzazengi* in zazen posture
9:00   Lights out

These periods of concentrated practice become part of the rhythm of the lifestyle. No talking beyond absolute necessity is permitted during a *sesshin*. Many nuns look forward to this time, because it, in part, means diminished interaction with others. Most of the life in the monastery involves intense human relations, so the *sesshin* is a chance where nuns may rest from this more stressful aspect of life in the monastery. It has the effect of cleansing and rejuvenating everyone. Many novices mentioned to me that *sesshin* provide a chance to pause and see their path clearly again.

During their tenure in the monastery the nuns will participate in and perform many ceremonies, but among the most powerful and intimate are the ceremonies to Ānanda (J. Anan). There is a short version to be held on the seventh of the month. A longer and more elaborate version is held only rarely, the *Anan Kōshiki*. Only nuns perform this ceremony. It helps create a clearly defined sense of community of female monastics. Ānanda is special to the nuns; he is remembered for having interceded to Śākyamuni on behalf of the first women who wanted to enter the Buddhist order of renunciants. It is held that through Ānanda's persuasion, Śākyamuni established the order of Buddhist nuns. The nuns at Aichi Senmon Nisōdō perform a ritual in honor of Ānanda that Kankō-ni, one of the most powerful nuns of the Meiji period, formally designed. She based it upon earlier traditions that are no longer performed. Since Kankō-ni was the teacher of Mizuno Jōrin, one of the founding nuns of Aichi Senmon Nisōdō, this nunnery is dedicated to maintaining the ceremony.[41] The ceremony evokes a mood reminiscent of ancient India. In contrast to the quick, rhythmic and nontonal Japanese chants, the chants in homage to Ānanda's great compassion are colorful Indian-sounding melodies with a songlike quality. Sōtō nuns use this ritual to recreate the imagined sentiments of the first nuns. In this way, Sōtō nuns seem to establish a bond with these first courageous and committed women, a connection that transcends the centuries and cultures. Each round of chants and prostrations apparently draws out renewed understanding and heartfelt insight into their historical context. When the ceremonies I observed came to a close, each woman virtually glowed from her profound gratitude that she was a nun. This ritual is rare in a number of ways. It is a particularly evocative ritual that has a long (though scattered) history, and it is now known by just a small percentage of nuns. Nonetheless, it is a ritual that continues to empower a number of nuns today. It is a time of gratitude and communally renewing their commitment to life as monastic women.[42]

Aside from this highly specialized ritual, the year is filled with ceremonial rituals that are common to most Zen Buddhists. By participating in them, one gains a heightened awareness of the Buddhist tradition, especially Zen. Another ceremonial ritual that evokes a reflective spirit is the *Fusatsu* repentance ceremony (Skt. *Uposatha*).[43] This ceremony, traditionally performed on new and full moons, has been integral to the monastic tradition since shortly after the Buddha's passing.[44] The ritual is based upon the *Haradaimokusha* (Skt. *Prātimokṣa Sūtra*).[45] A solemn atmosphere is instantly created when each nun enters the worship hall after purifying her robes with the smoke from incense that is burning at the entryway. One's unfair thoughts, unkind words, poor attitude, and improper actions are easy to see in the monastery where there is a strict regimentation of ritual, hierarchy, and daily schedule, for there is no place to hide. Therefore, this ceremony of repentance is approached with gravity and relief. On most days it is easier to see the shortcomings of others, but on this day, no one seems to know one's own faults better than oneself. The ritual provides a chance for nuns to face themselves in front of the community and begin anew.

To start off the spring, Śākyamuni's birthday is celebrated on April 8 with many flowers. A memorial service for the two heads of Sōtō Zen, Dōgen and Keizan, is held on September 28 and 29. Shortly thereafter the legendary founder of Zen, Bodhidharma, is remembered on October 5. Although not celebrated by the general sect, the nuns take special time to celebrate the birthday of Buddha's mother on October 31. *Rōhatsu Sesshin*[46] ends on the Buddha's Enlightenment Day, December 8. Dōgen's birthday is celebrated on January 26. The annual ritual calendar ends appropriately with a ceremony on February 15, marking the day when Śākyamuni Buddha entered *parinirvāṇa*. These ceremonies bring one deeper into the Zen Buddhist world. Through them one becomes more aware of its important figures and the significant moments in Buddhist history. In this way one becomes more deeply involved with the Buddhist Community.

Graduation is the final ceremony before returning to the general society as a fully trained nun. For those who have had advanced training, this means leaving the monastery after five to seven years. Others decide to graduate after the two years required for the basic degree necessary to head a temple. In all cases, these years of training have inevitably been filled with a myriad of experiences, feelings, and insights into their own hearts. Most nuns come to see this as a noble life through which they persevered. Every nun I questioned mentioned that they did not leave the same as they entered. During the graduation ceremony I attended in 1989, the abbess noted that the graduates had begun to be polished—having become rounder, smoother, and brighter through near constant interaction with the other nuns, teachers, and laity affiliated with the monastery. She was quick to add, however, that there was no graduating from Buddhist practice.[47]

A nun may become involved in various activities for the laity while she practices in her own temple. Some of the important ones are also held at the monastery, including sūtra copying (*shakyō*), Sunday Zen activities (*Nichiyō-sanzenkai*), and Dharma lineage (*Hōmyaku-e*) precept classes and ceremony.[48] While still in training, however, the novices can only assist in the activities. Once a month the worship hall is opened up for sūtra copying.[49] It is an activity, like all activities for the laity, primarily attended by laywomen. The most commonly chanted sūtra in Zen is the *Heart Sūtra*, and so it is no surprise that this is the sūtra everyone copies. Although it is an extremely profound text, it is also the shortest sūtra. A space is also left for people to write down their prayers. It provides a little sacred space and time for people to be close to the Buddhist world and themselves as they face a figure of Kannon (the bodhisattva of compassion) shrouded in clouds of incense, while carefully brushing each stroke of the *Heart Sūtra* onto thick cotton paper. After offering their copies onto the altar, a nun, usually Kitō Sensei, who would quietly sip tea and engage in conversation with those who approached her. For some, she was the reason they had come. She poured compassion on the troubled, the wounded, and the lonely. She apparently increased people's joy with her smile of understanding. It was easy to notice that most people would leave a little more peaceful than when they arrived. This is one of the subtle ways in which a nun helps others, just by sitting there and letting people come and open their hearts.

Another activity open to the public is the *Nichiyō-sanzenkai*. One Sunday each month is set aside to invite anyone to experience a day of Zen lifestyle. It is not as personal as the quiet time of sūtra copying, for there are always dozens of women (and a few men) who come from near and far to participate in this. Some women would even travel on a train all night to attend. It is not because there are no such activities in their vicinity (Tokyo). They are drawn to Aoyama Shundō's teachings and the nuns' community. The abbess gives two instructional and inspirational talks during this day of zazen and Zen-style eating. Through discussion with participants and a survey I conducted of laity who attended activities at the nunnery, I learned that most people are physically and spiritually challenged by the day, but they still find it worth the effort. They keep coming back for more. This is an opportunity for the novice nuns to learn how to interact and help the laity. It is also a chance for novices to be reminded of their own progress, for they were once in the position of those whose legs ached and could not enjoy eating due to the profusion of details to remember during the meal.

The Dharma Lineage Ceremony is the most involved and time-consuming of the ceremonies for the laity. This is a ceremony where laity can receive the precepts and a precept name (*kaimyō*), usually reserved for the deceased or the ordained. The entire ceremony takes seven days. At the Nagoya monastery, the nuns follow the common pattern of meeting once a month for seven months. The ceremony consists of an extremely abbreviated version of monastic training. At all of these day-long ceremonies, there are lessons given by eminent teachers from around the country. One ritual in which the laity participates is for the repentance of wrongdoings. They also take the same sixteen precepts as the monastics, although they remain laypeople. At the end of this elaborate ceremony, filled with high teachers in ornate robes performing complicated and fascinating rituals, the visitors receive a precept name and a certificate that establishes them in the Zen spiritual lineage. Most temples do not perform this elaborate ceremony, for it is demanding in terms of time, money, energy, complexity of ritual, and in seriousness. The nuns at the Nagoya monastery, therefore, are fortunate to have the rare opportunity to learn the intricacies of this solemn ceremony. It places them in the important position of being among a select group who are able to assist with this ceremony when they graduate.

The most popular ritual in the annual calendar of the nuns of Aichi is an ancestor worship rite called Jizō Nagashi, held on July 7.[50] Jizō, a bodhisattva (Skt. Kṣitigarbha-bodhisattva), is frequently depicted standing in the image of a clean-shaven monastic holding a staff. He vowed to deliver all people from this suffering world and to empty the hells. He is particularly known for saving all beings in the period between Śākyamuni Buddha of the past and Maitreya Buddha of the future.[51] Therefore, nuns of Aichi Senmon Nisōdō created this ritual, primarily for lay members of the community, as part of the ancestor rites that occur all over the country during the summer months of July and August.[52] The nuns designed a day that involves a short trip to a large temple and a boat ride on a lake that is conducive to reflection upon one's deceased family members[53] and the meaning of life in the face of death. Before this day arrives, nuns and laity alike have the names of their ancestors written on individual memorial tablets. Ten busloads of devotees gather in the morning; buses numbered four and nine are conspicuously missing, however, for homonyms of these numbers are "death" and "suffering," respectively. The nuns cultivate a sense of community among the people in each bus by leading everyone in Buddhist songs and chants. A sense of pilgrimage is quickly established—the air filled with the mixture of joy and adventure, reflection and prayer—among the sea of new and old faces. Between rounds of the *Heart Sūtra* and chants to Jizō, newcomers are naturally swept into the ring of sharing candies, a thermos of tea, and homemade *umeboshi* (pickled plums) and the exchange of details about recent aches and pains, illness, deaths, marriages, and births. The year I attended, the temple we were going to was Myōgon-ji in Toyokawa (more famous for its shrine to the fox deity, Inari). Before arriving at the temple, the people show all the signs that they have become comfortable in their identity as the Nisōdō pilgrims.

At the temple, the abbess leads the worship ceremony in deep coral-colored robes while other nuns play cymbals, drums, and bells. The voices of dozens of nuns merge together as they recite the names of each and every person being remembered that day. After the nuns have formally paid respect to literally thousands of ancestors, the abbess offers some advice. She begins by explaining the five offerings that help an ancestor: candle, incense, flowers, food, and drink.[54] More powerful than these, however, is Jizō who cares for all beings upon death. The abbess says that he is especially known for his concern for children, so his qualities are commonly likened to those of a mother who constantly tries to ease the suffering of her children. The abbess gently reminds those present that in order to effectively help like Jizō, you must practice becoming like water. She explains that this waterlike quality enables you to fill the need no matter what the shape. After the ceremony comes to a close, all 450 people eat lunch in the temple. Upon boarding the spacious boat heading out into the large lake—this year it was Hamanako and last year it was Lake Biwa—everyone chants the *Heart Sūtra* followed by seven repetitions of a *darani* to Jizō: *Onkākākabisanmaeisowaka*.[55] For the remainder of the boat ride a solemn mood is maintained by the nuns singing a somber song of homage to Jizō. Once the boat is out in the middle of the lake, everyone moves to the edge of the boat facing the mountains, now veiled in clouds. With the song of homage accompanying their personal prayers, in a natural gesture of respect each person raises to their forehead the five little slips of rice paper with the image of Jizō printed on them and slowly lets each of their five slips float off their fingertips and flutter in the air. Memories of the devotees' loved ones are stirred with each piece slipping off and into the sea of paper whirling in the wind.

As the rice-paper Jizōs dissolve into the water, the intent is that the suffering over their own loss should also melt in their hearts, which are now renewed and healed through this ritual. In creating this unique ritual and drawing upon traditional practices and images, the nuns reveal their concern with the nature of the human heart as it tries to heal in the awareness of death. Performing this ritual on water makes people aware of the image of water, flowing harmoniously with its surroundings. As I stood on the boat amid the pilgrims, it seemed to me somehow fitting to have nuns lead this ritual, for they resemble Jizō—a clean-shaven monastic with the heart of a mother.

Some rituals are only performed once in a lifetime, while others are repeated daily, monthly, or annually, but all play a significant role in the lives of the nuns. Performing rituals helps define what it means to be a nun, for both the woman herself and for the people around her. Rituals assist her through various phases of growth and development. In turn, the nuns attempt to help others through various aspects of their lives by performing rituals that quietly heal, that honor loved ones, and that celebrate life.

Educational Curriculum and Degrees

As described in chapter 3, the founding nuns saw education as the key to solving their problems.[56] Although the lessons gained from their responsibilities in running the monastery divisions and performing rituals are essential, the education at the monastery provides them with skills and knowledge necessary for leading people in a Zen Buddhist way. It sharpens their minds and grounds them in relevant Buddhist philosophy and history. Practical courses also prepare them to be self-sufficient members of the Buddhist clergy.[57] As a result of their perseverance and strong vision, the monastery now offers elementary through advanced levels of training. Their various programs give nuns the flexibility to meet the needs of women who come with different backgrounds and have different goals. Some have a temple waiting for them and need to return with the necessary skills and qualifications as soon as possible, while others have little background and only one thing clear: they must practice. All of them, regardless of their situation, must meet a basic standard of education and training in the monastery in order to graduate and be granted authorization to head a temple.

Since the monastery offers both monastic training and Buddhist textual education, a nun may simultaneously qualify for various monastic and religious teaching ranks.[58] The requirements for monastic leader ranks involve Buddhist practice, most of which may be acquired at a certified monastery. Religious teaching ranks are achieved by studying Buddhist texts, history, and philosophy. In the case of requirements for the teaching ranks, some of the requirements may be met at a monastery, but many achieve the necessary background through Buddhist universities, primarily Komazawa University and Aichi Gakuin University. The basic requirements for both types of ranks often occur in conjunction with each other, for the monastery is designed to train one in Buddhist practice and offers academic courses to fulfill the religious teaching requirements.[59] Depending upon the circumstances, the minimum requirements can take as little as six months to complete, and the advanced degrees can take a lifetime to accomplish.

Monastic Leader Ranks (highest to lowest)

1. Great Preceptor (*Daioshō*): One who has established a Dharma banner by formally practicing in a monastery for a set term, usually one hundred days (*kessei-ango*).
2. Preceptor (*Oshō*): One whose name has been enrolled in the register of monastics who have been officially recognized by the two Head Temples as a monastic who has been given Dharma transmission by his or her teacher (*zuise*).
3. Meditation Hall Leader (*Zagen*): One who has done advanced practice and has become a recognized monastic skilled in the fundamentals of monastic life (*risshin; kessei-ango*).
4. Assistant Meditation Hall Leader (*Jōza*): One who has received ordination (*tokudo*) and whose name is enrolled in the register of monastics.

Religious Teacher Ranks (highest to lowest)

1. Supreme Head Master (*Daikyōsei*)
2. Head Master (*Gon Daikyōsei*)
3. Head Teacher (*Daikyōshi*)
4. Associate Head Teacher (*Gon-Daikyōshi*)
5. Full Rank Teacher (*Seikyōshi*)
6. First Rank Teacher (*Ittōkyōshi*)
7. Second Rank Teacher (*Nitōkyōshi*)
8. Third Rank Teacher (*Santōkyōshi*)
9. First Rank Assistant Teacher (*Ittōkyōshiho*)
10. Second Rank Assistant Teacher (*Nitōkyōshiho*)

The requirements for the various monastic and teaching ranks include degrees offered through the official sect monasteries. The requirements are complex, leaving room for significant individual variance. In general, for basic ranks, the average monastic stays two years; for intermediate ranks five years is common.

Degrees Conferred by Monastery

1. Preparatory Curriculum Degree (*Yoka*): two years if the monastic has no high school diploma
2. Standard Curriculum Degree (*Honka*): two years if the monastic has a high school diploma
3. Research Curriculum Degree (*Kenkyūsei*): three years after obtaining Standard Curriculum Degree
4. Advanced Curriculum Degree (*Tokusō*): two years after obtaining Research Curriculum Degree

The first degree, the Preparatory Curriculum Degree (*Yoka*), requires two years of training at the monastery while completing a high school education. Most women today, however, enter with a high school diploma, so they enter straight into training for the Standard Curriculum Degree (*Honka*). During these two-year programs the nuns learn to chant the sūtras, perform the various necessary ceremonies and rituals, cook Japanese vegetarian food (*shōjin ryōri*), clean, sew religious garments, take tea and flower lessons, do zazen, and take a number of academically oriented courses on Buddhist texts. The third level of advancement is a two- to three-year program for the Research Curriculum Degree (*Kenkyūsei*). This is considered the level where the nuns refine what they have learned in the previous years. Since many ceremonies and rituals only occur once a year, it requires many years to perfect and deeply understand the complicated ritual motions and profound meaning embodied in the various ceremonies. They also study more advanced texts. The highest level of training offered at the Nisōdō is the Advanced Curriculum Degree (*Tokusō*). As with monks, most nuns do not complete this training, for it is a long and challenging program. Although they are still in training themselves, they become responsible for the younger nuns' training. Completing this training qualifies them for becoming a high level teacher.

The academic schedule is based upon a three-semester system. The first semester is from April 8 to July 20. The second semester, the longest in duration, begins September 1 and runs through December 24. A shorter term from January 8 to March 31 marks the third semester of their year. During recess periods from the monastery, the nuns return to their home temple and their own teacher in order to study and assist with affairs there.

Among the required activities for all levels of nuns is taking courses in a number of Buddhist texts. At Aichi Senmon Nisōdō, high monastic teachers (*Rōshi*) from other temples come to the monastery to teach these courses. The curriculum is designed to cover all the important texts. The basic texts are studied in the first year, while advanced texts are studied at certain times in successive years.[60] Among the texts studied in the first year is the *Gakudōyōjinshū* [Points to Watch in Practicing the Way] by Dōgen. It is vital for the nuns in training, for it covers fundamental issues such as the necessity of arousing Bodhi-mind, the importance of finding a true teacher, and the basics of harmonizing body and mind. Mano Rōshi was a male Zen Master, slight in build, who was in his late eighties at the time I was there. In a voice that quivered with experience, he plainly said to the novices who were still adjusting to life within the monastery walls, "If you want to be comfortable, then all becomes painful. Wanting to be comfortable is not practice."[61] He later analyzed the word for monastery: *sōrin*. Part of the word includes the character for forest. In a forest, trees grow straight up. Likewise, in a forest of humans, people grow straight too.[62] In other words, to establish yourself straight on the path, monastery life is helpful, for it creates an environment where people must live so close together that there is no direction in which to grow but straight up. The study of Buddhist texts is a vehicle through which the nuns receive essential information to help them on the monastic path. The texts are not studied for their historical significance or their philosophical importance, but for their deep insight into how one leads a Buddhist life.

Keizan Jōkin's (1268–1325) text, *Zazen-yōjinki* [Key Points on Zazen], is read with keen interest for, among numerous essential things, it instructs the new nuns on more mundane aspects of zazen, such as how to keep from getting sleepy (focus your mind on your hairline). It describes the kind of clothing suitable for zazen—not luxurious, not rags, but comfortable—and cautions one to eat moderately lest one get sick. Breathing techniques are also described to help enable one to find harmony of body and mind. Dōgen's *Shōbōgenzō Zuimonki*, understood to be recorded by Koun Ejō (1198–1280), is also scrutinized, because it is a text which recounts lectures Dōgen gave to his disciples in training at Kōshō-ji. The main teaching of this text instructs the disciples how to see impermanence and egolessness. Although the majority of the nuns do not have the time, training, or inclination to analyze these texts in technical philosophical terms, they grasp the texts' core in an embodied sense as they learn to move through the activities of each day according to these teachings.

In addition to the high teachers brought from outside, the abbess also frequently lectures on central Buddhist teachings. Her teachings invariably hit their mark, for they are born out of her own experience of the monastic life. She knows the concerns and questions that a novice encounters, and she also knows how to transform their doubts into inspiration. On one occasion she explicated the foundation of Sōtō Zen teachings: Dōgen's understanding of the relationship between practice and original enlightenment.[63] She begins with saying that no matter which way you throw grass seeds, they will all grow towards the sun, because they are naturally designed to do this. The seeds' full (Buddha) nature is not manifested, however, if they do not have water and sunshine. Humans are the same, she explains. Practice is to us as water and sun are to plants. We must practice so our original enlightenment can be realized.[64] That is why you cannot do whatever you like to realize your Buddha-nature. Your original enlightenment, she stresses, is only realized in practice. Although all activities can be done as practice, practice is not doing just anything. Practice is doing activities in accordance with the Dharma—with efficiency, no waste, no excess, and respect, and in harmony with the natural interdependence of all. Returning to the water and sun image, The abbess explains the reason the Japanese character for Dharma includes the "water" radical in its composition[65]: water moves gracefully from high to low and fills each place it encounters with no resistance. Moreover, unlike humans who complain at rising early, the sun rises on time every morning with no exception. In educating the novice nuns, the abbess urges them to live like water and sun.

Practice takes many forms. The form is not what links each of the distinct activities. Activities nuns include in their practice—poetry writing, sewing garments, preparing tea, arranging flowers—are similar in that they are done in the spirit of not differentiating between self and object. In Dōgen's words, this is shushō ittō—practice and enlightenment are one. Creative process and enlightenment are simultaneous.

At Aichi Senmon Nisōdō, along with the traditional Zen training which includes zazen, chanting sūtras, studying Buddhist texts, sewing, cooking, and cleaning, the nuns include flower arranging (kadō), calligraphy (shodō), and tea ceremony (chadō) as integral elements of their training. Mastery of these contemplative arts is not an ornamental supplement to their training; it is required for receiving the certificates of graduation the monastery offers. The nuns take tea and flower lessons throughout their tenure in the monastery. The teachers of these arts are also nuns. They teach not only the basic skills of the arts, but they also teach the philosophy, more commonly called kokoro (heart-mind) in these circles, which accompanies these arts. They are arts that simultaneously train the body, mind, and heart. This philosophy is based on the orientation that the body, mind, and heart are one. One quickly discovers that to perform these arts with beauty requires a pure spirit that draws on the deepest resources of one's *kokoro*. These arts are included in monastic training, because the nuns maintain that to teach the hand to pour water into the tea bowl is to teach the heart the way of compassion and wisdom.[66]

The educating of nuns also includes the study of Chinese poetry (*kanshi*). This foundation in reading Chinese poetry enables nuns to gain a broader perspective and interpretation of Buddhism as it interplays with other aspects of culture. Buddhist sermons, *hōwa*, are also practiced, for the nuns will be expected to give sermons on various occasions throughout their career once they leave the cloistered walls of the monastery. One of the favorite classes, *dōwa* (children's stories), challenges the nuns to express their understanding of Buddhist teachings in a simple and creative way. The nuns take turns telling stories to each other. On every occasion I observed, the ones listening enjoyed reverting to childhood innocence for a brief respite from the more intense aspects of their training.

Sewing Buddhist garments is also a basic activity within the monastery. Incense is lit and silence is maintained as nuns seek to become one with the garments they carefully stitch with a simple needle and thread. They learn to sew all the garments necessary for a nun. This includes a *kesa*, *rakusu*, *zagu*, *koromo*, and kimono. Most nuns begin with sewing a *rakusu*, a miniature, symbolic version of a *kesa*. *Kesa* are the only robes worn by the ordained in Theravadin countries, as it was in the days of early Buddhism. But as Buddhism moved to cooler climates and sundry cultures, the robes of monks and nuns also underwent appropriate transformations. The Chinese added the *koromo*, a long-sleeved robe, and the Japanese added another layer underneath, the kimono. Nuns and monks also began to include working, whether it be tilling fields, cooking meals, or cleaning floors, as an essential dimension of Buddhist practice. Since it was cumbersome to work with so many layers, the modified *kesa*, the *rakusu*, was developed. Zen nuns frequently sew *rakusu* for their beloved teachers and friends. The tiny stitches required for making a *rakusu* are seen as an expression of the commitment one has to the Dharma; thus, to offer a *rakusu* as a gift is a highly symbolic gesture. Once one masters the intricate pattern of a *rakusu*, one can advance to the complicated, but meaningful, project of sewing one's own *kesa*. This is usually preceded, however, by the sewing of the *zagu*, or kneeling mat, since it is a much less involved piece. Many of the nuns then go on to sew their own *koromo* or kimono, but this requires a great amount of time. During their tenure at the monastery this is usually not reasonable. But all the nuns learn how to sew tiny stitches in straight lines. The abbess, Aoyama, frequently reminds them that this is the same way one follows the path of Buddhism—taking tiny steps in a straight line of pure concentration on the Dharma. In this way, sewing is practice.

Go-eika, or its Sōtō sect version, *baika*, is becoming an increasingly necessary art for the nuns to acquire, for it has become extremely popular among the laity. *Baika* is a recently developed form of singing songs based upon the scriptures. The singing is accompanied by a bell and chime which the singer strikes in rhythm with the melody. As in all Japanese arts, there is an elaborate and meticulous pattern of ritual-like motion that helps the singer enter into a contemplative and focused state appropriate for putting Buddhist scriptures to song. All nuns graduating from the monastery must be trained to lead groups of interested devotees. Some of the nuns choose to concentrate on this art and become advanced teachers, while others choose tea or flower arranging as their specialization.

These arts are included in their practice because they are necessary skills for performing the various activities in a temple. It is, however, perhaps no coincidence that most of the arts nuns practice are also the arts expected of a proper Japanese woman. Monks do not have an institutional structure that requires practice of these traditional arts as nuns do. Although at all temples flowers must be arranged and tea served to guests, monks usually defer these tasks to their wives, whereas nuns must do these activities on their own. Another aspect of the nuns' involvement in these traditional arts gives insight into the nuns' contribution to general Japanese society.

Many nuns teach tea or flower lessons in their temples. The students are not necessarily Buddhists, but they are women interested in refining their skills and hearts. Teaching these traditional arts not only allows the nuns to make an impact upon the cultivation of Japanese women, it also serves as a means by which nuns may earn an acceptable form of income. Most temples run by nuns do not have parishioners, or *danka*, so they must find other means of support. An investigation into the role of the traditional arts in the lives of the nuns is a multifaceted issue. Through the traditional arts nuns reveal the beauty of their spirit, their independence in running a temple, the sociological factors that impinge upon their lives, their economic ingenuity, and their contribution to preserving traditional culture in contemporary Japanese society.

Learning to live like a Buddha, assert the nuns, requires one to understand with one's body; therefore all the teachers place strong emphasis on using the teachings in everyday life. An intellectual understanding is not primary in this training—indeed knowledge for the sake of knowledge is considered a waste. Intellectual knowledge can also be an obstacle to one living according to the Dharma. Aoyama constantly warns that to just study and not practice the teachings amounts to nothing.[67] Mano Rōshi emphasizes that satori is not a thing. It is an experience, an activity. Therefore, if it is not done with one's body, it cannot be understood. While moving the body, he explains, one can begin to gain a sense of what enlightenment is. There is no other way to know.[68] In other words, there is no enlightenment outside the body.

The Aesthetics of Discipline

Over the course of the years studying the nuns' lives, I was continuously struck by the pervasiveness and importance placed on beauty. The following are my reflections as I have tried to understand the role of beauty in Zen nuns' lives.

Beauty is not the aim of the nuns' Buddhist path. It is a byproduct of the nuns manifesting Buddhist teachings in their actions. Upon observation, it seems that beauty naturally appears when an activity is so refined through disciplined practice that the dichotomy between subject and object, or process and result, dissolves.

In other words, the total unification of flower and flower arranger occurs when the disciplined art of flower arranging is mastered. When a discipline is mastered, it becomes what the nuns describe as "Buddha activity" (*gyōbutsu*). "Buddha activity" manifests as beauty, for the nuns claim it is action that embodies the truth. In Zen practice, this is expressed as actions of respect, efficiency, and necessity. It is action that is true to the nature of reality as described by Buddhist teachings, the reality that all is interrelated and impermanent.

According to the *Vinayapiṭaka*, monastic discipline is an expression of the Dharma. In Zen parlance, disciplined activity is "Buddha activity." Dōgen used the phrase "practice is enlightenment." In other words, undisciplined activity is activity that expresses one's ignorance of the reality that all is interrelated and impermanent. Senior nun teachers frequently allude to this teaching and remind novices that delusion about reality leads to acting as if the self is the center. This delusion results in acts of passion and hatred of mind and body. "Ugliness" is manifested in such acts as waste, disrespect, laziness, and selfishness. Ugliness appears when the Dharma is not manifest in action. On the contrary, beauty appears when the Dharma is manifest in action. In activities from cutting carrots to making offerings on an altar, the nuns' monastic training inculcates the notion that discipline is action of the mind and body that is not centered on the self. Novices learn through experience that without delusion about self, hatred and passion do not arise. Each activity is designed to prove that the wisdom of inter-relatedness and impermanence results in acts of compassion. Such fancy words are not heard around the monastery as often as their concrete expressions like "do not be wasteful" and "treat all things with respect."

It became obvious to me that the meaning of "Buddha activity" was encoded in the details of the monastic structure, ritual activity, and procedures for daily tasks. By training in the monastery, then, one can practice "Buddha activity." Upon watching advanced nuns, it seemed like those who followed the correct procedures, those whose actions appeared "enlightened," flowed naturally from a profound understanding of necessity, respect, and impermanence.[69] Sometimes, senior nuns would invoke Dōgen to explain their actions, citing that he described many procedures that concretely teach just what necessity, respect, and imper-manence mean in daily activity. Such carefully designed actions can be called ritual, performing truth. The assumption at the core of their monastic life is that through repetitive training one can cultivate the form of enlightened action.

These nuns reflect deep insight into the profound capacity of the body. They would agree with Martha Graham, who taught dancers that "movement never lies."[70] Both know that genuine understanding is evident in bodily expression.[71] The nuns draw upon Dōgen's extremely intricate instructions on how to perform nearly every action commonly done in the monastery, inferring that focusing on the form of the body is an expedient means of teaching and learning how to act as a Buddha. These regulations about minutiae in daily life are considered con-crete ways to live according to the sixteen precepts Dōgen gave his disciples.[72] The Zen nuns follow Dōgen's mode of Buddhist monasticism that stresses somatic knowledge, which is consonant with his nondualistic worldview. Intellectual knowledge requires establishing a subject and object dichotomy. The nuns are keenly aware that intellectual forms of knowledge do not necessarily change one's actions in accordance with the cognition of the intellect. (This seems to be the reason behind their suspicion of scholars.) They believe that training the body is an expedient method for dissolving a bifurcation of mind and body, for in teaching the body how to act, one is less prone to dichotomize between subject and object.[73] The nuns' practice of Dōgen's teachings and regulations illustrates their belief that perfecting the form of an action is an effective way to experience the nondualistic world where practice *is* enlightenment.

Aoyama conveys the basic teaching that practice is enlightenment in various simple ways. She uses a common illustration to make the point that even the posture of one's body affects the mind. For example, while wearing pajamas, one generally feels relaxed in both body and mind, yet when wearing formal clothing and sitting straight, one's mind is naturally sharper. The mind sees things more starkly when the body is in a stark posture.[74] She argues that this is one of the fundamental reasons zazen, a form of practice that often causes aching legs, has endured through the centuries. She lives her life as an example of the teaching that beautiful action is created by a disciplined body, for a disciplined body moves according to the fundamental qualities of beauty: respect, efficiency, and imper- manence. According to the abbess, beauty is a bodily experience.

Many of the actions in the monastery are done by people everywhere, like sitting, eating, sleeping, bathing, cooking, and cleaning. In monastic life, each of these common activities is refined to an art form, for each activity is an opportunity for enlightenment. It is not a matter of sitting, eating, and cleaning in any fashion one pleases. The nuns stress that these actions must be done in accordance with the Buddhist teachings. Since monastic discipline is based upon Buddhist teach- ings, abiding by the discipline is Buddha activity. In order to perform each act as Dharma, nuns must be utterly respectful and constantly aware of the interrelat- edness of all things. The monastic discipline requires monastics to eat like a Bud- dha. The quantity of food is meticulously calculated so there is not too little or too much. After eating, each person cleans her own bowls with the aid of a pickle to wipe and tea or hot water to rinse. The pickle and liquid are then eaten, thereby ensuring no waste (which would be inefficient and disrespectful). Cooking pots and the residual food on them are treated with similar respect; they are licked clean. (Unlike individual eating utensils, cooking utensils are washed afterwards with an absolute minimum of detergent.) The nuns claim that by following the prescribed activities with ritual exactness (*sahō*[75]) in the monastery day in and day out, they begin to realize enlightenment in those acts. Since habit formation depends on training the body in specific ways, the monastic discipline reaches into nearly all aspects of life. The strictness with which they are adhered to de- termines the results, for the nuns maintain that it is not a matter of whether or not one comprehends the meaning of Buddha-nature. You either act according to Buddha-nature or do not. Discipline is a manifestation of a nun's awareness of truth. If a nun is perfectly disciplined, enlightenment and beauty permeate every aspect of her life.

The monastic lifestyle teaches nuns what necessity and respect are by making the nuns aware of the interrelatedness of all events in the moment and the impermanence of the moment. Doing only what is necessary teaches them simplicity and patience. All around the monastery it is evident that efficient skills develop according to the demands of necessity. Necessity also dictates sufficiency, where there is no room for self-indulgence.[76] Acting out of necessity, then, trains a nun to see how her own actions affect the environment and precludes actions that would benefit herself at the expense of others. Those around her also help pressure her into awareness of how her action affects others. Strict control of her bodily movements, with relentless attention to detail, is also encouraged by her seniors with sometimes zealous tenacity. The aesthetic of respect is taught through persistent attention to the numerous regulations that are rooted in the interpretation of reality that all existents are Buddha-nature. The following simple example reflects the extent to which respect is expected of nuns in the monastery. When a nun uses a rag to wipe a table, she is to treat the rag and the table with the same respect she should give Śākyamuni Buddha. While the table and rag are all Buddha-nature, they each have distinct purposes and needs. A nun shows respect to the table by carefully wiping it with a clean rag, not one that was used to wipe the floor. A nun shows respect to a rag by washing it thoroughly when finished cleaning with it and hanging it up so that it may dry properly, rather than making the rag sit in a dirty heap that will begin to smell. Respect is not an abstract emotion. Nuns are trained to understand that respect is doing what is necessary in an efficient manner.

Monastics learn that acting with deep respect according to the demands of necessity requires a nun to be focused solely upon the present moment. By paying keen attention to the present, she can learn the nature of impermanence. The nuns I studied teach that since beauty springs from the realities of life, the disciplines of necessity and respect also teach a nun the beauty of impermanence. This view is not unique to Zen nuns. From ancient times, Japanese have cultivated an aesthetic where impermanence is a vital element. Cherry blossoms are a poignant example of the Japanese understanding of the beauty of impermanence. These blossoms are prized for their beauty not merely for their delicate pink petals, but more for the fact that they dare to burst forth into the spring air with such profusion in the face of imminent death. In Indian Buddhist teachings, ignorance of impermanence is the source of suffering, but in Japanese culture, impermanence is a characteristic of beauty. In Japan, then, impermanence is not seen primarily as a source of suffering, but impermanence is a source for experiencing sublime beauty. This highly refined aesthetic finds beauty in the ephemeral nature of reality. According to the logic of this aesthetic, beauty is a quality of Buddha-nature.

In the context of traditional Japanese culture, beauty and discipline are inextricably interwoven. Without one, the other does not exist. Discipline is not perfect without beauty, and beauty does not occur without the perfection of discipline. To reach perfect discipline, the dichotomy between self and object must dissolve. This is the core of Dōgen's understanding of enlightenment as reflected in the lives of contemporary Sōtō Zen nuns.

Out of a shared orientation to the world, traditional Japanese art masters have passed down their insights by disciplining their students to perfect beauty. They stress that the creation of beauty requires cultivating the heart and training the body in the necessary skills of the art. By refining the form, the heart is also refined.[77] A master can quickly discern a disciple's level of discipline by seeing the art forms she or he has produced. Perfecting the discipline of a particular art form demands one understand the art of living. When the discipline of living is mastered, beauty blossoms.

One manifestation of the discipline of living is found in drinking, one of the most fundamental and natural activities in life. Concentrating on this basic activity, Japanese have refined the activity in such a way that learning the ritualized form of making and drinking tea can awaken one to the present moment as one learns to move efficiently and respectfully. It takes on the qualities of art. The various contemplative arts, however, are commonly understood in their Rinzai Zen formulation where art is a means to enlightenment. Indeed, Zen arts flourished within the Rinzai sect, where practice is done *in order to become* enlightened. In this scheme, art is understood as an expedient means (Skt. *upāya*) to actualizing enlightenment. Zen arts as a form of practice resonates with certain aspects of the "Six Arts" of the Confucian tradition: ritual, calligraphy, music, arithmetic, archery, and charioteering.[78] Heavy emphasis is placed on discipline of the body to perform rituals so purely that they become a natural response.[79] The Confucian tradition also recognizes that teaching the body is better than words, because teaching ritual disciplines the body. The perfection of form involves extreme discipline. Once disciplined, one can have freedom and go beyond the self. Rinzai Zen arts and the Six Arts in the Confucian tradition, however, differ in aim and purpose from the nuns' Zen practice based on Dōgen's teachings. In Rinzai Zen and the Confucian tradition, the purpose of disciplining the body is to become enlightened and to cultivate the budding sprouts of sagehood, respectively. In Dōgen's type of Zen, in contrast, Buddha-nature is already here and now—one just needs to actualize it. The nuns in the monastery are taught that for Dōgen, practice is not a means to the end, it is enlightenment itself. When practice is enlightenment, so, too, is the Buddha-nature of all things realized.

Therefore, in Sōtō Zen tea is not *for* something other than drinking. It is not a process that leads to something else. Each gesture is done with grace and efficiency for a concrete purpose in accomplishing the immediate task of serving and drinking tea. Strict attention is directed to detail so one develops powers of concentration on the concrete activity in the present moment. These are the basic tools of Buddha-nature—concentration on acting efficiently and respectfully in the present.

The distinction between Rinzai and Sōtō approaches should not, however, be overemphasized. The seven rules of drinking tea espoused by Sen no Rikyū (1521–1591), the renowned tea master who remained a Rinzai layperson, are in consonance with Sōtō focus on the primacy of necessity and respect:

> Make a delicious bowl of tea; lay the charcoal so that it heats the water; arrange the flowers as they are in the field; in summer suggest coolness, in winter, warmth; do everything ahead of time; prepare for rain; and give those with whom you find yourself every consideration.[80]

Rikyū holds that "in all of these we imitate the acts of the Buddha." "To take pleasure in the splendor of a dwelling or the delicate flavors of food belongs to worldly life. It is enough if the dwelling one uses does not leak and the food served suffices to stave off hunger: this is the teaching of the Buddha and the essential intent of tea."[81] The nuns' tea ceremony teacher notes that tea, like all activities — eating, cleaning, cooking — is an activity that you perfect by doing. Most of the time lessons concentrate on teaching the body the proper motions. She occasionally mentions that once the basic motions are under your control, it becomes obvious that without focused concentration deriving from the inner core of your being (heart, spirit), the form of the body cannot be perfected. If the entire being, heart, mind, and body are not fully engaged in the present moment, she underscores, perfection is not attained and beauty is elusive.

On rare moments when the tea ceremony teacher expounds on the virtues of the tea ceremony,[82] she explains how it is an expedient activity for teaching someone how to act in the refined manner of a Buddha. It is designed to cultivate four virtues — harmony (*wa*), respect (*kei*), purity (*sei*), and tranquillity (*jaku*). Refinement of necessary motion is cultivated in the tea ceremony. In refining a motion, the harmonious interrelatedness of all things becomes clear. Harmony is another way of referring to the Buddhist understanding of the interdependent nature of the phenomenal world. The teacher explains that when someone becomes aware of this harmony, the natural response to others is respect. Respect for each of the utensils means handling them gracefully and purposefully, for they too are Buddha-nature. Refining an act is also an expression of respect, she said. Purity extends from using clean utensils to purifying the heart and mind of vain concerns. Washing your hands at a well outside the tea hut is intended to remove the dust of the world from your hands and your heart; stooping through the low door to enter the tea room, you are to leave social rank and status outside. Only then do you enter the tea room to drink tea with friends as a simple human being. Refinement is to purify an action of all extraneous elements, leaving only tranquillity — life as it is. Creating tranquillity in the tea room is an opportunity to experience emptiness, to accept impermanence with grace. Desire, she explains, is a common obstacle to this beauty, so you must train your body to know sufficiency by cultivating patience (*gaman*). The opposite of patience is selfishness, born out of an ego that perceives the world revolving around itself, but patience leads to selflessness. Patience cannot be taught through the mind; it must be learned through the body. The slow pace of activities in the tea room disciplines you in the art of patience and opens the door to the world of the beauty of impermanence. Most of the time, however, these teachings are silent; a nun learns them through observing her teacher and fellow students, and especially by doing the actions with her own body.

I came to the conclusion that monastic practice is disciplined training in formal arts and the art of daily living. Sōtō nuns make it an explicit dimension of a nun's training, for it is in teaching art classes that perfection of body–mind harmony is cultivated. The art classes are designed to manifest the sublime beauty of efficiency, respect, and impermanence. When using the lessons in the tea room as a model for all activity, Aoyama teaches that one enters the world in which "emptiness is form and form is emptiness."[83] It demands focusing on presentational immediacy. In numerous ways, a nun is reminded in the monastery that when she is focused on the present, she can move like water and be *sunao*. Nuns see *sunao* as the virtue of accepting life-as-it-is with no resistance from the self-centered ego. Having this virtue enables one to respond to the present moment with compassion. One, however, cannot work at being *sunao*. *Sunao* is a natural result of having the strength and wisdom to accept whatever happens. Monastic discipline leads to experiencing beauty in each of these moments. Beauty must be learned through refining the body, because beauty is an experience of truth. Perfection of action transforms life into art.[84] For these nuns, a beautiful act is honed efficiency and respect. The perfection of discipline is beauty. In other words, beauty is "Buddha activity" manifest.

Monastic life is compelling, because it can be transformative. Through training the body, it concretely teaches what Buddha-nature is in all aspects of life. Women of all ages with various motivations and a broad range of backgrounds tumble together in their commitment to monastic Buddhist life. Through disciplined training, their bodies and minds understand the words Dōgen wrote in *Ikka Myōju* [One Bright Pearl]: "When one is a total body, there is no obstruction for it, it is graciously smooth and tumbles freely."[85] This is the key to the nuns' success in living according to their experience of Dōgen's tradition. Each day in the monastery is dedicated to actualizing Buddha activity by disciplining daily activities: from cleaning and performing rituals, to cooking, and sitting, and studying the *Shōbōgenzō*. Through its structure, regulations, curriculum, practices, and human relations, the monastery serves as a crucible in which discipline melts down the facade of individuated selves to realize the beauty of the Buddhist teachings.

FIVE

Motivations, Commitments, and Self-Perceptions

I was in full possession of body, speech, and mind.
With the root of craving uprooted,
I have become cool and quenched.[1]

W hy would a woman who has a successful career, the economic means to purchase whimsical and professional clothing, and the liberty to choose her own leisure activities—take English conversation classes, travel abroad, play tennis—want to relinquish this comfort and freedom to live an austere and regimented life with all its accompanying hardships and restrictions? Is she just a social anomaly who does not understand, or cannot handle, the complexity of the modern world? In a society where ultramodern conveniences in transportation and communications abound and many pursue economic prosperity as a panacea, what value is there in a woman who has committed her life to Buddhist teachings and traditional monastic life? Are her contributions significant and meaningful? What does *she* think of life as a twentieth-century Sōtō Zen Buddhist nun in Japan?

Answers to my questions about nuns' monastic experience could not be found in Sōtō Zen texts or institutional regulations. All Sōtō Zen monastics, male and female alike, begin the monastic path with a clean-shaven head and black robes when they take the same sixteen vows. Over the years, variations in the color and quality of robes begin reflecting a person's level in the religious hierarchy. Nevertheless, from a quick glance at the external appearance of traditional robes and clean-shaven heads, it is sometimes difficult to discern whether a monastic is male or female, or even whether the monastic is from the tenth, thirteenth, or twentieth century. Work clothes differ only in how worn they are. The doctrines of the Sōtō sect are uniform nationwide. Especially in the last century, the renewed interest and study of Dōgen's texts has brought together the teachings throughout the sect's temples and monasteries to focus upon the *Shōbōgenzō*.[2] Resulting from the concerted efforts of the nuns, during the last few decades all regulations issued by the sect headquarters are equal for men and women, including requirements for teaching and monastic ranks, temple status, and educational opportunities. Scriptures used in ritual ceremonies like the morning and evening services are standardized, and temples throughout the country rely upon the scripture book published by the sect headquarters. This book contains many texts important to the Sōtō sect, including the *Kannon-gyō*, the *Heart Sūtra*, a number of *darani* (Skt. *dhāraṇī*),[3] and the lineage list of Sōtō Zen masters. Sōtō Zen monasteries may vary in certain details and style, but they are basically similar.

My 1989–1990 survey and interview data offers a rare window on the self-perception of a significant number of nuns. These female monastics appear generally engaged with acting in accord with their vision of the "genuine" Zen monastic life. An example of their commitment to tradition is that, although for nearly 100 years the sect has officially permitted monks and nuns to marry,[4] a high percentage of monks acted upon these regulations[5] and the overwhelming majority of nuns did not. Traditionally monastics took a vow of celibacy, and laity took a vow to not engage in sexual misconduct. With the official permission to marry, monastics interpret their vows differently. The difference in response to the regulation on marriage and the divergence in interpretation of monastic vows has also led to a different temple lifestyle. Marriage comes with a host of other activities not commonly associated with monastic life: raising children, taking responsibility for supporting the family economically, and passing a temple on through hereditary channels. Monastics who do not marry have a temple lifestyle that is closer to the traditional monastic life. The changes in the activities of monastics spurred my inquiry into the nuns as a distinct group within the Buddhist structure. Such examination is indispensable for a more comprehensive understanding of Buddhism in modern Japan.

Although there are ebbs and flows, as indicated by the number of Sōtō monastic women over the last few decades—2,000 in 1911,[6] 2,380 in 1931,[7] 3,239 in 1958,[8] and 1,000 in 1990[9]—these women created enduring waves that continue to affect Japan today. Many of these women perceive their monastic experience to be fundamentally different from that of their male counterparts, especially in terms of motivation and attitude towards monastic vows in daily life.[10] A profile of the nuns is emerging through these data, thus elucidating the practical and cultural functions of Sōtō nuns in Japanese society.

While researching twentieth-century Sōtō Zen nuns in Japan, I heard many of them articulating a positive evaluation of their lives as nuns. I also observed many acting in ways that suggest this. What had been described as subservient, oppressive, and submissive activity by some scholars was apparently experienced by many nuns as unfair treatment that has been or is being rectified, opportunities to dissolve the ego, and patient understanding of others' misunderstanding of the Buddhist path. This chapter will focus primarily on how Zen nuns interpret their own lives. The answers are intricately tied to the method used to understand them. Data available through textual sources are minimal. The types of things available through public records or documents available through libraries (including documents at Sōtō sect headquarters) offer quantitative data such as the number of nuns, how many are in which rank, and educational level. Culling through Sōtō Zen texts and institutional regulations tells only part of the picture.

In order to understand the perspective of monastic women, obtaining firsthand information was a priority. To listen to nuns speak in their native tongue and observe them while living among them are the only methods by which the knowledge necessary for understanding their motivations, commitments, and self-perceptions can be harvested. Without direct interaction, the available statistics and materials would only dimly reflect their vitality, creativity, and the richness of their lives. Listening to the voices and seeing the actions of numerous Zen nuns reveals a commitment to monastic life that resists characterizations of nuns as inferior members of the monastic community or women who could not thrive in the "real world."

Ethnographic data are indispensable to assess the significance of the data available and to provide more information. Aware that the nature of information sought required personal interaction and responses, and that many Sōtō Zen nuns are suspicious of the intentions of scholars, my first task was to gain their trust. In 1990, I spent four months cloistered in the main Sōtō Zen nuns' monastery and another nine months living in an apartment of one of the monastery's teachers, located in a temple near the monastery. Since then, I have continued close contact with many of these nuns. It was only after spending six months living closely with Sōtō nuns that I compiled a series of questions that would help elicit a broader and deeper understanding of the various aspects of a nun's life. The abbess of the largest nunnery, Aoyama Shundō, reviewed the questions and slightly modified them. Only after having received her approval and permission did I send surveys to 150 Sōtō nuns all over the country.[11] A representative group of nuns was chosen according to the criteria of age, region, and involvement in various activities. The response rate was overwhelming. Not only did nearly 40% return the long and involved survey, but they wrote lengthy and detailed responses.[12] Only one survey was returned with just the multiple choice answers circled, with no written comments. Most, however, were filled with expressions of gratitude for a meaningful life as a nun. A number of nuns wrote honestly about the hardships of this life, and several offered their prayers for this work.[13] In addition to the survey responses, hours of intensive interviews and conversations with teachers and elders in the nuns' community helped me gain a fuller picture of the conditions of Sōtō nuns in contemporary Japan. After having received permission from the abbess, I also conducted extensive interviews of all the novices with whom I was in training. They helped me understand the motivations of women who choose to commit their lives to Zen training in the modern age. This is the first scholarly inquiry into the subjective experience of Zen nuns, a rare glimpse into their personal backgrounds, motivations, values about religious practice, attitudes towards monks, perceptions of society's views of them, thoughts on social responsibility, and self-reflections on life as a Zen nun.

Aiming to deepen the understanding of various aspects of the lives and attitudes of Sōtō Zen nuns, this chapter concentrates upon my analysis of the roles, meaning, and praxis of nuns in contemporary Japanese institutional, social, and cultural context. My inquiry seeks to develop an interpretive analysis of Sōtō Zen nuns' niche in modern Japanese Buddhism. The numerous quotes from interviews and survey responses of nuns remain anonymous, except where permission was sought and granted. For the purpose of making some of the stories of novice nuns more accessible, I used fictitious names. The only actual names used are the teachers' names. Allowing the monastic women to speak for themselves, albeit in my translation, enables readers to at least passively enter into the conversation.

The material we are dealing with in this chapter is based primarily on their construction of their personal history. That they describe their lives in such positive terms tells us about the meaningfulness they experience in their lives. So it is not surprising that the responses do not show the tensions of daily life in the monastery spelled out, as done in chapter 4. That information was primarily based on participant-observation, not their own assessment of their lives. All nuns I spoke with on the matter, however, did say that human relations were the most difficult part of the practice, but none elaborated with details of those experiences. This tells us that the details are not important to them. What is important for us to note is that the participant-observation method yielded the struggle and process involved in negotiating the ideals, while the interviews and surveys yielded the positive evaluations. This highlights the need for both methods.

The nuns' responses to interview or survey questions are sometimes quite similar, but their range is also rich with diversity in background, motivation, personality, age, and notions of Buddhist practice. As with all members of society, monastics are also constantly affected by, adapting to, and shaping the world around them. Their actions over the years, however, reveal a sustained commitment to simplicity, hard work, and caring for others. On the whole, their reflections upon their lives as Zen nuns are positive and suggest that it is a meaningful and fulfilling life. Since the majority of nuns expressed such positive views—despite having endured hardships due to unfair sect regulations and years of war—this suggests that these nuns are trying to live according to Buddhist teachings. The one that they invoke most frequently is: suffering is diminished when each event is seen as an opportunity to practice. Their stories and comments animate the rich and colorful detail of their individual lives.

The vast majority of nuns I interviewed and surveyed suggested that their main concern is in leading meaningful lives, and they happen to find the lifestyle of a Zen nun the most fulfilling. For them, it is the most expedient way to their goal. They do not interpret obstacles such as unfair treatment as a poor reflection on themselves. Rather, the discriminatory treatment is invariably seen as a resource that affords them the opportunity to get closer to their articulated goal of living compassionately and gratefully. They seem to have a keen awareness that the fundamental problem in doing such is reifying the self. So, the nuns use the unfair sect regulations and any person who might have treated them unfairly as a reminder that the nuns themselves are still in need of more practice. In a number of notable ways, nuns responding with increased commitment to pare down the ego in the face of unfair treatment did not lead to increased oppression by the

male-dominated sect institution. Instead, the nuns' actions frequently led to increased opportunities, egalitarian regulations, and a higher education. Precisely
because it is part of their serious Buddhist practice, they are not inclined to ad-
vertise how they accomplished so many things. So, they have not written about
it. Talking with the nuns who experienced this was the only way to learn of their
quiet and effective method of dealing with oppressive treatment.

Changing Life Patterns of
Twentieth-Century Zen Nuns

Reflecting the rapidly changing social structure and cultural values, differences
that have arisen between women who entered the monastery during the first half
of the century versus those who have entered more recently are particularly apparent in the circumstances surrounding their decision to commit themselves to
a monastic life. The other phases in the life of a nun—ordination, training, temple
life, and the role as an elder in the community, whether formally or informally
teaching and leading—have not changed as much. To highlight the two major
patterns in the twentieth century, this discussion of the motivations of nuns is
divided into two parts, nuns ordained before 1960 and after 1960.

One pattern is represented by the older generation who entered the temple at
a young age. Before 1960, the nuns' community was constituted primarily of
women who came from large families that had a close relationship with a temple
long before a daughter would consider the monastic life. When a family had many
children, these families that had a close relationship with a temple considered it
a pious and reasonable thing to let a child go to the temple to be raised as a
monastic. Roughly 60% of the women ordained before 1960 had a family-related
reason for entering the monastic life.[14] The vast majority of these women took
their monastic vows in their mid-teens and entered the monastery for an average
of five years of training. Their young bodies learned the monastic way of life
without much question or resistance. To wake up meant to wake up early. To
clean meant to clean impeccably and constantly. Their bodies became accustomed to a strict way of life, so they could endure more later in life. Upon graduation they would assist their teacher in running her temple. Eventually the temple would be passed along to the disciple to head. She, in turn, would take in a
disciple. Today these nuns are the leaders of temples.

The other pattern has arisen during recent decades. Since 1960, the pattern
and context of women who enter the monastic life has shifted significantly. The
size of families has rapidly decreased. Hasekawa, the current abbess of Toyama
Senmon Nisōdō, explains that after the war people have had fewer children. Before
the war, the average farming family had eight children; now the average is two.
The reasons for families having fewer children vary, but the nuns say that the
primary cause for the decrease in the number of women entering the monastic
life is the trend toward smaller families. Most families are reluctant to let their
only daughter become a nun. Therefore, a daughter who desires to pursue the

life of a nun usually explores the depth of her commitment before she faces her family. This phenomenon yields fewer novitiates, but invariably results in women being clearly determined and highly motivated to lead a monastic life.

Another factor that contributes to the diminishing numbers of novitiates is the expanding gap between modern life and monastic life. The average household has a markedly more comfortable lifestyle than in the past, so it is harder for people to commit themselves to the austere life of a monastic. Fewer people are choosing the monastic lifestyle,[15] for it is radically different from the comforts and freedoms to which they have become accustomed. The monastic life is not harder than it was before, reflected Abbess Hasekawa; it is only harder in contrast to the average lay life.[16] Many people are daunted by the difficulty, leaving only the extremely determined and dedicated to undertake the monastic path.

A third type of fundamental change in monastic life of women in modern Japan is the increase in the age of the average novice, which in the early 1990s was forty-three years. Most of the women are near this age, but there are a few cases of rather young (nineteen) and quite old (seventy) novices. The trend toward entering at more mature ages means that the more recently ordained women bring a wealth of diverse life experiences with them, such as marriage, children, and careers. These women also enter with a higher level of education, reflecting the general increase in Japanese educational levels nationwide.

Women who enter at a more advanced age have a harder time adjusting to the rigorous pace of monastic life. As an abbess, Hasekawa tries to find a balance between demanding strict adherence to the monastic discipline and understanding the changing circumstances of incoming novices. Primarily, this means placing fewer physical demands on the novices. The former abbess of Niigata Senmon Nisōdō, Nakamura Busshin (b. 1903), has sentiments similar to those of Hasekawa.[17] Nakamura reflected that, in general, the training is not as intense as before. Like Hasekawa, she also attributed this to the standard of living in Japan today having dramatically increased in the last few decades.

A fifth point is that most female novitiates have not had any notable affiliation with temple life before pursuing the monastic path. The contribution of these factors results in a striking difference between the recent novitiates and the women ordained before 1960. The situation is more complex now. These differences reflect emerging differences in the motivations of the two distinct patterns.

The following responses from nuns represent those in the first pattern; their ages range from 51 to 70. Their responses to the question on motivation for becoming a monastic confirm that their families, the primary decisionmaking body, had personal connections that led to a daughter's ordination. The response of one elderly nun clearly indicates that her parents had determined that she would become a nun, for when questioned about her motivation in deciding to become a nun she replied, "I do not know, since I was an infant."[18] At age 70, however, she has not wavered from the course she had been set upon by her parents. She was not the only one who entered the monastic life because of her parent's will; other nuns responded to inquiries of their motivation to become a nun in a similar fashion. One nun who went on to attain the monastic equivalent to a master's degree (*kenkyūsei*) flatly stated that she had no motivation, "since I entered the nun's temple when I was something under five years old."[19] Another woman who had been a nun for nearly five decades remembers going to her aunt's, a nun, "and it happened naturally."[20] It is evident that this was not an unusual course. Another accomplished nun's recollections of the events around her entry into the monastic life are analogous; she recounts this significant turning point in her life in some detail:

> I have six siblings. When I was five, my parents thought it would be good to have one child become ordained. On August twenty-second my father took me to the temple for annual ancestor rites. The monk said I looked O.K., so I stayed until the twenty-sixth helping out. Having *"en"* (a profound connection) things stayed like that, and I became a nun.[21]

Another woman replied that her motivation was due to the unfortunate circumstance that her mother died when she was quite young.[22] The responses do not suggest what the parents' motivations were in choosing the monastic life for their daughters. It is likely that it was a combination of religious and socioeconomic reasons. The circumstances under which these nuns first entered the temple life, however, did not guarantee that they would remain a monastic for the duration of their lives. So, what we do learn from the responses is that the nuns who entered the monastic path because of parental decision did not reject it after becoming an adult. Many of the responses suggest that they have no regrets for having lived their life as a nun. On the contrary, the majority of these nuns express gratitude for their lives as monastics.

Although the decision to become a monastic was often a family decision, at least during the first half of this century, there was sometimes room for individual choice in the matter. This became clear in a number of the responses elderly nuns gave to the question of their motivation to be a monastic. Many indicated that when it became a family matter to have a child go to the temple, the girls who eventually became nuns said they, rather than their siblings, had clearly chosen to go to the temple. In such cases, one child had usually shown keen interest and curiosity in temple life. A seventy-six-year-old nun declared with conviction that "Since I have a number of relatives who are ordained Buddhists, I entered the Buddhist gate on my own accord at age ten."[23] With a hint of precocity a nun definitively affirms that "It was my wish when I was five."[24] Another nun reflects that "as a child my heart was moved by the compassion of a nun."[25] Some nuns admit that, as is typical of children, they were attracted by the flowing robes of the nuns, while others were drawn into the mysteries of the incense and Buddhist carvings. More than one nun laughed while divulging her untold reason for being attracted to the temple was that she would receive special cakes whenever she went to the temple. Though the beginnings may have been naive in some instances, as they matured in their practice they maintained their sometimes inexplicable commitment to lead a monastic life. This tells us that the children probably came from families where the value of Buddhist teachings was a priority. Monastic life was a positive option, not an escape. To have made such a definite decision at a young age, many of them must have had a respectable level of confidence in themselves and the monastic path. Even if the responses do not express the complete circumstances involving their decision to become a monastic, they do reflect a high value of monastic life and a distinct level of self-confidence.

Only a few women said their families forced them against their will. The pain is still perceptible in the words of a nun who did not understand why her parents had decided she lead the life of a monastic. "When I was six I was received by a temple. It seemed like I was forced into it. I thought that it was because I was not suitable for marriage."[26] Another nun reflects a certain tone of anger, "Since I was the daughter of a temple, I was ordered by my parents."[27] Nonetheless, she has remained a nun for nearly fifty years. These nuns did not mince words in their responses. This suggests that their misunderstanding and anger are genuine. It is quite possible that they might not be alone in having had bad experiences with their families' authoritarian decisions. Others may not have written about it because they no longer harbor ill feelings about the situation, and they did not want to bring it up in a formal survey. Or perhaps some may not have indicated their negative feelings because they value the ideals of the monastic tradition, and they did not want the image tainted in a public investigation. I have no data to support my speculations, but they seem like important possibilities.

Many nuns developed deep motivating forces that compelled them to devote their entire lives to the discipline of Buddhist monastic life. Den Taikan, writing in 1923, denounced the simplistic notions that people have in regard to a woman's motivation to become a nun. Taikan affirms that the critical element is that nuns have faith in themselves as nuns.[28] A fifty-nine-year-old university graduate who went on to attain the highest degree the monastery offers (*tokusō*) explains her motivation for becoming a nun: "I thought that since I have received life, I wanted to lead a life without regrets. I looked for that way, and this is the result of my search."[29] Her comments indicate the seriousness with which she understands the significance of her life and the value of Buddhist monastic life.

Other women who were deeply affected by World War II also found profound meaning in monastic life. One seventy-year-old nun discloses that, "since many of my relatives were killed in the war, [I entered] for the purpose of Buddhist service for the repose of the dead."[30] As might be expected from a tragedy of that war's magnitude, she was not alone:

> Many people passed away, both domestically and abroad, during World War II. I became a renunciant to mourn for these people's enlightenment. However, after I graduated from university, since the society was in a precarious state of affairs, I thought of participating in the movement to educate, and I did Buddhist work (*samu*) as an educator.[31]

In the face of the tragedies of war, both of these nuns found Buddhist monastic life valuable. Their explanations do not indicate that they saw monastic life as an escape from the tragedies. The monastic life seems to offer them a way to go on living, not just for themselves, but also for those who died.

One nun who was born after the war, graduated from the university, and also graduated with the highest degree offered by the monastery, gave a basic Buddhist response. She stated that her reason for committing herself to the monastic Buddhist life was due to a "sense of impermanence (*mujōkan*)."[32] According to Buddhist teachings, impermanence is the fundamental characteristic of reality. In this context, it is appropriate, if not ideal, that one renounce householder life to devote oneself to realizing enlightenment. Here, renunciation is not viewed as an escape from the difficulties and problems in life. On the contrary, it is viewed as a positive response that reflects their awareness of the need to learn more about what is important in life.

The second pattern of monastic women comes from more diverse backgrounds and experiences than those in the first group. The motivations of women who have sought ordination more recently reflect that many women are first establishing their independence from their parents before considering the monastic life. Put another way, the majority of women who seek ordination today have had their own careers and/or families first. Ironically, most of the women do not come from a family with relations to a temple, but a number of these women felt that they had finally "returned home" when they entered a temple.

A middle-aged nurse named Tamura was typical of the women who have no direct connection with a religious person or institution, yet are searching for deeper meaning and peace in their lives. Tamura's life was characterized by the emotional overload and physical fatigue that often accompanies hospital emergency room work. Although the level of skill, discipline, and commitment required of a medical professional who specializes in emergency cases rivals in degree and importance that of a nun, she was not satisfied with her life. This immediately tells us that her values in life are not limited to typical secular concerns, for either career—nurse or nun—is considered both worthy and respectable. Knowing nothing about Zen, she leafed through the Tokyo telephone book in quest of a deeper peace. To squeeze more activity into her already strained schedule made convenient times and quick access of paramount importance. The difference between Rinzai and Sōtō Zen was immaterial to her. Though unaware at the time, Tamura's fate was sealed when she discovered that the branch temple of the Sōtō sect's Head Temple, Eihei-ji Betsuin, was convenient to the hospital in which she worked. Having never done zazen, she was excited to attend the weekly Wednesday sittings. "It fit with what I respect." Tamura reflected back to that first time when the pain was so great that she could not sit properly:

> I was in a life where everything was hectic, and to immediately leave that and instantly enter this world was wonderful. It was an ineffable feeling. After we finished zazen, three monks served tea and cakes to everyone. My heart was dried out. I kept wondering, is there really this kind of world? I liked it.[33]

The environment was precisely what she had been seeking. It was not that she did not have a meaningful life as a nurse, but she knew there was more and her desire ran deep. Tamura's decision to become a renunciant does not sound like a negative evaluation of her life as a nurse so much as it sounds like a positive view of the life of a monastic. Zen seemed to offer her more than she had in her already meaningful life. It was the awareness of a fuller life that drew her to renunciation.

Tamura's story indicates that the monastic women's community has shifted to a more intentional community. Unlike the nuns who were committed to monastic life as children, women now are exploring various possibilities. The experience of Sasaki is another example that suggests this trend. When she was in her early forties, she had a career in the municipal government. Sasaki began pursuing a religious path, in part because people described her as "a fish out of water."[34] She says of herself:

> When I became a nun I was like a fish in water. You can tell that I am happy to be a nun just by looking at me. I thought the same when I shaved my head. I feel like I have become more myself. When I had hair and worked in the society, I did not feel right. When I became a nun, I felt like, 'Oh, this is where I belong.' It feels like I have returned to my native home (*furusato*).[35]
>
> When I shaved my head I did not cry at all. When I vowed to take refuge in the Buddha, tears just gushed and gushed. When I held my hands up together in worship and faced the Buddha, the tears flowed freely. My teacher came and wiped my face with a handkerchief. I was so happy!! I cried. If you do not have that kind of feeling, you should not become a monastic.[36]

Her warning that one should not become a monastic unless one feels this kind of peace and happiness indicates that her motivation to become a nun was not born out of a rejection of her life as a municipal worker so much as a recognition that her life would be better as a nun. Although it appeared to be a radical step, she experienced it as a homecoming. Many of Sasaki's fellow employees in the government office probably cannot imagine that their colleague would feel it is more natural to have a shorn head and lead an austere and regimented life, but she is a lucid example of the profound meaning the commitment to Buddhist teachings can have to someone even amid earthquake-proof skyscrapers and commuter rails that run like clockwork.

Tamura and Sasaki are not alone in their view that there is a sublime life outside the glossy finish of late twentieth-century urban Japan. Another woman, Nagawa, who was in training at the same time as Tamura and Sasaki, had also left a full career behind because the life of a monastic had more meaning to her. Nagawa, like the others, did not have any background in Buddhism until she was approaching the age of fifty. Her first exposure to Buddhist monastic life was through the books of the abbess, Aoyama Shundō. As she was returning from a business trip, Nagawa was in a bookstore looking for a book to read while riding the "bullet train" home, and her eye caught the title of Aoyama's book on tea and zen. Having a deep interest in the traditional arts, she became thoroughly absorbed in the book. Upon arriving at her home station, she immediately went to her local bookstore and ordered all of Aoyama's books. She learned about the women's monastery from the jacket on one of the books. After reading all the books, she called the abbess in November. The abbess's usual response to these types of telephone calls is first to invite the caller to a Zen retreat before speaking with her in depth;[37] there are far more such inquiries than she can manage. If the person is genuinely serious, she always finds time to meet. Enduring a Zen retreat is a clear indication of the level of one's sincerity. Knowing nothing more than the dates of the retreat, Nagawa arranged her business schedule accordingly, and on December first she set off to the monastery in Nagoya. She admits later that had she known it was the most difficult retreat of the year, *Rōhatsu Sesshin*, she would have politely put it off until January. She remarks, "I did not know anything when I first sat. My body did not feel like my own."[38] When she left home, her intention was to do the retreat so she could have a conversation with the abbess, and she never dreamed that she would have the feelings that she did:

> In one week I decided. I told Aoyama Sensei that I would come back in three months. Aoyama Sensei said that I must still return for the monthly retreats. I agreed. In the end it took me four months to finish my job and return. Looking back it seems unbelievable that I could have changed so much in that time. I feel impermanence so clearly now.
>
> Before I did this, I had been raised as the youngest child in a very spoiled manner. Although there was talk of marriage, I thought that if I had gotten married like that I would ruin my life. Even though I knew it would be an inconvenience to everyone, I wanted to go out in the world once. I could have passed as a cute bride, but I wanted to do more. At that time my personality changed a bit. There were many times, of course, that I wanted to cry, but I always told myself that I would take time to cry after I hurdled this mountain. Or, I will cry after I cross this river. I came this far with rarely shedding a tear. Now, at every retreat, things penetrate me so deeply, and I cry so much that I wonder what happened to the me that once did not cry. I cannot stop the tears now. It seems like I have returned to my natural self.
>
> Since I decided to become a monastic, the most difficult thing has been to suppress my own ego and ideas. Up until now, I had been the highest ranked female employee of my company, just under the president. Therefore, I am very accustomed to giving orders. But, until now, I had never been used to just answering "yes." There is nothing that is simple, because my life has changed 180 degrees. The first pain is waking up in the morning. Also, there is the pain of meal time. Sitting is also painful. I have had to change from a life where up until now I freely sat in soft chairs, and now I must sit on hard wood! Without a cushion! There hasn't been anything comfortable, but this is what I desired. So, it does not turn into suffering. It feels like coming home.[39]

It is quite stunning to hear that a successful career woman who had no prior significant experiences with monastic Buddhism could know after tasting this life for just one week—the most intense week of the year—that this was her true home. After devoting decades of her life to developing a respectable career and triumphing over the challenges of being a businesswoman, she had the perspicuity to see what she really wanted: to be a Zen Buddhist nun.

Her reflections reveal that she had a desire to seek something more from life than that which was readily apparent. She knew that marriage, the most conventional and accepted path, would not lead her to her "home." She succeeded in her choice to be a professional business woman, although she does not deny that following this more uncommon path was difficult. She did not find "home" or her "natural self" here either, but she did not relent. A brief encounter with the monastic life was all she needed to recognize what she had been seeking for decades. The more "permanent" paths of marriage and career were abandoned for the environment in which she feels most natural, a life that appreciates impermanence. It seems that another part of the appeal of the monastic path is that suffering is a significant facet of it. Unlike the Indian Buddhist view, suffering is not the negative result of ignorance of impermanence. In Nagawa's worldview, shared by many in Japan, suffering is understood as the key to maturity and beauty. Suffering is a necessary ingredient; it is the key to bliss. In Zen monastic life, Nagawa found her natural self in the impermanent home where beauty is the cultivated fruit of suffering.

Another woman the same age as Nagawa took a longer path to being a nun, but no less deliberate. Yamada first arrived in Nagoya for a Zen retreat eight years before she was finally ordained; she was stunned to find the abbess of the monastery was a nun she had seen on television years before. Reminiscing over that time sparked enthusiasm in her voice and a reverential warmth in her eyes, "I thought she was a beautiful person, and that if I was going to become a nun I would like to have her as my teacher. I did not want to be initiated at a monk's temple."[40] Yamada had decided as a young girl that she wanted to become a nun and lead a life of solitude. With the conviction that she had found the right place, she told Aoyama about her hopes of becoming a nun. As usual, Aoyama did not mince words in her response, "Frankly, the desire or dream to become a nun would not be enough to become a nun." "She told me to commute to the monthly retreats for a year." Even though the number of nuns is rapidly diminishing, it is clear that Aoyama is not moved to attract women who are not absolutely serious. Eight years of commuting by all-night train to the monthly Zen retreats at the women's monastery in Nagoya culminated when she finally pleaded with the abbess, "Please let me stay. I will not find peace otherwise. I have been here ever since."[41]

These stories of women who left their careers to become nuns illustrate that the profile of many nuns first entering the nunnery has undergone a considerable shift. Rather than having been raised in a temple environment—like the majority of women who were ordained before 1960—nuns now frequently enter the monastery from a lay family. Indeed, 56% of the women who became monastics before 1960 had a blood relation who was a monastic. Aunts were the primary link, which suggests a lateral pattern of heredity. Moreover, just forty years ago the average entering age of a nun was sixteen years, but the average entering age by 1990 had risen to forty-three years. These facts alone suggest the various other differences in the composition of the novice nuns now versus that in the 1950s. The majority of women entering now have had their own families or careers before taking their robes, whereas in the past the tender age at which most women shaved their heads precluded other life experiences. The women now give up other concrete options as they make their conscious and mature decisions to commit their lives to Buddhist monasticism.

Although the differences are substantive, these nuns do seem to share some similarities with the forest monks Michael Carrithers studied in Sri Lanka. They both want more than the secular world offers:

> Indeed, if we are to seek a single socially effective cause, which would underlie a single dominant motive among the welter of motives through which renunciation is initiated, it would be this, that to become a forest monk is a heroic and laudable choice, a destiny that appeals to romance and high hopes rather than to misery and desperation to escape.[42]

Monastic life is not *against* something so much as it is *for* something more. Monastic life involves a great deal of serious effort, and it is unlikely that someone who is not genuinely committed to it will continue along that path, especially in a climate where there are numerous options. Again, Carrithers' observations about the life of forest monks in Sri Lanka could apply to the life of Sōtō Zen nuns in modern Japan: ". . . the life is both physically and mentally difficult, and those who truly cannot organize themselves, or who are seriously disordered, soon fall away."[43] Aoyama gives a common illustration to drive her point home in a lecture she delivered at the women's monastery in Nagoya during a Zen retreat on October 3, 1989. She cautioned that if you became a nun as an escape, you will not find peace. You would give up after the first trial. "Just like when you button a shirt, if you start with the wrong button, you will have wrong buttons all the way down."

The types of women who choose to become a nun in the late twentieth century in Japan are predominantly women who were already successful people. Their choice to become a monastic makes sense if one understands the depth of their religious values. In this also, Carrithers' findings and my data suggest that relatively conservative and strict modes of monastic life have similar features. Carrithers found that three of nine forest monks not only would have been successful in anything they chose, but they would also be influential. He concludes that each of them chose to become a forest monk because it is a noble life.[44]

Moreover, the writings of nuns from ancient India and the reflections of nuns in modern Japan also have common elements. Although a direct comparison between these two groups of nuns—divided by numerous centuries, seas, and countries—is not intended, contemporary Sōtō Zen nuns make the point that both groups of nuns reflect a strong commitment to a Buddhist life of renunciation.[45] I. B. Horner's interpretation of the women of the *Therīgāthā* suggests that the women seeking the monastic life in ancient India were sincerely pursuing a deeper and more meaningful life:

> They [almswomen] thought of it [entry into the Order] as securing the means of self-realization and a larger and fuller field for mental activity, more vital than that of the domestic circle. . . . They were animated solely by the desire for a real search for enlightenment, for it was the religious life as such that they recognized to be their genuine vocation. They did not seek it as an escape from an existence which they could no longer endure; but knew it to be the life they would prefer above all other to lead. . . . Renunciation is looked upon as a privilege where Freedom, Insight, Peace are to be the gains.[46]

This resonates with contemporary Zen nuns, regardless of the likely differences in what constitutes "a deeper and more meaningful life." It is notable, nonetheless, that women for dozens of centuries in disparate cultures have found the life of a Buddhist nun to be profoundly meaningful.

The formal survey responses from Zen nuns, young and old, novitiates and mature elders, were confirmed by their actions: Their commitment to living in accord with Buddhist teachings is genuinely deep. None entertain delusions that becoming a nun will dissolve all their problems. They know it is not a life of physical or spiritual comfort, for it is not an easy path to freedom, insight, and peace. Cultures have flourished and waned, societies have undergone radical transformation of governmental structures and economic systems, but the necessity for relentless discipline and serious desire required to continue on the path of a Buddhist renunciant has remained steadfast over the millennia.

Aoyama, the current abbess of the women's monastery in Nagoya, reflects on her understanding of the life of a renunciant. She admits that she chose the life of a renunciant precisely because her desire ran so deep.[47] She wants eternal bliss and nothing less. With the knowledge born out of experience, Aoyama notes that you will work very hard when you deeply desire something. You will lose sleep and persevere. What monastics want is greater than money, fame, and family. Śākyamuni wanted it deeply, too, according to Aoyama's interpretation. He advised that one should not remain with one's family when pursuing this path, but it is important to be with others who are on the same path. There is strength in numbers.[48] Even Aoyama admits it is hard to wake up early every morning after minimal sleep when all alone, but it is easier when you are in a group that does so. This is the fundamental principle behind a communal monastic life. Aoyama elaborates on her insight into human nature and the meaning of renunciation:

> Renunciation is a 180-degree transformation of the value of things. One feels that all happiness is possible if only there is money, so one runs around to obtain money. However, the world is not that well designed. Human beings, gratefully, are not made that way.
>
> Even when one's every wishes are granted just as one likes, those with a heart will hear the wind in the depth of their breast. Once one senses this doubt, those who begin to hear the sound of this wind will hear it evermore. This is the gate to religiosity. Renunciation is the path of those who understand this gate. Renunciation is the path of those who seriously understand the joy of truth.
>
> People think of themselves as adorable. For one's whole lifetime one will not change. But no one knows when it will end. Everyone wants to live to the fullest and live without regrets. People who renunciate are resolved to being happy. Nuns do not abandon the world; rather, we clearly recognize this world with respect. It is not casting off the world, but understanding unequivocally the genuine joy of this world. This is renunciation.[49]

Aoyama's pithy definition of renunciation also offers insight into the aims and types of people who renunciate. She indicates that those who become renunciants are those who are unsatisfied, and they want to experience genuine happiness. The route to happiness is exactly the opposite of the conventional aims in which householders are engaged. She claims, however, that renunciation does not necessitate leaving the world. Joy can be found in the world. The key is to respect life. In so doing, the truth will emerge, accompanied by bliss. Aoyama's description of renunciation clearly states that renunciation is not a negative action. The foundation of her values is based on Buddhist teachings; to her, therefore, renunciation is a positive step toward a more meaningful and fulfilling life. Indeed, she views renunciation as the highest path.

Table 5-1 Family
background of Sōtō
Nuns

Agrarian	48%
White collar	30%
Temple	19%
Labor	3%

A general overview of the women's family background, education, and accomplishments in teaching and monastic ranks will help fill out the picture of who these monastic women are (tables 5.1 and 5.2). In the older generation that responded to the questionnaire and the younger generation that was interviewed, one-third of the women came from farm families. This is not unexpected, since the Sōtō sect is primarily traditionally composed of people with an agrarian background (48%). In addition, 30% were from white-collar families, while 19% were from temple families—meaning that the nun's father was a priest—and 3% were engaged in labor. With little exception, the recent novices have at least completed high school. One-third of the older generation went through *Joshi Kōtōshogakkō*, which was the minimum of the national compulsory education, comparable to high school.[50] The level of education of nuns also seems to correspond to parental levels of education and stature in society.[51]

Nuns are now eligible for the full range of degrees and certificates offered by the Sōtō sect. They authorize the recipient to teach at various levels and hold positions of responsibility in the temple hierarchy. The results of my 1990 survey of Sōtō monastic women show that the average rank of female monastics had increased over the last four decades (table 5.3). In 1950, 1,245 nuns ranked at some level of religious teacher.[53] An overwhelming majority of the nuns (94%) was qualified to be the lowest rank of teacher, that is, Third Rank Teacher (*Santō Kyōshi*). By 1990 the tides had shifted. Almost one-half of the nuns (46%) had attained the Second Rank Teacher (*Nitō Kyōshi*) level by 1990, whereas in 1950 less than 5% had attained that degree. Likewise, 31% were First Rank Teacher (*Ittō Kyōshi*) in 1990, when only 1% were at that rank in 1950. The progress of monastic women is most clearly seen in the statistic that 23% of the nuns in 1990

Table 5-2 Highest Secular
Education of Sōtō Nuns in
1990

Middle School	5%
Jogakkō	26%
High School	44%
Jr. College	10%
Undergraduate	13%
Graduate School	2%

Table 5-3 Religious Teacher Ranks (highest to lowest)

	1950	1990
Supreme Head Master (*Daikyōsei*)		
Head Master (*Gon Daikyōsei*)		
Head Teacher (*Daikyōshi*)		2%
Associate Head Teacher (*Gon Daikyōshi*)		2%
Full Rank Teacher (*Seikyōshi*)		19%
First Rank Teacher (*Ittō Kyōshi*)	1%	31%
Second Rank Teacher (*Nitō Kyōshi*)	5%	46%
Third Rank Teacher (*Santō Kyōshi*)	94%	
First Rank Assistant Teacher (*Ittō Kyōshiho*)		
Second Rank Assistant Teacher (*Nitō Kyōshiho*)		

had attained even more advanced ranks, while no nuns in 1950 were included in these higher ranks.

The various monastic titles authorize monastics to head the commensurate level of temple and perform special rituals. In terms of these ranks the nuns in 1990 also fared much better than their 1950 counterparts (table 5.4). For example, 55% of nuns in 1990 had won the respected monastic rank of Preceptor (*Oshō* when in 1950 only 11% were granted this title. Only 2% of the nuns in 1990 had the title Monastic Hall Leader (*Zagen*), just below Preceptor (*Oshō*), while 43% in 1950 were kept at this rank. No nun in 1990 was in the lowest rank, Assistant Monastic Hall Leader (*Jōza*), but almost a majority of nuns (46%) in 1950 filled this rank. A compelling example of the changes in recent decades is the fact that 43% of Sōtō nuns had won the highest monastic title, Great Preceptor (*Daioshō*), by 1990, but no nun was granted this title in 1950.

These figures represent the marked increase in monastic women's educational opportunities, but they also reflect that by 1990 the requirements for the various degrees became equal for men and women. In 1950, the requirements were not only steeper for women, but in many cases, no matter how competent or qualified a monastic woman was, she was not permitted to attain the higher levels. It is fair to conclude, then, that women in the 1990s have better opportunities and greater official recognition for their achievements than the women forty years ago, but this does not lead to the conclusion that the women forty years ago were any less competent, capable, and hard working. It is, rather, due to their tremendous perseverance, concerted effort, and insight into Buddhist teachings that they were

Table 5-4 Monastic Ranks (highest to lowest)

	1950	1990
Great Preceptor (*Daioshō*)		43%
Preceptor (*Oshō*)	11%	55%
Monastic Hall Leader (*Zagen*)	43%	2%
Assistant Monastic Hall Leader (*Jōza*)	46%	

successful in changing the sect regulations regarding degrees and in improving educational facilities for monastic women today.

These nuns do not sound or act oppressed. They do not indicate that they think there is something they cannot do because they are women.

Buddhist Practice: Meaning and Action

Sōtō Zen nuns today are taught that Dōgen's fundamental teaching about Buddhist practice is: Practice *is* enlightenment (*shushō ittō*). His explicit and detailed instructions about many daily activities clarify a common misunderstanding. Throughout any given day in the monastery they are reminded that this does *not* mean *all* activity is enlightenment. Had he meant "all activity is enlightenment," there would be little meaning in monastics vowing to live in accord with any precepts. Yet Dōgen did predicate his monastic life on sixteen precepts, and they have continued to be the foundation of Sōtō Zen monasticism. In the last century, however, the meanings of the precepts have been questioned, challenging the very fabric of monasticism itself.

I asked the nuns a number of questions designed to elicit their interpretation of the meaning of practice. Their responses led me to further questions. Where do nuns stand on the issue of precepts? What do they think practice means? Do they try to live according to Dōgen's teachings? Perhaps the better question to ask is: What do their actions tell us about how they interpret Dōgen's teachings? How has this shaped their activities and involvement with society?

Aoyama, along with the vast majority of nuns in modern Japan, maintains that it is more important to keep the standards high than to dilute the demands of monastic life in order to increase numbers.[54] This was made clear in the nuns' responses to questions regarding the meaning and importance of abiding by the monastic discipline. The survey results showed that the majority of nuns (73%) considered that abiding by the precepts is meaningful in contemporary society. Another 15% thought it was not meaningful, and 12% did not know whether or not it was meaningful. These figures reflect that the clear majority of Sōtō Zen nuns take Dōgen's teachings to heart, for their founder held that "keeping the precepts and devotion to the Way are inseparable with the monastic life."[55] He explains why it is imperative to observe the precepts: "To guard against evil and prevent oneself from doing wrong." Dōgen adds that he knows it is not an easy path. Although all monastics take the same precepts, how the precepts are interpreted varies.

Responses to the survey question: "Do you think there is meaning in maintaining the precepts in contemporary Japan?"[56] suggested that many nuns do not devote much time deciding whether or not it is important to maintain their vows, they just consider living according to their vows to be "part of the definition of being a renunciant."[57] Others reasoned that "if you do not follow the precepts, then there is no value in being a renunciant. Especially if you are intent on maintaining the true Dharma, you cannot save people headed towards confusion and chaos in the contemporary society."[58] Another compelling reason for maintaining the precepts came from the wisdom of a nun who has lived through seventy years of change, including war, illness, and hard work. "If you abide by the precepts, then you can see the proper path."[59] She seemed to be suggesting that the precepts serve as an anchor that keep one from floundering in a sea of sometimes tumultuous change. The responses of Sōtō nuns led to the conclusion that for them to follow the precepts is not simply a matter of following tradition. It is a decision to lead a meaningful and effective monastic life.

Among the 15% of the nuns who did not think there is primary value in the precepts, many of their reasons were still based upon a concern for leading a meaningful and effective life. One middle-aged nun reasoned that "it is more important to maintain a humanitarian lifestyle and to be concerned with civilization than to follow the monastic regulations."[60] One nun who had not made a final decision about whether or not the precepts are appropriate for the current society shared her reasoning:

> You must heed regulations before you can understand them. Just like clothing, you cannot tell whether it fits or not just by looking at it displayed on a hanger. You must try it on to know where it does not fit properly. Regulations are the same. You must try them on for yourself. It also is important to see how other people "wear" the regulations. Only then might you be able to discern where some regulations might be inappropriate.[61]

She gave no indication when, if ever, she might find any of the precepts inappropriate, but her approach reflects patience and trust in the traditional Buddhist practices. Her mind was open, but she did not want to rush such an important change.

Male and female monastics alike traditionally took a vow of celibacy, for it is included in Dōgen's sixteen precepts required for ordination. As explained previously, in the late nineteenth century, the Japanese government instituted regulations for Japanese monastic Buddhists that equally permit male and female monastics to marry. By 1935, 80% of Sōtō Zen "male monastics" acted upon the Japanese government's permission for monastics to marry. Many monastics now choose to interpret the vow regarding sexual conduct in the same way it is interpreted for the laity: To not engage in sexual misconduct. They no longer regard celibacy as a necessary vow of the monastic discipline. This is a significant change in the definition of monasticism in Japan, highlighting the data that indicate monks are in the forefront of this change. Many monastics claim that celibacy does not affect one's ability to live according to Buddhist truth (Dharma). Whether or not this is true is another matter, and it is not the issue I am addressing. I introduce the issue of celibacy because one's view on celibacy is a clear indication of whether one is more "traditional" or more "modern." Although most nuns interpret their vows to extend to celibacy, four cases of Sōtō Zen monastic women marrying have appeared after 1990. Three nuns involved were married within ten years after becoming a nun, one remained married when she became a nun. In all but one case the marriage was to a monk. In one of the cases a non-Japanese woman was involved. These cases amount to less than 0.4% of Sōtō Zen nuns.[62] In other words, single nuns constitute the overwhelming majority.

Over the last few years in numerous conversations with scholars, laity, feminists, office workers, housewives, and elderly people in various regions in Japan, I found that the impressions people have of why nuns do not marry fall into a few distinct lines of reasoning. Some declare this as clear proof of social discrimination, concluding that there is still a double standard that operates against women. Most people, however, are not aware that the actual regulations are equal. Many think the regulations discriminate against women by not permitting them to marry. Those who know that the true regulations are equal *still* argue that the fact that women monastics do not marry is due to unfair social pressure for nuns to remain traditional. Another possibility rarely mentioned was that women *choose to maintain* their traditional Buddhist vows and do not *want* to marry. From this viewpoint, some monastics' choice to marry is more appropriately seen as a modern reinterpretation of monasticism, and the vast majority of nuns' choice to remain single is not fundamentally an indication of discrimination against nuns.[63]

Contrasts between monks and nuns are useful to make, because they reveal how nuns position themselves in the Zen monastic landscape. The majority of male monastics come from a "monastic" family. They are groomed since childhood to take over the family temple from their father. In this sense, the women's monastic community today is more "intentional" than the male monastic community, because women sought out this life from among other alternatives. This is not to say that men and women who choose ordination with substantial support and even pressure from their families do not make a serious commitment, but there seems to be a different attitude toward the monastic life and Buddhist practice between those monastics who left other lifestyles and made an individual decision to live a monastic life and those who enter the monastery with inherited responsibilities that include siring the next heir. One nun does not hesitate to express her opinion on the matter. "If in Japan there are actually any who follow Buddhist truth, they are only nuns. Most monks are only concerned with ceremonies and services."[64] This criticism of monks tells us that this nun values monastics who do more than ceremonies and services. She is likely interpreting "Buddhist truth" to include monastic celibacy and maintaining a temple lifestyle that includes doing zazen and all one's own cooking, cleaning, and serving.

Indeed, almost all Sōto nuns are and were single. Out of forty-eight Sōtō nuns who responded to this question on the survey, forty-five had never been married, one was a widow, one was divorced, and one was married. As might be expected following the high statistics of unmarried women, only a handful have children. With only a few exceptions, most of these are adopted children, some of whom are being cultivated as disciples. Despite the fact that regulations permit male and female monastics to marry, especially for the purpose of cultivating an heir to the temple, nuns do not choose to marry. Until the late 1980s, marriage was not entertained as a desirable alternative to nuns, so there has been little public discussion of the matter. Celibacy was taken for granted. In the last few years, a few lone voices have broached the question of the possible merits of marriage for a nun, citing that the lack of heirs for the temples has become a serious problem. The vast majority of nuns enter the discussion on the side of maintaining the monastic tradition of celibacy, for it enables nuns to lead a full monastic life rather than one divided between family and temple responsibilities. A significant number of novices in the 1980s have left family life, because they preferred monastic life. These new nuns join the chorus in favor of celibacy.

In order to do this successfully, most nuns are agreed that one must "have an attitude of a renunciant." According to the abbess Aoyama, to be a renunciant means not to pursue worldly things and not to behave in worldly ways.[65] In keeping with Dōgen's teachings, most nuns draw a clear distinction between the lifestyle of a renunciant and a householder. Dōgen devoted one chapter to the "Virtue of Renouncing the World" (*Shukke Kudoku*) in which he stated with no apology that "it is clear that devotion to the Buddhist Way is extremely difficult, if not impossible, for a householder. A renunciant, on the other hand, removed from the seeds of suffering and illusion, can be fully devoted to practice."[66] The primary reason Dōgen maintains that undivided attention to the Buddhist Way is difficult for the householder is that a householder must concentrate on earning a living and providing financial support for the household. Dōgen explicitly notes that he is not insinuating that there are ontological reasons that preclude nonmonastics from realizing enlightenment, only that he understands that in a pragmatic sense it is a greater challenge to realize enlightenment as a householder. Most nuns indicated that they realized that in order "to have a heart of compassion,"[67] they must remove self-serving and selfish patterns of behavior, which is precisely what the monastic life is designed to accomplish.

By remaining celibate they not only keep their monastic vows, but by maintaining a single life, they are also freed to devote themselves to various important projects. Kojima Kendō prevailed over the Sōtō sect administration because of her indefatigable energy and indomitable courage. Her contributions to nuns in the twentieth century, including work in Hawaii, would not have been possible had she been circumscribed any more than she already was by androcentric institutions and regulations. Another nun of the same generation, Taniguchi Setsudō, was able to mother dozens of orphans because of her lifestyle as a Buddhist nun. It gave her the freedom and the strength to establish the still thriving orphanage, Lumbini-en.[68] The effectiveness and significance of Aoyama's numerous books, and her occasional television appearances, have already been discussed. With these activities on top of her responsibilities as an abbess and the head of a temple, Muryō-ji, in Nagano prefecture, Aoyama would clearly be limited in her capacity to reach people in many parts of the world if family obligations were included. For Kitō Shunkō, her international effectiveness would have been precluded had she had a family, because it would have been virtually impossible to care for a family during the four years she spent helping establish the Japanese Temple in Bodh Gaya, India. Yet another nun who has had an impact throughout Japan and in other foreign lands is Okamoto Kōbun, a teacher of sewing monastic robes. She is one of the only monastics qualified and competent to teach this traditional and venerated practice of hand-sewing one's own monastic robes.[69] These are only a few highlights of the contributions and activities of a handful of important nuns in this century. It is hard to imagine them being as effective if they had house-holder responsibilities. Being celibate, they have realized their potential and accomplished many things.

This issue of the marital status of monastics is another clear example of how ethnographic data can provide information to make the statistics mean something quite different from what they appear. The larger historical context, cultural impulses, and personal aims must be examined to understand the significance of the statistics on monastic marriage. The reasons for the differences are woven into the fabric of Japanese history and sewn in the hearts of participants in that history. Monks and nuns have responded to modern developments in distinct ways, revealing divergent aims. In short, the vast majority of nuns maintain a "traditional" view of the vow on sexual conduct.

Another basic feature of monastic life that has pervasive consequences is the issue of keeping the head shaven or letting the hair grow. There is no precept requiring a nun to shave her head. It is a tradition that has continued for more than 2,000 years, for monastics have found it to be effective in certain important ways. Notable consequences accompany a monastic's decision whether or not to shave one's head. Many male monastics, though not all, do not keep their heads clean-shaven after their training period. In response to this, one nun flatly admits that she thinks that "it is bad that monks let their hair grow."[70] Again, for this study, the value of a nun's criticism of monks is that it informs us about what she thinks is important. The following comments shed light on why she would draw such a conclusion. Zen nuns who maintain clean-shaven heads say that it is liberating, despite (or perhaps because of) the cultural history that prizes women with long hair. One seasoned nun noted the significance and practicality of a clean-shaven head:

> It is a sign of self-awareness that one has become a nun. If you had the same appearance as a layperson, you would not be able to make the distinction in your own heart. Besides, when your head is shaven, living is much easier. When you wake up in the morning you do not have to worry about combing your hair or anything. You do not have to put on cosmetics. As far as clothing, there is no concern for what is in fashion.[71]

A number of nuns echoed this practical reasoning. They thought that if one begins to grow one's hair out, it would become increasingly difficult to determine what was appropriate. Another nun explains that "the act of shaving your head serves to reconfirm that you are a nun."[72] They seem to be saying that it is easier to be a monastic when it is not ambiguous. A further benefit that many mentioned was that "when one maintains the appearance of a nun it helps, if even just a little, to suppress one's ego-self."[73] Beyond practical concerns, tonsure is an effective method to help one practice the Buddhist teachings.

Another nun, who has a keen concern for the responsibility monastics bear in helping those in need, added her reflections upon why she keeps her head shaven:

> Just having a shaven head brings many people to you who will initiate speaking about many things. A person who has hair is not treated the same, because

others feel it is not appropriate to speak with unrelated persons about certain topics. Most people feel that when talking to regular people, there is nothing they can do about it or they will not understand. But, as a nun they come to you.[74]

In this quiet yet persistent way nuns make their presence felt wherever they may be. The quality of modern life is subtly affected by these spontaneous events that offer hope and guidance. A traditional appearance helps society identify a traditional monastic with all its attendant expectations. Tonsured heads and monastic robes are a visible expression of one's concern for placing priority on maintaining tradition.

In an environment where novel interpretations of monasticism are openly explored, nuns are being perceived as bearers of the traditional interpretation of monastic precepts and lifestyle. One nun observed that "there are more people who are beginning to think that nuns are keeping the Buddhist truth (Dharma) alive—more than monks."[75]

An activity that the nuns of Aichi Senmon Nisōdō pursued expresses their preference for traditional monasticism. Even when traditional Japanese architecture is overshadowed by modern and economical concrete structures, in 1972 the nuns of Aichi undertook a major project to repair and rebuild the monastery that has become a landmark of their commitment to traditional monastic training and aesthetics. Beginning with nothing more than zeal, they successfully galvanized various people and resources in the effort to build traditional monastic facilities. It required a nationwide effort in which Tanaka Dōrin and Katō Shinjō, two of the leaders of the Aichi Nisōdō at the time, rallied support from graduates of the Nisōdō from around the country. Teachers and novices alike went on alms-gathering rounds to make their dream of a complete monastery complex a reality. With the cooperation and support of countless laypeople around the country, especially the generous donations of the layman Furukawa Tamesaburō, by October 1973 the nuns had received enough funding to complete the massive project. In succession they repaired the Main Worship Hall (*hondō*), built new living quarters, and erected a new front gate (*sanmon*) in time for their Seventieth Anniversary ceremonies.[76] This architectural project is a tribute to their genuine concern to continue leading and training women in the traditional monastic mode. For their Eightieth Anniversary they again appealed to the generosity of thousands of people in order to do much-needed repairs. They had the vision that the monastery would become a place for women around the world to come and seek the truth, and a place in Japan where those with peaceful hearts would congregate.[77]

Nuns would be the first to admit, however, that practice does not require any particular facilities. The attitude with which each and every activity is done is more important. "Practice is not the *type* of activity, but it is what is done within the *heart*."[78] Although this statement can be construed to justify a wide range of activities, the nun who wrote this explanation of practice also wrote that it was meaningful to maintain the precepts in contemporary Japan. Evidence that many nuns agree with Dōgen's nondualistic orientation is apparent in the following comments that were made in response to the survey questions concerning monastic practice.[79] "Everything in everyday life is to be done diligently one by one. Practice is not something special."[80] Ceremonies are not more important than daily tasks. "Every activity between wake-up and lights out is important for the life of a renunciant. Practice is acting, being, sitting, sleeping."[81] It is when these daily activities are done in accord with the Buddhist teachings that mundane actions become practice. Displaying awareness of the reality of life, one nun simply responded, practice is "daily cleaning."[82] Another nun states a similar understanding of the content of practice, though more emphatically: "If one cannot do the things right in front of oneself, like cooking and cleaning, then that person is not the image of a monastic. If the person who is supposed to be the teacher cannot make even one dish, then that person is not useful wherever he or she goes."[83]

The survey responses reflect that nuns are aware of an underlying assumption that practice takes diverse forms. "It depends on each individual."[84] What many nuns suggested is that there is no limit to practice. It does not depend on a particular form like doing zazen in full- or half-lotus posture. It is primarily, as another nun mentioned, a matter of the heart, for "there are people who cannot fold their legs. Although sitting zazen is important for those who have the capacity to sit, for people who cannot, the people are more important than zazen."[85] In other words, zazen is not an absolute paradigm. This insight helps nuns open up their hearts to various people and their circumstances. A hallmark of genuine Zen adepts is their ability to live and breathe Buddhist teachings so they become one with their bodies. One nun even articulates her commitment in these terms: Practice is "to make the Truth part of my body."[86] For most Zen nuns, practice is doing nothing more than what is necessary. They do not reify certain activities over others, nor do they establish a hierarchy of what is more important or religious. In this they affirm what their founder taught in numerous writings, including *Zenki* [Total Activity], *Senmen* [Wash the Face], *Busshō* [Buddha-Nature], *Gyōbutsu Iigi* [The Refined Activities of Buddha Action], *Gyōji* [Ceaseless Practice], *Senjō* [Rules for the Lavatory], and *Tenzo Kyōkun* [Instructions for the Cook].

In Buddhist practice in India, as reflected in the writings of the early almswomen monastics in the *Therīgāthā*, quelling sensory desires was seen as essential to winning ultimate freedom. Zen nuns, on the contrary, train themselves in order to refine all senses in the name of Buddhist practice. Many observers of Buddhism have noted that Japanese Buddhists were deeply affected and shaped in aesthetic realms far more than those in the early monastic life in India. There is no distinct dichotomy between aesthetic experience and religious experience in Japan. A clear demonstration of the difference in orientation toward Buddhist teachings between Japan and India is that the monastic discipline formulated in India prohibits monastics from participating in music, dance, and dramatic forms of activity. Dōgen did not include these in his sixteen precepts, nor are they included in most other Japanese Buddhist sects' rules. A salient quality of Japanese Buddhism is its positive and affective appreciation of the subtleties in the phenomenal world. Dōgen extended this nondualistic orientation to his understanding that enlightenment is in the here and now—the key lies in the way an activity is executed. Nuns who root themselves in this tradition maintain this nondualistic view of ultimate reality. Integrating the arts into their formal practice is a clear manifestation of this.

Sōtō Sect Nun Association records for 1984 reveal that Zen nuns were actively engaged in traditional arts: sixty-six nuns taught tea at their temples, ninety-one taught pilgrim hymn singing (*baika*), seventy-nine taught flower arranging, and fourteen taught calligraphy.[87] The records on nuns' temple activities, and my time spent with the monastic women, left me with the impression that these activities are included precisely because the women saw these arts as a basic aspect of their Zen practice.[88] The curriculum in the training monasteries reflects this deliberate concern to cultivate these arts as a part of practice, and the survey and interview responses bore out the view that nuns *want* to be engaged in these arts.

Sōtō nuns fought for many things early in this century, including institution-alizing their "women's" activities. They designed their own curriculum, and they integrated these arts into their monastic training because they are skills that mo-nastics need in running their own temples upon graduation. One nun made it quite clear: "I think you must be able to do tea ceremony and flower arranging. Now monks have their wives do it, but as monastics they should do it." Here we see a nun clearly expressing the value of self-sufficiency and celibacy. Moreover, another nun explained the necessity of these skills, suggesting that they can also refine the heart and body of a monastic, regardless of gender:

> It is not so much that monastics must preserve these traditions, but these traditions are part of the life of being a monastic in Japan. There are flowers in various parts of the temple, and if there is a gathering, tea is served. It is a natural part of the life. The heart is deeply affected by the way the body moves.[89]

While art is a practice that refines the harmony of body and mind, art classes can also be a source of income. Conversations with elderly nuns suggested that there was a time when teaching tea ceremony and flower arranging classes in their temples was a primary source of income for many. The survey results from 1990 indicated, however, that for most nuns it is no longer such a source of income (but 17% of the nuns responding still receive their primary income from teaching art classes). Furthermore, numerous nuns continue to offer art classes, which provides a supplement to their main income. The increase in nuns' opportunities to receive higher monastic ranks has resulted in 65% receiving their primary in-come from temple services, that is, performing various ceremonial rituals either at their own temple or assisting in the temple of others. Due to a general decline in monastic numbers both male and female, the demand upon each individual monastic to perform ceremonies has increased. The remaining 18% of Sōtō nuns surveyed in 1990 had "other" sources of primary income, including administering nursery schools and alms gathering.

Nuns are also active beyond the bounds of their temple walls; this became clear in their responses to the survey question: "What kind of social responsibility do you think nuns have?" The types of activities outlined in their comments indicated that Zen nuns are engaged in a range of activities that are aimed at reaching out to help people. From their responses it is notable that many nuns are devoted to education at all levels, from educating the general society, to university students, to kindergartners. Another dimension of their social concern occurs at a more intimate level. Nearly all nuns surveyed suggested that one of their primary social responsibilities is to listen attentively to the needs of others and to help them find peace in their daily lives. A significant number of nuns are also active in volunteer work, primarily focusing on the needs of orphans and the elderly, a manifestation of their general concern to help people. In these ways, nuns make a concerted effort to fill a vital niche in modern Japanese society.

A nun who graduated from university (at a time when it was uncommon for a woman to receive such a high level of formal education) held that her responsibility is "to explain the Buddhist way of seeing and way of thinking."[90] The most common format for formally offering Buddhist teachings is to have lectures at one's temple. One nun stressed these must be "lectures from the heart, on the foundation of Buddhist teachings."[91] More than one nun was aware that "there are many people these days who, even though they are materially blessed and lead luxurious lifestyles, have rotten hearts." They hope to "make this world a little brighter and point people in the direction of leading humane lives."[92]

This requires nuns "to be active in the education of families."[93] In both formal and informal ways, nuns do just that. One nun expressed enthusiasm that she was teaching at the university level: "I am a university professor, and I am enjoying even working with foreign students."[94] At other levels nuns showed their insight into the importance of education. "I am putting in tremendous effort from my heart to help educate young people and adolescents who will one day become adults. This is a way to help improve society."[95] Numerous nuns work with the youngest members of society and "through the kindergarten activities, we educate the parents."[96]

Despite their efforts, many nuns feel that they are not understood by society, as clearly articulated by a university-educated, fifty-year-old nun: "Many people think that we have abandoned the world. Few people understand the meaning of our lives."[97] From her perspective, monastics have a role in the world, and the intimation that monastics have abandoned the world seems to resound of irresponsibility in her ears. Her sentiments are understandable, for nuns have not abandoned the world. Except for the period in which nuns are in strict training, nuns are actively engaged with society. Aside from large monastic complexes, temples have historically served and continue to be centers of community life. According to the 1990 survey, at least thirty-seven nuns ran orphanages or nurseries and seven held regular Zen retreats for the laity. There were twenty-eight other varieties of activities that the nuns regularly held at their temples, including two nuns who were Girl Scout leaders, four who ran women's associations, and one who was heading an association for the elderly. These institutionalized activities are supplemented by the subtle and profound ways in which nuns help people in very personal ways.

An incomplete impression of ordained Sōtō Zen Buddhists was fostered by the 1984 Sōtō Sect survey of 1,800 laypeople, which cited that only 8% of the people go to priests for spiritual reasons, whereas 78% see priests concerning mortuary rites.[98] An assessment of the survey by Sasaki Kōkan[99] indicates that the monks' involvement in popular rites has dominated, for "temple priests were not regarded as religious teachers, but rather as ritualists whose role was to carry out ceremonies related to the death process."[100] In the spring of 1990, I conducted a survey of sixty-eight laypeople who have contact with nuns through nuns' activities open to the laity, like zazen retreats and sūtra copying. A group of Sōtō laity emerged who do not correspond to the pattern from the 1984 Sōtō Sect survey. The results of my more limited survey cannot be directly compared to the survey of the sect administration, but it points to areas of activity in the sect that perhaps have gone undetected by the central administration. My survey of laity in the Nagoya area seems to represent a subset within the Sōtō sect. These people all had some contact with a Sōtō nun prior to participating in the survey. None of the sixty-eight people who responded to the survey were seeking nuns for mortuary rites, but this is not surprising. Sect regulations prohibited nuns from performing funerals until nuns successfully changed this regulation earlier in the twentieth century. Despite nuns now having authorization to perform these rites, it is understandable that families are not inclined to "move" their ancestors from one temple to another. Thus, nuns' temples have yet to become centrally engaged in funerals. Due to the decrease in monastics in general, however, nuns are actively involved in assisting mortuary rites.

Keeping in mind the context of my 1990 survey, the most common response offered by laity who turned to nuns for personal conversations was that nuns are better listeners, like mothers. Most of the people who went to nuns for help were female (90%) and middle-aged (average age fifty-four), and they primarily discussed their concerns about family, children, marital problems, and elderly parents. They also sought nuns' advice when they were confused, depressed, and at a turning point in their lives. Nuns perceive part of their role as a monastic is to create an atmosphere where people can feel comfortable and open with personal conversation. My survey of laity confirmed that many nuns must be successful in their efforts, providing an atmosphere where laity feel it is easier to speak with nuns rather than monks: 62% of the surveyed laity responded that it was easier to speak with nuns rather than monks, 1.5% thought it was easier to speak with a monk, 7.5% did not know, and 27% thought there was no difference. Of these respondents, 61% thought nuns were more serious than monks, but no one thought that monks were more serious than nuns.

It is not surprising that many laypeople turn to nuns for personal counseling, in light of the fact that more than 80% of the nuns surveyed indicated that their role and obligation to society was to "be a kind and womanly listener to anything and everyone."[101] Furthermore, nuns stress that it is of premium importance "to listen carefully to what the person you are talking to is saying, so one can help them gain a sense of peace."[102] It seems the majority of the concerns people bring to nuns involve family. "Sympathy toward housewives and the elderly" seems to make up most of these discussions. As one nun summed it up, nuns do their best "to mediate and offer succor by spreading a fresh morning breeze and showing a compassionate smiling face."[103] One nun intimates that some of these matters are only discussed with nuns. "Many constantly oblige me by coming to me to discuss their family situations and say things they cannot say to monks."[104] Another nun,

Kojima Kendō Sensei leading a 700th Memorial Service for Koun Ejō at Eihei-ji Temple in 1980. She was the first nun on record to perform the role of head celebrant at this temple founded by Dōgen.

Kojima Kendō Sensei's Zen painting and calligraphy at age ninety-three. "Not A Thing."

Kojima Kendō Sensei
and Kitō Shunkō Sensei
in front of the altar at
Kōrin-ji, site of the official
Sōtō nunnery in Nagoya.

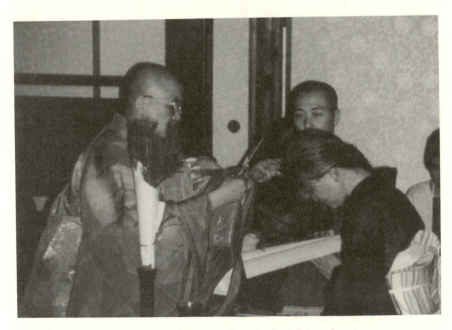

Abbess Aoyama Shundō performing a female disciple's ordination ceremony.

The bell tower and Zen Meditation Hall of Aichi Senmon Nisōdō in Nagoya.

Nuns practicing zazen in Zen Meditation Hall of Aichi Senmon Nisōdō.

Airing the Zen meditation cushions ("Sunbathing the Buddhas").

Abbess Aoyama Shundō performing ritual of *Perfection of Wisdom Sūtra*.

Novice nuns of Aichi
Senmon Nisōdō on alms
rounds in Nagoya.

Cooking as Zen practice.

Celebrating Christmas at Aichi Senmon Nisōdō,
on behalf of author's western presence.

Novice nun cleaning
the garden of memo-
rial stones.

Okamoto Sensei, novice, and laywomen (right to left) in
"sewing practice" at 4:00 A.M.

Seventy-three-year-old
novice nun.

Flower arranging as Zen practice.

Tomio Sensei, teacher
of *baika* hymns.

Kuriki Kakujō Sensei, tea ceremony teacher,
in front of her Nagoya temple, Seikan-ji.

Group portrait from "Entering Monastery Ceremony" for new nuns on April 7, 1990, at Aichi Senmon Nisōdō.

who evidently has also experienced many people coming to her with personal concerns, offers an explanation of why she thinks this is a common occurrence. "It seems that the laity have a much easier time talking with nuns than with monks. Because it seems as though people look at nuns like they look at a mother."[105] My limited survey of laity confirms her view. Not only does this tell us how the role of a nun is interpreted in modern Japan, but it also shows what people expect of a mother figure: to listen with compassion and understand with wisdom.

The character of these interactions is perhaps best described as intimate relationships of mutual concern. Although many nuns feel it is their responsibility "to enter into the world of the general people of the society," most wind up "talking together and sharing each others' joys and sufferings while becoming good friends."[106] What this response seems to reflect is that some nuns have a sense of responsibility that as a monastic they must go into the world and make a difference, but the result is that the "world" is composed of people like themselves who have good and bad times. In this unpretentious way, nuns are committed to living in the world. Many aim simply "to interact with people warmly and make a bright society."[107] Nuns also have a deep effect upon each other. One novice comments how she learned how to resolve one of her biggest trials—anger—by noticing how her senior behaved. "I felt like I had been saved, just by her mere presence. I thought, 'there is potential for real human beings to become like her.' "[108]

Before one can effectively act upon one's commitment to "civilize society"[109] or make significant contributions by "volunteer[ing] and participate[ing] in social movements,"[110] most nuns claim "the first thing is that one attain peace oneself. Subsequently, one must understand the confusion of the world, suffering, and fear."[111] Many nuns explained that without the wisdom and peace that accompany practice, it would be hard to be effective in helping others with their problems. According to Buddhist teachings, ignorance is understood to be the source of suffering. Therefore, good intentions alone are not useful in helping others. Training in the monastery is designed to cultivate the peace and wisdom necessary to be effective and caring members of the society.

To open one's heart to others enables one "to be a harbor for society people." In *For the Sake of the World*, Henry and Swearer contend that now, more than ever, monastics have a special role to play in society. Those who lead monastic lives can "bear witness to the deepest human capacities they discover in the contemplative experience. In the face of rampant secularism and materialism, the monastic contribution to personal and social well-being has become increasingly important, if not imperative."[112] Aware of their vital role in modern society, many nuns open not only their hearts, but also their temples. Although an uncommon view, one elderly nun asserts that "Amadera, nun's temples, are all contemporary *kakekomidera*—temples for women to find refuge, especially from men."[113] It does not come as a surprise that one of the responsibilities that nuns hold is one of the bodhisattva vows: "Save all sentient beings."[114]

One nun unambiguously asserts what many laypeople and monastics alike think: "I think that nuns today are the ones who abide by the precepts and we are true heirs of the Buddha Dharma."[115] The abbess of Toyama Nisōdō reflects, however, that nuns are not inherently better than monks.[116] If they had what monks had—wealthy temples, children, money, power, rank—nuns would be much less effective. Her observation supports the analysis that nuns perceive being traditional as being good. That nuns are more traditional than monks is a multifaceted issue. In part, it is due to choice. As the survey responses prove, many nuns see the value of traditional monastic practice, for it is in accord with Buddhist teachings. Many have found it genuinely effective in leading a meaningful Buddhist life. From the perspective of historical development, it seems that choosing traditional monastic discipline has also served as a method for nuns to gain recognition and respect. It seems to have helped them win parity in sect regulations. Nuns are also "traditional" as a result of discriminatory practices. I qualify this usage of traditional because both Dōgen's writings and the nuns' interpretation of Dōgen's writings state that women and men are equal in practice. So, the practice of discrimination against nuns is not "traditional." Nevertheless, discriminatory regulations have arisen. These regulations and social pressure made it difficult, if not impossible, for nuns to explore different modes of monastic living. That developments in the twentieth century are leading toward nuns increasing their rank and power might explain why a few nuns are choosing to marry. Before they had status in the eyes of the male-dominated institution, being traditional was the most efficient route to acknowledgment. The fact that nuns are now exercising their prerogative to marry is a strong indication they have enough stature to choose between traditional and modern ways. They are not as bound to their gender as before. To have choice is a clear indicator of greater equity. Within this context, however, the vast majority still choose traditional monasticism.

The nuns surveyed expressed a strong concern for maintaining a relatively traditional interpretation of the precepts. This extends to various practices, including tonsure. Most hold a view of practice that is in accord with Dōgen's teachings. Including the arts of tea ceremony and flower arranging as explicit features of their practice shows not only their aesthetic sensibilities, but it is a practical matter also. These arts help refine one's actions, which is a necessary aspect of interpreting that practice is enlightenment. Many nuns act upon their view that practice involves being concerned about members of the society. They interact with the people who seek them out at an intimate level, and a significant sector of the nuns' community reaches out to people in numerous ways, including educating in various formats, assisting elderly, and caring for orphans. In these ways nuns make significant and important contributions to society. The prevailing number of nuns have made a clear commitment to uphold traditional monastic practice, not because they are merely conservative, but because they find inimitable value in it.

Nuns' Views on Monastic Life

What do nuns think about how society views them? Of all the nuns surveyed, 62% thought that they were respected by society, and 22% thought that they were *highly* respected by society. Only one nun responded that nuns were not respected by society at all, while another few percent were either not sure or thought nuns received little respect. The statistics signify that, on the whole, these women do not feel society perceives them as inferior. It also confirms the view that nuns have a high level of confidence and self-respect. The predominant number of nuns do not act or express themselves in a way that would suggest they think that they are social anomalies. They do not pity themselves, nor do they think society pities them. These nuns know they make valuable contributions to society, and they recognize that they are appreciated.

Respect from general society, however, does not necessarily translate into fair treatment. Parity in regulations does not guarantee equity either. Discrimination against nuns still occurs. It is not uncommon for discrimination to occur particularly regarding matters that regulations do not control or areas that are difficult to enforce. Some nuns cited specific instances. As might be expected, economic disparity is the most prevalent kind of discrimination. Many nuns attested to the fact that "there is discrimination in temple offerings (*fuse*)."[117] Despite the egalitarian sect regulations, the tension in a statement offered by a sixty-five-year-old nun suggests that some monks do not realize that this means nuns must be treated equally: "Up until now there was discrimination concerning every facet. Since monks and nuns are the same Buddhist renunciants, they should mutually respect each other, and it is important that nuns are not monk's tea servers."[118] The frustration nuns feel about being treated in subservient ways reflects that they have a clear understanding of their abilities and role in the community. They know that they should be treated equally, and they have not simply waited for monks to realize this. They changed the regulations, but they cannot change the attitude and actions of the monks. But this has not diminished their self-respect.

The fact of discrimination and the nuns' perception of it are not necessarily the same thing. Nuns surveyed were divided down the middle about whether or not they were the recipients of discrimination. Given the reality that nuns were subjected to unfair sect regulations until the late 1950s,[119] it is surprising that so many nuns would say that they have not experienced discrimination. Many will admit that "there is discrimination in terms of division of labor,"[120] but despite the inequity, many nuns interpret their lives in a positive light. Many also acknowledge that things are much better than before.[121] One nun even expresses acceptance of the situation. "I am satisfied with the present lifestyle."[122] A nun who teaches in the university says with no reservation, "Socially I have been accepted on many levels, and I feel proud to be a nun." The following seventy-year-old nun exudes strength, while her age betrays that she has experienced intense hardship. Her question indicates that she does not have sympathy for those who feel pity for themselves: "Is not the reason people think they are the recipient of discrimination because their own effort is not sufficient and they walk right into it?"[123] She assesses her life this way. "I cannot say that it has been an even path, but I have pride in the fact that I applied as much effort as I could to have the strength to not be defeated by monks."[124] Her remark about whether nuns receive discrimination from monks, then, is put in context. It is not that she has not been the brunt of unfair treatment or regulations, but she has not let that stand in her way of living according to her vision of Buddhist truth. Most of the comments on discrimination do not indicate that nuns habitually see themselves as poor and passive victims of an oppressive system or misogynist individuals. At a fundamental level, many nuns approach problems in life as opportunities and resources for greater growth, so their perception of discrimination cannot be gauged with a conventional "worldly" measure. The fact that many nuns do not stress their experiences of being discriminated against tells us more about the nuns' strength as Buddhist practitioners than it does about the level of discrimination.

Nuns do speak candidly about a problem that can be measured in simple numbers. There is a shortage of nuns to run the nuns' temples.[125] This is the topic of conversation at numerous formal and informal gatherings of nuns. One nun spoke for the vast majority of nuns today: "The thought of not having been able to raise a successor is heartrending."[126] The source of the problem is complex, and there is no *deus ex machina* in sight. In the face of these dire circumstances, most nuns just persevere with their integrity intact and their commitment to Buddhist truth unflinching. The prevalent view is that it is better to have nuns who are genuinely committed to traditional monastic life than have a larger quantity. With this priority, there is not much nuns can do. Applying pressure, like that used in the hereditary system, has resulted in novel interpretations of monastic life. Nuns know that choosing the life of a renunciant and committing to a traditional interpretation of monastic discipline is something only an individual can decide.

All go through a difficult phase when becoming a monastic, but it is a good life worth persevering for, crying for, suffering for, intones the former abbess of Niigata Senmon Nisōdō, Nakamura Busshin.[127] She recalls her early years as a nun when she thought she had chosen the wrong path for herself. But, since she decided to do it on her own, having not buckled under opposition from her family, she could not complain or waver from the path she chose. Another example of the kind of commitment and determination commonly found in nuns reflects the caliber of monastic women today:

> I am a full seventy-six years old and I will pass each day persevering for others and for myself. Even though I have become an elderly nun, I will not be dependent on other people at all as long as I have life. Even though I am an elderly person, I lead people and together we make special and important pilgrimages to temples.[128]

This kind of spirit is echoed in the words of another respondent: "I think, isn't it not good to have an adventurous side and to try and take the challenge of anything?"[129]

As illustrated in the nuns' remarks, despite hardships and failures, not just a few nuns expressed gratitude for the benefits of a nuns' life: "Although when I was young it was quite difficult, I am grateful for the lifestyle of being a nun now that I know old age. I am grateful to my body that I entered this path of faith."[130] Another nun speaks honestly about her lack of consistent gratitude, but she still strives to do her best: "Every day, day in and day out, I cannot practice with joy and gratitude, but wherever I am granted to be, I try to put my whole being into doing what is necessary."[131] One nun reflected on her awareness that she has many things for which to be thankful, but she also recognized that she has to continue to improve herself:

> Since I was a child I have been granted the Buddha's food. As expected, I am passing every day grateful that I have become a nun and I think it is good. Every day is a good day. I think that even today I must try and advance as a disciple of the Buddha, because although I am a nun, I still have dust.[132]

Her final words indicate that some might think that she is pure, because she is a nun. Although she denies this assessment, it reveals the difference between how she thinks she is perceived by others and how she perceives herself. Overall, her comments tell us that she is generally pleased with her life as a nun.

The overwhelming majority of nuns express unreserved joy when reflecting on their lives as nuns. The following chorus can act as testimony: "I think it was a fantastic life."[133] "I think it is a wonderful path."[134] "Only that I am merely thankful and *gasshō*."[135] "I am grateful for my life as a nun who lives in society, and, more than anything, I feel joy and gratitude."[136] "Since I committed myself to this path (*hosshin*), I look back and have joy from my heart and a sense of living a worthwhile life."[137]

> When I was very young, I came to a nun's temple as an adopted child because I had *en*, a deep connection. It has been about forty-six years that I have been passing every day as a disciple of the Buddha being freely in game/fun samadhi. It has been a grateful day by day. No suffering.[138]

What is the source of their joy? Does it derive from their Buddhist experience? The comments seem to indicate that their joy does derive in large measure from their commitment to Buddhist teachings. The Buddhist path itself is understood as something that brings gratitude and joy. It is what has made their lives meaningful. This positive interpretation of their own lives seems to make it easier for them to accept discrimination and hardship. One nun goes so far as to say she has "no suffering."

Many nuns take this gratitude and joy and give it to others in the society. A number agree with the nun who said: "I think from now on nuns increasingly must go out into society and touch the greater society, making it brighter and healthier."[139] Affirming this view, another nun asserted: "I think it is necessary for nuns to turn their eyes more and more towards social welfare and serve the society."[140] Indeed, many have felt that call and responded with concrete results as they maintain meaningful monastic lives: "Looking back on my life as a nun I find the highest joy in having spent half my life nursing the Buddha's children and having been engaged in a social enterprise of value. I am filled with the feeling of deep gratitude for having lived a complete life as a nun."[141]

In summary, the value nuns place on monastic tradition is evident in the choices monastic women make in their lives. Their survey and interview responses and their actions suggest that many find the practices laid down by Buddhist tradition, especially Dōgen, meaningful. Sōtō Sect regulations do not restrict nuns from marrying or letting their hair grow, yet nearly all choose to keep the vow of celibacy and the practice of tonsure.[142] Most explained that they considered these actions basic to the definition of being a monastic. Taking their commitment to Buddhist teachings seriously is not experienced as a burden nor as merely clinging to old-fashioned ways. In the rush to keep up with the future, most nuns see that living a life according to these ancient teachings is even more important, because they help one understand the nature of human society. There is an underlying sense that a number of nuns feel that a person must know profound peace in order to help others usher in the new age. The preference for traditional monastic life and the self-perception of a significant number of nuns in the late twentieth century is articulated in the following assessment offered by a novice who gave up a successful business career to don the robes of a monastic. Evidently, she is of the view that traditional monastics are more respected, and nuns are more traditional:

> I think that since monks are beginning to get the reputation of not being very disciplined, society will begin to see that nuns are more disciplined, and then the nuns will receive more respect from society. There will come a time when people will think that nuns are the only ones who practice diligently.[143]

Exuding a positive evaluation of monastic life, the survey responses reveal that these women have the confidence that they can make a valuable difference. They did not let the attempts of the male-dominated sect administration undermine their effectiveness or inhibit them from acting in accord with their interpretation of Dōgen's teachings. Although a broad range of activities and attitudes is represented among nuns, one thing they have in common is that their brand of monasticism is life-affirming. Leading lives of aesthetic refinement, nuns keep Japanese aesthetic traditions alive as well as an aspect of their Buddhist values. They express few complaints or regrets about their lives. On the contrary, the most frequently used word in the survey in response to an inquiry about the reflections of life as a nun is "gratitude."

Gratitude is the key to the nuns' disciplined practice. Each event, whether it be cutting carrots, carrying heavy tables up the stairs, or being blamed for some infraction, is an opportunity for practice. The challenge is to respond to negative experiences in a manner that accords with the fundamental teaching to respect each person and object as an enlightened being. Accepting this teaching and moving with carefully disciplined physical and verbal gestures are required. When the circumstances to which one is responding, however, include structural oppression, unfair regulations, unjust treatment, or jealous rage, just knowing that it is possible to use difficult situations to further one's practice and acting in a polite manner are usually not enough to transform one's negative experiences into positive ones. Most nuns hold that if one responds with gratitude, even viscerally intense negative events can become a source of empowerment for a person. Nuns' extensive use of the "gratitude conjugation" facilitates their ability to cultivate gratitude. It is not surprising, then that "gratitude" was the most commonly used word in the survey responses of nuns who have lived through an era of institutionalized oppression. The majority of these same nuns also responded that they did not consider themselves victims of sexual discrimination.

The data reveal that Sōtō Zen nuns have a high respect for traditional monastic life. Women in other traditions, contexts, and time periods who have been dismissed as oppressed and unfortunate have found their lives important and meaningful as well. The Personal Narratives Group has found that "while . . . women might be defined as 'marginal' from the perspective of a society's dominant norms and established power relations, the women so defined did not necessarily experience themselves as marginal."[144] The women's lives as seen through the poetry of the *Therīgāthā* suggests that women in ancient India had the resolve to take control of their lives and not let themselves be pushed by the tides of suffering. They persisted and found liberation and joy. Many monastic women in modern Japan are similarly strong, dedicated, and determined to lead meaningful lives. Their gender as female monastics in modern Japan does not preclude them from full devotion to Buddhist teachings, for they have defined it as a gender with the qualities of a plum blossom—strong enough to be gentle in the harshest conditions.

Referring to the general situation of nuns, a seventy-three-year-old nun wrote on her survey response: "Please do not write this into nonchalant sentences. I am worried that to put it in print will somehow make it seem insignificant."[145] I share her concern. With all due respect, I include the following story, for it poignantly demonstrates how many Sōtō Zen nuns lead exemplary, yet ordinary, lives devoted to Buddhist teachings. This significant moment in the life of Sōtō Zen nuns in modern Japan was not found in headlines heralding the remarkable event, nor was it recorded in a compilation of eminent monastics. It was not even a story passed freely around in the oral lore of the community. I eventually received it orally from a nun who plays a supporting role in the story, but only after having studied directly under her tutelage for one year. This story highlights the nature and importance of ethnographic research:

> In a small, inconspicuous nun's temple in Nagoya, a hardy Zen nun, Nogami Senryō, tried to live according to Dōgen's teachings with her entire being. Though little known beyond the temple compound walls, her daily life was plain testimony to her supreme realization of Buddhist truth. She dedicated herself to caring for this nun's temple, Seikan-ji, while training a quiet but alert nun, Kuriki Kakujō. Kuriki, the current head nun of Seikan-ji, arrived under Nogami's tutelage at the age of eight. With a sense of awe, respect, and a hint of trepidation, Kuriki remembers how Nogami raised her on the classical Zen dictum: "*Zadatsu Ryūbō*. (Die sitting. Die standing.) This is the way of a monastic."[146]

Interpreted as an indication of the deceased's level of spiritual attainment, since ancient times, various cultures have had a fascination with the posture of a person at the moment of death. In Zen, *Zadatsu Ryūbō* represents death postures considered absolute proof of enlightenment, although no one can verify how many people have actually succeeded in this. Dōgen used this classical Zen dictum to stress that practice means to do all activities with steady attention to reality here and now. According to Dōgen, practice is not for the purpose of creating sages out of ordinary people, because the distinction between an ordinary person and a sage is false. All are Buddha-nature. Therefore, he admonishes, "*Zadatsu Ryūbō.*"

Nogami practiced this each morning as she sped—palms flattened on the damp, neatly folded rag—down the wooden floor in the hallway collecting each particle of dust, after each meal as she wiped her bowl clean with a piece of pickled radish, and every afternoon as she pulled tiny weeds from the white-stone garden. Her body understood that enlightenment meant tolerating nothing less than perfect completion of each activity. Strictly adhering to Buddhist truth, she commanded those around her, but especially herself, to approach everything in the spirit of *"Zadatsu Ryūbō."* She repeated this like a *mantra* as she strove to live each moment with pure and relentless concentration. On the seventeenth day of a crisp November afternoon in 1980, Nogami's adamantine voice pierced the silence, "It's time for *Zadatsu Ryūbō!*" Not knowing what to expect, Kuriki rushed to the dim hallway where she saw Nogami slowly walking toward the bronze sculpture of Śākyamuni Buddha sitting full-lotus posture on the altar in the Worship Hall. Arriving in time to witness the stout, ninety-seven-year-old nun in simple black robes take a final step to perfect her stance, Kuriki reached out to embrace her and pealed, "Congratulations!" as Nogami died standing.[147]

This nun had attained one of the highest achievements in the Zen tradition, yet it was not widely publicized. This confirms the need for more ethnographic research. While not all Zen nuns reach the level of Nogami Senryō, the survey results and interview responses overwhelmingly suggest that Zen nuns do interpret their own lives positively, even in the face of unfair treatment. Relying only on texts and statistics, one could interpret Zen nuns as misfits who finally got more egalitarian treatment only after recent reforms. Yet texts found not in libraries, but in storage chests in nuns' temples, and stories told only after lengthy relationships reveal that the majority of Sōtō Zen nuns are not submissive. These nuns have found expedient and effective methods for reaching their goal: To live meaningful Buddhist lives. These nuns both re-create traditions of Zen culture that began to blossom in the Kamakura Period (1186–1333) and cultivate methods and expressions that are unique to women committed to monasticism in modern Japan.

SIX

Conclusion

Innovators for the Sake of Tradition

Before I met Kitō Shunkō in Bodh Gaya, I had not encountered Japanese Zen Buddhist nuns anywhere in the texts I read. Once I knew nuns were vital and active in Japan, their accomplishments became obvious in numerous places. Androcentric bias was the reason that the contributions of women I came to know in person and through historical documents and oral history had been neglected. It became clear to me as well that the practically exclusive focus on textual sources for an academic study of Zen Buddhism was also part of the reason nuns have not appeared in the basic academic literature on Zen. This is not because nuns do not appear anywhere in the original texts, but rather that they were not seen as important by academics. When working with English translations of Japanese texts, the reason is primarily because nongendered words for "person" and "monastic" were consistently translated as "man" and "monk."

Anthropological methods were essential to discovering the important contributions of Sōtō Zen nuns. The participant-observation, interviews, and surveys gave me access to their history of triumph over the male-dominated sect institution's regulations and structures and insight into what their religious practice entails; this combined method also enabled me to see how nuns interpret their own lives. This then equipped me to use the available texts and statistics within the context of the nuns' activities. For example, just looking at the changes in the sect regulations does not explain who made these changes. One might assume that the sect leaders—men—did it. This conclusion would be made especially if one had an androcentric bias. In the course of my field research, however, I met a number of the women who were actually responsible for the changes.

Moreover, in analyzing the field data, the relationship between the actual daily life in the monastery and the ideals of the community became clear. As might be anticipated, participant-observation yielded more information about the nuns' daily life, and interviews and surveys yielded more information about their ideals. I used the information gathered from one method to inform me about the other. This gave me a clearer sense of the way in which the ideals of the community are negotiated in daily life. The participant-observation data showed the difficulties and tensions that accompany monastery life. It was the key to understanding that the core of the nuns' practice is in dealing with human relations. Knowing their ideals in turn helped explain how they could take negative situations and express them in positive terms. Thus, the information gained through interviews and surveys made more sense. When these nuns reflected on their personal histories, they invariably described their experience as nuns in affirmative terms—despite having lived through difficult and unfair circumstances. Indeed, the nuns lavishly articulated the ideals of their community, especially in the surveys. This confirms that the participant-observation method, as well as interview and survey methods, need to be employed to get a balanced picture of their lives. Without the participant-observation data informing us about the nuns' real-life complexities, we would only get a picture of the end result, which at times sounds too positive to be true. On the other hand, if we only saw how nuns dealt with interpersonal relationships, we would not have learned that upon leaving the training monastery many nuns were able to apply their practice of taking things as a resource for growth—and actually experience difficult circumstances like misogynist regulations and oppressive structures—yet remember their lives as something for which to be grateful. Most did not even acknowledge that they had been discriminated against.

Oppression can elicit a diversity of responses. I have been concerned with both the perception of detached observers and the perception of those who are the target of oppression, in this case Sōtō Zen nuns. People often assume that those who are the target of oppression experience it negatively. People who are the targets of oppression often come to see themselves as deserving victims and act as if they were inferior. My field research disproves this in the case of Sōtō Zen nuns. Instead, Sōtō nuns changed their situation to make it closer to their vision of monastic life. They accomplished this by living according to their understanding of Buddhist practice. Their religious values instruct them not to blame external conditions, but rather to seek opportunities for expressing gratitude. The pervasiveness of the "gratitude conjugation" in their habits of speech has a powerful and positive influence on their interpretation and expression of their experiences. Gratitude is what provides the refined polish to their hearts. Although this is the key to their lives, it would not have come to light without ethnographic research.

My research revealed that several impressions about nuns are unfounded. Over the years I have heard several images about nuns in various academic and casual conversations. I have also found them implied in various texts. Sometimes the text suggests these impressions by the line of analysis used when addressing nuns and sometimes by lack of mention. The impressions outlined here are a synthesis of these sources.

The first impression, "Because nuns are oppressed, they are weak," is rejected by citing their achievements. Despite unfair regulations that officially kept nuns out of sect-authorized training institutions at the beginning of the century, these nuns trained themselves, eventually establishing their own official monasteries. Then, even though the nuns started the twentieth century with their highest rank being lower than the lowest monks' rank, they were effective in changing the sect ranking regulations. After a few decades of concerted effort, they now enjoy complete parity in all monastic and teaching ranks. To establish their equal position within the sect, they had to become leaders in educational and institutional reform. To facilitate this process, they organized an official group to express their concerns in sect politics and began publishing various journals for and by nuns. They did not act like nor did they perceive themselves to be oppressed victims of discriminatory practices. They turned their unfair situation into an opportunity to freely practice their interpretation of Buddhist teachings. Oppression by the institution did not make them act as if they really were less deserving than the monks. Instead, the women changed the structure of the institution.

The same evidence that refutes the first impression also negates the reciprocal second impression—"Because nuns are weak, they are oppressed." The cause of the nuns' being oppressed was not their weakness. They showed great strength, first in their successful efforts to train, practice, and teach themselves with little sect support, and second in their triumph over misogynist sect regulations.

The third impression about nuns, "The number of nuns is small, so they do not play a significant role in Zen Buddhism or Japanese society," is rejected on the basis of an examination of nuns' activities and an analysis of their contributions. The establishment of five training monasteries for women (three are still open) is a significant development for Zen Buddhism, as is the major reform of its sect regulations. Functioning as counselors for laity is a significant role nuns play in both Zen Buddhism and in Japanese society. Also, people often feel reluctant to seek assistance with personal problems, yet my survey of laity showed that many are more willing to discuss their personal problems with a nun. By responding to the needs of the laity, nuns fill a vital niche. Furthermore, nuns' traditional dress, language, and eating habits, as well as their engagement in tea ceremony, flower arranging, calligraphy, and poetry writing, help to maintain these aspects of Japanese culture that are waning in the society's drive to modernize. The numbers of nuns involved in these activities may be relatively small, but that does not diminish the importance of their contributions. Cultural contributions are not a matter of quantity. They are a matter of quality.

Fourth, the impression that "Nuns have not made any real gains in the twentieth century, because they are only able to do what the monks used to do from the thirteenth through nineteenth centuries," is not supported by research in the field. Characterization of monastic Buddhist practice in modern Japan depends on the perspective from which the past century's developments are viewed. Analysis proceeds from two major vantage points. One is concerned with secular values that are deeply imbedded in the society. The other is based upon values integral to the Buddhist monastic tradition. When comparing the activities of females and males, if the standard is set by secular society, entirely different results ensue than if the standard is based upon traditional monastic Buddhist values. The secular view finds that nuns are victims of a male-dominated system, because it assumes that what monks do is better and that nuns accept that.

Most nuns do not marry but most monks do, and this is one of the points that a secular line of analysis could claim as proof that nuns are not faring as well as monks. Monks' marrying enables the practice of passing their temples by inheritance. By remaining celibate, nuns increasingly have trouble finding successors. Feminists see this as discrimination against women. Many casual observers draw a quick conclusion that nuns do not marry because only unmarriageable women enter a nunnery in the first place. Among those who know that the 1872–1873 revision of regulations governing the lives of monks and nuns allowed both male and female monastics to marry, many people still interpret the nuns' decisions as an indication that society will not accept married nuns even if the sect administration will. This is the secular view of equality, marriage, and human worth.

My interviews and survey results show clearly that nuns do not use modern monks as models. It also became obvious that nuns have deliberately pursued a path different from most monks in the twentieth century. Nuns are following a traditional paradigm of monastic living; this means that most nuns choose to adhere to monastic regulations that include celibacy, diet, cleaning, and cooking in their daily practice. When examined from a Buddhist perspective, twentieth-century developments illuminate the power and loyalty of Zen nuns and their substantive contributions.

Having viewed Sōtō Zen nuns from historical, anthropological, cultural, and Buddhist perspectives, I am convinced that the significance of Sōtō Zen nuns is evident in at least three realms: traditional monasticism, traditional Japanese culture, and advancing women's opportunities. The Sōtō sect regulations permit monastics of both sexes to interpret the monastic tradition with considerable flexibility. The community of nuns shows strong commitment to their interpretation of a traditional paradigm of Zen monastic Buddhism. Moreover, their choice to maintain a traditional monastic lifestyle has significant ramifications for Japanese culture. The nuns' community represents a sector of modern society that honors traditional patterns of behavior. They deliberately retain firm roots in the customs and values that have been cultivated for hundreds of years. Traditions are central in their everyday lives. Their nunnery is one of the few places in modern Japan where one can experience or observe traditional Japanese culture in daily life. Furthermore, Sōtō Zen nuns are a leading example of the educational, occupational, and social advancements that Japanese women have made during this century. Their most distinguished roles are as preservers of traditional Buddhist monastic life and bearers and transmitters of traditional Japanese culture.

Preservers and Creators of Buddhist Tradition

My research results portray nuns as preservers and creators of Buddhist tradition. Four of the hypotheses affirmed by the data can be summed up in this section. The arguments and analysis of the data overlap, because the issues are interrelated. Hypothesis one: "Women in Japanese Buddhist history did not act as though they were defeated by oppressive conditions." The nuns' Buddhist practice is the reason for this. As seen in the data gathered through participant-observation, the nuns' ideal—to be strong enough to be as beautiful as a winter blooming plum blossom—is cultivated through their discipline of human relationships. This practice entails trying to use each situation as an opportunity to "polish" one's heart, and it does so by focusing the problem on the self. One does not begin by blaming. When the focus is on how one responds to the situation and not why the situation is the way it is, it leads to positive action rather than negative complaints. In this way, nuns work at paring down their delusions, desires, and aversions. It is no wonder, then, that the participant-observation data established that the discipline of human relationships is at the core of their practice. This is how they are trained to take even negative situations and transform them into opportunities for Buddhist practice. It does not mean that the nuns were treated fairly at all times; there were oppressive regulations and unfair treatment of nuns in Japanese history. The survey and interview data confirmed, however, that these nuns represent their own history and experience in terms of meaningful Buddhist practice. The nuns were able to overcome the obstacles, because they are dedicated preservers of Buddhist practice.

Furthermore, Sōtō Zen nuns serve as a model for all women who seek liberation. In two generations they went from a position of little opportunity and recognition to a position of full and official acceptance by the male-dominated sect institution, complete with independent institutions for nuns. As innovative pioneers in their struggle to lead traditional monastic lives, nuns serve as a model for all women who seek to make choices about their lives. They turned the unfair practices that circumscribed their lives into an opportunity to become stronger and clearer about the lives they wanted to lead. Their success is proof that oppressive circumstances are not an indication of weakness. On the contrary, those who have triumphed over oppression commonly acquire a keen ability to see what is significant and important. One might even say that Sōtō nuns are strong because acting in the face of discrimination honed their strength and vision to be creative preservers of Buddhist tradition.[1]

Hypothesis two: "In their fight for institutionalizing egalitarian regulations, twentieth-century Sōtō nuns acted as though they were only asking for what history had told them was their due." They saw their history as one filled with valiant nuns, not one that was against women. Their interpretation of history is based on the facts that the first ordained Buddhists in Japan were women and that many important women in Japanese history were nuns. Nuns had been treated with respect in Japanese history in part because many had come from the imperial family. There was not a sense that nuns were the outcasts and poor of society. Twentieth-century nuns began their fight with dignity, drawing upon the dignity of the women who preceded them. They were part of a long tradition of dedicated Buddhist women.

Sōtō Zen nuns in modern Japan preserve the tradition of female Buddhist renunciants begun in India in the sixth century B.C.E. Like these women, Sōtō Zen nuns in modern Japan had to create new traditions in order to participate more fully in the community of Buddhist renunciants. Moreover, they claim that treating women as equals is part of traditional Zen monasticism. In order to preserve this tradition, they first had to systematically revise sect regulations to be in accord with Dōgen's teachings of egalitarianism. They made unprecedented strides in educational possibilities as the twentieth century saw the first nuns educated and graduated from the Sōtō sect's prestigious Komazawa University.[2] Sōtō nuns also formed their own organization in 1944, *Sōtō-shū Nisōdan*, which has since published its own journal, *Otayori*. They went from only being permitted ranks lower than the lowest monk's to being granted the highest title, *Daioshō*. These achievements of Sōtō nuns were always ahead of or synchronous with women in the secular sphere in winning reforms in education, economic opportunities, and self-determination. In the midst of these significant advancements, these nuns maintain the traditional quality of monastic Buddhism. More accurately, they had to disencumber themselves from the unfair practices that had encroached into the sect's regulations over the centuries. Only after they were treated equally could the tradition be lived as they claim Dōgen intended it.

Hypothesis three: "Sōtō nuns use distinctive strategies to establish legitimacy, relevance, and power in the twentieth century." In the twentieth century, the relationship between the monastic order and the social order is complex. Nuns' choices of how to respond to the demands of the twentieth century and their choices of aims are other examples of how they are preservers and creators of Buddhist tradition. Their choices to keep heads shorn, to wear monastic clothing at all times (not just at ceremonies, as many monks do), to be celibate, and to train themselves in traditional arts are evidence that they want to maintain the patterns of the past. Insofar as Sōtō nuns maintain a clear distinction between monastic and lay patterns of life, they represent Dōgen's vision of traditional monastic life. These women do not deem it desirable to lead a lifestyle closer to that of the laity. Indeed, nuns were able to get parity in sect regulations and establish their own training monasteries by following their understanding of Dōgen's teachings. Basing their vision of Zen monastic life upon traditional monastic values, their dominant mode of monastic life is traditional. This enables them to be legitimate bearers of their tradition. Their relevance in the modern age is especially clear in their role as counselors to laity. Their power to be effective in helping people derives from the authority and respect granted to them because they are recognized as genuine teachers of Buddhist values.

The results of my field research confirm Bernard Faure's insight that "it is time for Chan scholarship . . . to stress 'anthropological' multiplicity, since earlier scholarship has tended to stress the 'atheological' unicity of Chan 'classical' orthodoxy."[3] The activities and practices that actually are included under the Zen umbrella are diverse. Monastic women in the sect were not consulted, so the sect did not discover that most Sōtō nuns have religious or spiritual reasons for wanting to uphold traditional monastic practices. The practices of most monastic women (as revealed in observations of their training) and their attitudes about monastic practice (expressed in interviews and surveys) lead to the impression that traditional values are central to their lives. As the interviews indicated, many nuns recognize traditional monastic life as their "real home." It is not experienced as an escape or reversal. The result is that there are now two patterns of ordained Sōtō Zen Buddhists: traditional and modern. Women are primarily traditional.

Hypothesis four: "Most twentieth-century women became Sōtō nuns because they *wanted* to lead traditional monastic lives." The survey and interview responses revealed that the common motivation to become a Sōtō Zen nun was due to their desire to live a monastic lifestyle. The fact that most nuns actually do live a traditional monastic lifestyle is confirmation of the depth of their motivation and commitment. Many openly articulated the rationale that if they had wanted to lead a life like the laity, there was no reason to be ordained as a monastic. Having had to fight so hard, it is clear that Sōtō nuns were deliberately choosing reforms that enabled them to uphold the tradition over reforms that entailed modifying the tradition. They were not and are not, however, engaged in an equalitarian[4] battle to act like monks. Most nuns do not want to live like "monks." They merely want to practice as they interpret Dōgen had intended all monastics to practice. For them, celibacy is not only a monastic vow to be adhered to, it is a preferred virtue. Furthermore, the results of the interviews and surveys suggest that Sōtō nuns view their male counterparts' activities as a degeneration of monastic Buddhism. This type of reflection underscores the value they place on traditional practices. Nuns continue to be concerned with living according to Dōgen's vision of Buddhist monastic life.

Sōtō Zen nuns preserve the role women have played in the development of Japanese Buddhist tradition. It began with women being the first ordained Japanese Buddhists and it continues through women innovatively maintaining their position as monastic Buddhists, overcoming the challenges of this time period.

Bearers and Transmitters of Traditional Japanese Culture

Viewing the nuns' activities in sociohistorical context reveals that the traditional life Sōtō Zen nuns maintain embodies aspects of aesthetic qualities that hark back to the aristocratic culture of the Heian Period. This was a time in which the appreciation of beauty was cultivated through refining the senses to subtle differences in shades and hues of colors, scents, and delicately rich turns of phrase that evoked more than described.[5] Renewed appreciation of these qualities in Japanese culture arose in the face of rapid westernization in the middle Meiji years (1880–1890s).[6] In the search for a new identity in the sea of change, many people developed a heightened awareness of the value of traditional Japanese ways. The 1890s saw a revival of interest in flower arranging, tea ceremony, and Noh drama.[7] In this context, then, the Sōtō nuns' 1903 decision to integrate the traditional arts into their curriculum for training nuns was not merely a matter of appealing to traditional expectations for women. They were tapped into the pulse of a nation that was zealously trying to preserve its own refined traditions. They helped transmit this revival of traditional Japanese arts by teaching them in their nunneries. Many nuns also actively taught these arts in their temples, like a nun named Tetsugan-ni who was admired by the people in her neighborhood because she had many students who studied flower arranging, tea ceremony, and sewing with her.[8] Sōtō Zen nuns actively participated in the Meiji construction of "traditional Japanese Buddhism and culture."[9]

Nuns' involvement in the arts did not, however, begin in the Meiji period. Zen, especially the Rinzai sect, and Japanese art have had an intimate relationship that can be traced back to the Kamakura Period, although the Muromachi Period is better known as a period in which "Zen Art" flourished. Tea ceremony began as a practical method to help a monastic remain alert while engaged in Zen practice. An aesthetic of Zen art evolved out of an emphasis upon the person engaged in the execution of an act. Flower arranging as a spiritual discipline evolved in conjunction with the tea ceremony as a subtle yet beautiful reminder of the impermanent nature of life. The artistic spirit of Zen in action, attention to minute detail in daily living, was captured in Noh drama and developed into a distinct performing art.

Today, the arts as a living tradition, combining usefulness and beauty, can be found as central qualities in these Sōtō Zen nuns' lives. Other Japanese are engaged in the traditional arts, but few make these arts central to their daily pattern of life. Most of the traditional arts in contemporary Japan are experienced in the context of a classroom or reserved for special occasions. Nuns' temples and monasteries are some of the few places in contemporary Japan where one can find beauty and discipline cultivated and refined in ordinary activities like removing slippers, peeling apples, and cooking radishes. Sōtō nuns maintain a relatively traditional lifestyle in the midst of a technologically progressive society, with the tea ceremony and flower arranging as integral aspects of many nuns' daily lives. The nuns also help preserve the traditional arts of Japan by teaching them in their original spirit: training for the body, mind, and heart. Contemporary Japanese society leaves little room for traditional arts and Buddhist values, yet a small number of quality Sōtō Zen nuns keep these alive. Those who want to study the roots of traditional Japanese arts will find a Sōtō Zen nunnery an important resource.

Maintaining a tradition requires careful attention to detail. Being a transmitter of it demands a comprehensive understanding of and experience with the intricate mechanisms that comprise the tradition. In obvious and subtle ways, the nuns' choice of clothing, patterns of speech, and preferred behavior suggest that they are qualified bearers of the cultural and artistic traditions of Japan. Their physical appearance and use of language are obvious indications of their concern for tradition. With one glance across a crowded train station platform, one can pick out a nun immediately, for her traditional monastic robes and *zōri* sandals (not to mention her shorn head) stand in distinct contrast to the western-style clothing that is worn by the vast majority of the population. With one quick conversation, her ease in correctly conjugating the most complicated and polite forms of Japanese sounds practically musical against the drone of truncated and fumbled attempts pervasive in Japan today.

In a way, Zen nuns are quintessential models of traditional Japanese women. They affirm the value of virtues, such as patience, strength, and beauty. Many nuns have perfected the art of serving with grace and bowing humbly in the face of various demands. Although this skill has been denigrated by western feminists as an indication of women succumbing to male dominance, monastic women do not interpret it this way. Instead, they interpret such behavior as the mark of a disciplined heart and body, where the ego is pared down and the rough edges rounded off. They understand that this derives from insight into Buddhist wisdom and the ways of compassion. Nuns know that to effectively cultivate such skills requires tremendous discipline. That is why most nuns exceed the minimum requirements for training at a monastery. The average time nuns spend in monastery training is five years. They explain that this is important, so that even after leaving the high-pressured communal life they will be able to maintain their discipline. As the participant-observation data revealed, the discipline of human relationships is at the core of their practice. It is in learning how to respond to other people (without first thinking how you are hurt or helped by the interaction) that enables nuns to take any situation as an opportunity for Buddhist practice. These nuns think that to treat another person with kindness is the mark of a "polished" heart. On numerous occasions I heard nuns explain that kindness from a well-disciplined person is not dependent upon how the other person treats you. They recognize that the "gentler" virtues are signs of discipline, strength, and clarity.

In *Recreating Japanese Women*, Jennifer Robertson intimates that many women in Japanese history became nuns as a way of rejecting the conventional female gender roles.[10] This is not the case with Sōtō Zen nuns. When they established their own training facilities, the nuns chose to institutionalize as an integral part of their practice the main traditional arts that defined a woman as refined, particularly the tea ceremony and flower arranging. Their choices reveal that they relish the discipline of the monastic life and the traditional arts. They perceive themselves as being part of a long history of women who have surmounted the obstacles that challenge one's ability to be gracious, patient, strong, and beautiful. They know it is not easy. To continue their commitment to these traditions is a testament that they think traditional Japanese culture has value in modern times.

Therefore, hypothesis five is established: "The aesthetic dimension to Sōtō nuns' practice helps maintain and transmit traditional Japanese culture in modern Japan." The nuns' presence is critical, for their actions bear and their monasteries and temples transmit some of the most refined and highly revered traditions that Japanese culture has to offer. They provide depth to the society through their religious commitment, and they also serve as reminders of what it means to be a "traditional Japanese." A number of Japanese lay Buddhists commented to me that Sōtō Zen nuns should be recognized as "Living Treasures" of traditional Japanese Buddhism and culture.

Like the story of the first ordained Buddhists in Japan, the story of Sōtō nuns in this century illuminates a vital stream in Japanese society and culture. Including their activities and accomplishments gives a more accurate account of each of the scholarly contexts: monasticism, women and religion, Buddhist historiography, Japanese religion, Zen Buddhism, and religious discipline. As adherents to traditional monastic Zen Buddhism, they serve as moral and spiritual leaders of society. Indeed, interviews, surveys, and living with the nuns enabled me to verify that they do not see themselves as powerless victims of oppression. This raises the historiographical issue that leads us to consider the self-perceptions of women historically, and not just how they have been viewed by others, primarily men.

The story of Sōtō Zen nuns helps bring to the surface the lasting role of women in Japanese religion. Women continue to make important contributions to Japanese religious life as they participate in it and create it according to their own understanding. Focusing on the nuns, we see that a traditional paradigm of Zen monastic life is not a matter of the past, but is alive in the present day as nuns engage in their daily activities their religious discipline. Indeed, over the millennia, the monastic way of life has compelled people to leave their homes for austere practices. Like the women in Śākyamuni Buddha's time, women in modern Japan still find the renunciant's lifestyle worth the effort. In order to live as a traditional monastic in modern Japan, however, they had to fight for fair treatment—which included instituting new practices, publishing journals, modifying sect regulations, and establishing new institutions. From this vantage point hypothesis six is clear: "In order to accomplish their goals, Sōtō Zen nuns in twentieth-century Japan became innovators for the sake of tradition."

The history of women in Japanese Buddhism is filled with courageous acts and personal victories—from the first ordained Buddhist in the sixth century, to the inclusive spirit of the Kamakura Period, to the perspicacity and determination of nuns in the Tokugawa Period, to the leaders in educational and institutional reforms in the twentieth century. The events highlighted here only begin to suggest a dim outline of the contours of a landscape that is rich with the suffering and triumphs of centuries of women devoted to Buddhist living. This is only a clue to the treasures buried in Japanese Buddhist history—a history waiting to be discovered.

Notes

CHAPTER ONE

1. Daniel Patte, *Discipleship According to the Sermon on the Mount* (Valley Forge, Penn.: Trinity Press, 1996), p. 24. Patte labels his two categories "Traditional Scholarly Interpretations" and "Exemplary Critical Interpretations." After discussion with him, I renamed the first category "Customary Scholarly Interpretations" so as not to confuse readers of my text, where "traditional" is used in a much different way.

2. Ann Gordon, "The Problem of Women's History," in *Liberating Women's History: Theoretical and Critical Essays*, ed. Berenice A. Carroll (Urbana: University of Illinois Press, 1976), p. 85.

3. Elisabeth Schüssler Fiorenza, "The 'Quilting' of Women's History: Phoebe of Cenchreae," in *Embodied Love: Sensuality and Relationship in Feminist Values*, ed. P. Cooey, S. Farmer, and M. Ross (San Francisco: Harper & Row, 1983), p. 40.

4. Margot Duley and Mary Edwards, eds., *The Cross-Cultural Study of Women: A Comprehensive Guide* (New York: The Feminist Press at the City University of New York, 1986).

5. Ifi Amadiume, *Male Daughters, Female Husbands: Gender and Sex in an African Society* (London: Zed Books, 1987), p. 4.

6. Ibid., pp. 7–8.

7. I. B. Horner, *Women under Primitive Buddhism: Laywomen and Almswomen* (New York: Dutton, 1930); Hellmuth Hecker, *Buddhist Women at the Time of the Buddha* (Kandy, Sri Lanka: Buddhist Publication Society, 1982); Kathryn A. Tsai, "The Chinese Buddhist Monastic Order for Women: The First Two Centuries," in *Women*

in China: Current Directions in Historical Scholarship, ed. Richard Guisso and Stanley Johannesen (Youngstown, N.Y.: Philo Press, 1981), pp. 1–21.

8. Alan Sponberg, "Attitudes toward Women and the Feminine in Early Buddhism," in *Buddhism, Sexuality, and Gender*, ed. Jose Cabezon (Albany: State University of New York Press), p. 8.

9. Margot Duley, "Women in China," in *Cross-Cultural Study of Women*, ed. Margot Duley and Mary Edwards (New York: The Feminist Press at the City University of New York, 1986), p. 244.

10. Bernard Faure, *The Rhetoric of Immediacy: A Cultural Critique of Ch'an/Zen Buddhism* (Princeton, N.J.: Princeton University Press, 1991), p. 243.

11. Mircea Eliade, ed., *Encyclopedia of Religion* (New York: Macmillan, 1987).

12. Keith Crim, ed., *Perennial Dictionary of World Religions* (San Francisco: Harper & Row, 1981).

13. Diana Paul, *Women in Buddhism* (Berkeley: University of California Press, 1985), p. 78.

14. *Bhikkhuni* is Pāli for nun; *bhikṣuni* is the Sanskrit word.

15. Patrick Henry and Donald Swearer, *For the Sake of the World: The Spirit of Buddhist and Christian Monasticism* (Minneapolis: Fortress Press, 1989), pp. 157–158.

16. See Tess Bartholomew, *Women Under the Bo Tree* (Cambridge: Cambridge University Press, 1994), and Chatsumarn Kabilsingh, *Thai Women in Buddhism* (Berkeley, Calif.: Parallax Press, 1991).

17. The sixteen precepts include the three precepts of faith, also known as the three treasures (faith in the Buddha, Dharma, and Saṇgha), the three precepts of purity (to eradicate all evils, to exert for all things that are good, and to liberate all sentient beings), and (7–16) the ten major precepts (not to destroy life, not to steal, not to commit sexual acts, not to lie, not to deal in intoxicating liquors, not to report the wrongdoings of anyone among the four groups (monks, nuns, laymen, and laywomen), not to covet, and not to revile each of the three treasures).

18. Sallie B. King, "Egalitarian Philosophies in Sexist Institutions: The Life of Satomi-san, Shinto Miko and Zen Buddhist Nun," *Journal of Feminist Studies in Religion* vol. 4, no. 1 (Spring 1988): 19.

19. Ibid., p. 20.

20. Kyōko Nakamura, "Women and Religion in Japan," *Japanese Journal of Religious Studies* vol. 10, nos. 2–3 (June–Sept. 1983): 115–121; Robert Ellwood, "Patriarchal Revolution in Ancient Japan: Episodes from the *Nihonshoki* Sūjin Chronicle," *Journal of Feminist Studies in Religion* vol. 2, no. 2 (Fall 1986): 23–37; Chiyoko Higuchi, *Her Place in the Sun: Women Who Shaped Japan*, trans. Sharon Rhoads (Tokyo: East Publications, 1973); Chieko Irie Mulhern, *Heroic with Grace, Legendary Women of Japan* (Armonk, N.Y.: M. E. Sharpe, 1991).

21. Helen and William McCullough, *A Tale of Flowering Fortunes: Annals of Japanese Aristocratic Life in the Heian Period*, 2 vols. (Stanford, Calif.: Stanford University Press, 1980), assert that in most respects Japanese Heian Buddhism did not differ from the Buddhism of the Six Dynasties in China, except that the Japanese had a preoccupation with impermanence in nature and human affairs. Ivan Morris, in *The World of the Shining Prince* (Oxford and New York: Oxford University Press, 1964), p. 123, concurs with the McCulloughs' observation that "the Buddhist stress on evanescence has had a major influence on the literature of the Heian period and later. It is characteristic of the Japanese absorption with nature that their *memento mori* should be . . . live, poignant images like the scattering of blossoms or the yellowing of autumn leaves, which served to remind them that all beautiful things must soon pass away."

22. Joseph Kitagawa describes this orientation a "seamless" worldview. He explains how Japanese myths suggest the "sacredness of the whole universe" which is a "community of living beings." *Religion in Japanese History* (New York: Columbia University Press, 1966), pp. 12–13.

23. For more background, see Heinrich Dumoulin, *Zen Buddhism: A History*, vols. 1 and 2, trans. James Heisig and Paul Knitter (New York: Macmillan, 1990).

24. Dōgen, *Shōbōgenzō*, "*Busshō*," in *Dōgen Zenji Zenshū* vol. 1, edited by Ōkubo Dōshū (Tokyo: Chikumashobō, 1969): 14–35.

25. Takakusu Junjirō and Watanabe Kaigyoku, eds. *Taishō shinshū daizōkyō* vol. 82, 2584 (Tokyo: Taishō issaikyō kankōkai, 1924–1934); pp. 319–342.

26. This is not unlike the intent of the monastic regulations codified in the *Vinayapiṭaka*. See John Holt's discussion of this in his book *Discipline: The Canonical Buddhism of the* Vinayapiṭaka (New Delhi: Motilal Banarsidass, 1981).

27. One concern when determining appropriate terminology in reference to the use of "nun" in the West involves the increasing number of western women who are committed to the monastic Buddhist path and who bring with them a dissatisfaction about the English term "nun." The basis of their discontent lies in the association of the term with Catholic nuns, who are not allowed to perform the Mass. Since Buddhist nuns are equal to monks, a counterargument might stress using the term nun for Buddhists, and thereby raise the status of the appellation. Although historically there have been differences in the vows of male and female adherents to Buddhism, in Sōtō Zen, female and male monastics take the same vows. Western women who have committed themselves to Sōtō Zen Buddhist monastic life want this to be clear.

28. For further information on the Buddhist Saṇgha, see: Sukumar Dutt, *Buddhist Monks and Monasteries of India: Their History and Their Contribution to Indian Culture* (London: Allen and Unwin, 1962), p. 23; Hirakawa Akira, "The Twofold Structure of the Buddhist Saṃgha," *Journal of the Oriental Institute* vol. 15, no. 2 (Dec. 1966): 131–137; Nakamura Hajime, *Genshi Bukkyō no Seiritsu* (Tokyo: Shunjūsha, 1969); Holt, *Discipline*.

29. The feminine suffix *ni* used in "nun" becomes inverted in Japanese, going from the Chinese *sengni* to the Japanese *nisō*.

30. "Buddhist Community" or *seng-chia* is pronounced *sōgya* in Japanese.

31. Kumiko Uchino, "The Status Elevation Process of Sōtō Sect Nuns in Modern Japan," *Japanese Journal of Religious Studies* vol. 10, nos. 2–3 (June/Sept. 1983): 177–194.

32. Personal Narrative Group, ed. *Interpreting Women's Lives: Feminist Theory and Personal Narratives* (Bloomington: Indiana University Press, 1989).

33. Miriam Levering, "The Dragon Girl and the Abbess of Mo-Shan: Gender and Status in the Chan Buddhist Tradition," *Journal of the International Association of Buddhist Studies* vol. 5, no. 1 (1982): 19–35.

34. The description of monastic and academic training levels used in this book reflects the system used before reforms made in 1995. The old system did not make it clear how much time a person actually spent doing disciplined practice in a monastery, because academic training could be calculated in when configuring what monastic training level one belonged to. The new system clarifies this ambiguity. It makes a sharp distinction between monastic training and academic training. This system will enable nuns to be duly recognized for their dedication to monastic training.

35. Richard Jaffee, "Neither monk nor Layman: The Debate over Clerical Marriage in Japanese Buddhism, 1868–1937." (Ph.D. diss., Yale University, 1995).

36. Ishii Shūdō, "Recent Trends in Dōgen Studies," trans. Albert Welter, in *Komazawa Daigaku Kenkyūjo* no. 1 (March 1990): 263.

37. Ian Reader, "Transformation and Changes in the Teaching of the Sōtō Zen Buddhist Sect," *Japanese Religions* vol. 14, no. 1 (Dec. 1985): 28–48.

38. Trinh Minh-Ha, *Women, Native, Other* (Bloomington: Indiana University Press, 1989), p. 107.

39. Koun Ejō, *Shōbōgenzō Zuimonki*, trans. Shōhaku Okumura (Kyoto: Kyoto Sōtō Zen Center, 1987), p. 112.

40. Sōtōshū Nisōdan, *Sōtōshū Nisō Meibō*, 1984. Although not all Sōtō nuns are members of the Sōtōshū Nisōdan, the figures based on information from their records represent the clear trend that few young women become Sōtō nuns. There are approximately 400 nuns in the Jōdo sect, 300 in the Rinzai sect, and some representatives in the Nichiren, Tendai, and Shingon sects. It is extremely difficult, however, to obtain an accurate count on the number of monastic women in each sect; the statistics recorded in the *Shūkyōnenkan* [Annual Record of Religion] (Ministry of Education, Tokyo) designates all professional religious affiliations under the category *kyōshi*, or teacher. The definition of female teacher (*onna kyōshi*) has broadened considerably in recent years. Before World War II this term referred primarily to monastic women, but now it also includes female lay teachers. The people included in my figures were based upon a traditional definition of monastic women: shaven heads, monastic robes worn in daily life, trained at least for a year at a training temple, and celibate. If the same standards were applied to the calculation of the number of monks, their number would be much lower than currently recorded.

41. See chapter 4 for a detailed explication of the specifics.

42. Bernard Faure, *Chan Insights and Oversights: An Epistemological Critique of the Chan Tradition* (Princeton, N.J.: Princeton University Press, 1993), p. 151.

43. See Faure, *Chan Insights and Oversights*, p. 99.

44. Ibid., pp. 114–115.

45. Keizan draws on the *Ching te ch'uan teng lu* (J. Keitoku Dentōroku) and the *Wu teng hui yüan* (J. Gotō egen) in his *Denkōroku*. *Taishō*, vol. 82, 2585, pp. 343–411. English translation by Francis H. Cook, *The Record of Transmitting the Light: Zen master Keizan's 'Denkoroku'* (Los Angeles, Calif.: Center Publications, 1991).

46. *Taishō*, vol. 82, 2585, p. 349.

47. Dōgen, *Shukke Kudoku. Taishō*, vol. 82, 2582, p. 282.

48. The original text does not designate the robes as "monks'." This is an example of how the false impression is inculcated that monks are the norm.

49. Cook, *Record of Transmitting the Light*, pp. 44–45. I have made a few modifications to this translation. The original text is in *Taishō*, vol. 82, 2585, p. 350.

50. A male cannot spend the night at a monastery for women.

51. There is an excellent discussion of the relationship of the researcher and the results of the research in James Clifford and George Marcus, eds., *Writing Culture: The Poetry and Politics of Ethnography* (Berkeley: University of California Press, 1986) and James Boon, *Other Tribes, Other Scribes: Symbolic Anthropology in the Comparative Study of Cultures* (Cambridge: Cambridge University Press, 1982); I will defer to their expertise on the subject and not repeat their theories and insights here.

52. Alfred North Whitehead, *Adventures of Ideas* (New York: Free Press, 1933); Whitehead, *Process and Reality*; Corrected edition, ed. David Ray Griffin and Donald Sherburne (New York: Free Press, 1978); Whitehead, *Modes of Thought* (New York: Free Press, 1938).

53. E. Valentine Daniel, *Fluid Signs: Being a Person the Tamil Way* (Berkeley: University of California Press, 1984).

54. Dōgen, "Uji" [Being Time], in *Shōbōgenzō. Taishō*, vol. 82, 2582, p. 47. Translations are mine.

55. Danny Jorgensen, in *Participant Observation Method* (Newbury Park, Calif.: Sage Publications, 1989), p. 76, warns that "Age, ethnicity, and gender are grounds for much social distance. Rapport requires that these distances be bridged."

56. Other scholars have voiced this concern, including George Marcus and Michael Fischer, *Anthropology as Cultural Critique: An Experimental Moment in the Human Sciences* (Chicago: University of Chicago, 1986), p. 21.

57. Insider and outsider correspond to the cognitive anthropological terms emic and etic, respectively. Emic and etic derive from the linguistic terms "phonemic" and "phonetic." Emic is internal to a language or culture and derived from etic, which poses as universal or scientific. Since these are actually relative terms, Geertz's experience-near and experience-far come closer to capturing the relative nature of the phenomenon. This helps unravel the relationship of the researcher to the research. For further discussion see Marcus and Fischer, *Anthropology as Cultural Critique*, pp. 30–31.

58. For those who know me, my hair turned dark brown when I was five.

59. I concur with James Boon, who, in *Other Tribes, Other Scribes* asserts that writing about experiences of self in "other" cultures and being a voice of "other" people is a tricky business. It is the business of tricksters.

60. Since my academic training has occurred primarily in western institutions, I associate my American qualities with academe. I do not, however, want to make any hidden insinuations that there is anything inherent in American culture that is more scholarly than in Japanese culture.

61. The most explicit example of this occurred when I gave a presentation (in Japanese) of my research-in-progress at a Japanese academic conference on "Japanese Women and Buddhism" at the end of my field research year in Japan.

62. Living on a continuum between cultures offers a rare vantage point from which to explore and interpret various scholarly questions. Kirin Narayan, a German-American Indian with western academic training, describes a similar experience in her book *Storytellers, Saints, and Scoundrels* (Philadelphia: University of Pennsylvania Press, 1989), pp. 8–9: "My shifting identifications worked their way into this text. . . . Rather than being a discovery of the exotic, this work is in many ways a deepening of the familiar."

63. Anthropologist Emiko Ohnuki-Tierney is among the leaders in this investigation. Consult her article, " 'Native' Anthropologist," *American Ethnologist* vol. 11, no. 3 (August 1984): 584–586.

CHAPTER TWO

1. *Kami* are the deities of the indigenous Japanese religious tradition primarily connected with Shintō. They are commonly referred to as animistic or nature deities, for there are mountain *kami*, wind *kami*, and tree *kami* among the myriads.

2. I have found no records that indicate who offered the original ordination ceremony. It was likely a Buddhist monastic visiting Japan from Korea. Given that the three women first received a novice ordination when they arrived in Paekche, the precise status they had before they left Japan is unclear. The Buddhist ordination

tradition allows for adaptations in ordination process when meeting the requirements for regular ordination are impossible. In any case, the important point to stress in the context of this book is that twentieth-century Sōtō Zen nuns recognize these three women as the first ordained Japanese Buddhists.

3. *Nihongi*, trans. by W. G. Aston (Rutland, VT: Charles E. Tuttle Co., 1972), vol. 2, p. 101. *Shūkai* edition of *Nihongi* v. XX, p. 14.

4. *Nihongi*, vol. 2, p. 101. *Shūkai* edition v. 20, p. 14. *Gangōji Garan Engi* in *Jisha Engi*. Compiled by Sakurai Tokutarō, Hagiwara Tatsuo, Miyata Noboru (Tokyo: Iwanami Shoten, 1975), p. 11.

5. *Gangōji Garan Engi*, p. 12. *Nihongi*, vol. 2, p. 113. *Shūkai* edition v. 21, p. 8. *Kamitsumiya no Shōtoku no Nori no Ohokimi no Taisechi*. In *Shōtoku Taishi Shū*. Compiled by Ienaga Saburō, Fujieda Akira, Hayashima Kyōshō, Tsukishima Hiroshi (Tokyo: Iwanami Shoten, 1975), pp. 355–378. The Great Imperial chieftain told envoys from Paekche to take nuns, including Zenshin, to study the precepts.

6. *Nihongi*, vol. 2, p. 113. *Shūkai* edition, v. 21, p. 8.

7. This is a temple headed by a woman. *Ama* means nun and *tera* (or *dera*, depending on the sound of the previous syllable) means temple. There is no equivalent in English, since there is no such situation, so I maintain the transliteration.

8. *Nihongi*, vol. 2, p. 118. *Shūkai* edition, v. 20, p. 14.

9. The *Nihongi*, v. 2, pp. 65–67 (*Shūkai* edition v. 19, p. 33–36), notes the date King Song (-myong) of Paekche sent Emperor Kinmei a present of a Buddhist sculpture and scriptures at 552 C.E. According to the *Gangōji Engi*, p. 8, this event took place in 538 C.E. For more detailed information see Tamura Enchō, "Japan and the Eastward Permeation of Buddhism" in *Acta Asiatica* No. 47 (1985): 1–30.

10. Paekche was becoming isolated in the Korean peninsula due to the increasing military power of both the Silla and Koguryo forces. The Yamato court had aided Paekche in the past, and King Song was concerned to maintain this support, in part through the offering of rare gifts.

11. Tamura, "Japan and the Eastward Permeation of Buddhism," pp. 17–19, surmises this from the records in the *Nihongi* and *Gangōji Engi*.

12. For further information on this issue see Fukuyama Toshio, *Nihon Kenchikushi no Kenkyū* [History of Japanese Architecture] (Kyoto: Sōgeisha, 1980), p. 343; Mochizuki Nobunari, *Nihon Jōdai no Chōkoku* [Sculpture in Ancient Japan] (Osaka: Sōgensha, 1943), p. 147; *Daianji Garan Engi Narabini Ruki Shizaichō* [Materials on the History of the Legends about the Buildings of Daianji] Sonyō, Kyōgi, compiled by Reinin (Tokyo: Nihon Bunka Shiryo Center, 1997); Tamura Enchō, *Nihon Bukkyōshi*, vol. 4 (Kyoto: Hōzōkan, 1983).

13. Tamura, "Japan and the Eastward Permeation of Buddhism," p. 8.

14. For a more detailed discussion of the distinction between "indigenous deities" (*kunitsu-kami*) and "foreign deities" (*adashi-kami*) see Tamura, ibid., pp. 20–23.

15. A *miko* is a person with shamanic powers. Women, or virginal maidens, are frequently found to have these powers. Rarely are there accounts of male *miko*. In ancient Japan, the most renowned *miko* was Empress Himiko, reflecting the power women had in spiritual as well as governmental realms (more accurately phrased, the powers of spirit and government were not distinctly bifurcated).

16. *Nihongi*, vol. 2, p. 101. *Shūkai* edition, vol. 20, p. 14.

17. *Gangōji Garan Engi*, p. 12–13.

18. Ibid., p. 14.

19. Hirakawa Akira, "The History of Buddhist Nuns in Japan," in *Buddhist-Christian Studies*, vol. 12 (1992):150. The ten precepts of a male or female novice (Skt.

śrāmaṇera or *śrāmaṇerikā*) are: (1) refrain from taking life, (2) refrain from taking what is not given, (3) refrain from telling lies, (4) refrain from sexual activity, (5) refrain from taking intoxicants, (6) refrain from singing, dancing, and entertainments, (7) refrain from using ornaments and cosmetics, (8) refrain from using high or luxurious seats and beds, (9) refrain from handling gold and silver, and (10) refrain from taking untimely food. (See Karma Lekshe Tsomo, "Translator's Introduction to 'The History of Buddhist Nuns in Japan' " in *Buddhist-Christian Studies*, vol. 12 (1992):143–146, for a succinct overview of Buddhist precepts.)

20. The number of precepts required of a probationary nun varies. They are basically the same as the first five of the novice plus an additional precept to abstain from taking food after midday. After successfully training for two years, a woman of at least twenty years of age may be ordained a full nun (*bhikṣuṇī*). Part of the rationale for requiring women to enter a probationary period is to allow for a woman to determine absolutely whether or not she is pregnant. Two years is clearly *more* than sufficient time.

21. Hirakawa, "History of Buddhist Nuns," p. 150. It is unclear which school of vinaya these nuns were engaged in, but Hirakawa speculates that it might have been the Daśabhāṇavāra Vinaya or the Caturvarga Vinaya.

22. *Nihongi*, vol. 2, p. 118. *Shūkai* edition, vol. 20, p. 14. It is likely that Miroku Bosatsu (*Maitreya bodhisattva*) was enshrined at Sakurai-ji, for the *Gangōji Engi* (p. 11) recounts that this was the bodhisattva worshipped by Soga no Umako.

23. *Nihongi*, vol. 2, p. 154. *Shūkai* edition, vol. 22, p. 38.

24. Shufunotomo, *Amadera: Kazari O Otoshita Nyonintachi* (Tokyo: Dainihon Insatsu, 1989), p. 38.

25. Takagi Yutaka, *Bukkyō-shi no Naka no Nyonin* (Tokyo: Heibonsha, 1988), pp. 51–53. He bases his analysis upon the records in the *Nihongi* and *Shoku Nihongi*.

26. *Nihongi*, vol. 2, p. 145. *Shūkai* edition, vol. 22, p. 28.

27. *Nihongi*, vol. 2, p. 348. *Shūkai* edition, vol. 29, p. 29.

28. *Nihongi*, vol. 2, p. 349. *Shūkai* edition, vol. 29, p. 30.

29. *Nihongi*, vol. 2, p. 379. *Shūkai* edition, vol. 29, p. 64.

30. See Takagi, *Bukkyō-shi no Naka no Nyonin*, p. 45, for other examples of this type of activity.

31. In 645 the Japanese legal system converted to a Chinese patrilineal model. However, for the following few centuries, social norms defied the legal system. Children continued to take the mother's name and the husband would go to the wife's home for marriage.

32. In general, the Japanese language does not have many sex-specific titles. A title usually just tells what role the person has.

33. *Nihongi*, vol. 2, p. 352. *Shūkai* edition, vol. 29, p. 33.

34. Mikoshiba Daisuke, "Kōmyōshi no Bukkyō Shinkō: Sono Bukkyōteki Kankyō to Kokubunji · Kokubunniji Sōken e no Kanyo nitsuite," in *Ama to Amadera*, ed. Ōsumi and Nishiguchi (Tokyo: Heibonsha, 1989), pp. 74–103.

35. See Takagi, *Bukkyō-shi no Naka no Nyonin*, pp. 89–97, for a more complete discussion of the major contributions Empress Kōmyō made to Buddhism.

36. *Kokushi Daijiten*, p. 681.

37. Some have tried to suggest that nuns were responsible for absolution of sins, because women have more sins. The notion of women having more sins was not in currency until the latter half of the ninth century. Furthermore, the *Shoku Nihongi* states that both monks and nuns studied the *Konkōmyō-kyō* and the *Lotus Sūtra*. Therefore, Yoshida Kazuhiko, in "Ryūnyo no Jōbutsu," *Sukui to Oshie* (Tokyo: Hei-

bonsha, 1989), p. 59, concludes that the sins of the country were being absolved at the Hokke Metsuzaishi-ji.

38. Tajima Hakudō, *Sōtō-shū Nisō-shi* (Tokyo: Sanyo-Sha, 1955), pp. 119–121.

39. Ibid., p. 127. For a more detailed discussion of the issue see Nishiguchi Junko, "Nihonshijō no Josei to Bukkyō: Nyonin Kyūzaisetsu to Nyonin Jōbutsu o megutte" in *Kokubungaku Kaishaku to Kanshō*, vol. 56, no. 5 (May 1991): 19–25. Only toward the end of the ninth century did interpretations of the Nāga princess story begin to raise the question as to whether the story was actually saying that females had to become males in order to be enlightened.

40. Mikoshiba Daisuke, "Kōmyōshi no Bukkyō Shinkō," in *Ama to Amadera*, ed. Ōsumi and Nishiguchi (Tokyo: Heibonsha, 1989), p. 101. Tajima, *Nisō-shi*, p. 130.

41. Seiichi Iwao, ed., *Biographical Dictionary of Japanese History* (New York: Kodansha International, 1978), p. 44.

42. Tajima, *Nisō-shi*, p. 126.

43. *Kamitsumiya no Shōtoku no Nori no Ohokimi no Taisechi*, p. 360.

44. It has gained notoriety for the elegant Buddhist sculpture of Maitreya that is enshrined there.

45. Tsuchiya Megumi, "Ganshu to Ni," in *Ama to Amadera*, ed. Ōsumi and Nishiguchi (Tokyo: Heibonsha, 1989), p. 176.

46. Kyōko Nakamura, *Miraculous Stories from the Japanese Buddhist Tradition: The Nihon Ryōiki of the Monk Kyōkai* (Cambridge: Harvard University Press, 1973), p. 72.

47. Interview with Aoyama Shundō in Nagoya, Japan, in July 1992.

48. Kawamura Kōdō, ed., *Shohon taikō Eihei Kaisan Dōgen Zenji Gyōjō Kenzeiki* (Tokyo: Taishūkan Shoten, 1975), p. 4.

49. *Taishō*, vol. 82, 2582, p. 20.

50. Ibid., p. 91.

51. This view of Buddha-nature also kept Dōgen out of the discussion of the Degenerate Age of the Dharma (*mappō*), because such a concept presupposes that Buddha-nature is something that one must acquire.

52. All English translations from the *Raihaitokuzui* are from Hee-Jin Kim, *Flowers of Emptiness: Selections from Dōgen's Shōbōgenzō* (Lewiston, N.Y.: Edwin Mellen Press, 1985), pp. 287–294. *Taishō*, vol. 82; 2582, p. 33.

53. *Taishō*, vol. 82; 2582, pp. 33–34.

54. He draws upon stories he heard about prominent and highly respected nuns in China. He refers by name to Myōshi-ni, who had seventeen monks as her disciples and authorized their enlightenment during the ninth century, and Massan Ryōnen-ni, known for being the teacher of the great Chinese Zen master Kankei Shikan Zenji.

55. *Taishō*, vol. 82; 2582, p. 35. The translation offered by Kim has been modified according to the research of Miriam Levering, a specialist on Zen in Sung China. The original Chinese text does not add qualifications that are found in Kim's translation. The major difference is that Kim's text suggests only subordinate nuns gather to hear the teachings of an abbess, but the original Chinese states that *all* subordinates, male and female alike, gather for the teachings. Miriam Levering, "Women in Sung Ch'an: A Preliminary Report on the Record," paper presented at a conference on Medieval Zen in Cross-Cultural Perspective at Shilai University, Los Angeles, June 14–15, 1992.

56. *Taishō*, vol. 82; 2582, p. 35. Brackets appear in Kim's text.

57. Kim, *Flowers of Emptiness*, p. 293, note 18 [*Dōgen Zenji Zenshu* 1: 612]. The *Himitsu Shōbōgenzō* is accepted by Dōgen scholars as authentically written by

Dōgen. It received this appellation because it was kept secretly at Eihei-ji for many years.

58. Brackets appear in Kim's text.

59. *Taishō*, vol. 82; 2582, p. 35.

60. Ishikawa Rikizan, "Dōgen no 'Nyoshin Fujōbutsu Ron' Nitsuite Jūni Makibon *Shōbōgenzō* no Seikaku o Meguru Oboegaki," *Komazawa Daigaku Kenkyūjo Nenpō* vol. 1 (March 1990): 88–123.

61. Kasahara Kazuo, *Nyonin Ōjō Shisō no Keifu* (Tokyo: Yoshikawa Kōbunkan, 1975), p. 196.

62. Hokoya Noriaki, *Hongaku Shisō Hihan* (Tokyo: Daizōshuppan, 1989).

63. Tagami Taishū, *Dōgen no Iitakatta Koto* (Tokyo: Kodansha, 1985).

64. Junko Minamoto, *Women, Religion, and Sexuality*, ed. by Jeanne Becher (Geneva: World Council of Churches, 1990), p. 162.

65. King, "Egalitarian Philosophies in Sexist Institutions," pp. 20–21.

66. *Taishō*, vol. 82; 2582, p. 282.

67. Kawamura Kōdō, *Shōbōgenzō no Seiritsushiteki Kenkyū* [Formative and Historical Studies of *Shōbōgenzō*] (Tokyo: Shunjū-sha, 1986), p. 379.

68. An important example of this concerns the establishment of the Nuns' Order. Although Śākyamuni did not leave any writings, he is "quoted" in texts written after his demise that the Dharma will decline 500 years earlier if women enter the order, but the concept of Dharma ages of decline did not arise until 200 years after Śākyamuni passed on. Therefore, the misogynist statement was proven to have been added to the tradition at a later time, and it is not an indication of the founder's views of women.

69. This text was compiled by 500 arhats 400 years after Śākyamuni passed on.

70. *Taishō*, vol. 82; 2582, p. 281.

71. Funaoka Makoto, *Dōgen to Shōbōgenzō Zuimonki* (Tokyo: Hyoronsha, 1980).

72. Ibid., p. 138.

73. Ibid., p. 134.

74. Kōdō, p. 337.

75. Ishikawa Rikizan, "Chūsei Bukkyō ni okeru Ni no Isō Nitsuite: Tokuni Shoki Sōtō Shūkyōdan no Jirei o Chūshin toshite," *Komazawa Daigaku Zen Kenkyūjo Nenpō* no. 3 (March 1992): 141–153.

76. Bernard Faure, "The Daruma-shū, Dōgen, and Sōtō Zen." *Monumenta Nipponica* vol. 42 (Spring 1987): 22–55.

77. Tajima Hakudō, *Dōgen Keizan Ryō Zenji no Nisōkan* (Nagoya: Sotō-Shū Kōtō Nigakurin Shuppanbu, 1953), pp. 16–17.

78. *Eihei Kōroku vol. 10* in *Dōgen Zenji Zenshū*, vol. 2, p. 190.

79. *Eihei Kōroku vol. 8* in *Dōgen Zenji Zenshū*, vol. 2, p. 155.

80. *Eihei Kōroku vol. 10* in *Dōgen Zenji Zenshū*, vol. 2, p. 191.

81. *Eihei Sansogyōgōki* in *Sōtō-shū Zensho*, Shiden jō, Ed. Sōtōshū Zensho Kankōkai (Tokyo: Sōtōshū Shūmuchō, 1970–1973), p. 3.

82. Cited in Tajima, *Zenji*, pp. 30–31.

83. *Eihei Kōroku vol. 2* in *Dōgen Zenji Zenshū*, vol. 2, p. 42.

84. Daibutsu-ji was the name of Dōgen's temple in Echizen before he renamed it Eihei-ji.

85. Some rigidly theory-oriented scholars might see Dōgen's ritual activity as contradicting his philosophical teachings, but this example entices one to imagine Dōgen in the context of a complex society with a variety of concerns.

86. *Eihei Kōroku vol. 5* in *Dōgen Zenji Zenshū*, vol. 2, p. 97.

87. Buddhist lineage is explained in terms comparable to family lineages. The teacher is the "parent" and the disciples are the "children." Therefore, a "Dharma aunt" is a female monastic who has the same teacher as the given disciple's teacher.

88. There is no documentation that records why Dōgen would travel to Kyoto when he was ill. The most popular explanation is that he knew he was near death and wanted to return to his home town to die.

89. Tajima, *Zenji*, pp. 21–25.

90. Ibid., p. 14.

91. *Sōtōshū Zensho*, Shūgenka, p. 525.

92. William Bodiford, "The Growth of the Sōtō Zen Tradition in Medieval Japan," (Ph.D. diss., Yale University, 1989), p. 195. He cites *Gikai sōki* (1309:10:3), compiled by Keizan Jōkin, in *Zoku Sōtōshū Zensho* vol. 2 (1974–1977), shingi, 1a.

93. *Sōtōshū Zensho*, Shūgenka, p. 516.

94. In Sōtōshū *Komonjo* 1:125–26.

95. Kohō Chisan, ed., *Jōsai Daishi Zenshū*, reprinted and enlarged (Yokohama: Dai Honzan Sōjiji, 1976), p. 410.

96. Keizan Jōkin, *Bussō shōden bosatsukai kyōjumon*, transmitted August 28, 1328 to Ekyū in *Dōgen Zenji Zenshū*, vol. 2, ed. Ōkubo Dōshū (Tokyo: Chikuma Shobō, (1970), pp. 282–285. The quote is cited in Bodiford, p. 200.

97. Tajima, *Zenji*, p. 63.

98. Ekyū-ni is recorded in Keizan's *Bussō shōden bosatsukai kyōjumon* in *Sōtōshū Komonjo*, jo, pp. 324–325.

99. Ekyū-ni, En'i-ni, and Shozen-ni are recorded in the *Tōkokusan jinmiraisai okibumi* in *Sōtō-shū Zensho*, Shūgenka, p. 153. Shozen-ni and En'i-ni are also mentioned in the *Eikō-ji* in *Sōtōshū Komonjo*, jo, pp. 122–123.

100. *Tōkokusan jinmiraisai okibumi* in *Sōtōshū Komonjo*, jo, pp. 120–121. *Sōtōshū Zensho*, Shūgenka, p. 504.

101. Tajima, *Zenji*, p. 55.

102. Bodiford, "Growth of the Sōtō Zen Tradition," p. 464.

103. See Heinrich Dumoulin, *Zen Buddhism: A History, Japan* vol. 2 (New York: Macmillan, 1990), pp. 207–214, for information concerning these Zen masters.

104. Ishikawa Rikizan, "*Sōtōshū Nisōshi* o meguru Shomondai," paper delivered at Kenkyūkai: Nihon no Josei to Bukkyō, August 28, 1991, Kyoto, Japan.

105. *Ama Soitsu Kishinjō* (Oct. 26, 1371), in *Sōtōshū Komonjo* vol. 1:53. Noted also in Tajima, *Sōtō-shū Nisō-shi*, p. 205.

106. The text can be found in the *Zenrin gashō shu* in *Zoku Sōtōshū Zensho* vol. 2 (1974–1977): Shingi, 21a.

107. Tajima, *Zenji*, p. 58.

108. The names of nuns are in italics. The figure does not include all the male disciples, but it includes all the known female disciples. The Chinese characters or *kanji* for the people can be found in the glossary (Appendix B). For a lineage chart that includes only male disciples see Dumoulin, *Zen Buddhism: A History*, vol. 2, pp. 457–458.

109. *Nihon Sōtō shū Nisō Keifu*. Cited in Tajima, *Nisō-shi*, p. 312.

110. *Higo Daiganji Hokke Shosha Tōmei*, in *Sōtōshū Zensho*, Konseki, p. 537.

111. *Higo Daiganji Shōmei*, in *Sōtōshū Zensho*, Konseki, p. 537.

112. *Shinsanjisekitōkō*, vol. 6 in *Higo Bunken Sōsho*, vol. 3 (Tokyo: Ryūbunkan, 1909), p. 96.

113. Sōitsu-ni, Myōjun-ni, Genshu-ni, and Honshō-ni are recorded in *Jōseki yuimotsu bunpaijō* in *Sōtōshū Komonjo*, Shū, pp. 5–6.

114. All of Gasan's nun disciples, including Myōzen-ni, are recorded in *Shogakuzan Sōjijizenji Nidai Jōseki Oshō Shihō Shidai* in *Nihon Bukkyōshi*, chūsei hen ni, pp. 343–344.

115. Sōki-ni and Ryōso-ni are recorded in *Haitō no Goninzu*, nos. 42 and 43 of *Shōbō Jūzan Nenpu*.

116. *Gessen Ryōin Zenji Gyōjōki*, in *Zoku Sōtōshū Zensho*, Shingi, p. 36.

117. *Ama to Amadera*, p. 60.

118. Bodiford, "The Growth of the Sōtō Zen Tradition," p. 465.

119. Cited in Ishikawa Matsutarō's *Onna Daigakushū* [Collected Manuals for Female Education] (Tokyo: Heibonsha, 1977), pp. 20–21.

120. For an excellent overview of various dimensions of women's lives in Japan since the onset of the Tokugawa feudalism, see Gail Lee Bernstein, ed., *Recreating Japanese Women, 1600–1945* (Berkeley: University of California Press, 1991).

121. Kyōko Nakamura, "Revelatory Experiences in the Female Life Cycle," *Japanese Journal of Religious Studies* vol. 8, nos. 3–4 (Sept.–Dec. 1981): p. 191.

122. Tajima, *Nisō-shi*, pp. 226–227. For further information on this topic see also Takagi Kan, *Enkiridera Mantoku-ji Shiryōshū* (Tokyo: Seibundō, 1976). Also see Sachiko Kaneko and Robert Morrell, "Sanctuary: Kamakura's Tōkei-ji Convent" in *Japanese Journal of Religious Studies* vol. 10, nos. 2–3 (1983): 195–228.

123. Yoshie Ueda, *Chōmon Nisō Monogatari* (Tokyo: Kokusho Kankōkai, 1979), pp. 69–74.

124. Daihonzan Eihei-ji, *Eihei-ji Shi* (Tokyo: Taishūkan Shoten, 1982), shitamaki, p. 1263.

125. Tajima, *Nisō-shi*, p. 233.

126. In Japanese, the two aims are *kannagara* versus *bummei kaika*. For further discussion of the issues, see Joseph Kitagawa, *Religion in Japanese History* (New York: Columbia University Press, 1966), p. 204.

127. A clear example of this phenomenon is documented in photographs from that time. Seikyōsha members (a conservative group) are photographed in kimono, while Min'yūsha members (a progressive group) wear western suits. Kenneth Pyle's book *New Generation in Meiji Japan: Problems of Cultural Identity, 1885–1895* (Stanford, Calif.: Stanford University Press, 1969) contains reproductions of these photos and a lengthy discussion of the issues. The matter of clothing as an indication of concern for traditional culture is now also played out in the monastic world. Monastic women continue to wear their traditional robes all the time, whereas many monastic men only don the robes for explicitly religious activities.

128. Kitagawa, *Religion in Japanese History*, p. 254.

129. For further discussion of Fukuzawa, see Irokawa Daikichi, *The Culture of the Meiji Period*, trans. and ed. Marius Jansen (Princeton, N.J.: Princeton University Press, 1985), pp. 59–68. For an in-depth look at Yukichi's views on women, see Eiichi Kiyooka, trans. and ed., *Fukuzawa Yukichi on Japanese Women: Selected Works*, intro. Keiko Fujiwara (Tokyo: University of Tokyo Press, 1988).

130. See Ueda, *Chōmon Nisō Monogatari*, p. 77, for a more contextualized analysis of the issue.

131. H. J. J. M. Van Straelen, *The Japanese Women Looking Forward* (Tokyo: Kyojun Kwan, 1940), p. 90.

132. Nakamura, "Revelatory Experience," p. 194.

133. For an in-depth discussion of education as a vehicle for westernization in Meiji Japan, see Michio Nagai, "Westernization and Japanization: The Early Meiji Transformation of Education," in *Tradition and Modernization in Japanese Culture*, ed. Donald Shively (Princeton, N.J.: Princeton University Press, 1971). For a close look at one of the women who participated in the imperially sponsored program to send women to the United States to study, see Yoshiko Furuki, *The White Plum: A Biography of Ume Tsuda, Pioneer in the Higher Education of Japanese Women* (New York: Weatherhill, 1991).

134. I hope that this chapter has shown enough evidence to lead to the awareness that women throughout Japanese history have been engaged in seeking and winning fair treatment. Upon hearing about the women's movement in the West, one late-nineteenth-century Japanese feminist commented on the unfortunate circumstances western women have to deal with, and she considered her own country more advanced.

135. Tajima, *Nisō-shi*, p. 329.

136. Nakamura, "Revelatory Experience," p. 194.

137. Ibid., p. 191.

138. See Murakami Senshō, *Shinshū Zenshi* (Tokyo: Heigo Shuppansha, 1916), pp. 8–11, for details. Cited in James Ketelaar, *Of Heretics and Martyrs in Meiji Japan: Buddhism and Its Persecution* (Princeton, N.J.: Princeton University Press, 1990), p. 203.

139. See Kishimoto Hideo, *Meiji Bunka-shi Shūkyō-hen* (Tokyo: Obunsha, 1956), pp. 542–43. Also see Ueda, *Chōmon Nisō Monogatari*, p. 78.

140. At the core of the government's decision to change these regulations was the desire to remove political ties between the State and Buddhist institutions. State and religion had become tightly interwoven during the Tokugawa Period. See Ketelaar, *Of Heretics and Martyrs*, p. 6, for a more contextualized discussion of the issue.

141. There is, however, historical and philosophical precedent for this decision. In accordance with Shinran's (1173–1262) interpretation of Buddhism and his understanding that he was living in the age of *Mappō* (Degenerate Age of the Dharma), he openly married. He called himself neither monastic nor lay (*hisō hisoku*). Since then, monks from the True Pure Land sect have frequently chosen the option to marry. This practice spread to other sects, but Zen did not formally acknowledge the marriage of monks until the turn of the twentieth century. Researchers should be careful to note that Japanese Buddhist sects across the board now practice the marriage of monks, not just the Pure Land Buddhist monks. The book by Patrick Henry and Donald Swearer, *For the Sake of the World* (Minneapolis, Minn.: Fortress Press, 1989), refers to only Pure Land. In order to gain a more accurate picture of the significance of nuns, one must be aware that nuns are the only monastics who, as an institution, continue to abide by the ancient monastic regulation of celibacy.

142. Kitagawa, *Religion in Japanese History*, p. 203.

143. Tajima, *Nisō-shi*, p. 334.

144. Irokawa, *The Culture of the Meiji Period*, trans. Marius B. Jansen (Princeton, N.J.: Princeton University Press, 1985), pp. 117–178.

145. Ibid., p. 197.

146. Ibid., p. 67.

147. For another perspective on the contributions of women in Japanese history, see Kagotani Machiko, *Josei to Cha no Yu* (Tokyo: Tankōsha, 1985), which views history through the lens of tea.

CHAPTER THREE

1. Hiratsuka wrote this in the inaugural edition of *Seitō* [Bluestockings], the first published journal written for and by women. Cited in Mulhern, *Heroic with Grace*, p. 227.

2. For more information about this movement, see Laurel Rasplica Rodd, "Yo-sano Akiko and the Taishō Debate over the 'New Woman,' " in *Recreating Japanese Women, 1600–1945*, ed. Bernstein, pp. 175–198.

3. Carmen Blacker, *Catalpa Bow: Shamanistic Practices in Japan*, second ed. (London: Allen & Unwin, 1986).

4. See Chapter 4 for detailed explanation of the range and types of degrees available.

5. In 1872 the government officially designated Sōji-ji and Eihei-ji as the head temples of the Sōtō sect. During this time of change, the male-dominated Sōtō Zen institution did not initiate reforms to bring equality to monastic women.

6. Ueda, *Chōmon Nisō Monogatari*, pp. 79–80.

7. *Terakoya* were common in the Tokugawa Period, and they made a positive contribution to a community by offering an education to youths.

8. This information was passed on to me through oral history. Many elderly nuns today recall how their teachers and teacher's teachers taught young children in their temples.

9. For more detailed information on the various degrees offered by the training monastery, see the section "Education: Degrees and Curriculum" in chapter 4.

10. Ishikawa Rikizan, an eminent scholar of Zen Buddhism at Komazawa University, invited me to attend a field research trip to this temple. He was particularly interested in determining more about the temple's historical origins, and he had learned that the temple possessed a black storage chest which contained various original documents that had been spared through the centuries. It was an exciting moment when, in the presence of the two elderly nuns now running the temple, a letter was found that was stamped with the original seal of Hideyoshi. In that instant Yōrin-an became an incontrovertibly important historical temple, reflecting its grand stature extending over four centuries.

11. Information taken from the original certificate kept in storage at Yōrin-an.

12. July 1992 interview with Hori Taiō, the current head of Saikō-ji (formerly Ryūsen-kutsu).

13. The renaming of nuns' temples was part of the sect's reforms to treat male and female monastics equally. Temples with a nun as head had not been classified as full temples. The most common appellation was *"an"* or hermitage. *"Kutsu"* suggests a cave, a common place in nature for Buddhist practice.

14. Minami Kifun is the name of the region in which this Yakushi-dō is located. Since Yakushi-dō is a common name for Buddhist temples, the region name frequently becomes part of the name by which such temples are identified.

15. In 1941 the sect administration gave approval to rename Yakushi-dō as Kōrin-ji, thus raising it to full-ranking temple status.

16. Ōgishi Sakichi, *Gyōten Sōrin no Hibiki: Kifun Yakushi-dō to Aichi Senmon Nisōdō no Rekishi* [Echoes from the Dawn of a Zen Monastery: The History of Kifun Yakushi-dō and Aichi Senmon Nisōdō] (Nagoya: Kaikoku Kōsoku Insatsu, 1981), p. 17.

17. During the Sengoku Period (late sixteenth century), the region was known as Owari no Kuni. Later, it was called Higashi Kasugaigun.

18. In September 1990, I went to visit the original site of the nuns' school, where the bamboo grove is still lush. A larger temple building standing on this site has replaced the original small building. The original building was moved to a nearby temple compound.

19. With one glance at the original building, the harsh reality of the nuns' early years and the height of their zeal was immediately apparent. It was hard to imagine how thirty people could fit into such a tiny space. Led by Kitō Shunkō and a laywoman, Ōgishi Emiko, I visited the original building and site in August 1990.

20. *Miso* soup is a soybean paste soup. It is a staple in the Japanese traditional diet that is complemented with rice to provide an efficient source of protein.

21. One *ri* = 2.44 miles.

22. *Rokujūnen no Ayumi*, p. 8.

23. For further details of their daily schedule and lifestyle, see Yamaguchi's description cited in Sakichi Ōgishi, *Gyōten Sōrin no Hibiki: Kifun Yakushi-dō to Aichi Senmon Nisōdō no Rekishi* (Nagoya: Kaikoku Kōsoku, 1981), p. 24.

24. Ōgishi, *Gyōten Sōrin no Hibiki*, p. 27.

25. This small temple still stands in Nagoya. In the summer of 1992, Kitō Shunkō, who had lived through this time period, walked me from this temple to Umemoto Kinzaburō's home, to the old site of the Yanagihara Nisōdō. This made it easy to imagine how the events must have transpired.

26. Today the region has been redeveloped, and a traditional Japanese cakes store (*manjū-ya*) currently stands at the site of the old front gate of the Nisōdō.

27. To give a sense of the social climate, on January 25, 1911, Kanno Suga was executed for treason against the emperor. She had fought for a socialist solution to women's problems. "She apparently had seen nothing that encouraged her to believe socialism or socialists would provide real solutions to women's problems; women would have to shed their own blood in their own behalf." Sharon Sievers, *Flowers in Salt* (Stanford, Calif.: Stanford University Press, 1983), p. 150. Likewise, monks did not sweat for nuns.

28. A memorial tablet that enshrines the three nuns now stands at the current site of the Nisōdō in Shiroyama-chō, Nagoya.

29. Cited in Ōgishi, *Gyōten Sōrin no Hibiki*, p. 22.

30. Cited in ibid., p. 16.

31. *Rokujūnen no Ayumi*, p. 23.

32. Recounted in Ōgishi, *Gyōten Sōrin no Hibiki*, p. 23.

33. *Rokujūnen no Ayumi*, p. 33. For point of reference, in 1935 there were 2,382 nuns and 28,093 monks in the Sōtō Sect.

34. The memorial stone still stands on the original site of the Nisōdō, which was Andō Dōkai's temple Kōrin-ji.

35. *Rokujūnen no Ayumi*, p. 57, and personal interview with Kitō Shunkō, Sōtō Zen nun, head of Gensen-ji in Nagoya, Japan, in August 1992.

36. These events were relayed to me in an interview with Kitō Shunkō, who had lived through this experience. Interview in Nagoya, Japan, in August 1992.

37. Aichi Senmon Nisōdō, *Jōrin: 80 nen no Ayumi* (Tokyo: Bukkyō Shorin, 1983), p. 12. In interview with Kitō Shunkō, she affirmed the courage of her teacher Hori Mitsujō.

38. The *Monju-bosatsu* from the meditation hall of the Yanagihara Nisōdō was donated by the nuns to Zenshū-ji in Los Angeles, where it is enshrined today. *Rokujūnen no Ayumi*, p. 107.

39. After I left the monastery, I lived in an apartment in a nuns' temple that is

located across the street from Kentoku-ji, now near the center of Nagoya's shopping district.

40. The current location is Shiroyama-chō, Chikusa-ku, Nagoya, Japan.

41. Aichi Gakuin is a university established by the Sōtō Sect in Nagoya. Its Tokyo counterpart is Komazawa University.

42. They retained this arrangement until 1974, at which time the majority of novices entered with high school diplomas.

43. From interviews with Aoyama Shundō and Tomio Chie in Nagoya, Japan, in November 1989. Both of them were in training at the nunnery during this period.

44. *Rokujūnen no Ayumi*, p. 60.

45. Ibid., p. 116.

46. Cited in Ōgishi, *Gyōten Sōrin no Hibiki*, p. 24.

47. The photographs of all the abbesses of the nunnery are hanging in order of succession in the main worship hall of Aichi Senmon Nisōdō.

48. This story was relayed in an interview with Kitō Shunkō in Nagoya, Japan, in August of 1992.

49. There were three other smaller Nisōdō established (in Nagano, near Eihei-ji, and in Tokyo), but none of them are extant today.

50. In the Indian tradition, alms gathering was done for both ritual and practical reasons. As a mark of being a renunciant of the world, the monastic discipline (*vinaya*) did not allow monastics to work. They relied upon the generosity of the laity. Developing a reciprocal relationship, the laity received merit for being generous to a worthy person while the monastics received the sustenance. Monastics in East Asia, especially those following Zen, consider work part of their monastic practice. In keeping with this East Asian interpretation, Sōtō nuns' practice of alms gathering is primarily only continuous with the ritual aspects of alms-gathering practice found in the Indian tradition. It is a practice primarily for developing qualities in the monastic, and it is only by way of consequence that they receive food and/or money for their efforts. There are a few rare exceptions, however; one nun surveyed responded that alms gathering was her primary source of income.

51. Interview with Abbess Hasekawa in Toyama, Japan, in July 1990. I stayed at Toyama Nisōdō for a few days to observe and learn about their monastery activities.

52. Interview with Nakamura Busshin Ekō, former abbess of Niigata Nisōdō, in Niigata, Japan, in July 1990. I stayed at the nunnery for a number of days.

53. Kojima Kendō, *Bikuni no Jisei: Fune ni Kazamu* (Tokyo: Josei Bukkyō-sha, 1985). Interviews with Kojima Kendō held during July of 1990 in Toyama, Japan.

54. From conversations with Kojima Kendō at Lumbini-en in Toyama, Japan, on July 9, 1990.

55. Mizuno Jōrin, "Kyōiku wa Shōrai no tame," *Jōrin* no. 2 (June 1923): 10.

56. Taniguchi Setsudō-ni Tsuitōshū Henshū Iinkai [The Taniguchi Setsudō Memorial Collection Editorial Committee], *Jikō Mugen: Taniguchi Setsudō-ni o Shinonde* [Infinite Compassionate Light: Remembering Taniguchi Setsudō-ni] (Toyama, Japan: Shakai Fukushi Hōjin Lumbini-en, 1987). This book details the activities and extraordinary life of Taniguchi, an illustration of a nun who made a difference in twentieth-century Japan.

57. Found in *Shōbōgenzō* fascicle "Bosatsu no Shishōbō" [The Four Ways a Bodhisattva Acts].

58. Laurel Rasplica Rodd, "Yosano Akiko and the Taishō Debate over the 'New Woman,'" p. 198.

59. His posthumous name is *Niso Dōkō Fūshō Kokushi*.

60. This was their second meeting at Eihei-ji.

61. Interview with current abbess of Niigata Nisōdō, Nakamura Ryoen, in July 1990, Niigata, Japan.

62. Her teacher was Harada Sōgaku.

63. Interview with Sasakawa Ryōsen, current head of Sōtō-shū Nisōdan, in January 1990, Tokyo.

64. Nuns' use of Dōgen's texts in their fight for equality was probably only possible after Watsuji Tetsurō rediscovered Dōgen and examined the significance of the Shō-bōgenzō.

65. Cited in Tajima Hakudō, Sōtō-shū Nisō-shi (Tokyo: Sanyo-sha, 1955), p. 439.

66. Cited in ibid., p. 440. Hōchi is the standard level of temple. The vast majority of temples in Japan are this rank. Monastic women could only be head of sub-temples (originally heisōchi, but renamed junhōchi), the rank below hōchi.

67. The complete list of resolutions can be found in Sōtō-shū Nisō-shi, pp. 440–443.

68. The nuns' actions are typical; Japanese Buddhist history is filled with examples of Buddhists who organized their concern for the well-being of the country, especially during times of strife.

69. The Sōtōshū Nisō-shi was published in 1955.

70. Kojima, Bikuni no Jisei, p. 155.

71. The other four were the promotion of labor unions, democratization of school education, the abolition of regulations that legalized secret investigations and trials, and the democratization of the economic structure.

72. For more detailed information consult: W. G. Beasley, The Modern History of Japan, third rev. ed. (Tokyo: Charles E. Tuttle Company, 1963), pp. 285–286. For a thorough discussion of the cultural and linguistic complexity of the constitution, see Kyoko Inoue, MacArthur's Japanese Constitution: A Linguistic and Cultural Study of its Making (Chicago: University of Chicago Press, 1991).

73. Cited in Sōtō-shū Nisō-shi, p. 443.

74. Cited in ibid., p. 445.

75. Kojima, Bikuni no Jisei, p. 164.

76. Interview with Kitō Shunkō in Nagoya, Japan, July 1990.

77. In 1947, the Constitution required universities to accept women. See Itō Tsuneko, "Sengo Kaimei to Fujin Kaihō" (Postwar Reforms and Women's Liberation), in Nihon Josei-shi, vol. 5 (Tokyo: Tokyo University Press, 1982), p. 298.

78. A literal translation of shōkōshi is "incense ritual celebrant." It refers to the person who leads the ceremony, offers the incense, sits in the center, and does prostrations on behalf of everyone. This position reflects high honor and respect.

79. In June 1993 the Nisōdan decided that nuns would honor Dōgen's memory at Eihei-ji, holding a ceremony similar to the one they hold at Sōji-ji. The ceremony is to be held each year on September 27 or 28, to honor Dōgen's death anniversary (Dōgen died on September 29, 1253).

80. Interview with Kuriki Kakujō, head nun of Seikan-ji in Nagoya, Japan, in August 1990. She also showed me a photograph of the event with Katō wearing a yellow robe.

81. Interview with Kojima Kendō in Toyama, Japan, in July 1990.

82. Kojima gave me her copies of Hanahachisu.

83. I met a few of them when I was in Bodh Gaya in 1987. They spoke in superlative terms about the kindness of Kitō Sensei. I was duly impressed with their level of Japanese.

84. When I interviewed her in June 1990, she recounted how she was sorry she was unable to arrive in time due to uncontrollable delays in travel arrangements.

85. Interview with Kitō Shunkō in Nagoya, Japan in August 1990.

86. For more detailed information on this event, see Igawa Etsudo, ed. "Kōjunshin tadahitotsu," *Otayori* no. 76 (Sept. 1980): 2–13.

87. Kojima, *Bikuni no Jisei*, p. 156.

88. Ibid., p. 157. Ten years earlier, the Nisōdan journal, *Otayori*, published an article by Aoyama Shundō that explicates how Sōtō nuns had almost accomplished their goals of equalitarian treatment by the Sōtō sect administration and regulations. See Aoyama Shundō, "Nansō Nisō no Sabetsu: Hanseiki no Higan ga Minoru," *Otayori* no. 57 (Aug. 1979): 4–9.

89. Interview with Kuriki Kakujō, head nun of Seikan-ji in Nagoya, Japan, in August 1990.

90. In Japanese, it is the difference between making *kubetsu* (distinctions) where necessary, but not promoting *sabetsu* (discrimination).

91. Kojima, *Bikuni no Jisei*, p. 130.

92. Interview with Aoyama Shundō at Muryō-ji in Shiojiri, Nagano, Japan, on July 8, 1990.

93. Aoyama Shundō, "Sermon on *O-bon* and a Mother's Love," delivered at Myōgon-ji, Toyokawa, Japan on July 7, 1992.

94. Aoyama Shundō, *Kokuhatsu-tachite Irishi Michi* (Tokyo: Seirin-ji, 1990), p. 60.

95. Aoyama, *Kokuhatsu*, p. 101.

96. Aoyama Shundō, *Nori no Kemanshō: Hokekyō o Ajiwau* (Tokyo: Hakujusha, 1984), p. 6.

97. Conferring a doctoral degree in the Japanese higher education system is not exactly the same as that practiced in the higher education system of the United States. In the Japanese system, one must often wait long after the completion of all requirements to prove one's scholarly ability before a doctoral degree, or the status of *hakase*, is granted.

98. Aoyama Shundō, *Imani Inochi Moyashite: Watakushi o Sutete Dō Michi o Hirakuka* (Tokyo: Kōsei Shuppansha, 1987), p. 89.

99. Aoyama Shundō, *Zen Seeds: Reflections of a Female Priest*, trans. Patricia Daien Bennage (Tokyo: Kōsei, 1990), p. 160. She wrote the poem in the year the theme of the Emperor's poetry contest was "bridge." She drew upon two metaphors from Buddhist sources. One is from the T'ang dynasty. Zen master Chao-chou explains that enlightenment is open to all, just as a bridge does not distinguish between donkeys and horses, but unconditionally lets all cross over it. Aoyama combined this with an extension of the early Buddhist "raft" metaphor where enlightenment is understood to be a quest to get to the other shore.

100. I attended the 1989 and 1990 Zen no Tsudoi.

101. This book has been translated into English under the title *Zen Seeds*.

102. See bibliography for a more complete list of Aoyama Shundō's books.

103. For more detailed information on this project, see Kadowaki Kakichi and Jan Van Bragt, eds., *Tōzai Reisei Kōryū no Seika* (Tokyo: Sekai Shūkyōsha Heiwa Kaigi Nihon Giinkai, 1985) and Jan van Bragt, "An East-West Spiritual Exchange," *The Eastern Buddhist* vol. 13, no. 1 (Spring, 1980): 141–150.

104. Aoyama, *Kokuhatsu*, p. 16. Although words can be obstacles to understanding the truth, Aoyama does not claim that words cannot be a viable medium for teaching the truth.

105. Aoyama, *Zen Seeds*, p. 34.

106. Aoyama, *Utsukushikihitoni* (Tokyo: Kabushikigaisha Pantaka Shuppan, 1983), p. 28.

107. Cited in Aoyama, *Ikasarete, Ikashite, Ikiru* (Tokyo: Shunjūsha, 1989), pp. 18–19.

108. Aoyama Shundō, *Kokuhatsu*, p. 19.

109. Aoyama Shundō, *Ikasarete*, p. 33.

110. Aoyama Shundō, *Zen Seeds*, p. 82.

111. Aoyama Shundō's lectures at Aichi Senmon Nisōdō, Fall 1989. Recorded by Paula Arai.

CHAPTER FOUR

1. The matrix for this form of Buddhist practice is found in the Ch'an tradition of China. In part, Confucian influences explain the concern for group harmony through a hierarchical scheme. For further inquiry see Heinrich Dumoulin, *Zen Buddhism: A History, India and China*, vol. 1, trans. James Heisig and Paul Knitter (New York: Macmillan Publishing Co., 1988).

2. Victor Turner, *The Ritual Process: Structure and Anti-Structure* (Ithaca, N.Y.: Cornell University Press, 1969), p. 113.

3. For further elaboration on the discrepancy between common western assumptions about Zen and its actual practice in Asia, see Robert E. Buswell, Jr., *The Zen Monastic Experience: Buddhist Practice in Contemporary Korea* (Princeton, N.J.: Princeton University Press, 1992). The most explicit discussion of this issue can be found on pp. 3–20 and 217–223.

4. For a closer look at Zen monastic life, also see: Martin Collcutt, *Five Mountains: The Rinzai Zen Monastic Institution in Medieval Japan* (Cambridge, Mass.: Harvard University Press, 1981); Griffith T. Foulk, "The Zen Institution in Modern Japan," in *Zen: Tradition and Transition*, ed. Kenneth Kraft (New York: Grove Press, 1988), pp. 157–177; Nishiyama Eshin, *Unsui: A Diary of Zen Monastic Life*, ed. with intro. by Bardwell Smith (Honolulu: University of Hawaii Press, 1973); David Preston, *The Social Organization of Zen Practice: Constructing Transcultural Reality* (Cambridge: Cambridge University Press, 1988); Daisetz T. Suzuki, *The Training of the Zen Buddhist Monk* (Reprint. Berkeley: Wingbow Press, 1974).

5. The purpose and structure of Zen and Catholic monasteries differ. Catholicism includes two "professional" paths: monastic and priestly. Modern-day Sōtō Zen "professionals" are technically monastics, although many function primarily as liturgical leaders.

6. Hee-Jin Kim, "Monastic Asceticism: The Way of Ritual and Morality," in *Dōgen Kigen—Mystical Realist* (Tucson: University of Arizona Press, 1975), pp. 228–308, offers a solid discussion of these issues.

7. *Hōrō* is the religious age of a monastic. The day of your ordination ceremony becomes your birthday as a monastic Buddhist.

8. Uchiyama Kōshō, *The Zen Teachings of "Homeless" Kōdō* (Kyoto: Kyoto Sōtō Zen Center, 1990), p. 150.

9. This is a striking example of Dōgen's understanding of sufficiency, since water was abundant in the regions where he lived and taught. One might also interpret Dōgen's keen attention not to waste as a strict interpretation of the vow not to steal. Since we are all related, stealing is not simply a matter of taking what is not given, but it is also using more than what is needed.

10. A Zen monk, Victor Sōgen Hori, once told me how he was reprimanded by

his Zen master for not teaching the novices how to cook a certain dish that he had requested. The monk quickly retorted to the master, "But I do not know how to cook that dish myself, how am I supposed to teach others?" The master replied, "That is no excuse! I know very little, and yet I must teach all of you everything!" He also recounts this incident in "Teaching and Learning in the Rinzai Zen Monastery," *The Journal of Japanese Studies* vol. 20, no. 1 (Winter 1994): 21.

11. Holt, *Discipline*, p. 22.

12. Ibid., p. 30.

13. Ibid., p. 103.

14. *Ama* means female Buddhist monastic or nun, and *san* is a suffix indicating respect. This is a warm title in common usage. The term *nisō* is a more technical term that is used in writing or in formal discussions. It is not used to call someone, although *nisō-san* is used as a more formal version of *ama-san*.

15. *Mañjuśrī-bodhisattva* in Sanskrit. He is a symbol of wisdom.

16. *Avalokiteśvara-bodhisattva* in Sanskrit. I refer to this bodhisattva using the endearing honorific title, for this reflects the everyday language of the monastic women.

17. I was one of three laywomen living at the nunnery for four months. My fluency in Japanese and familiarity with Japanese culture facilitated my ability to adapt to the rhythm of life at the nunnery as well as conduct all my interviews and research without the aid of an interpreter. Most of the following text derives from my observations while participating in this life and from the journal I kept during that period.

18. The daily schedules of Zen monasteries vary. Some monasteries do a few more rounds of zazen, while others do less. Aichi Senmon Nisōdō stands out in that it holds a *sesshin* with intensive zazen and teachings once a month. Eihei-ji and Sōji-ji, the Head monasteries of the Sōtō sect, only hold a few *sesshin* per year.

19. The monastic regulations that developed in India included that a monastic was not to eat after the noon hour. Monastics gathered alms for sustenance. As the tradition was transported to China, however, gathering alms was not easily accepted. Therefore, Chinese monastics introduced tilling their own fields as part of their monastic Buddhist practice. With such physical labor, it was not reasonable to maintain the "middle path" and not eat after noon. So, the practice of incorporating an informal "medicine meal" late in the day developed. This tradition came to Japan from China.

20. This was perhaps the most difficult aspect of the practice for me. Having not been raised sitting on the floor in formal *seiza* posture—lower half of legs tucked neatly under upper half of legs—I squirmed a lot. By the end I did succeed in developing calluses on the top side of my feet, but not as big as those of the nuns. This is also a sign of the nuns' decision to maintain Japanese tradition. Many in modern Japan now use chairs for sitting.

21. For pragmatic reasons, laundry is permitted on other days. There is not enough space for everyone to hang their clothes to dry.

22. Nuns generally retain this rhythm of life after leaving the nunnery. They continue to rise early, clean their own temple daily, chant sūtras, arrange the flowers, and cook. I have yet to meet a lazy Zen nun.

23. The names of novices in training are pseudonyms. The names of the teachers are actual.

24. Aoyama Sensei passed her exam with a perfect score.

25. *Keigo*, or honorific language, is the highest stratum of Japanese language, and it is the most complex level of speech. The conjugation of verbs and certain nouns differ from "ordinary" speech. Many elders in Japan today are concerned that young

people do not know the proper usage of this level of speech. For a more detailed discussion of *keigo* and modernization, see Roy Miller, "Levels of Speech (*keigo*) and the Japanese Linguistic Response to Modernization," in *Tradition and Modernization in Japanese Culture,* ed. Donald Shively (Princeton, N.J.: Princeton University Press, 1971), pp. 601–665.

26. Donald Shively, ed., *Tradition and Modernization in Japanese Culture* (Princeton, N.J.: Princeton University Press, 1971), p. 505.

27. Jack Goody, *The Interface Between the Written and the Oral* (Cambridge: Cambridge University Press, 1987), p. 3.

28. Ōgishi, *Gyōten Jōrin no Hibiki,* pp. 35–36.

29. The abbess writes in her "Abbess Diary" that we "go straight by winding along." Aoyama Shundō, "Dōchō Nikki," *Zen no Kaze* vol. 1 (March, 1981), p. 85.

30. See Holmes Welch, *The Practice of Chinese Buddhism 1900–1950* (Cambridge, Mass.: Harvard University Press, 1967), chapter 1, for a more complete description of the traditional division of labor in a monastery.

31. Aoyama, *Imani Inochi,* pp. 53–54.

32. Arnold van Gennep, *The Rites of Passage,* trans. Monika B. Vizedom and Gabrielle L. Caffee (London: Routledge and Kegan Paul, 1909).

33. The following discussion of ordination and precept ceremonies of nuns is based upon my inquiries and my observation of these ceremonies during the spring and summer of 1990 in Aichi and Nagano prefectures.

34. There are numerous layers of the bridal kimono. They are both functional and symbolic. The first kimono is pure white to symbolize the death of the bride to the family in which she was raised. The second layer is bright red, a symbol of her birth into her new family with her husband. Over these inner garments are decorative slips and an ornate outer kimono.

35. Relations with family and friends are rarely entirely terminated, but during the first several years after ordination, many women have only minimal contact.

36. For an overview of Buddhist precepts for nuns, see Chatsumarn Kabilsingh, *A Comparative Study of the Bhikkunī Pāṭimokkha* (Varanasi: Chaukhamba Orientalia, 1984). Kabilsingh does not, however, include a discussion of the precepts commonly taken by Japanese nuns. Documents on nuns' precepts in Japanese Buddhist history are only just beginning to be uncovered. One thing is certain, however: nuns of the Sōtō Zen tradition in Japan take the same precepts as the monks, namely the sixteen precepts followed by Dōgen.

37. On the basis of Kagamishima Genryū's article "Endokai to Zenkai," Bodiford concludes that "no tradition of abbreviated precepts existed in China"; "Growth of the Sōtō Zen Tradition," p. 394. In thirteenth-century China, the distinction between Mahāyāna and Theravada was a matter of orientation and attitudes. Precepts were not questioned; they were uniformly administered (Bodiford, p. 375). Saichō changed the view of precepts in Japan. For a thorough discussion of this issue, see Paul Groner, *Saichō: The Establishment of the Japanese Tendai School* (Berkeley, Calif.: Berkeley Buddhist Studies Series, 1984).

38. According to Bodiford, "Growth of the Sōtō Zen Tradition," p. 393, Dōgen did not include fifty-eight precepts from the *Bonmōkyō* that are administered in Tendai. Bodiford (p. 394) identifies three main influences on Dōgen's sixteen precepts: (1) Tendai practice of observing only Mahāyāna precepts, (2) Chinese Ch'an insistence on precepts realized only in daily life, and (3) an abbreviated ordination ceremony based on a reduced number of bodhisattva precepts.

39. Aoyama Shundō, the abbess, explained the precepts to me on the eve of an

ordination ceremony she was to perform, August 7, 1990, at her temple, Muryō-ji, in Nagano, Japan.

40. A few times a year, Aichi Senmon Nisōdō holds *Mugon Sesshin* (silent retreats). The lectures are replaced with zazen.

41. Interview with Aoyama Shundō on July 8, 1990, in Nagoya, Japan.

42. For more information on the Anan Kōshiki, see my chapter, "Japanese Buddhist Nuns' Ritual of Gratitude and Empowerment" in *Women Changing Contemporary Buddhism* (forthcoming).

43. Nakamura Hajime, *Genshi Bukkyō no Seiritsu* (Tokyo: Shunjūsha, 1969), pp. 348–356; Jean Przyluski, "Uposatha," *Indian Historical Quarterly* vol. 12 (Sept. 1936): 383–90.

44. Charles Prebish, "The Vinaya Piṭaka," in *Buddhism: A Modern Perspective*, ed. Charles Prebish (University Park: Pennsylvania State University Press, 1975), pp. 49–53.

45. Kabilsingh, *A Comparative Study of Bhikkhuni Patimokkha*; Charles Prebish, *Buddhist Monastic Discipline: The Sanskrit Prātimokṣa Sūtras of the Mahāsāṃghikas and Mūlasarvāstivadins* (University Park: Pennsylvania State University Press, 1975).

46. *Rōhatsu Sesshin* is a retreat held December 1–8 every year. It is considered the most intensive retreat of the year.

47. Although I did not become ordained, nor did I have any intention of seeking ordination, the abbess, Aoyama, gave me a special certificate of graduation for having lasted the four months cloistered in the monastery. After countless times of wondering whether I had been an interruption to the nuns' training, tears of relief and joy naturally welled up in my eyes when the abbess looked deep into them, handed me the certificate, and softly whispered, "Congratulations." She told me she had decided to accept me into the monastery after I told her the reason I wanted to study nuns; namely, because I had found the living Dharma in the nun and teacher, Kitō Shunkō. I maintained a certain degree of decorum during those months due to Kitō Sensei's kindness and understanding. I am embarrassed, however, that a ceremony was made out of my inadequate and brief efforts, which are in stark contrast to the years of training to which the nuns are committed. However, my own difficulties in lasting a mere four months made it viscerally clear how deep the commitment of these women who graduate must be.

48. The Dharma lineage is structured similar to blood lineages (*ketsumyaku*). Teachers are like parents and disciples are like children. The Dharma lineage structure also expands to include "grandparents," "cousins," "aunts," and "uncles." More technically, a Buddhist lineage, or *Kechimyaku*, can be divided into two distinct lineages. One is the lineage of direct transmission of the Dharma between teacher and disciple (J. *Hōmyaku-e*), and the other lineage is the lineage of the conferment of precepts from preceptor to novice (J. *Kaimyaku*). *Japanese-English Buddhist Dictionary* (Tokyo: Daitō Shuppansha, 1965), p. 166.

49. *Shakyō* was highly developed in the Heian period with focus upon the *Lotus Sūtra*. The *Lotus Sūtra* itself says that the sūtra should be copied, for it is an act that results in accruing merit.

50. I attended the Jizō Nagashi in 1992.

51. *Jizō Hongan-kyō*, vol. 2 (Taishō, vol. 13).

52. The festivals and rituals are part of *O-bon*. Many texts on Japanese Buddhist practice include a discussion of this festival, including a colorful account in Ian Reader's *Religion in Contemporary Japan* (Honolulu: University of Hawaii Press, 1991), pp. 96–101.

53. This ritual includes *mizuko*, unborn fetuses. For a discussion of aborted *mizuko* and Japanese Buddhism, see William LaFleur, *Liquid Life: Abortion and Buddhism in Japan* (Princeton, N.J.: Princeton University Press, 1992).

54. These are traditional offerings that are given out of respect with the hopes that they will make the deceased more comfortable.

55. From *Dainichi-kyō*.

56. Mizuno Jōrin, "Kyōikuwa Shōrai no tame," *Jōrin* no. 2 (June 1923): 7.

57. In an interview with Aoyama Shundō on July 8, 1990, she pointed out that before 1903 nuns could not receive degrees to acknowledge the level of their practice and training; however, they went because they wanted to be renunciants. Strong teachers attracted numerous disciples.

58. The requirements for the various religious teaching ranks are complex. They can be found in the *Sōtō Shūmuchō Kitei*.

59. Variance may occur when a nun receives a high level of academic education in a Buddhist university and then receives a correspondingly high academic rank, but her monastic rank would not be equivalent without the appropriate years spent in training at the monastery or serving in a temple.

60. See the *Nisō-shi* (p. 407) for a detailed chart of which texts are studied at what level.

61. From my notes taken at a lecture at Aichi Senmon Nisōdō on December 7, 1989.

62. From my notes taken at a lecture at Aichi Senmon Nisōdō on December 19, 1989.

63. From my notes taken at a lecture at Aichi Senmon Nisōdō on October 3, 1989.

64. The metaphor drawing upon the images of grass seeds, sun, and water suggests a few strands of Buddhist theories of primordial ground: the *Tathāgatagarbha* theory of Buddha-nature and the *Nirvāṇa Sūtra* metaphor of a mango seed that must ripen with sun and water to become sweet fruit. Dōgen employs the seed and water metaphor in his fascicle on Buddha-nature, *Busshō*, but he qualifies the explanation by ending that "this is the thought of ordinary people." Aoyama, indeed, sees ordinary people as her audience, and her use of metaphors is effective. Although her example is closer to the concept of Buddha-nature of Dōgen's teacher (all sentient beings *possess* Buddha-nature) rather than Dōgen (all existents *are* Buddha-nature), my understanding of her explanation is that she was trying to stress practice to the novices. She was not intending to reinterpret Dōgen's teachings. For more information about the *Tathāgathagarbha* theory of Buddha nature, see Sallie B. King, *Buddha Nature* (Albany: State University of New York Press, 1991), pp. 48–56.

65. From my notes taken at a lecture at Aichi Senmon Nisōdō on November 5, 1989.

66. There are numerous books that discuss the tea ceremony. Aoyama has written two: *Chazen Kanwa* [Quiet Talk on Zen Tea] (Tokyo: Nakayama Shobo, 1978) and *Shōrai ni Kiku: Zen no Michi Cha no Michi* [Listen to the Wind in the Pine: The Path of Zen, the Path of Tea] (Tokyo: Hakujusha, 1992). A text highlighting the historical contributions of women is Kagotani Machiko, *Josei to Cha no yu* (Tokyo: Tankōsha, 1985). Texts in English include Okakura Kakuzō, *The Book of Tea* (New York: Dover Publications, 1964) and Sōshitsu Sen XV, *Tea Life, Tea Mind* (Tokyo: Weatherhill, 1979).

67. From my notes taken at a lecture at Aichi Senmon Nisōdō on October 3, 1989.

68. From my notes taken at a lecture at Aichi Senmon Nisōdō on September 14, 1989.

69. Shigenori Nagatomo elaborates on the topic implicit in this discussion, Dō-gen's concept of "total functioning," in his book *Attunement through the Body* (Albany: State University of New York Press, 1992), p. 172.

70. Martha Graham, *Notebooks* (New York: Harcourt Brace Jovanovich, 1973), p. xv.

71. Thomas Rohlen asserts that in the Japanese definition of adulthood: "There is no more powerful symbol of the perfected inner life than that of outward composure. . . . To be neat, proper, and orderly—whether in housekeeping, factory routines, personal relations, or daily ceremonies—is to possess the necessary will, energy, and attention." From "The Promise of Adulthood in Japanese Spiritualism," in *Adulthood*, ed. by Erik Erikson (New York: Norton, 1978), p. 136.

72. Further discussion of the relationship between Dōgen's sixteen precepts, his monastic regulations, and ethics can be found in Christopher Ives, *Zen Awakening and Society* (Honolulu: University of Hawaii Press, 1992), pp. 53–56.

73. Shigenori Nagatomo explicates the reasons for this phenomenon, as outlined by Ichikawa Hiroshi and Yuasa Yasuo, in his book *Attunement through the Body*, p. 253.

74. Aoyama, *Shōrai*, p. 59.

75. The methods are so refined that Kim translates the word *sahō* as "ritual conduct." Hee-Jin Kim, *Dōgen Kigen—Mystical Realist*, p. 237.

76. Yanagi Soetsu, *Unknown Craftsman: A Japanese Insight into Beauty* (Tokyo: Kodansha, 1972), p. 143.

77. Aoyama, *Shōrai*, p. 55.

78. Wing-Tsit Chan, trans. and comp., *A Source Book in Chinese Philosophy* (Princeton, N.J.: Princeton University Press, 1963), p. 17, n. 10.

79. Tu Wei-Ming, *Confucian Thought: Selfhood as Creative Transformation* (Albany: State University of New York Press, 1985), pp. 97–98.

80. Cited in Soshitsu, *Tea Life, Tea Mind*, pp. 30–31.

81. Sen no Rikyū, *Namboroku*. Cited in Tanikawa Tetsuzo, "The Esthetics of Chanoyu, Part I," in *Chanoyu Quarterly* no. 23 (1980): 42–43.

82. I took tea ceremony lessons for one year from Kuriki Kakujō, one of the nuns who taught the tea ceremony at the monastery.

83. Aoyama, *Shōrai*, pp. 42, 54. The quote is from the *Heart Sūtra*.

84. Nishida Kitarō, *Art and Morality*, trans. David Dilworth and Valdo Viglielmo (Honolulu: The University of Hawaii Press, 1973), p. 161.

85. From *Dōgen*, vol. 1, ed. by Terada Tōru (Tokyo: Iwanami Shoten, 1980), p. 105. Cited in Nagatomo, *Attunement through the Body*, p. 168.

CHAPTER FIVE

1. Susan Murcott, *The First Buddhist Women: Translations and Commentary on the "Therigatha"* (Berkeley, Calif.: Parallax Press, 1991), p. 26.

2. William LaFleur. "Dōgen in the Academy," in *Dōgen Studies*, ed. William LaFleur (Honolulu: University of Hawaii Press, 1985), pp. 1–20; Carl Bielefeldt, "Recarving the Dragon: History and Dogma in the Study of Dōgen," in *Dōgen Studies*, pp. 21–53. Dōgen's texts are central to the curriculum of Sōtō Zen monasteries in Japan.

3. *Darani* are syllables that are regarded as embodying special religious or mystical power.

4. As recorded in the *Shūkyō seido chōsa shiryō*, ed. Mombushō Shūkyō Kyoku (Tokyo: Hara Shobo, 1977), on January 22, 1873, the nuns' regulations were adjusted

to match the monks' regulation, which had been modified shortly before in April 1872. James Ketelaar addresses this issue briefly in his text, *Of Heretics and Martyrs*, pp. 5–6. One of the sixteen vows is to not engage in sexual misconduct, which for a monastic traditionally means celibacy.

5. By 1935, 80% of "male monastics" in the Sōtō sect were married.

6. Japan Ministry of Education, comp., *Sōtō Shūmukyoku Chōsa* in *Bukkyō Nenkan* (Tokyo: Gyōsei Keiei Kyōkai, 1911).

7. Japan Ministry of Education, comp., *Sōtō Shūmukyoku Chōsa* in *Bukkyō Nenkan* (Tokyo: Shūmukyoku Chōsa, 1935).

8. *Sōtō Shūmuchō Chōsa shuho no. 198 choshū*. Cited in Takagi, *Nisō-shi*, p. 486.

9. Japan Ministry of Education, comp., *Shūkyōnenkan* (Tokyo: Gyōsei, 1990).

10. For an overview of the general state of male Zen monastics in modern Japan, see Ian Reader, "Zazenless Zen? The Position of Zazen in Institutional Zen Buddhism," in *Japanese Religions* vol. 14, no. 3 (Dec. 1986). Reader acknowledges that "a result of this hereditary system is that many who become priests do not necessarily wish to do so . . ." (p. 5).

11. See Appendix A for an English translation of the cover letter and survey.

12. Among sociologists, a response rate of 33% to a survey is considered a great success. Furthermore, a survey that is primarily quantitative, requiring checking one of a set number of choices, generally receives more responses than one that is primarily qualitative and requests elaborating on a number of issues. Despite these concerns, I designed the survey to allow for detailed and personal answers. Because I had received approval from the abbess and I was attending a well-known, respectable university, my intuition told me that the nuns would take this as an opportunity to express their views in a manner they had never been requested to do before.

13. Although I clearly explained in a cover letter the academic nature of the survey and my interest in nuns (see Appendix A), some even hoped I would still consider becoming a nun.

14. Statistics from Spring 1990 Sōtō Nun Survey.

15. In 1990, 52% of Sōtō nuns were born before 1928.

16. Interview with Hasekawa in Toyama, Japan, on July 8, 1990. I stayed at the Toyama monastery for a number of days. I participated in a few of their regular activities, observed their daily pattern of life, and spoke with each of the novices in training.

17. Interview with Nakamura Busshin (b. 1903) in Niigata, Japan, on July 14, 1990. During the few days that I was at the Niigata Nisōdō, I participated in some of their regular activities, observed their daily pattern of life, and interviewed a novice in training.

18. Spring 1990 Sōtō Nun Survey Response No. 122, document in the collection of P. K. R. Arai. All survey responses were translated into English by P. Arai.

19. Spring 1990 Sōtō Nun Survey Response No. 51, document in the collection of P. K. R. Arai.

20. Spring 1990 Sōtō Nun Survey Response No. 116, document in the collection of P. K. R. Arai.

21. Spring 1990 Sōtō Nun Survey Response No. 62, document in the collection of P. K. R. Arai.

22. Spring 1990 Sōtō Nun Survey Response No. 94, document in the collection of P. K. R. Arai.

23. Spring 1990 Sōtō Nun Survey Response No. 29, document in the collection of P. K. R. Arai.

24. Spring 1990 Sōtō Nun Survey Response No. 148, document in the collection of P. K. R. Arai.

25. Spring 1990 Sōtō Nun Survey Response No. 134, document in the collection of P. K. R. Arai.

26. Spring 1990 Sōtō Nun Survey Response No. 102, document in the collection of P. K. R. Arai.

27. Spring 1990 Sōtō Nun Survey Response No. 35, document in the collection of P. K. R. Arai.

28. Den Taikan, "The Problem of Nuns' Education," *Jōrin*, no. 2 (June 1923).

29. Spring 1990 Sōtō Nun Survey Response No. 18, document in the collection of P. K. R. Arai.

30. Spring 1990 Sōtō Nun Survey Response No. 37, document in the collection of P. K. R. Arai.

31. Spring 1990 Sōtō Nun Survey Response No. 67, document in the collection of P. K. R. Arai.

32. Spring 1990 Sōtō Nun Survey Response No. 121, document in the collection of P. K. R. Arai.

33. Interview with nun in Nagoya, Japan, on December 22, 1989.

34. Interview with nun in Nagoya, Japan, on November 24, 1989.

35. The word *furusato* connotes an emotional and nostalgic place filled with family, friends, and a familiar landscape.

36. Interview with nun in Nagoya, Japan, on November 24, 1989.

37. The Sōtō sect as an institution does not encourage its followers to do zazen. The administration's film, *Eiheiji*, intended to be an introduction to Zen life, depicts zazen to be so severe that it would be unreasonable to expect the average person to practice it. See Reader, "Zazenless Zen?" p. 20. Aoyama, however, does not follow this line of reasoning. She will not speak seriously with anyone until they have done a significant amount of zazen. This shows a marked difference between male and female Sōtō Zen monastics' understanding of themselves and their role in society.

38. Interview with nun in Nagoya, Japan, on November 8, 1989.

39. Ibid.

40. Interview with nun in Nagoya, Japan, on November 14, 1989.

41. Ibid.

42. Michael Carrithers, *The Forest Monks of Sri Lanka: An Anthropological and Historical Study* (Delhi: Oxford University Press, 1983), p. 15.

43. Ibid., p. 17.

44. Ibid., p. 16.

45. Drawing connections between themselves and the nuns of ancient India, Sōtō nuns perform the *Anan Kōshiki*, a ceremony that ritually brings all nuns together as one group of Buddhist disciples. See description of this ceremony in chapter 4.

46. I. B. Horner, *Women under Primitive Buddhism* (New York: Dutton, 1930), p. 199.

47. Aoyama Shundō, *Ikasarete, Ikashite, Ikiru* (Tokyo: Shunjūsha, 1989), p. 28.

48. Aoyama Shundō, *Imani Inochi Moyashite: Watakushi o Sutete Dō Michi o Hirakuka* (Tokyo: Kōsei Shuppansha, 1987), p. 229.

49. Aoyama Shundō, "Shukke to Nisō," in *Hibiki*, p. 38.

50. For further information on Japanese education systems see Tokiomi Kaigo, *Japanese Education: Its Past and Present* (Tokyo: Kokusai Bunka Shinkōkai, 1968).

51. One must, of course, allow for changes in the standard of education in regard to the time period under question.

52. Statistics quoted are from the survey I conducted in Japan in the spring of 1990.

53. Tajima Hakudō, *Sōtō-shū Nisō shi* (Tokyo: Sanyo-sha, 1955), pp. 486–88.

54. Aoyama Shundō, *Imani Ikiru*, p. 81.

55. Dōgen, "Shukke Kudoku" in *Shōbōgenzō*, translated by Nishiyama and Stevens, with modifications by the author.

56. Since celibacy is one of the precepts, the responses to this question also reveal the respondents' views toward celibacy.

57. Spring 1990 Sōtō Nun Survey Response Nos. 58 and 26, documents in the collection of P. K. R. Arai.

58. Spring 1990 Sōtō Nun Survey Response No. 62, document in the collection of P. K. R. Arai.

59. Spring 1990 Sōtō Nun Survey Response No. 37, document in the collection of P. K. R. Arai.

60. Spring 1990 Sōtō Nun Survey Response No. 51, document in the collection of P. K. R. Arai.

61. Interview with nun in Nagoya, Japan, on November 8, 1989.

62. This statistic is based upon the number of Sōtō Zen nuns officially recorded in the *Shūkyōnenkan*: 1,071 Sōtō Zen nuns in 1985. In 1988, the Sōtō sect stopped making a distinction between male and female monastics, so it is not possible to tell the number of monks versus nuns from official documents. As a point of reference, the number of Sōtō Zen male monastics in 1985 was 15,790.

63. Ian Reader, *Religion in Contemporary Japan* (Honolulu: University of Hawaii Press, 1991), p. 88, describes the contemporary Buddhist situation as being based upon a hereditary system of priesthood, but it fails to add even a word of qualification that this is a description of male Buddhist professionals and does not include women. In other portions of Reader's text (p. 91), he explains activities of the "priesthood" in which monastic women also participate.

64. Spring 1990 Sōtō Nun Survey Response No. 35, document in the collection of P. K. R. Arai.

65. Aoyama, *Nori no kemanshō: Hokekyō o Ajiwau* (Tokyo: Hakujusha, 1984) p. 224.

66. Dōgen, "Shukke Kudoku" in *Shōbōgenzō*, trans. Nishiyama and Stevens. In an effort to be more accurate and reflect the inclusive language of the original, I modified the translation. I translated *zaike* as "householder" instead of "layman," and I translated *shukke* as "renunciant" instead of "monk."

67. Spring 1990 Sōtō Nun Survey Response No. 1, document in the collection of P. K. R. Arai.

68. The orphanage is named after the site where Śākyamuni was born, a garden in Lumbini, Nepal.

69. Very few monks are engaged in the practice of sewing their own robes. Instead, most buy them in local stores.

70. Interview with nun in Nagoya, Japan, on November 21, 1989.

71. Interview with nun in Nagoya, Japan, on November 14, 1989.

72. Spring 1990 Sōtō Nun Survey Response No. 128, document in the collection of P. K. R. Arai.

73. Spring 1990 Sōtō Nun Survey Response No. 44, document in the collection of P. K. R. Arai.

74. Interview with nun in Nagoya, Japan, on November 12, 1989.

75. Interview with nun in Nagoya, Japan, on November 14, 1989.

76. *Hachijūnen no Ayumi*, p. 15.

77. *Hachijūnen no Ayumi*, p. 17.

78. Spring 1990 Sōtō Nun Survey Response No. 47, document in the collection of P. K. R. Arai.

79. See survey questions 12 and 16 (Appendix A).

80. Spring 1990 Sōtō Nun Survey Response No. 49, document in the collection of P. K. R. Arai.

81. Spring 1990 Sōtō Nun Survey Response No. 1, document in the collection of P. K. R. Arai.

82. Spring 1990 Sōtō Nun Survey Response No. 9, document in the collection of P. K. R. Arai.

83. Interview with nun in Nagoya, Japan, on November 12, 1989.

84. Spring 1990 Sōtō Nun Survey Response No. 118, document in the collection of P. K. R. Arai.

85. Spring 1990 Sōtō Nun Survey Response No. 90, document in the collection of P. K. R. Arai.

86. Ibid.

87. Sōtō-shū Nisōdan, *Sōtō-shū Nisōdan Meibo*, 1984. This document records the name of each nun in the Sōtō sect, her temple's name, her status in the temple, birthdate, address, telephone number, and temple activities. A similar document that largely overlaps with the *Nisōdan Meibo* is put out by Tokubetsu Nisōdō Aichi Senmon Nisōdō, *Jōrin Kaiin Meibo*, 1983. Aside from the above information, the *Jōrin Kaiin Meibo* includes the nuns' year of graduation from Aichi Senmon Nisōdō. The documents are published in conjunction with major anniversaries.

88. Upon hearing that Sōtō Zen nuns integrate the traditional "women's arts" into their Zen practice—sewing, cooking, flower arranging, the tea ceremony—Nakamura Kyōko, an anthropologist who is a pioneer in the study of women and Japanese religion, suggested this reveals that monastic women have been historically discriminated against and they have done their best to turn it into something positive, rather than resisting it. From conversations with Nakamura Kyōko at the Center for the Study of World Religions, Harvard University, Cambridge, Mass., on August 8, 1991.

89. Interview with a nun in Nagoya, Japan, on November 9, 1989.

90. Spring 1990 Sōtō Nun Survey Response No. 18, document in the collection of P. K. R. Arai.

91. Spring 1990 Sōtō Nun Survey Response No. 94, document in the collection of P. K. R. Arai.

92. Spring 1990 Sōtō Nun Survey Response No. 58, document in the collection of P. K. R. Arai.

93. Spring 1990 Sōtō Nun Survey Response No. 37, document in the collection of P. K. R. Arai.

94. Spring 1990 Sōtō Nun Survey Response No. 86, document in the collection of P. K. R. Arai.

95. Spring 1990 Sōtō Nun Survey Response No. 73, document in the collection of P. K. R. Arai.

96. Spring 1990 Sōtō Nun Survey Response No. 62, document in the collection of P. K. R. Arai.

97. Spring 1990 Sōtō Nun Survey Response No. 89, document in the collection of P. K. R. Arai.

98. These figures are cited in Reader, *Religion in Contemporary Japan*, p. 89.

99. Sasaki Kōkan, "Kaisetsu — Shuyō na mondai o megutte," in *Shūkyōshūdan no Ashita e no Kadai*, ed. Sōtō-shū Shūseichōsa Iinkai (Tokyo, 1984), p. 365.

100. Sasaki's assessments are outlined in Reader, "Zazenless Zen?," p. 12.

101. Spring 1990 Sōtō Nun Survey Response No. 29, document in the collection of P. K. R. Arai.

102. Spring 1990 Sōtō Nun Survey Response No. 135, document in the collection of P. K. R. Arai.

103. Spring 1990 Sōtō Nun Survey Response No. 9, document in the collection of P. K. R. Arai.

104. Spring 1990 Sōtō Nun Survey Response No. 47, document in the collection of P. K. R. Arai.

105. Interview with a woman about to take the tonsure, in Nagoya, Japan, on November 9, 1989.

106. Spring 1990 Sōtō Nun Survey Response No. 147, document in the collection of P. K. R. Arai.

107. Spring 1990 Sōtō Nun Survey Response No. 134, document in the collection of P. K. R. Arai.

108. Interview with nun in Nagoya, Japan, on December 22, 1989.

109. Spring 1990 Sōtō Nun Survey Response No. 33, document in the collection of P. K. R. Arai.

110. Spring 1990 Sōtō Nun Survey Response No. 94, document in the collection of P. K. R. Arai.

111. Spring 1990 Sōtō Nun Survey Response No. 121, document in the collection of P. K. R. Arai.

112. Henry and Swearer, *For the Sake of the World*, p. 22.

113. Spring 1990 Sōtō Nun Survey Response No. 35, document in the collection of P. K. R. Arai.

114. Spring 1990 Sōtō Nun Survey Response No. 318, document in the collection of P. K. R. Arai.

115. Spring 1990 Sōtō Nun Survey Response No. 121, document in the collection of P. K. R. Arai.

116. Interview with Hasekawa, abbess of Toyama Nisōdō in Toyama, Japan, on July 1990.

117. Spring 1990 Sōtō Nun Survey Response No. 54, document in the collection of P. K. R. Arai.

118. Spring 1990 Sōtō Nun Survey Response No. 386, document in the collection of P. K. R. Arai.

119. See chapter 3 for a sketch of the types of discrimination nuns endured.

120. Spring 1990 Sōtō Nun Survey Response No. 121, document in the collection of P. K. R. Arai.

121. Chapter 3 includes a discussion of what opportunities were available before the reforms of the 1950s and 1960s.

122. Spring 1990 Sōtō Nun Survey Response No. 128, document in the collection of P. K. R. Arai.

123. Spring 1990 Sōtō Nun Survey Response No. 122, document in the collection of P. K. R. Arai.

124. Ibid.

125. An overview of the reasons monastics are declining in number can be found in chapter 4.

126. Spring 1990 Sōtō Nun Survey Response No. 39, document in the collection of P. K. R. Arai.

127. Interview with Nakamura Busshin in Niigata, Japan, on July 14, 1990.

128. Spring 1990 Sōtō Nun Survey Response No. 29, document in the collection of P. K. R. Arai.

129. Spring 1990 Sōtō Nun Survey Response No. 86, document in the collection of P. K. R. Arai.

130. Spring 1990 Sōtō Nun Survey Response No. 16, document in the collection of P. K. R. Arai.

131. Spring 1990 Sōtō Nun Survey Response No. 73, document in the collection of P. K. R. Arai.

132. Spring 1990 Sōtō Nun Survey Response No. 91, document in the collection of P. K. R. Arai.

133. Spring 1990 Sōtō Nun Survey Response No. 2, document in the collection of P. K. R. Arai.

134. Spring 1990 Sōtō Nun Survey Response No. 1, document in the collection of P. K. R. Arai.

135. Spring 1990 Sōtō Nun Survey Response No. 135, document in the collection of P. K. R. Arai. *Gasshō* (Skt. añjali): a joining one's palms together as a physical expression of reverence, gratitude, welcome, and respect.

136. Spring 1990 Sōtō Nun Survey Response No. 70, document in the Collection of P. K. R. Arai.

137. Spring 1990 Sōtō Nun Survey Response No. 73, document in the collection of P. K. R. Arai.

138. Spring 1990 Sōtō Nun Survey Response No. 49, document in the collection of P. K. R. Arai.

139. Spring 1990 Sōtō Nun Survey Response No. 111, document in the collection of P. K. R. Arai.

140. Spring 1990 Sōtō Nun Survey Response No. 354, document in the collection of P. K. R. Arai.

141. Spring 1990 Sōtō Nun Survey Response No. 62, document in the collection of P. K. R. Arai.

142. The practice of tonsure is effective in Japan, because people in general society recognize a tonsured person as one who has made a deep commitment to Buddhist practice. As one nun cited in her interview response, being tonsured makes it easier for people to turn to her for assistance, because there is an expectation that those who are tonsured are supposed to be helpful. In a society where a shaved head does not necessarily carry religious significance, the practice of tonsure might be an obstacle.

143. Interview with nun in Nagoya, Japan, on November 8, 1989.

144. Personal Narratives Group, *Interpreting Women's Lives*, p. 12.

145. Spring 1990 Sōtō Nun Survey Response No. 75, document in the collection of P. K. R. Arai.

146. In the Buddhist tradition, there have been a number of adepts who have proven their state of enlightenment by passing away in the full-lotus position of meditation. Dōgen used the phrase *Zadatsu Ryūbō* in his text *The Way of Zazen Recommended to Everyone* (J. *Fukanzazengi*), which he wrote shortly after returning from China (1227) with the intention of making the true Buddhist teachings available to all people. Bernard Faure, in *The Rhetoric of Immediacy*, discusses death postures of Zen masters and one case of a master who died standing.

147. From an interview with Kuriki Kakujō at Seikan-ji Temple in Nagoya, Japan on July 17, 1990.

CHAPTER SIX

1. This perspective is more poignant when expressed in Japanese, because it is imbued with humility, elegance, and penetrating insight into the interrelated nature of reality: *Nisō wa sabetsu no okagede rippadesu.*

2. Along with Tsuda Ume, Fukuzawa Yukichi, and a few others, Sōtō nuns were in the forefront of the fight for education for women. For detailed information about women's higher education in purely secular institutions, see the following texts: Eiichi Kiyooka, ed. and trans., *Fukuzawa Yukichi on Japanese Women* (Tokyo: University of Tokyo Press, 1988); Furuki, *The White Plum*; Sharon Sievers, *Flowers in Salt: The Beginnings of Feminist Consciousness in Modern Japan* (Stanford, Calif.: Stanford University Press, 1983).

3. Faure, *Rhetoric of Immediacy*, p. 320.

4. In this case I mean "equalitarian" and not "egalitarian." Nuns wanted to be treated fairly, but they did not strive to be equal or the same as monks.

5. Murasaki Shikibu's *Genji Monogatari* is a novel from the Heian period that describes (and is itself an example of) this world where aesthetic appreciation was actively cultivated. Secondary sources that explore this aspect of Japanese culture include Ivan Morris, *The World of the Shining Prince: Court Life in Ancient Japan* (New York: Peregrine Books, 1969) and Norma Field, *The Splendor of Longing in the 'Tale of Genji'* (Princeton, N.J.: Princeton University Press, 1987).

6. Donald Shively, "The Japanization of the Middle Meiji," in *Tradition and Modernization in Japanese Culture*, p. 118.

7. Beasley, *Modern History of Japan*, p. 157. Formal governmental protection of cultural heritage in Japan actually began in 1871 when the Japanese government proclaimed that important old works of art should be protected. See Jan Fontein, ed., *Living National Treasures of Japan* (Boston: Committee of the Exhibition of Living National Treasures of Japan, 1982), p. 14. Valuable works of architecture, painting, sculpture, and applied arts began to be registered in 1897 when the "Law for Preservation of Old Shrines and Temples" was enacted. This law was expanded in 1929 as the "Law for Preservation of National Treasures" to include works of art not affiliated with shrines and temples. These various laws were unified in 1950 under the "Law for Protection of Cultural Properties." The law is defined to include the "Intangible Cultural Properties," namely the people who create the art forms. These people are popularly known as "Living National Treasures." One of the main purposes for the subsidies provided by the government to these "Treasures" is to help defray the cost of educating and training their successors (Fontein, *Living National Treasures*, p. 15).

8. Ōgishi, *Gyōten Sōrin no Hibiki*, p. 33.

9. See the analysis and discussion in Ketelaar, *Of Heretics and Martyrs*, of many Meiji institutions' concern to construct a convincing portrayal of a strong and coherent Japanese tradition.

10. Jennifer Robertson, "The Shingaku Women: Straight From the Heart," in *Recreating Japanese Women*, ed. Bernstein, pp. 99–101.

Appendix A

Questionnaire (English translation)

Dear Respondents,   April 12, 1990

My name is Paula Arai. I am currently a graduate student majoring in Japanese Buddhism at the Religion Department of Harvard University in the United States. I am interested in researching nuns, who can be called treasures of Japanese Buddhism, and I have taken "The Lifestyle and History of Nuns" as the theme of my doctoral dissertation.

Last year, for a period of four months, from September 1 through December 23, I received the honor of performing Buddhist practice with the nuns of Aichi Senmon Nisōdō. It was the first time for me to have such experiences with my own body, and I learned the wonder of nuns' attitude towards life. Now I am reading books and articles on nuns, and I am receiving instruction from professors of Komazawa University, Aichi Gakuin University, and Nanzan University.

For the purpose of sharing the beauty and importance of nuns with people abroad, I have composed a questionnaire on the current conditions of nuns in Japanese society. The results of the survey will appear in the journal *Otayori*.

Although it is hard to make a request to you nuns who are so busy, I humbly beseech your cooperation.

The results of the survey will only be used for this research. Further, since the responses will be without names, please respond freely. If there are questions that do not pertain to your situation, please do not answer them.

Although it only serves my convenience, I humbly request that your responses be returned by May 20.

Gasshō,

Paula Arai
Harvard University
Ph.D. candidate

Spring 1990 Survey of Sōtō Nuns

1. Year of Birth:

2. Highest Education level   Please circle one of the following:

    Elementary   Middle School   High School Jogakkō
    Jr. College   University   Other

3. Concerning your parents' employment and education

    Father: employment   Highest Education Level
    Mother: employment   Highest Education Level

4. Do you have any blood-relatives who are monastics?

    Yes   What relation?   No

5. Concerning your motivation to become a renunciant:

6. About Initiation *(tokudo)*

    a. Year:
    b. Teacher: Nun   Monk
    c. Location of Initiation: Prefecture/Fu
                                               Metropolitan Tokyo

7. About entry into the nunnery

    a. Name of the nunnery:
    b. Entry year:
    c. How many people did you enter with?
       Of that number, how many left before completion?
    d. Level upon graduation: Yoka   Honka   Kenkyū   Toku
       Other
    e. Date of Graduation:

8. Current Religious Rank: Jōza   Zagen   Oshō   Daioshō

9. Current Teaching Rank:

    Assist. Second Rank   Assist. First Rank   Third Rank
    Second Rank   First Rank Seikyōshi   Gon Daikyōshi   Other

10. What kind of social respect do you think nuns have today?

    a. Greatly respected   b. Respected
    c. Not very respected   d. Not at all respected   e. Other

11. Do you think there is meaning in maintaining the precepts in contemporary society?

Yes   No   I do not know
Why?

12. Which of the following items do you consider Buddhist practice?
Please mark a circle at the appropriate items.

                          Yes   No   I do not know
Tea Ceremony
Flower Arranging
Calligraphy
Sewing
Cooking
Cleaning
Other

13. Please respond regarding your temple's activities.

a. How many *danka* do you have?
   How many followers do you have?   Others?
b. Instructional activities: Sanzenkai   Sūtra Copying
                              Flower Classes   Tea Classes
                              Baika   Other

14. What is the main source of your income?

a. Temple associated activities
b. Teaching Arts
c. Other

15. Where are lay and monastics different?

a. Appearance
b. Approach to lifestyle
c. Precepts
d. Human Relationships

16. Of the following points, which do you think are most appropriate? Please place a circle accordingly.

                          Nuns   Monks   Both   Neither
Be Serious
Receive Respect
Maintain Buddhist Ways
Receive Discrimination

16. (*continued*)

	Nuns	Monks	Both	Neither

What is necessary for a monastic?
Daily Zazen
Daily Chanting
Tonsure
Knowledge of Buddhism
Celibacy
Other

17. Do you think nuns are discriminated against?

Yes (Please cite examples)   No

18. What kind of social responsibility do nuns have?

20. Marital Status:
a. Single
b. Separated: widow   divorced   Other

21. Children:
a. none
b. have   Number   age(s)

22. What was your occupation when you were a layperson?

Thank you for your help in the midst of your busy schedule.

If you have any other opinions, please write them out.

Appendix B

Glossary of Japanese Terms

Adachi Teikō　足立貞光

Aichi　愛知

Aichi Gakuin Daigaku
　愛知学院大学

Aichi Senmon Nisōdō
　愛知専門尼僧堂

aigo　愛護

ama　尼

amadera　尼寺

amanyūdō　尼入道

Ama Shōgun　尼将軍

Amaterasu　天照

Andō Daiken-ni　安藤大賢尼

Andō Dōkai　安藤道契

ango　安居

anja　行者

Aoyama Shundō　青山俊董

Asakusa　浅草

Ashikaga　足利

Asuka　飛鳥

baika　梅華

banka 晩課

Bendōwa 辨道話

Bikuniden 比丘尼伝

Bishō-dō 微笑堂

bodaishin 菩提心

Bommō-kyō 梵網経

bosatsukai 菩薩戒

Bosatsukai-ni 菩薩戒尼

Busshō 仏性

chadō 茶道

Chazen Kanwa 茶禅閑話

chiden 知殿

Chikusa-ku 千種区

Chisen-ni 知線尼

Chōei-ji 長栄寺

chōka fūgin 朝課諷經

Chōsei-an 長性庵

Chūgū-ji 中宮寺

Chūō-sen 中央線

Daibibasha-ron 大毘婆沙論

Daibutsu-ji 大仏寺

Daikyōsei 大教正

Daikyōshi 大教師

daimyō 大名

Dainichi Nōnin 大日能忍

Daitetsu Sōrei 大徹宗霊

danka 檀家

darani 陀羅尼

Daruma-shū 達磨宗

Denbō-e 伝法絵

Denkōroku 伝光録

Dōgen, Keizan Ryōzen-ji no Nisōkan
 to sono Eka no Nisō
    道元瑩山両禅師の尼僧観
        とその會下の尼僧

dōji 同事

dōwa 童話

Echizen 越前

Egi-ni 懐義尼

Eihei Dōgen 永平道元

Eihei-ji 永平寺

Eihei-ji Betsuin 永平寺別院

Eihei Kōroku Dai Hachi Hōgo
    永平廣録大八法語

Eihei Sansogyōjōki
    永平三祖行業記

Eihei Shingi 永平清規

Ejō 懐弉

Ekan Daishi 圓観大師

Ekyū-ni 恵球尼

Emperor Godaigo 後醍醐天皇

Empress Danrin 檀林皇后

Empress Suiko 推古天皇

en 縁

Engaku-ji 圓覚寺

En'i-ni 圓意尼

Enkiri-dera 縁切寺

Entsū-an 圓通庵

Erin-ji 恵林寺

Eshin bikuni 恵信比丘尼

Eshin-ni 恵信尼

Eshō 懐照

Eshun-ni 恵春尼

Ezen-ni 恵善尼

Fujiwara 藤原

Fukanzazengi 普勧坐禅儀

Fukugon-ji 福厳寺

Fukuzawa Yukichi 福澤諭吉

Furukawa Tamesaburō
　　古川為三郎

furusato 故郷

Fusatsu 布薩

fuse 布施

Fushukuhampō 赴粥飯法

Gakudō Yōjinshū 学道用心集

Gakumon no Susume 学問の進め

gaman 我慢

Gangōji Engi 元興寺縁起

Ganjin 鑑真

Gasan Jōseki 峨山紹碩

gasshō 合掌

Gensen-ji 玄泉寺

Genshu-ni 源珠尼

genzen sanga 現前僧伽

Gessen Ryōin 月泉良印

Gifu 岐阜

Gikai 義价

go-eika 御詠歌

Gohō-ji 護法寺

gokuraku 極楽

Gon Daikyōsei 権大教正

Gon Daikyōshi 権大教師

Gonen-ji 護念寺

goshō 五障

go-teishō 御提唱

gozan 五山

Gyōbutsu Iigi 行仏以威儀

Gyōji 行持

Gyōten Sōrin no Hibiki
　　暁天叢林の響

Hakuchōzan 白鳥山

Hakuju-an 柏樹庵

Hanahachisu 花はちす

Hasekawa　長谷川

hattō 法堂

Hayakawa Kenryū　早川見龍

Heian 平安

heisōchi 平僧地

Hieizan 比叡山

Higashi-ku 東区

Himiko 卑弥呼

Himitsu Shōbōgenzō
　　秘密正法眼蔵

Hiratsuka Raichō 平塚らいてう

hisō hizoku 非僧非俗

hōben 方便

Hōbutsu-ni 法仏尼

hōchi 法地

Hōi-ni 法位尼

Hōji-ji 法持寺

Hōjō Taira Masako　北条平政子

Hōjō Tokimune 北条時宗

Hokke Daimokusho 法華題目書

Hokke Metsuzaishi-ji
　　法華滅罪之寺

Hōmyaku 法脈

Hōmyaku-e 法脈會

hōmyō 法名

hondō 本堂

Hōnen 法然

honka 本科

Honshō-ni 本韶尼

Hori Mitsujō 堀密成

Hori Tokujō-ni 堀徳成尼

Hōryū-ji 法隆寺

hosshin 発心

hōwa 法話

Ichijō Chikō Jōnin　一条智光上人

ikasarete itadakimasu
　　行かされて頂きます

Ikejiri-ji 池後寺

ikiru 生きる

Ikka Myōju　一顆明珠

ikkyū nikyōshi 一級尼教師

*Imani Inochi Moyashite:
Watakushi o Sutete Dō
Michi o Hirakuka*
　　今にいのち燃やして：
　　私を捨ててどう道を開くか

Inari 稲荷

ino 維那

Ishikawa Rikizan 石川力山

ittō kyōshi 一等教師

ittō kyōshiho 一等教師補

jaku 寂

Ji 時

Jimmu Tennō 神武天皇

Jizō Nagashi 地蔵流し

Jōa-ni 成阿尼

Jōdo-shū 浄土宗

jogakkō 女学校

Jōjū-ji 浄住寺

Jōkin Hotsuganmon 紹瑾発願文

Jōnin-ni 浄忍尼

Jōrin 業林

Jōrinkai 業林会

josei kyōshitsu 女性教室

junhōchi 準法地

kadō 華道

Kaibara Ekken 貝原益軒

kaichin 開枕

kaidan 戒壇

kaimyō 戒名

Kakekomi-dera 駆け込み寺

Kakuan 覚安

kakuchi 各地

Kakuōzan 覚王山

Kakushin-ni 覚信尼

Kakuzan-ni 覚山尼

Kamakura 鎌倉

Kametani Esan 亀谷恵参

kami 神

kanbun 漢文

Kanbyō-ni 観苗尼

Kangan Giin 寒厳義尹

Kankō-ni 観光尼

kanni 官尼

Kannon 観音

Kannon-gyō 観音経

Kannon-ji 観音寺

Kansai 関西

Kansai Nigakurin 関西尼学林

kanshi 漢詩

Katō Shinjō-ni 加藤真成尼

kei 敬

Keiai-ji 景愛寺

keigo 敬語

keisu 磬子

Keizan Jōkin 瑩山紹瑾

Keizan Shingi 瑩山清規

kenkyūsei 研究生

Kentoku-ji 乾徳寺

kesa 袈裟

Kiesanmon 帰依三宝

kimono 着物

kinhin 経行

Kitō Shunkō 鬼頭春光

Koide Yūzō 小出有三

Kojima Kendō 小島賢道

kokoro 心

Kokubun-ji 国分寺

Kokubun-niji 国分尼寺

Kokuhatsu Tachite Irishi Michi
  黒髪たちて入りし道

Kokuon-ji 国恩寺

Komazawa Daigaku 駒沢大学

Kōmyō 光明

Kondō Shuken 近藤疏賢

Konkōmyō-kyō 金光明經

Konkōmyō Shitennō Gokokushi-ji
  金光明四天王護国之寺

Kōrin-ji 香林寺

koromo 衣

koseki 戸籍

Kōshō-ji 興聖寺

koto 琴

Koun Ejō 孤雲懷弉

Kōya 高野

Kurata Baigaku 倉田梅岳

Kuriki Kakujō 栗木覚成

kyōshi 教師

Lumbini-en ルンビニ園

Manō Rōshi 真野老師

Mantoku-ji 満徳寺

mappō 末法

Massan Ryōnen-ni 末山了然尼

Matsukijima 松木島

Meiji 明治

Menzan Zuihō 面山瑞方

miko 巫女

Minami Kifun 南気噴

Miroku Bosatsu 弥勒菩薩

miso 味噌

Miyata Baie 宮田梅恵

Mizuno Jōrin 水野常倫

mokugyo 木魚

Monju-bosatsu 文殊菩薩

Mononobe 物部

Mugaku Sogen Zenji
  無極志玄禅師

mujōkan 無常観

Muromachi 室町

Muryō-ji 無量寺

Myōgen Soshin 妙玄祖真

Myōgon-ji 妙厳寺

Myōhō-ni 妙法尼

Myōjun-ni 妙準尼

Myōkoku-ni 妙国尼

Myōshin-ni 妙心尼

Myōshō-ni 明照尼

Myōzen-ni 了禅尼

Nagano 長野

Nagazawa Sozen 長沢祖禅

Nagoya 名古屋

Nakamura Busshin 中村仏心

Nakamura Sen'e 中村仙恵

Nakamura Sengan 中村仙巌

Namu Amida Butsu 南無阿弥陀仏

nansō 男僧

Nara 奈良

nehan 涅槃

ni 尼

Nichibutsu-ni 日仏尼

Nichiren 日連

Nichiyō-sanzenkai 日曜参禅会

Nidaioshō 尼大和尚

nigakurin 尼学林

Nihon Shoki 日本書紀

Niigata 新潟

Niigata Nisō Gakurin 新潟尼僧学林

Niigata Senmon Nisōdō 新潟専門尼僧導

niji gozan 尼寺五山

Nijōza 尼上坐

nikyū nikyōshi 二級尼教師

Ningen Kokuhō 人間国宝

Ninkai-ni 忍戒尼

ninyūdō 尼入道

Ni-oshō 尼和尚

Nishuza 尼首座

nisō 尼僧

Nisōdan 尼僧団

nitō 二等

nitō kyōshi 二等教師

nitō kyōshiho 二等教師補

Nizagen 尼座元

Nori no kemanshō: Hokekyō o Ajiwau 法の華髪抄： 法句経を味わう

Nyodai-ni 如大尼

nyonin kekkai 女人結界

nyonin kinsei 女人禁制

nyūdō 入道

Odawara 小田原

Ōgishi Emiko 大岸恵美子

Ōgishi Sakichi 大岸佐吉

Okamoto Kōbun 岡本光文

Okazaki 岡崎

Okumura Taidō 奥村泰道

Ōmikami 大神

Onkākākabisanmaeisowaka
    奄訶訶訶尾三摩曳婆娑訶

onna kyōshi 女教師

Onna Daigaku 女大学

oshō 和尚

Ōtaka-machi Yakushidō
    大高町薬師堂

Otayori おたよ里

Pi-chiu-ni-chuan 比丘尼伝

Raihaitokuzui 礼拝得髄

rakusu 絡子

ri 里

rigyō 利行

Rinzai 臨済

rōhatsu 臘八

Rokujūnen no Ayumi
    六十年のあゆみ

Ryōnen-ni 了然尼

Ryōsō-ni 良宗尼

Ryūkai-in 龍海院

Ryūsen-kutsu 龍泉窟

Sada Kendō 久田賢道

sahō 作法

Saichō 最澄

Saijō-ji (Odawara) 最乗寺

Saikō-ji (Nagoya) 西光寺

Sakurai-ji 桜井寺

samu 作務

sankyū nikyōshi 三級尼教師

sanmon 山門

sanshō 三障

sanshō 三従

santō kyōshi 三等教師

sanzendōjō 参禅道場

Sawaki Kōdō 澤木興道

sei 清

Seikan-ji 清閑寺

Seikyōshi 正教師

seisō 清掃

Seitō 青鞜

seiza 正座

seng-chia 僧伽

seng-ni 僧尼

Sen'nichi-ni 千日尼

Senjō 洗浄

Senmen 洗面

sesshin 接心

shakaijigyō-bu 社会事業部

shakyō 写経

shibun-ritsu 四分律

shigen-bu 資源部

shihō sanga 四方僧伽

shike 師家

shingi 清規

Shingon 真言

Shinmyō-ni 心妙尼

Shinran 親鸞

shinrei 振鈴

Shinshō-ni 心正尼

Shintō 神道

Shiroyama-chō 城山町

Shōbōgenzō 正法眼蔵

Shōbōgenzō Zuimonki
正法眼蔵随聞記

Shōbō-ji 正法寺

Shochi-ni 證智尼

shodō 書道

shōgaku-bu 奨学部

Shōgaku-ni 正覚尼

Shōgaku Zenni 正覚禅尼

shoin 書院

shōjin ryōri 精進料理

shōkōshi 焼香師

Shoku Nihongi 続日本記

Shōmu Tennō 聖武天王

shōmyō 声明

Shōtoku Taishi 聖徳太子

Shozen-ni 性禅尼

shūdō-bu 修道部

Shūe-ni 修恵尼

shukke 出家

Shukke Kudoku 出家功徳

Shūkyō Nenkan 宗教年鑑

Shūritsu Nisō Gakurin
宗立尼僧学林

Shushōgi 修證義

shushō ittō 修證一等

sō 僧

Soga no Iname 蘇我の稲目

Soga no Umako 蘇我の馬子

sōgya 僧伽

Soitsu-bikuni 祖一比丘尼

Soitsu-ni 祖一尼

Sōji-ji 総持寺

Sōjijinidai oshō shōtō
総持寺二代和尚抄割

Sōkai 僧海

Sōki-ni 宗喜尼

Somyō-ni 素妙尼

Sonin-ni 祖忍尼

sōrin 僧林

Sōtō-shū Dai-ichi Nigakurin
　　曹洞宗第一尼学林

Sōtō-shū Kōtō Nigakurin
　　曹洞宗高等尼学林

Sōtō-shū Nigakurin 曹洞宗尼学林

Sōtō-shū Nisōdan 曹洞宗尼僧団

Sōtō-shū Nisō Gakurin
　　曹洞宗尼僧学林

Sōtō-shū Nisō Gokokudan
　　曹洞宗尼僧護国団

Sōtō-shū Nisō-shi 曹洞宗尼僧史

Sōtō-shū Shūmuchō 曹洞宗宗務庁

Sōtō-shū Zenkoku Nishū Daikai
　　曹洞宗全国尼衆大会

Sōtō Zen 曹洞禅

sunao 素直

Taihei-ji 太平寺

Tajima Hakudō 田島柏道

Takama Shūdō 高間宗道

takuhatsu 托鉢

Tamagawa Jitsubyō 玉川實苗

Tanaka Dōrin 田中道倫

Taniguchi Setsudō 谷口節道

tatami 畳

Teihokenzeiki Kōroku
　　訂補建撕記廣録

Teijitsu-ni 貞実尼

Teishin-ni 貞心尼

Temmu Tennō 天武天王

Tendai 天台

tenzo 典座

Tenzo Kyōkun: Suzuyakani Ikiru
　　典座教訓：すずやかに生きる

tera 寺

terakoya 寺小屋

Tetsugan-ni 哲巌尼

Tōdai-ji 東大寺

Tōkei-ji 東慶寺

Tokubetsu Nisōdō 特別尼僧道

tokudo 得度

tokudoshiki 得度式

Tokugawa 徳川

tokusō 特僧

Tomio Chie 富尾智恵

Toyama 富山

Toyama Nisō Gakurin
　　富山尼僧学林

Toyama Senmon Nisōdō
　　富山専門尼僧堂

Toyoyomi Hideyoshi 豊臣秀吉

tsubo 坪

Tsūgen Jakurei 通幻寂霊

Tsūgen-ji 通玄寺

Tsurumi Joshi
   Gakkō 鶴見女子学校

U Riki 宇理機

Uji 有時

umeboshi 梅干し

Umemoto Kinzaburō 梅本金三郎

Utsukushikihitoni Zen ni Ikiru Nisō no Kotoba
  美しき人に禅に生きる尼
   僧の言葉

waka 和歌

yakuseki 薬石

Yakushi-dō 薬石堂

Yamagushi Dōkin-ni 山口道吟尼

Yamaguchi Daikyū 山口大邸

Yamagushi Kokan 山口巨鑑

Yamatai 耶馬台

Yamato 大和

Yanagihara Jidai 柳原時代

yaza 夜座

yoka 予科

Yōkō-ji 永光時

Yōrin-an 養林庵

Yoshimizu Gakuen 吉水学園

zadatsu ryūbō 坐脱立亡

zafu 坐蒲

zagu 坐具

zazen 坐禅

Zazen Yōjinki 坐禅用心記

Zen Nihon Nisō Hōdan
  全日本尼僧法団

Zen no Tsudoi 禅の集い

Zenbō-ji 禅芳寺

zendō 禅堂

Zengo-ni 善悟尼

zenji 禅師

Zenki 全機

Zenmyō-ji 禅明寺

Zenmyō-ni 善妙尼

Zenni 禅尼

zenrin 禅林

Zenshin-ni 善信尼

Zenzō-ni 禅蔵尼

zōri 草履

zuise 瑞世

Bibliography

Adachi, Barbara. *The Living Treasures of Japan*. New York: Kodansha International, 1973.

Addiss, Stephan. *The Art of Zen*. New York: Abrams, 1989.

Amadiume, Ifi. *Male Daughters, Female Husband: Gender and Sex in an African Society*. London: Zed Books, 1987.

Amino, Yoshiko. "Yūjo to Hinin Kawaramono." In *Sei to Mibun*. Ed. Miyata Noboru. Tokyo: Shunjūsha, 1989: 93–128.

Anesaki, Masaharu. *Art, Life, and Nature in Japan*. Rutland, Vt.: Charles E. Tuttle, 1973.

Aoyama, Shundō. *Chazen Kanwa*. Tokyo: Nakayama Shobo, 1978.

———. *Hana Ujō*. Tokyo: Shufu no Tomosha, 1997.

———. *Ikasarete, Ikashite, Ikiru*. Tokyo: Shunjūsha, 1989.

———. *Imani Inochi Moyashite: Watakushi o Sutete Dō Michi o Hirakuka*. Tokyo: Kōsei Shuppansha, 1987.

———. *Kokuhatsu-tachite, Irishi Michi*. Tokyo: Seirin-ji, 1990.

———. *Michi o Mitomete*. Tokyo: Shufu no Tomosha, 1992.

———. *Mouhitori no Watakushi e no Tabi*. Tokyo: Yayoi Shobo, 1997.

———. *Nori no Kemanshō: Hokekyō o Ajiwau*. Tokyo: Hakujusha, 1984.

———. *Shōrai ni Kiku: Zen no Michi, Cha no Michi*. Tokyo: Hakujusha, 1992.

———. *"Tenzo Kyōkun": Kōwa*. Tokyo: Hakujusha, 1995.

———. *Tenzo Kyōkun: Suzuyakani Ikiru*. Tokyo: Daizō Shuppan, 1987.

———. *Utsukushikihitoni Zen ni Ikiru Nisō no Kotoba*. Tokyo: Pantaka, 1983.

———. *Zen no Manazashi*. Tokyo: Suzuki Shuppan, 1996.

Aoyama Shundō and Hiro Sachiya. *Zen no Chie: "Shōbōgenzō Zuimonki" ni Manabu.* Tokyo: Suzuki Shuppan, 1994.

Bode, Mabel. "Women Leaders of the Buddhist Reformation." *Journal of the Royal Asiatic Society of Great Britain and Ireland* vol. 25 (1893): 517–566, 763–798.

Bodiford, William. "The Growth of the Sōtō Zen Tradition in Medieval Japan." Ph.D. diss., Yale University, 1989.

Bodiford, William. *Sōtō Zen in Medieval Japan.* Honolulu: University of Hawaii Press, 1993.

Boon, James. *Other Tribes, Other Scribes: Symbolic Anthropology in the Comparative Study of Cultures, Histories, Religions, and Texts.* Cambridge: Cambridge University Press, 1982.

Boucher, Sandy. *Turning the Wheel: American Women Creating the New Buddhism.* San Francisco: Harper & Row, 1988.

Bregman, Lucy. "The Interpreter/Experiencer Split: Three Models in the Psychology of Religion." *Journal of the American Academy of Religion* vol. 46, no. 2 (1988 Suppl.): 115–148.

Brewer, Eileen Mary. *Nuns and the Education of American Catholic Women, 1860–1920.* Chicago: Loyola University Press, 1987.

Brinker, Helmut. *Zen in the Art of Painting,* trans. George Campbell. London: Arkana, 1987.

Brock, Peggy, ed. *Women, Rites, and Sites: Aboriginal Women's Cultural Knowledge.* Sydney: Allen and Unwin, 1989.

Brock, Rita Nakashima, Paula Cooey, and Anne Klein, eds. "The Questions That Won't Go Away: A Dialogue About Women in Buddhism and Christianity." *Journal of Feminist Studies of Religion* vol. 6, no. 2 (Fall 1990): 87–120.

Buswell, Robert, Jr. *The Formation of Ch'an Ideology in China and Korea: The 'Vajrasamādhi-Sūtra' A Buddhist Apocryphon.* Princeton, N.J.: Princeton University Press, 1989.

———. *The Zen Monastic Experience: Buddhist Practice in Contemporary Korea.* Princeton, N.J.: Princeton University Press, 1992.

Bynum, Caroline Walker. *Holy Feast and Holy Fast: The Religious Significance of Food to Medieval Women.* Berkeley: University of California Press, 1987.

Campbell, Joseph. *Spiritual Disciplines.* Princeton, N.J.: Princeton University Press, 1960.

Carman, John, and Streng, Frederick, eds. *Spoken and Unspoken Thanks: Some Comparative Soundings.* Cambridge, Mass.: Center for the Study of World Religions, 1989.

Carmody, Denise Lardner. *Religious Woman: Contemporary Reflection on Eastern Texts.* New York: Crossroad, 1991.

———. *Women and World Religions.* Second ed. Englewood Cliffs, N.J.: Prentice Hall, 1989.

Carr, Anne E. *Transforming Grace: Christian Tradition and Women's Experience.* New York: Harper, 1990.

Carrithers, Michael. *The Forest Monks of Sri Lanka: An Anthropological and Historical Study.* Delhi: Oxford University Press, 1983.

Carroll, Berenice A., ed. *Liberating Women's History: Theoretical and Critical Essays.* Urbana: University of Illinois Press, 1976.

Chan, Wing-Tsit, trans. and comp. *A Source Book in Chinese Philosophy.* Princeton, N.J.: Princeton University Press, 1963.

Christ, Carol, and Judith Plaskow, eds. *Weaving the Visions: New Patterns in Feminist Spirituality*. New York: Harper, 1989.

Clifford, James, and George Marcus, eds. *Writing Cultures: The Poetics and Politics of Ethnography*. Berkeley: University of California Press, 1986.

Collcutt, Martin. *Five Mountains: The Rinzai Zen Monastic Institution in Medieval Japan*. Cambridge, Mass.: Harvard University Press, 1981.

Creel, Austin B., and Vasudha Narayanan, eds. *Monastic Life in the Christian and Hindu Traditions: A Comparative Study*. Lewiston, N.Y.: Edwin Mellon Press, 1990.

Crihfield, Liza. "The Institution of the Geisha in Modern Japanese Society." Ph.D. diss., Stanford University, 1978.

Cook, Francis. *How to Raise an Ox: Zen Practice As Taught In Zen Master Dōgen's Shōbōgenzō*. Los Angeles: Center Publications, 1978.

Crowther, Paul. *Art and Embodiment: From Aesthetics to Self-Consciousness*. Oxford: Oxford University Press, 1993.

Daihonzan Eihei-ji. *Eihei-ji Shi*. Tokyo: Taishūkan Shoten, 1982.

Daniel, E. Valentine. *Fluid Signs: Being a Person the Tamil Way*. Berkeley: University of California Press, 1984.

Davis, Winston. *Japanese Religion and Society: Paradigms of Structure and Change*. Albany: State University of New York Press, 1992.

deBary, William, ed. *Sources of Japanese Tradition*, vol. 1. New York: Columbia University Press, 1958.

di Leonardo, Micaela, ed. *Gender at the Crossroads of Knowledge: Feminist Anthropology in the Postmodern Era*. Berkeley: University of California Press, 1991.

Dōgen. *Dōgen Zenji Zenshū*. 2 vols., ed. Ōkubo Dōshū. Tokyo: Chikuma Shobō, 1969–1970.

Duley, Margot and Mary Edwards, eds. *The Cross-Cultural Study of Women: A Comprehensive Guide*. New York: The Feminist Press at the City University of New York, 1986.

Dumoulin, Heinrich. *Zen Buddhism: A History*, 2 vols., trans. James Heisig and Paul Knitter. New York: Macmillan Publishing Company, 1990.

Dumoulin, Heinrich, and John C. Maraldo, eds. *Buddhism in the Modern World*. New York: Collier Books, 1976.

Dutt, Sukumar. *Buddhist Monks and Monasteries in India: Their History and Their Contribution to Indian Culture*. London: George Allen and Unwin, 1962.

———. *Early Buddhist Monachism*. New York: Asia Publishing House, 1960.

———. "The Vinayapitakam and Early Buddhist Monasticism in its Growth and Development." *Journal of the Department of Letters* vol. 10 (1923).

Earhart, H. Byron. *Japanese Religion, Unity and Diversity*. Third ed. Belmont, Calif.: Wadsworth Publishing Company, 1982.

Eliade, Mircea. *The Sacred and the Profane: The Nature of Religion*, trans. Willard Trask. New York: Harcourt Brace Jovanovich, 1959.

———. *Symbolism, the Sacred, and the Arts*, ed. Diane Apostolos-Cappadona. New York: Crossroad, 1990.

———, ed. *Encyclopedia of Religion*. New York: Macmillan, 1987.

Eliade, Mircea, and Joseph Kitagawa, eds. *The History of Religions: Essays in Methodology*. Chicago: University of Chicago Press, 1959.

Ellwood, Robert, and Richard Pilgrim. *Japanese Religion: A Cultural Perspective*. Englewood Cliffs, N.J.: Prentice Hall, 1985.

Ellwood, Robert. "Patriarchal Revolution in Ancient Japan: Episodes From The *Ni-honshoki* Sūjin Chronicle." *Journal of Feminist Studies in Religion* vol. 2, no. 2 (Fall 1986): 23–37.

Falk, Nancy. "An Image of Women in Old Buddhist Literature—The Daughters of Māra." In *Women and Religion*, ed. Judith Plaskow and Joan Romero. Missoula, Mont.: Scholars Press for the American Academy of Religion, 1974: 105–112.

———. "The Case of the Vanishing Nuns: The Fruits of Ambivalence in Ancient Indian Buddhism." In *Unspoken Worlds: Women's Religious Lives in Non-Western Cultures*, ed. Nancy Falk and Rita Gross, pp. 155–165. San Francisco: Harper and Row, 1982.

Falk, Nancy, and Rita Gross. *Unspoken Worlds: Women's Religious Lives in Non-Western Cultures*. New York: Harper & Row, 1980.

Faure, Bernard. "Bodhidharma as Textual and Religious Paradigm." *History of Relig-ions* vol. 25, no. 3: 187–198.

———. *Chan Insights and Oversights: An Epistemological Critique of the Chan Tra-dition*. Princeton, N.J.: Princeton University Press, 1993.

———. "The Daruma-shū, Dōgen, and Sōtō Zen." *Monumenta Nipponica* vol. 42 (Spring 1987): 22–55.

———. *The Rhetoric of Immediacy: A Cultural Critique of Ch'an/Zen Buddhism*. Princeton, N.J.: Princeton University Press, 1991.

———. "Zen and Modernity." *Zen Buddhism Today* vol. 4 (1986): 81–91.

Field, Norma. *The Splendor of Longing in the "Tale of Genji."* Princeton, N.J.: Prince-ton University Press, 1987.

Findly, Ellison Banks, and Yvonne Yazbeck Haddad, eds. *Women, Religion, and Social Change*. Albany: State University of New York Press, 1985.

Fiorenza, Elisabeth Schüssler. *In Memory of Her: A Feminist Theological Reconstruc-tion of Christian Origins*. New York: Crossroad, 1983.

———. "The 'Quilting' of Women's History: Phoebe of Cenchreae." In *Embodied Love: Sensuality and Relationship as Feminist Values*, ed. Paula Cooey, Sharon A. Farmer, and Mary Ellen Ross, pp. 35–49. San Francisco: Harper & Row, 1983.

Fontein, Jan, ed. *Living National Treasures of Japan*. Boston: Committee of the Ex-hibition of Living National Treasures of Japan, 1982.

Friedman, Lenore. *Meetings with Remarkable Women: Buddhist Teachers in America*. Boston: Shambala, 1987.

Fujikawa, Asako. *Daughter of Shinran*. Tokyo: Hokuseido Press, 1964.

Fukuyama, Toshio. *Nihon Kenchikushi no Kenkyū*. Kyoto: Sōgeisha, 1980.

Funaoka, Makoto. *Dōgen to Shōbōgenzō Zuimonki*. Tokyo: Hyōronsha, 1980.

Furuki, Yoshiko. *The White Plum: A Biography of Ume Tsuda, Pioneer in the Higher Education of Japanese Women*. New York: Weatherhill, 1991.

Geertz, Clifford. *The Interpretation of Cultures*. New York: Basic Books, 1973.

Gilligan, Carol. *In a Different Voice*. Cambridge, Mass.: Harvard University Press, 1982.

Gluck, Carol. *Japan's Modern Myths, Ideology in the Late Meiji Period*. Princeton, N.J.: Princeton University Press, 1985.

Gluck, Sherna, and Patai Daphne, eds. *Women's Words: The Feminist Practice of Oral History*. New York and London: Routledge, 1991.

Gold, Ann Grodzins. *Fruitful Journeys: The Ways of Rajasthani Pilgrims*. Delhi: Oxford University Press, 1989.

Golde, Peggy, ed. *Women in the Field: Anthropological Experiences*. Second ed., ex-panded and updated. Berkeley: University of California Press, 1986.

Gombrich, Richard, and Gananath Obeyesekere. *Buddhism Transformed: Religious Change in Sri Lanka.* Princeton, N.J.: Princeton University Press, 1988.

Goody, Jack. *The Interface Between the Written and the Oral.* Cambridge: Cambridge University Press, 1987.

Graham, Martha. *Notebooks.* New York: Harcourt Brace Jovanovich, 1973.

Groner, Paul. *Saichō: The Establishment of the Japanese Tendai School.* Berkeley, Calif.: Berkeley Buddhist Studies Series, 1984.

Grosjean, Yasuko Morihara. "Japan: The 'Silent Victims' Speak." *Journal of Feminist Studies of Religion* vol. 3, no. 2 (Fall 1987): 107–113.

Gross, Rita, ed. *Beyond Androcentrism: New Essays on Women and Religion.* Missoula, Mont.: Scholars Press for The Academy of Religion, 1977.

———. "Buddhism and Feminism: Toward Their Mutual Transformation." *The Eastern Buddhist* vol. 19, nos. 1–2 (Spring and Autumn 1986): 44–58; 62–74.

Guisso, Richard, and Stanley Johannesen, eds. *Women in China: Current Directions in Historical Scholarship.* Youngstown, N.Y.: Philo Press, 1981.

Hammitzsch, Horst. *Zen in the Art of the Tea Ceremony,* trans. Peter Lemesurier. Wiltshire, Great Britain: Compton Press, 1979.

Hardacre, Helen. *Kurozumikyō and the New Religions of Japan.* Princeton, N.J.: Princeton University Press, 1986.

———. *Shintō and the State, 1868–1988.* Princeton, N.J.: Princeton University Press, 1989.

Havnevik, Hanna. *Tibetan Buddhist Nuns: History, Cultural Norms and Social Reality.* Oslo: Norwegian University Press, 1989.

Hecker, Hellmuth. *Buddhist Women at the Time of the Buddha.* Kandy, Sri Lanka: Buddhist Publication Society, 1982.

Heine, Steven. *A Blade of Grass: Japanese Poetry and Aesthetics in Dōgen Zen.* New York: Peter Lang, 1989.

Henry, Patrick, and Donald Swearer. *For the Sake of the World: The Spirit of Buddhist and Christian Monasticism.* Minneapolis, Minn.: Fortress Press, 1989.

Herrigel, Gustie. *Zen in the Art of Flower Arrangement,* trans. R. F. C. Hull. London: Arkana, 1958.

Higuchi, Chiyoko. *Her Place in the Sun: Women Who Shaped Japan.* Trans. Sharon Rhoads. Tokyo: East Publications, 1973.

Hirakawa, Akira. "The History of Buddhist Nuns in Japan." *Buddhist-Christian Studies* vol. 12 (1992): 147–158.

———. *Monastic Discipline for the Buddhist Nuns: An English Translation of the Chinese Text of the Mahāsaṃghika-Bhikṣuṇī-Vinaya.* Patna: Jayaswal Research Institute, 1982.

———. "The Twofold Structure of the Buddhist Saṃgha." *Journal of the Oriental Institute* vol. 15, no. 2 (Dec. 1966): 131–137.

Hisamatsu, Shin'ichi. *Zen and the Fine Arts,* trans. Gishin Tokiwa. San Francisco: Kodansha International, 1971.

Hokoya, Noriaki. *Hongaku Shisō Hihan.* Tokyo: Daizōshuppan, 1989.

Holt, John. *Discipline: The Canonical Buddhism of the Vinayapiṭaka.* New Delhi: Motilal Banarsidass, 1981.

Hoover, Thomas. *Zen Culture.* London: Routledge, 1977.

Hori, Victor Sōgen. "Teaching and Learning in the Rinzai Zen Monastery." *The Journal of Japanese Studies* vol. 20, no. 1 (Winter 1994): 5–35.

Horner, I. B. *Women under Primitive Buddhism.* New York: Dutton, 1930.

Hurvitz, Leon, trans. *Scripture of the Lotus Blossom of the Fine Dharma.* New York: Columbia University Press, 1976.

Ienaga, Saburō, and Shunshū Akamatsu, eds. *Nihon Bukkyōshi.* Kyoto: Hōzōkan, 1976.

Ienaga, Saburō, Akira Fujieda, Kyōshō Hayashima, and Hiroshi Tsukishima, eds. and comps. *Shōtoku Taishi Shū.* Tokyo: Iwanami Shoten, 1975.

Imaide, Taitsu. "Hōnen Shōnin to Yūjo." *Nihon no Josei to Bukkyō Kenkyū* vol. 2 (1985): 26–29.

Inoue, Kyoko. *MacArthur's Japanese Constitution: A Linguistic and Cultural Study of its Making.* Chicago: University of Chicago Press, 1991.

Irokawa, Daikichi. *The Culture of the Meiji Period,* translation ed. by Marius B. Jansen. Princeton, N.J.: Princeton Unviersity Press, 1985.

Ishida, Zuikō. "Bikuni Kaidan." *Nihon Bukkyō Shisō Kenkyū* vol. 2 (1986).

Ishii, Kyōdō, ed. *Shōwa Shinshū Hōnen Shōnin Zenshū.* Kyoto: Heirakuj-ji Shoten, 1955.

Ishii, Shūdō. "Recent Trends in Dōgen Studies," trans. Albert Welter. *Komazawa Daigaku Kenkyūjo* no. 1 (March 1990).

Ishikawa, Matsutarō. *Onna Daigakushū.* Tokyo: Heibonsha, 1977.

Ishikawa, Rikizan. "Chūsei Bukkyō ni okeru Ni no Isō Nitsuite: Tokuni Shoki Sōtō Shūkyōdan no Jirei o Chūshin toshite, Part 1." *Komazawa Daigaku Kenkyūjo Nenpō* no. 3 (March 1992): 141–153.

———. "Chūsei Bukkyō ni okeru Ni no Isō Nitsuite: Tokuni Shoki Sōtō Shūkyōdan no Jirei o Chūshin toshite, Part 2." *Komazawa Daigaku Kenkyūjo Nenpō* no. 4 (March 1993): 63–80.

———. "Dōgen no 'Nyoshin Fujōbutsu Ron' nitsuite Jūni Makibon *Shōbōgenzō* no Seikaku o Meguru Oboegaki." *Komazawa Daigaku Kenkyūjo Nenpō* vol. 1 (March 1990): 88–123.

Ives, Christopher. *Zen Awakening and Society.* Honolulu: University of Hawaii Press, 1992.

Iwamoto. *Bukkyō to Josei* [Buddhism and Women]. Tokyo: Daisanbunmeisha, 1980.

Jaffee, Richard, "Neither Monk nor Layman: The Debate over Clerical Marriage in Japanese Buddhism, 1868–1937." Ph.D. diss., Yale University, 1995.

Jansen, Marius, ed. *Changing Japanese Attitudes toward Modernization.* Tokyo: Charles E. Tuttle, 1965.

Japanese-English Buddhist Dictionary. Tokyo: Daitō Shuppansha, 1965.

Johnson, Penelope D. *Equal in Monastic Profession: Religious Women in Medieval France.* Chicago: University of Chicago Press, 1991.

Jorgensen, Danny. *Participant Observation: A Methodology for Human Studies.* Applied Social Research Methods Series, vol. 15. Newbury Park, Calif.: Sage Publications, 1989.

Joseishi Sōgō Kenkyūkai, ed. *Nihon Joseishi,* 5 vols. Tokyo: Tokyo University Press, 1982.

———, ed. *Nihon Josei Seikatsushi.* Tokyo: Tokyo University Press, 1990.

Juergensmeyer, Mark. "Monastic Syndrome in the Comparative Study of Culture." In *Monastic Life in the Christian and Hindu Traditions: A Comparative Study,* ed. Austin B. Creel and Vasudha Narayanan, pp. 541–561. Lewiston, N.Y.: Edwin Mellon Press, 1990.

Kabilsingh, Chatsumarn. *A Comparative Study of Bhikkhuni Patimokkha.* Varanasi: Chaukhamba Orientalia, 1984.

———. *Thai Women in Buddhism.* Berkeley, Calif.: Parallax Press, 1991.

Kadowaki, Kakichi, and Jan Van Bragt, eds. *Tōzai Reisei Kōryū no Seika*. Tokyo: Sekai Shūkyōsha Heiwa Kaigi Nihon Giinkai, 1985.

Kagotani, Machiko. *Josei to Cha no Yu*. Tokyo: Tankōsha, 1985.

Kaigo, Tokiomi. *Japanese Education: Its Past and Present*. Tokyo: Kokusai Bunka Shinkōkai, 1968.

Kajiyama, Yūichi. *Kū no Shisō*. Kyoto: Jinbun Shoin, 1983.

―――. "Women in Buddhism." *The Eastern Buddhist* (new series) vol. 15, no. 2 (Autumn 1982): 53–70.

Kamens, Edward. *The Buddhist Poetry of the Great Kamo Priestess: Daisaiin Senshi and Hosshin Wakashū*. Ann Arbor, Mich.: Center for Japanese Studies, The University of Michigan, 1990.

Kaneko, Sachiko, and Robert Morrell. "Sanctuary: Kamakura's Tōkei-ji Convent." *Japanese Journal of Religious Studies* vol. 10, nos. 2–3 (1983): 195–228.

Kasahara, Kazuo. *Nyonin Ōjō Shisō no Keifu*. Tokyo: Yoshikawa Kōbunkan, 1975.

Kasulis, T. P. *Zen Action/Zen Person*. Honolulu: University Press of Hawaii, 1981.

Katagiri, Dainin. *Returning to Silence: Zen Practice in Daily Life*. Boston: Shambala Press, 1988.

Kato, Shuichi. *Form, Style, Tradition: Reflections on Japanese Art and Society*, trans. John Bester. Tokyo and New York: Kodansha International, 1971.

Kawamura Kōdō, ed. *Shohon taikō Eihei Kaisan Dōgen Zenji Gyōjō Kenzeiki*. Tokyo: Taishūkan Shoten, 1975.

Kawamura, Kōdō. *Shōbōgenzō no Seiritsushiteki Kenkyū*. Tokyo: Shunjū-sha, 1987.

Keene, Donald. *Appreciations of Japanese Culture*. Tokyo and New York: Kodansha International, 1971.

Keizan. *The Record of Transmitting the Light: Zen Master Keizan's 'Denkoroku'*, trans. Francis H. Cook. Los Angeles: Center Publications, 1991.

Kenkyusha's New Japanese-English Dictionary. Ed. Koh Masuda. 4th ed. Tokyo: Kenkyusha, 1974.

Ketelaar, James Edward. *Of Heretics and Martyrs in Meiji Japan: Buddhism and Its Persecution*. Princeton, N.J.: Princeton University Press, 1990.

Khantipalo, Bikkhu. *Banner of the Arhants: Buddhist Monks and Nuns from the Buddhist Time till Now*. Kandy, Sri Lanka: Buddhist Publication Society, 1979.

Kim, Hee-Jin. *Dōgen Kigen—Mystical Realist*. Tuscon: The University of Arizona Press, 1975.

―――. *Flowers of Emptiness: Selection from Dōgen's Shōbōgenzō*. Lewiston, N.Y.: Edwin Mellen Press, 1985.

King, Sallie B. *Buddha Nature*. Albany: State University of New York Press, 1991.

―――. "Egalitarian Philosophies in Sexist Institutions: The Life of Satomi-san, Shinto Miko and Zen Buddhist Nun." *Journal of Feminist Studies in Religion* vol. 4 no. 1 (Spring 1988): 7–26.

―――. *Passionate Journey, The Spiritual Autobiography of Satomi Myodo*. Boston: Shambala, 1987.

King, Ursula, ed. *Women in World's Religions: Past and Present*. New York: Paragon House, 1987.

Kirk, Jerome, and Marc L. Miller. *Reliability and Validity in Qualitative Research*. Beverly Hills Calif.: Sage Publications, 1986.

Kishimoto, Hideo, ed. *Japanese Religion in the Meiji Era*, trans. John Howes. Tokyo: Toyo Bunko, 1956.

Kitagawa, Joseph. *On Understanding Japanese Religion*. Princeton, N.J.: Princeton University Press, 1987.

————. *Religion in Japanese History*. New York: Columbia University Press, 1966.

Kitagawa, Joseph, and Mark Cummings, eds. *Buddhism and Asian History*. New York: Macmillan Publishing Company, 1989.

Kiyooka, Eiichi, trans. and ed. *Fukuzawa Yukichi on Japanese Women: Selected Works*. Introduction by Keiko Fujiwara. Tokyo: University of Tokyo Press, 1988.

Klein, Anne C. "Finding a Self: Buddhist and Feminist Perspectives." In *Shaping New Vision: Gender and Values in American Culture*, ed. C. W. Atkinson, C. H. Buchanan, and M. R. Miles, pp. 191–218. Ann Arbor, Mich.: UMI Research Press, 1987.

————. "Primordial Purity and Everyday Life: Exalted Female Symbols and the Women of Tibet." In *Immaculate and Powerful: The Female in Sacred Image and Social Reality*, ed. Clarissa Atkinson, Constance Buchanan, and Margaret Miles, pp. 111–138. The Harvard Women's Studies in Religion Series. Boston: Beacon Press, 1985.

Kojima, Kendō. *Bikuni no Jisei: Fune ni Kazamu*. Tokyo: Meibun Insatsu, 1985.

Komazawa Daigakunai Zengaku Daijiten Hensanjo, ed. *Zengaku Daijiten*, 3 vols. 1978. Rev. ed. 1 vol. Tokyo: Taishukan Shoten, 1985.

Kondo, Dorinne. *Crafting Selves: Power, Gender, and Discourses of Identity in a Japanese Workplace*. Chicago: University of Chicago, 1990.

————. "The Way of Tea: A Symbolic Analysis." *Man* vol. 20 (1985): 287–306.

Koun, Ejō. *Shōbōgenzō Zuimonki*, trans. Shōhaku Okumura. Kyoto: Kyoto Sōtō Zen Center, 1987.

Kraft, Kenneth, ed. *Zen: Tradition and Transition*. New York: Grove Press, 1988.

LaFleur, William. *The Karma of Words, Buddhism, and the Literary Arts in Medieval Japan*. Berkeley: University of California Press, 1983.

————. *Liquid Life: Abortion and Buddhism in Japan*. Princeton, N.J.: Princeton University Press, 1992.

————, ed. *Dōgen Studies*. Honolulu: University of Hawaii Press, 1985.

Lang, Karen Christina. "Lord Death's Snare: Gender-Related Imagery in the Theragāthā and the Therīgāthā." *Journal of Feminist Studies in Religion* vol. 2, no. 2 (Fall 1986): 63–79.

Lavrin, Asuncion. "Women in Convents: Their Economic and Social Role in Colonial Mexico." In *Liberating Women's History*, ed. Berenice A. Carroll, pp. 250–277. Urbana: University of Illinois Press, 1976.

Law, Bimala Churn. *Women in Buddhist Literature*. Varanasi: Indological Book House, 1981.

Lawrence, C. H. *Medieval Monasticism: Forms of Religious Life in Western Europe in the Middle Ages*. Second ed. New York: Longman, 1984.

Lawson, E. Thomas, and Robert M. McCauley. *Rethinking Religion: Connecting Cognition and Culture*. Cambridge: Cambridge University Press, 1993.

Leacock, Eleanor Banks. *Myths of Male Dominance: Collected Articles of Women Cross-Culturally*. New York: Monthly Review Press, 1981.

Lebra, Joyce, Joy Paulson, and Elizabeth Powers, eds. *Women in Changing Japan*. Stanford Calif.: Stanford University Press, 1976.

Lebra, Takie. *Japanese Women: Constraint and Fulfillment*. Honolulu: University of Hawaii Press, 1984.

Leggett, Trevor. *The Warrior Koans: Early Zen in Japan*. Boston: Arkana, 1985.

Lerner, Gerda. "Placing Women in History: A 1975 Perspective." In *Liberating Women's History: Theoretical and Critical Essays*, ed. Berenice A. Carroll, pp. 357–367. Urbana: University of Illinois Press, 1976.

————. "Priorities and Challenges in Women's History Research." *Perspectives*: American Historical Association Newsletter, vol. 2, no. 4 (1988): 17–20.

Levering, Miriam. "The Dragon Girl and the Abbess of Mo-Shan: Gender and Status in the Ch'an Buddhist Tradition." *Journal of the International Association of Buddhist Studies* vol. 5, no. 1 (1982): 19–35.

————. "Lin-chi (Rinzai) Ch'an and Gender: The Rhetoric of Equality and the Rhetoric of Heroism." In *Buddhism, Sexuality, and Gender*, ed. Jose I. Cabezon, pp. 137–156. Albany: State University of New York Press, 1992.

Lewis, Jane. "Women Lost and Found." In *Men's Studies Modified: Impact of Feminism on the Academic Disciplines*, ed. Dale Spender, pp. 55–72. Oxford: Pergamon Press, 1981.

Maralso, John C. "Hermeneutics and Historicity in the Study of Buddhism." *The Eastern Buddhist* (new series) vol. 19, no. 1 (1986): 17–43.

Marcus, George, and Michael Fischer. *Anthropology as Cultural Critique: An Experimental Moment in the Human Sciences*. Chicago: University of Chicago Press, 1986.

Matsunaga, Alicia, and Daigan. *Foundations of Japanese Buddhism*, vols. 1 and 2. Los Angeles: Buddhist Books International, 1974.

Matsuo, Kenji. *Kamakura Shin Bukkyō no Seiritsu*. Tokyo: Kikkawa Kōbunkan, 1988.

————. "Kamakura Shin Bukkyō o Minaosu: Josei to Kamakura Shin Bukkyō." *Shunjū* vol. 7 (1992): 36–39.

McCullough, Helen, and William McCullough. *A Tale of Flowering Fortunes: Annals of Japanese Aristocratic Life in the Heian Period*, 2 vols. Stanford, Calif.: Stanford University Press, 1980.

McCormick, Peter J. *Modernity, Aesthetics, and the Bounds of Art*. Ithaca, N.Y.: Cornell University Press, 1990.

McDaniel, Jay, Paula Cooey, and William Eakin, eds. *After Patriarchy: Feminist Reconstructions of the World Religions*. Maryknoll, N.Y.: Orbis Books, 1991.

McDaniel, June. *The Madness of the Saints*. Chicago: University of Chicago Press, 1989.

Minamoto, Junko. *Kamakura Jōdo-kyō to Josei*. Kyoto: Nagata Bunshō-dō, 1981.

Ministry of Education. *Shūkyō Nenkan*. Tokyo: Ministry of Education, annually.

Mochizuki, Nobunari. *Nihon Jōdai no Chōkoku*. Osaka: Sōgensha, 1943.

Mombushō Shūkyō Kyoku, ed. *Shūkyō seido chōsa shiryō*. Tokyo: Hara Shobō, 1977.

Morgen, Sandra, ed. *Gender and Anthropology: Critical Reviews for Research and Teaching*. Washington, D.C.: American Anthropological Association, 1989.

Morris, Brian. *Anthropological Studies of Religion: An Introductory Text*. Cambridge: Cambridge University Press, 1987.

Morris, Ivan. *The World of the Shining Prince*. Oxford and New York: Oxford University Press, 1964.

Mulhern, Chieko Irie, ed. *Heroic with Grace: Legendary Women of Japan*. Armonk, N.Y.: M. E. Sharpe, 1991.

Murakami, Shigeyoshi. *Japanese Religion in the Modern Century*, trans. H. Byron Earhart. Tokyo: University of Tokyo Press, 1980.

Murcott, Susan. *The First Buddhist Women: Translations and Commentary on the 'Therigatha.'* Berkeley, Calif.: Parallax Press, 1991.

Nagatomo, Shigenori. *Attunement through the Body*. Albany: State University of New York Press, 1992.

Nakamura, Hajime. *Genshi Bukkyō no Seiritsu*. Tokyo: Shunjūsha, 1969.

————. *Indian Buddhism: A Survey with Bibliographical Notes*. Delhi: Motilal Banarsidass, 1987.

————, ed. *Bukkyō-go Daijiten*, 3 vols. (Reduced size ed.) Tokyo: Tokyo Shoseki, 1981.

Nakamura, Kyōko. *Miraculous Stories from the Japanese Buddhist Tradition: The Nihon Ryōiki of the Monk Kyōkai*. Cambridge, Mass.: Harvard University Press, 1973.

————. "Revelatory Experience in the Female Life Cycle: A Biographical Study of Women Religionists in Modern Japan." *Japanese Journal of Religious Studies* vol. 8, nos. 3–4 (Sept.–Dec. 1981): 187–205.

————, ed. "Women and Religion in Japan." *Japanese Journal of Religious Studies* vol. 10, nos. 2–3 (June–Sept. 1983): 115–121.

Nakane, Chie. *Japanese Society*. Berkeley: University of California Press, 1970.

Narayan, Kirin. *Storytellers, Saints, and Scoundrels*. Philadelphia: University of Pennsylvania Press, 1989.

Nattier, Jan. *Once Upon a Future Time: Studies in a Buddhist Prophecy of Decline*. Berkeley, Calif.: Asian Humanities Press, 1991.

Nefsky, Marilyn F. *Stone Houses and Iron Bridges: Tradition and the Place of Women in Contemporary Japan*. New York: Peter Lang, 1991.

Nihon Bukkyō Gakkai, ed. *Bukkyō to Josei*. Kyoto: Hyōraku-ji Shoten, 1991.

Nishida, Kitarō. *Art and Morality*, trans. David Dilworth and Valdo Viglielmo. Honolulu: The University of Hawaii Press, 1973.

Nishiguchi, Junko. "Eshin-ni Shojō." *Kyōto Joshi Daigaku Shigakkai* vol. 48 (March 1991): 203–214.

————. "Nihonshijō no Josei to Bukkyō: Nyonin Kyūsaisetsu to Nyonin Jōbutsu o megutte." *Kokubungaku Kaishaku to Kanshō* vol. 56, no. 5 (May 1991): 19–25.

Nishiguchi, J., and K. Ōsumi, eds. *Ama to Amadera* [Nuns and Nun Temples]. Tokyo: Heibonsha, 1989.

Nishiyama, Eshin. *Unsui: A Diary of Zen Monastic Life*, ed. with intro. by Bardwell Smith. Honolulu: University of Hawaii Press, 1973.

Ogawa, Masataka. *The Enduring Crafts of Japan: 33 National Living Treasures*, trans. Ralph Friedrich and Miriam F. Yamaguchi. Tokyo: Weatherhill, 1968.

Ōgishi, Sakichi. *Gyōten Sōrin no Hibiki: Kifun Yakushi-dō to Aichi Senmon Nisōdō no Rekishi*. Nagoya: Kaikoku Kōsoku, 1981.

Ohara, Jin. "Tennyo Jōbutsu setsu no Juyō nitsuite." *Nihon Bukkyō Shigaku* vol. 24 (March 1990): 13–28.

Ohnuki-Tierney, Emiko. " 'Native' Anthropologists." *American Ethnologist* vol. 11, no. 3 (August 1984): 584–586.

Okakura, Kakuzo. *The Book of Tea*. New York: Dover Publications, 1964.

Ōkubo, Dōshū. *Sōtōshū Komonjo*. 3 vols. Tokyo: Chikuma Shobō, 1972.

Ōmori, Sōgen, and Katsujo Terayama. *Zen and the Art of Calligraphy*, trans. John Stevens. London: Routledge and Kegan Paul, 1983.

Ortner, Sherry B. "The Founding of the First Sherpa Nunnery, and the Problem of 'Women' as an Analytic Category." In *Feminist Revisions: What Has Been and What Might Be*, ed. Vivian Patraka and Louise A. Tilly, pp. 98–131. Ann Arbor: Women's Studies Program, The University of Michigan, 1983.

————. "Is Female to Male as Nature is to Culture." In *Women, Culture, and Society*, ed. Michelle Z. Rosaldo and Louise Lamphere, pp. 67–89. Stanford, Calif.: Stanford University Press, 1974.

Ōsumi, Kazuo. " 'Nihon Bukkyō-shi ni okeru Josei' nitsuite no Oboegaki." *Chūo Gakujutsu Kenkyūjo Kiyō* no. 20 (Dec. 1991): 4–13.

Pai-Chang. *Sayings and Doings of Pai-Chang*, trans. Thomas Cleary. Los Angeles, Calif.: Center Publications, 1978.

Pao-Chang. *Pi-chiu-ni-chuan* [Biographies of Buddhist Nuns], trans. Li Jung-hsi. Osaka: Tohokai, 1981.

Parker, Joseph. "Playful Nonduality: Japanese Zen Interpretations of Landscape Paintings from the Ōei Era (1394–1427)." Ph.D. diss., Harvard University, 1989.

Patte, Daniel. *Discipleship According to the Sermon on the Mount.* Valley Forge, Penn: Trinity Press, 1996.

Paul, Diana. *The Buddhist Feminine Ideal: Queen Srimala and the Tathāgatagarbha.* Missoula, Mont.: American Academy of Religion, 1980.

———. *Women in Buddhism: Images of the Feminine in the Mahāyāna Tradition.* Berkeley: University of California Press, 1979.

Personal Narratives Group, ed. *Interpreting Women's Lives: Feminist Theory and Personal Narratives.* Bloomington: Indiana University Press, 1989.

Pilgrim, Richard. "The Artistic Way and the Religio-Aesthetic Tradition in Japan." *Philosophy East and West* vol. 27, no. 3 (1977): 285–305.

———. *Buddhism and the Arts of Japan.* Chambersburg, Penn.: Anima Books, 1981.

———. "Foundations for a Religio-Aesthetic Tradition in Japan. In *Art, Creativity, and the Sacred*, ed. Diane Apostolos-Cappadona, pp. 138–154. New York: Crossroad, 1989.

Prebish, Charles. *Buddhism: A Modern Perspective.* University Park: Pennsylvania State University Press, 1975.

———. *Buddhist Monastic Discipline: The Sanskrit Prātimoksa Sūtras of the Mahāsāṃghikas and Mūlasarvāstivadins.* University Park: Pennsylvania State University Press, 1975.

Preston, David. *The Social Organization of Zen Practice: Constructing Transcultural Reality.* Cambridge: Cambridge University Press, 1988.

Przyluski, Jean. "Uposatha." *Indian Historical Quarterly* vol. 12 (Sept. 1936): 383–390.

Pyle, Kenneth. *New Generation in Meiji Japan: Problems of Cultural Identity, 1885–1895.* Stanford, Calif.: Stanford University Press, 1969.

Reader, Ian. *Religion in Contemporary Japan.* Honolulu: University of Hawaii Press, 1991.

———. "Transformations and Changes in the Teachings of the Sōtō Zen Buddhist Sect." *Japanese Religions* vol. 14, no. 1 (Dec. 1985): 28–48.

———. "Zazenless Zen? The Position of Zazen in Institutional Zen Buddhism." *Japanese Religion* vol. 14, no. 3 (Dec. 1986): 7–27.

Reece, Robert, and Harvey A. Siegal. *Studying People: A Primer in the Ethics of Social Research.* Macon, Ga.: Mercer University Press, 1986.

Reischauer, Edwin O. *Japan: The Story of a Nation*, third ed. New York: Alfred A. Knopf, 1970.

———. *The Japanese.* Cambridge, Mass.: Harvard University Press, 1977.

Reiter, Rayna R., ed. *Toward an Anthropology of Women.* New York: Monthly Review Press, 1975.

Rhys Davids. *Psalms of the Early Buddhists.* London: The Pali Text Society, 1909.

Richardson, Herbert. *Nun, Witch, Playmate.* Lewiston, N.Y.: Edwin Mellen Press, 1971.

Richman, Paula. *Women, Branch Stories, and Religious Rhetoric in a Tamil Buddhist Text.* Syracuse, N.Y.: Citizenship and Public Affairs, Syracuse University, 1988.

Roberts, Helen, ed. *Doing Feminist Research.* London: Routledge and Kegan Paul, 1981.

Rodd, Laurel Rasplica, trans. *Nichiren: Selected Writings*. Honolulu: University of Hawaii Press, 1980.

Rohlen, Thomas. "The Promise of Adulthood in Japanese Spiritualism." In *Adulthood*, ed. Erik Erikson. New York: Norton, 1978: 129–149.

Ross, Nancy Wilson. *Three Ways of Asian Wisdom: Hinduism, Buddhism, and Zen and their Significance for the West*. New York: Simon and Schuster, 1966.

Sakurai, Tokutarō, Tatsuo Hagiwara, and Noboru Miyata, eds. and comps. *Jisha Engi*. Tokyo: Iwanami Shoten, 1975.

Sansom, G. B. "Early Japanese Laws, Part One." *Transactions of the Asiatic Society of Japan* Second Series vol. 9 (Dec. 1932): 67–109.

———. "Early Japanese Laws, Part Two." *Transactions of the Asiatic Society of Japan* Second Series vol. 11 (Dec. 1934): 117–147.

———. *Japan: A Short Cultural History*. Stanford, Calif.: Stanford University Press, 1931.

Schulenburg, Jane Tibbetts. "Women's Monastic Communities, 500–1100: Patterns of Expansion and Decline." *Signs: Journal of Women in Culture and Society* vol. 14, no. 21 (Winter 1989): 261–292.

Schuster, Nancy. "Changing the Female Body: Wise Women and the *Bodhisattva* Career in Some *Maharatnakutasutras*." *Journal of the International Association of Buddhist Studies* vol. 4 (1981): 24–69.

Scott, Joan Wallach. *Gender and the Politics of History*. New York: Columbia University Press, 1988.

Seiichi Iwao, ed. *Biographical Dictionary of Japanese History*. New York: Kodansha International, 1978.

Sekida, Katsuji. *Zen Training: Methods and Philosophy*. New York: Weatherhill, 1975.

Sharma, Arvind, ed. *Women in World Religions*. Albany: State University of New York Press, 1987.

Shively, Donald, ed. *Tradition and Modernization in Japanese Culture*. Princeton, N.J.: Princeton University Press, 1971.

Shufunotomo, ed. *Amadera: Kazari o Otoshita Nyonintachi*. Tokyo: Dainihon Insatsu, 1989.

Sievers, Sharon. *Flowers in Salt: The Beginnings of Feminist Consciousness in Modern Japan*. Stanford, Calif.: Stanford University Press, 1983.

Smith, Wilfred Cantwell. "Comparative Religion: Whither and Why?" In *The History of Religions: Essays in Methodology*, ed. M. Eliade and J. Kitagawa, pp. 31–58. Chicago: University of Chicago Press, 1959.

———. "Methodology and the Study of Religion: Some Misgivings." In *Methodological Issues in Religious Studies*, ed. Robert Baird, pp. 1–30. Chico, Calif.: New Horizons Press, 1975.

Sōshitsu, Sen XV. *Tea Life, Tea Mind*. Kyoto: Urasenke Foundation, 1979.

Sōtōshū Nisōdan, *Sōtōshū Nisō Meibo*. Tokyo: Sōtōshū Nisōdan Honbu, 1984.

Sōtōshū Shūseichōsa Iinkai, ed. *Shūkyōshūdan no Ashita e no Kadai*. Tokyo, 1984.

Sōtōshū Zensho Kankōkai, ed. *Sōtōshū Zensho*. 1929–1935. Rev. and enl. 18 vols. Tokyo: Sōtōshū Shūmuchō, 1970–73.

Spellman, Elizabeth. *Inessential Woman*. Boston: Beacon Press, 1988.

Spencer, John B. "The Aesthetic Ethics of Alfred North Whitehead." Ph.D. diss., University of Chicago, 1963.

Spender, Dale. *Men's Studies Modified: Impact of Feminism on the Academic Disciplines*. Oxford: Pergamon Press, 1981.

Spiro, Melford E. *Buddhism and Society: A Great Tradition and Its Burmese Vicissitudes*. New York: Harper & Row, 1970.

Sponberg, Alan. "Attitudes toward Women and the Feminine in Early Buddhism." In *Buddhism, Sexuality, and Gender*, ed. Jose I. Cabezon; pp. 3–36. Albany: State University of New York Press, 1988.

Spradley, James P. *Participant Observation*. New York: Holt, Rinehart, and Winston, 1980.

Spring Wind-Buddhist Cultural Forum. *Women & Buddhism* vol. 6, nos. 1, 2, and 3. (1986).

Suzuki, D. T. *The Training of the Zen Buddhist Monk*. Berkeley, Calif.: Wingbow Press, 1974.

——. *Zen and Japanese Culture*. Princeton, N.J.: Princeton University Press, 1959.

Swearer, Donald. "Contemporary Japanese Religion, An Interpretive Dilemma." *Japanese Religions* vol. 7, no. 4 (Dec. 1972): 35–49.

Tachibana, Maki. *Josei no tame no Bukkyō Nyūmon*. Tokyo: PHP Kenkyūjo, 1989.

Tagami, Taishū. *Dōgen no Iitakatta koto*. Tokyo: Kodansha, 1985.

Taira, Masayuki. "Chūsei Bukkyō to Josei." In *Nihon Josei Seikatsushi* vol. 2. Ed. Joseishi Sōgō Kenkyūkai. Tokyo: Tokyo Daigaku Shuppan Kai, 1990: 75–108.

——. "Josei Ōjō-ron no Rekishi-teki Hyōka o Megutte: Abe Yasurō-shi no Hihan ni Kotaeru." *Bukkyō Shigaku Kenkyū* vol. 32, no. 2 (1989): 94–109.

——. *Nihon Chūsei no Shakai to Bukkyō*. Tokyo: Hanawa Shobō, 1992.

Taishō Shinshū Daizōkyō, ed. Takakusu Junjirō, Watanabe Kaikyoku et al. 85 vols. Tokyo: Taishō Issaikyō Kankōkai, 1924–1934.

Tajima, Hakudō. *Dōgen Keizan Ryō Zenji no Nisōkan*. Nagoya: Sōtō-shū Kōtō Nigakurin Shuppanbu, 1953.

——, ed. *Rokujūnen no Ayumi* [A Path of Sixty Years]. Nagoya: Kingu Sha, 1963.

——. *Sōtō-shū Nisō-shi*. Tokyo: Sanyo-sha, 1955.

Takagi, Kan. *Enkiridera Mantoku-ji Shiryōshū*. Tokyo: Seibundō, 1976.

Takagi, Yutaka. *Bukkyōshi no naka no Nyonin*. Tokyo: Heibonsha, 1988.

Takahashi, Masanobu. *The Essence of Dōgen*, trans. Yuzuru Nobuoka. London: Kegan Paul International, 1983.

Takemi, Momoko. " 'Menstruation Sutra' Belief in Japan," trans. W. Michael Kelsey. *Japanese Journal of Religious Studies* vol. 10, nos. 2–3 (1983): 229–246.

Tambiah, Stanley. "At the Confluence of Anthropology, History, and Indology." *Contributions to Indian Sociology* vol. 21, no. 1 (1987) 187–216.

——. *World Conqueror and World Renouncer: A Study of Buddhism and Polity in Thailand Against a Historical Background*. Cambridge: Cambridge University Press, 1976.

Tamura, Enchō. "Japan and the Eastward Permeation of Buddhism." *Acta Asiatica* no. 47 (1985): 1–30.

Tanahashi, Kazuaki, ed. *Moon in a Dew Drop: Writings of Zen Master Dōgen*. San Francisco: North Point Press, 1985.

Taniguchi Setsudō-ni Tsuitōshu Henshū Iinkai. *Jikō Mugen: Taniguchi Setsudō-ni o Shinonde*. Toyama: Shakai Fukushi Hōjin Lumbini-en, 1987.

Terada, Tōru, ed. *Dōgen*. Tokyo: Iwanami Shoten, 1980.

Thich Nhat Hanh. *Miracle of Mindfulness: A Manual on Meditation*, rev. ed., trans. Mobi Ho. Boston: Beacon Press, 1975.

Trinh, Minh-Ha. *Woman, Native, Other*. Bloomington: Indiana University Press, 1989.

Tsai, Kathryn. "Chinese Buddhist Monastic Order." In *Women in China*, ed. R. Guisso and S. Johanneson, pp. 1–20. Youngstown, N.Y.: Philo Press, 1981.

Tsomo, Karma Lekshe, ed. *Sakyadhītā: Daughters of the Buddha*. Ithaca, N.Y.: Snow Lion Publications, 1988.

Tsunoda, Ryūsaku, trans. *Japan in Chinese Dynastic Histories*, ed. L. Carrington Goodrich. South Pasadena, Calif.: P.D. & I. Perkins, 1951.

Tu, Wei-Ming. *Confucian Thought: Selfhood as Creative Transformation*. Albany: State University of New York Press, 1985.

Turner, Victor. *The Ritual Process: Structure and Anti-Structure*. Ithaca, N.Y.: Cornell University Press, 1969.

Uchino, Kumiko. "The Status Elevation Process of Sōtō Sect Nuns in Modern Japan." *Japanese Journal of Religious Studies* vol. 10, nos. 2–3 (June–Sept. 1983): 177–194.

Uchiyama, Kōshō, and Dōgen. *Refining Your Life: From the Zen Kitchen to Enlightenment*, trans. Thomas Wright. New York: Weatherhill, 1983.

Ueda, Yoshie. *Chōmon Nisō Monogatari*. Tokyo: Kokusho Kankōkai, 1979.

Ushiyama, Yoshiyuki. *Chūsei no Amadera nōto* [Notes on Nun's Temples in Medieval Japan]. Nagano: Shinshū Daigaku Kyōiku Gakubu, 1990.

Van der Leeuw, Gerardus. *Sacred and Profane Beauty: The Holy in Art*. New York: Holt, Rhinehart, and Winston, 1953.

van Gennep, Arnold. *The Rites of Passage*, trans. Monika B. Vizedom and Gabrielle L. Caffee. London: Routledge and Kegan Paul, 1909.

van Straelen, H. J. J. M. *The Japanese Women Looking Forward*. Tokyo: Kyojun Kwan, 1940.

Weber, Max. *Sociology of Religion*; trans. E. Fischoff. Boston: Beacon Press, 1963.

Wei, Karen T. *Women in China: A Selected and Annotated Bibliography*. Westport, Conn: Greenwood, 1984.

Welch, Holmes. *The Practice of Chinese Buddhism, 1900–1950*. Cambridge, Mass.: Harvard University Press, 1967.

Whitehead, Alfred North. *Adventures of Ideas*. New York: The Free Press, 1933.

———. *Modes of Thought*. New York: The Free Press, 1938.

———. *Process and Reality*, corrected ed. David Ray Griffin and Donald W. Sherburne. New York: The Free Press, 1978.

Wijayaratna, Mohan. *Buddhist Monastic Life According to the Texts of the Theravada Tradition*, trans. Claude Grangier and Steven Collins. Cambridge: Cambridge University Press, 1990.

Willis, Janice, D. "Nuns and Benefactresses." In *Women, Religion, and Social Change*, ed. Ellison Banks Findly and Yvonne Yazbeck Haddad, pp. 59–86. Albany: State University of New York Press, 1985.

———, ed. *Feminine Ground: Essays on Women and Tibet*. Ithaca, N.Y.: Snow Lion Publications, 1987.

Yanagi, Sōetsu. *The Unknown Craftsman: A Japanese Insight into Beauty*, foreword by Shōji Hamada. Tokyo and New York: Kodansha International, 1972.

Yoshida, Shōkin. "Chūsei Zenrin niokeru Josei no Nyūshin." *Indogaku Bukkyō Kenkyū* vol. 21, no. 1 (1977): 1–13.

Zoku Sōtōshū Zensho Kankōkai, ed. *Zoku Sōtōshū Zensho*, 10 vols. Tokyo: Sōtōshū Shūmuchō, 1974–1977.

Index